ISBN 978-1-333-46622-0
PIBN 10507991

This book is a reproduction of an important historical work. Forgotten Books uses state-of-the-art technology to digitally reconstruct the work, preserving the original format whilst repairing imperfections present in the aged copy. In rare cases, an imperfection in the original, such as a blemish or missing page, may be replicated in our edition. We do, however, repair the vast majority of imperfections successfully; any imperfections that remain are intentionally left to preserve the state of such historical works.

English
Français
Deutsche
Italiano
Español
Português

www.forgottenbooks.com

Mythology Photography **Fiction**
Fishing Christianity **Art** Cooking
Essays Buddhism Freemasonry
Medicine **Biology** Music **Ancient
Egypt** Evolution Carpentry Physics
Dance Geology **Mathematics** Fitness
Shakespeare **Folklore** Yoga Marketing
Confidence Immortality Biographies
Poetry **Psychology** Witchcraft
Electronics Chemistry History **Law**
Accounting **Philosophy** Anthropology
Alchemy Drama Quantum Mechanics
Atheism Sexual Health **Ancient History**
Entrepreneurship Languages Sport
Paleontology Needlework Islam
Metaphysics Investment Archaeology
Parenting Statistics Criminology
Motivational

𝔑atural and 𝔄boriginal
HISTORY OF TENNESSEE.

[NOTE.—*The length of the errata is entirely owing to the defectiveness of the manuscript furnished the printer.*]

THE

NATURAL AND ABORIGINAL

HISTORY

OF

TENNESSEE,

UP TO THE

FIRST SETTLEMENTS THEREIN

BY THE

WHITE PEOPLE,

IN THE

YEAR 1768.

───────────────

BY JOHN HAYWOOD,

OF THE COUNTY OF DAVIDSON, IN THE STATE OF TENNESSEE.

───────────────

NASHVILLE:

PRINTED BY GEORGE WILSON.

1823.

2847

DISTRICT OF WEST TENNESSEE, *to wit:*

BE IT REMEMBERED, That on the twenty-second day of September, in the year of our Lord one thousand eight hundred and twenty-three, and of the Independence of the United States of America, the forty-eighth; JOHN HAYWOOD, of the said District, hath deposited in the office of the Clerk of the District Court for the District of West Tennessee, the title of a book, the right whereof he claims as author in the words following, to wit: "The Natural and Aboriginal History of Tennessee, up to the first settlements therein by the white people, in the year 1768. By JOHN HAYWOOD, of the County of Davidson, in the State of Tennessee."

In conformity to the act of Congress of the United States, entitled "An Act for the encouragement of learning, by securing the copies of maps, charts and books, to the authors and proprietors of such copies during the times therein mentioned," and also to the act, entitled "An Act supplementary to an act, entitled "An Act for the encouragement of learning, by securing the copies of maps, charts, and books, to the authors and proprietors of such copies during the times therein mentioned," and extending the benefits thereof to the arts of designing, engraving, and etching historical and other prints.

IN TESTIMONY WHEREOF, I have hereunto set my hand, and affixed the public seal of my office, the day and year aforesaid.

N A. McNAIRY,
Clerk of the District Court for the District of West Tennessee.

E. E. K.
5/7/32

CONTENTS.

CHAPTER I.

CHAPTER II.

CHAPTER III.

PREFACE

By clearing the woods, cultivation of the lands, and by the devastation which augmented population occasions, those remnants of antiquity are fast passing away, which indicate the situation and circumstances of this country in former ages. And since men of experience and learning, by an acquaintance with them, may make discoveries conducive to the advancement of science, for that reason, this attempt is made to preserve them in remembrance. Conviction that the aim is laudable, however imperfect the execution, has preceded the work. The same conviction has likewise determined, that correct statements concerning them, even in the rudest form, are preferable to their total extinction. Anticipation also expects from this publication an excitement of the public attention to the subject, more than it has hitherto attracted. Many articles of great value have been thrown away or destroyed, as useless, for want of such excitement; which, had they been preserved, might have eminently contributed to the enlargement of useful information. This work will be continued, and the investigations begun will be prosecuted, till some abler hand shall undertake it: and it is requested, that every friend to improvements in science will contribute all that is conveniently within his reach, to the encouragement of them. Discoveries suitable to this plan come slowly to light, and cannot all be embraced in the researches of a few years, nor even the greater part of them.

But by patient perseverance for some time, and by careful accumulation from many quarters of the country, with the assistance of friendly co-operators, there is reason to believe that a rich body of materials may be collected. They are strewn in profusion upon the face of the country and in the bowels of the earth; and when concentred in one common repository, will form, by arrangement, the ground-work and the evidences for a complete history of ancient ages, both geological and aboriginal. It is hoped that this publication will make known the objects of those inquiries which are making, as likewise the practicability of them, and at the same time will recommend them to public favour. The beginnings of very useful institutions are sometimes neglected, and even ridiculed, when the end to be attained is not understood; which afterwards become popular, when that is brought into view. This publication will develop the end; and, it is hoped, will procure, for the means essential to its success, both friends and patrons. It is but the first essay, the imperfect commencement, of a much more useful and a much more polished production. The earnest expectation is entertained, that it will have the effect to awaken attention, and of causing discoveries to be transmitted, in order that they may be recorded and perpetuated.

NATURAL AND ABORIGINAL

HISTORY OF TENNESSEE.

———:❊:———

CHAPTER 1.

THE History of Tennessee will be the more perfectly understood, if preceded by a brief statement
of the general face of the country, and of its natural productions. This subject, of course sub-di-
vides itself; and requires a description—First, of
the general appearance of the country: Secondly.
of its marbles, buhr stones and plaister of Paris:
Thirdly, of its salt waters: Fourthly, of its petrifactions, ores, volcanic formations, and poisonous
tracts. Its geological phenomena may be included
in a seperate article; which may be followed by a-
nother seperate article, exhibiting the vestiges, of
the aboriginal men of America: and this again, by
a view of the present races of Indians, who very
probably exterminated the aborigines. We shall
then come to the settlement of the country by the
white people, who at present occupy it; and to the
great exertions made by the Indians, to prevent or
defeat those settlements.

First, of the general appearance of the country:
East Tennessee is divided from North Carolina,
by the Unaca or White Mountains—Unica, in the
Cherokee language signifying white. The direction of the Mountain is southwest, bearing more to
the westward, than the other ridges of the Alligha-
nies. East of this, is another ridge, the course of
which diverges to the southwest. This latter, the
people of Tennessee lately contended to be the U-
naca; but the western ridge is now settled by treaty to be so. The Hiwassee breaks through this
mountain, and heads in North Carolina, toward the
Blue Ridge. Near to its head are very high lands.

A

Upon one of the, latter of these mountains, in a gap, through which the Indians pass, near the head of Brass Town creek, on a large horizontal rock, are representations of animal footsteps, which will be hereafter noticed. It is divided from West Tennessee by the Cumberland Mountain, bearing in the same direction nearly with the Unaca and the Mississippi. Between these large mountains, there are ridges running eastwardly and westwardly, directly from some point, near one of these mountains to some point near to the other; but not forming a junction with either. Between the ends of these ridges, and either of the mountains to the east or west of them, there is an interval or passage.— These ridges, extending from east to west, are at short distances from each other, forming valies between, and occupying all the rest of the country, from the northern to the southern boundary of the state.

On the eastern side, of the rich lands of West Tennessee, are the Cumberland Mountains, running northeast and southwest. On the western side of them, in the same direction, are other parallel high lands or ridges, at the distance of about one hundred and ten miles from the Cumberland Mountains. The traveller crosses the western rigde, at Paradice's going from Nashville to Clarksville; and at Robertson's, ten or twelve miles south of the former, in going from Nashville to Charlotte. In a northwardly direction, the ridge traverses the counties of Robertson, Sumner and Smith; and approaching the Cumberland River, crosses the Kentucky line, at a point west of the Cumberland Gap; and probably afterwards joins some spur of the Cumberland Mountain. Towards the south it extends to the Duck River ridge, which lies in the southern part of Dickson county; and also in the southern part of Williamson; and in the southern parts of Rutherford, and through a part of Warren, and terminates west of Collin's river, near to a spur on the east side, which connects with the main mountain, nearly west from Pikeville. The only interval being where Collins' river breaks through, and seems to seperate the two spurs, or ridges. In this space, which includes Davidson, Williamson, Rutherford, Wilson, Sumner, Warren, White, Jackson, and Overton, the relics of testaceous animals are much more abundant, than upon the high lands. Some of these relics, found upon the highlands, have been collected and preserved by the curious. The country between the highlands, and transverse ridges, of which there are others more to the south, and have been as far as the Muscle Shoals, are the rich lands of West Tennessee; the surface of which, is every where covered with great numbers of limestone rocks. The soil is black and of a different color, from the soils of the high lands, or of any other part of the state of Tennessee.— There is no portion of sand contained in its mould. Its texture is fine. The particles of earth which compose it, are like fine flour, except as to color.— In many places, are the beds, and banks of old creeks; in which there is now no water. And in common with the high lands, they present creeks, now flowing in beds and banks, which have been made by smaller quantities of water, than formerly flowed there. For on either side of the present banks, and at some distance from them, are larger and higher banks, which have been cut, into their present form, by strong currents of water, acting upon their sides. In many places on these high banks, the rocks have been made bare by the washing of waters; while those above their levels have been left covered with mould. It would seem, that after the whole of this large bottom was uncovered by drains, there still remained numerous streams, which long flowed and acted upon the surface.— these in their turn, have in a series of ages gradually withdrawn themselves; are still imperceptibly retiring; and will finally cease to run altogether, when the level of the ocean, shall be far enough below the bottom of the inland seas and lakes, to draw off the water from that part of their beds, which are not yet detected; and when other great reservoirs, which fill our rivers and creeks with water, shall be drained off into the ocean. That billows once rolled over this large plain, is too evident to admit of denial. Whether the waters which covered it, remained for some time infolded within the circle of these ridges, after the other neighbouring waters had retired to their native seats, before they could be discharged, by opening a passage to the ocean; or whether, when the waters in their neighborhood, retreated from their ancient habitations, to fill up the caverns and hollows, which the deluge had made by gulphs and inland seas, these were left imprisoned by the mountains and ridges, till they made a passage for themselves, and escaped to the ocean is not material. For whether the one or the other supposition be adopted, the result will be, in confirmation of the scriptural history; of the great deluge; and equally accounts for the many inequalities and protuberances made upon the crust of the globe, by the undulations and heavings of the waves. By the mighty rage of the waters, gushing and precipitated from their beds, by the near approach of the great comet, which rarified the air nearly to dissolution; excited the winds; set on fire every combustible material, not covered by the water—were possibly, as some believe, washed deeper the beds of the ocean; and were opened, those cavities which we see in all parts of the globe, in a direction from south to north; proving one uniform operation in the formation of all, and by a cause proceeding from the south. Such as the Baltic, Mediteranean, Adriatic, Eegean Sea, the Persian Gulph, that between Cape Jack and Cape Comorin; the Bay of Bengal, the Gulf of Siam, the yellow sea, the Channel of Tartary, the Sea of Ochotsk, the Gulfs of California, and Mexico, the Gulf of Bothnia, the White Sea, and Davis's Streights; all which seem to have been washed up, by waters running from south to north.— They carried with them to the northern regions, the equatorial and tropical plants, animals, weeds and trees, depositing them as far as the fiftieth degree of north latitude, where their remains are now every day found; whilst no such relics, and particularly none of northern growth, are found in regions south of the southern tropics. The western ridge before described, it is probable was opposed for some time after the recession of the waters below, to the passage of the Cumberland river and its tributaries, which were prabably elongated after the waters withdrew. This opposition probably continued till the waters of the lake, made by the supplies of the Cumberland, rose high enough to find the lowest part of the ridge, and proceeded through that passage, continually widening and sinking deeper, as the waters rushed over it, and carried off the constituent particles of the ridge, from the bottom and sides of the opening. The level of the water in the lake, lowered in proportion, till coming to the falls, as we now see them, near the mouth of the Big Harpeth, and Sycamore Creek; the whole lake was finally carried off. There was also an interior or circular ridge between the Cumberland Mountain, and the one before described, of the same circular form. Both these, will hereafter be particularly adverted to. It will be sufficient at present to say, that similiar remarks, to those above made, apply to the great lake, once formed, between the Duck River Ridge, on the one side and the Cumberland Mountain on the other; extending as far as the Muscle Shoals, and connected by a transverse ridge, which served to dam up the waters, till a passage was made by the workings of the Tennessee, and the whole lake was carried off. Should any one incline to doubt the decrease of waters, let him be desired to consider the evidences in favor of this proposition. There is a line of forts, beginning at the mouth of Catarangus creek, supposed to have been built on the brow of the hill; which appears to have once been the southern shore of Lake Erie. Since they were built, the waters have receded four or five miles. The surface between, is covered by a vegetable mould, made from the decay of vegetables; six, eight, or ten inches in depth. Many of the works on the Scioto, and the great Miami, had gateways and parallel walls, leading down to creeks, which once washed the foot of hills, from which the streams have now receded; have formed extensive and new alluvions, and have worn down their channels, in some instances, ten and even fifteen feet. The rivers have shifted their mouths, and in some places, their beds, almost universally, more to the south and west, than they were, when these ancient works were made. And perhaps this might be said with respect to all rivers, running into the Ohio and Mississippi. If this idea were followed up, it might possibly lead to a discovery of the cause, in the changed posture of the globe, or whatever else it may be. Has not the Mississippi changed its ancient beds or channels, for others more to the south? Did not the Cumberland at Nashville, once extend to the hill, on the north side opposite Nashville? Did not the small creek at colonel Joselin's on the southwest side of his plantation, once hold waters, up to the rocks on the banks on both sides, when the waters to fill it, must have been one hundred times more copious than they now are? The like may be observed of Whites' creek, Brush creek, and of every other creek in the country; and of the shores of the ocean. Did not these latter, once make salt, the waters between the Mississippi, and the oyster banks in this state, and Alabama, when all these rivers and creeks were full to their banks, and when their channels were not as deep as they now are? Against so many proofs of the fact, both on the ancient shores of ocean, and on the banks of all the rivers and creeks in the country, who can close his senses against conviction? Have not the waters of the Mississippi retired from the oyster ridges, between it and Tennessee?

To the same cause may possibly be referred, the praries, or barrens as they are called, and the appearances they exhibit in West Tennessee. In the counties of Montgomery and Stuart, is a part of the barrens, which are so extensive in the neighbouring counties of Kentucky. A great part of them is very fertile; and some part of them otherwise. These lands are flat and level, for one hundred miles and more in length, and breadth. No timber trees were upon them, and only a few saplings of ten or twenty years growth. Where the fire is kept from them, by the interposition of plantations, the young trees immediately spring up on the unburnt surface, and grow luxuriantly. Sometimes the barrens are seperated from the adjacent lands by the intervention of deep branches, and creeks, winding circuitously through them. In the bends are large timber trees, as tall as any in the forest, which adjoins the barrens; while on the outside of the creek, and to its very margin, the barrens are without a single timber tree of any sort.— Sometimes the barrens are intersected by swamps; in which trees of many descriptions stand thick, and as large as any in the forests. Sometimes small branches run through them, so obstructed in places by natural obstacles, as to overflow the lands on their sides. These overflowed spots, are covered with large trees. Very few mounds, are built upon the prairies or barrens. The roots of trees blown up in ancient ages, are no where visible; as they are abundantly in, the adjacent woodlands. Were not these barrens once covered with water; and afterwards with luxuriant grass, which being every year exposed to combustion, the soil has therefore produced no timber trees? This draining may have taken place at early periods; but probably long since the erection of those walled inclosures, which we see left in the other parts of the country, by the aborigines. It was since the settlement of the country by the aborigines; otherwise the annual growth of the barrens, would not every year have been burnt; but like the other parts of the country would have grown up in bushes and trees, undisturbed by the destructive interposition of human agency. If it be supposed, that trees once grew in the barrens, which have been consumed by fire, in some parching year, in the fall season, when the luxuriant grass had become combustible; why then were the adjoining woods left undisturbed? Why are not the roots of trees found here, which were blown up in ancient times, as they are found in the adjacent woods? Did not these praries emerge from water in times comparatively modern; and have they not been since kept under, by fire thrown into them annually, by the inhabitants who have been here, ever since their desiccation?

On Crossing Obeds River, thirteen miles east of the highest part of the Cumberland Mountain, are seen for the first time, in going from Nashville to Knoxville, some *scrubby pines*. From thence eastwardly, the pine trees increase both in number and size, as far as to Rogersville, and probably to the mountains on the eastern borders of this state.— Where the *pine* is first seen, there also appears in places, an intermixture of sand with the soil, which in a few miles further east. becomes a bed of sand. It seems to have been brought hither from a great distance; and to have rebounded from the side of Spencer's Hill, and to have settled in the country west of it, and its vicinity. Beds of sand like this appear no where in West Tennessee, except in the beds of rivers, which are exposed to view, in the summer. The top of Spencer's Hill, is a very high elevation, perhaps one of the highest, on the Cumberland Mountain. Upon its summit are large rocks, piled one upon another, deprived of all covering ; and are constantly kept clean by the rains and snows which melt upon them. The covering, which may have been once around and upon them, seems to have been swept away by overflowing waters.

THE rocks in West Tennessee, generally incline from southwest to northeast ; but in some instances, from northwest to southeast. In the banks of creeks and rivers, six or eight feet below the surface, they decline toward the north ; the part toward the south being the most elevated. In East Tennessee, the rocks, as well those on the surface, as those on the banks of creeks, uniformly incline from the southeast to the northwest, and have an elevation, of about forty-five degrees. Five miles west of Knoxville, near the house which Miller formerly occupied, on the north side of the road, and near the spring, is a very remarkable collection of rocks ; the edges of which are just far enough above the surface, to be seen, and to show their exact degree of elevation, towards the north. They are flat rocks, standing on the edges ; apparently ten or twelve layers of them. They are distant a few feet from each other, and are all exactly in the same degree of declination, from the zenith ; as if the whole had been moved in one and the same instant ; by one and the same shock ; and by one and the same cause, operating with the same force, exactly upon each.

IN both East and West Tennessee, are numerous cavities in the earth, called *sink holes*. Let us describe a few of them.

THERE is a hill, three hundred and fifty feet from the base to the summit—not a knob, but a ridge, which on the north joins Cumberland Mountain, and extends southwardly to the Tennessee River, which runs through it and finally joins the Alleghany Mountain, not far from the Oconee station.— The summit of this ridge, is in the county of Roane, northeast from South West Point. Upon the top of the ridge is a sink-hole, about six feet in diameter; in which is water about eight feet below the surface. In the water are fish; some of them from six to ten inches in length. It could not be fathomed, by three bed ropes tied to each other, and fifty feet of hickory bark added, with a heavy piece of lead affixed to the end, making in all three hundred and eighty feet at least. Not far from the sink-hole, is a spring at the side of the ridge; which when flushed by long and copious rains, has in it fish, of the same species with those found at the top. There must be some internal obstacle in the bowels of the earth, between the spring and the water in which the fish grow, which is overflowed in wet weather, and lets the water and fish over it. Near the water on the summit, eight feet below the surface of the earth, in a small platform, and nearly covered with dirt, was found a *conch*, of the size of the egg of a hen, and of the same form as those shells, which are commonly called *conch shells*.— There is a cave to the southwest of this sink, about half a mile on the southwest side of the ridge; the opening of which is fifty yards from the base of the ridge, and above it. There is a small apperture, after entering through which, there is a descent of fifteen feet, into an arched room, twenty by thirty feet in length and breadth; and from eight to ten feet in depth. Thence there is an opening into another room, and in it there is a cavern, into which if a stone be thrown, it will resound by the striking against the walls, the report becomming still less and less perceptible, till finally it seems to be too far below, to be heard from the surface. Every morning a smoke ascends from the opening, and continues till an hour or two after sunrise. In the first of these caves, depending from the arch, are various petrified drippings of water, or stalactites, like icicles. Directly under them, are petrified substances, made of water, in the form of dirt daubers nests; in other words rough, and converted into stone.— By some they are compared to cypress knees; and in some caves there are many of them. When candles are introduced, they exhibit a brilliancy of appearance to the representation of which, description is incompetent.

In Blount county, eight miles west of Maryville, is a spring, to the south of which is a ridge; and at the base of which is a sink hole. One standing on the side of the ridge, and looking through a fissure, into the rocks, may see water nearly upon a level with his breast; in which are fish. The spring is fifteen feet lower and one hundred and fifty feet from the spot, where the water is seen in the interior of the cave. This spring is unfathomable. The water is clear and of a bluish cast. Near the base of the ridge, is a sinkhole, in which there is no water.

In some sink holes in East Tennessee, water is at the bottom, fifteen or twenty feet or more, below the surface of the earth; and generally unfathomable. In some of them are great numbers of fish.— Sometimes it is observable, that there are many such sinkholes, in a course like that of a stream of water; one after another, all of them bottomless,* and containing fish. Sink holes, both in East and West Tennessee, are to be found in all parts of the country. They seem to have sunk in, from the surface toward the centre; wider at top, and narrower at bottom, They are from fifty to sixty yards in diameter, to ten or twelve feet.

In 1795, Joseph Ray was travelling from Holston in East Tennessee, to Sumner county in West Tennessee. Whilst he passed through the barrens in Kentucky, leading a horse by his side, the one that he rode sunk suddenly thirty or forty feet below the surface. He leaped from the sinking horse, and saved himself from going to the bottom, with the other. He went to Sumner county, and returned, and by means of assistance which he had ob-

* By bottomless is meant, not reached by any line, the inhabitants near them have made.

tained, he descended into the pit, where his horse had sunk, and found running water at the bottom of the pit. The horse had walked about in the cavern, but was dead.

ABOUT the last of May 1821, on Rock Creek, near the plantation of M'Cochrill, in Bedford county, in West Tennessee, a sudden subterraneous explosion took place. It heaved the earth upwards with great force, ejecting large rocks and small ones; throwing them against the trees which were near, bruising them so that they died. The sound of the explosion was like that of a large cannon; and the hole broken open by the eruption, was forty or fifty feet in diameter, and about fifty feet deep, having the appearance of a sink hole, and having within, a very rough and craggy appearance. A body of smoke was settled for several days at the bottom of the opening made by the eruption.

THROUGH all East and West Tennessee, caves are very abundant, on the sides of the mountains, knobs, hills and bluffs. Some of them are ten miles in length, and more. They are often filled with nitrous dirt, of which salt petre is made in large quantities, where the demand and prices given, make it profitable to work them. Many bones of the ancient inhabitants are found in them; and some skeletons in a state of preservation in the nitrous dirt within them.

THE whole of the country between the ridge west of the Tennessee, and the Mississsippi, is composed of the following strata.—First: soil mixed with sand; secondly, yellow clay; thirdly, red sand, mixed with red clay; fourthly, perfectly white sand, such as is seen on the shores of the Atlantic. Compared with the latter, there is no perceptible difference. The country on the south side of the Tennessee, near where that river crosses the southern boundary line of this state, and for many miles to the north west, and south is quite uneven; and exhibits the appearance of the ocean when agitated by a storm. To the south in many places are to be found immense banks of oyster shells; some of which are petrified. And in many places, oyster shells are to be found, upon the surface of the earth. These shells belonged to a species much larger. than any live oysters now to be taken, Some of the half shells weighed not less than two pounds.— These banks of Oyster shells, are not contiguous to any water course; but on high grounds, one hundred miles east of the Mississippi, and from two hundred to four hundred miles or more, north of the Gulf of Mexico.

Secondly—of the Marbles, Buhr stones and Plaister of Paris, in Tennessee.

Six miles south of Rogersville, on the lands of Judge Powell, is an abundance of fine marble, of various colors. There is a hill, two and a half miles east of north from Rogersville, wholly composed of marble; white, grey, and sometimes red. Also on the road eight miles west of Rogersville. Also on the north of Bean's Station, a mile from the top of Clinch Mountain. Also between Mr. Cain's and Knoxville· The marble here is white. Also on the south side of Knoxville, on the road leading from Sevierville to Knoxville.— Also between Campbell's Station and Mr. Merediths. Also between Blountsville and Jonesborough. South from Blountsville, on the south side of Holston, and two miles from it, is red marble. Also, large quantities in Jefferson county. A vien of grey and variegated marble extends along the north side of Clinch Mountain, for fifty miles; a great proportion of it very fine, and the vein of considerable breadth. The soil about is generally barren, or of a metallic color; easily washed into gullies.

In the mountains, on the eastern parts of East Tennessee, are inexhaustible stores of the Plaister of Paris, of the best quality; which may be carried down the Holston and its branches, to all the counties below whenever the exhausted state of their lands, shall be found to require reinvigoration.

SOME of the inner mountains above described; and particularly one lying fifteen miles to the north of Knoxville, are mountains of Buhr stone, which is acknowledged by the best Judges, to exceed all others of the like kind in the world

Thirdly of the Salt-Waters of Tennessee.

AT the foot of the Cumberland mountain, on the west side of it, almost every stream of water which runs from it, is found to be accompanied on its side, with other streams of salt water. Whence the inference has been made, that the Cumberland Mountain itself, is full of layers and rocks of salt. The streams of salt water, which flow from the Cumberland Mountain, are on the sides of rivers, at great depths below the fresh water; which is on the surface, or just below it. Salt water is also in other places, not in the neighborhood of fresh water streams, and far from the Cumberland Mountain; but the quantity of salt water is greater or less, in proportion, as the distance from the mountain is greater or less. The important circumstance, relative to salt water, and marvellously strange it is, if real, is this—that those streams so far below the surface, are found by *subterranean attraction*. In England it is called *Bletonism*; but in Tennessee, it is called by some *Cookism*; from the name of Mr. Cook, a resident of Kentucky, who has found a great number of subterranean streams in Tennessee, both of salt and fresh water. Mr. Cook attributes this quality, to some cause similar to that of magnetism: and its action upon twigs in the hands of some men, when on those in the hands of others it will not act at all, to sympathies, peculiarly bestowed by providence, for the purpose of making those essential discoveries, to which they lead; and, without which, the viens of subterranean waters, both fresh and salt, would be useless ; and the designs of providence, in creating them be disappointed. We know of its existence he says, as we know of magnetism ; not by any adeqnate cause we can assign, but by the numerous instances and proofs of its effects ; the only means of ascertaining that the unknown cause exists. These evidences may be advanced for the conviction of scepticism ; and for the accumulation of human knowledge, in relation to the invisible agents, which creative wisdom hath prepared, for the promotion and manifestation of its designs. Mr. Cook cites many instances, in proof of the real existence of this quality; which have no doubt occurred, as he is a man of truth. Whether success, was justly ascribed or not, to a magnetic cause, belongs not to the writer to decide. All he ought to say is, that a great majority of the people believe it. And that there is nothing more common than to search for water by this process; and to hear of the discoveries that have been made by it. We have the additional evidence, and very sensible remarks of Turner Lane esquire, of White county, upon this curious subject. He says, " the time once was, when when the amazing power of magnetism, or of attraction, was totally unknown to the world, and when it had not been discovered; that like qualities possessed the power of attracting, and by that power, producing an inclination, or tendency to each other. But the time of that profound ignorance has long since ceased to exist; for by mere casualty, one *Magnus,* a shepherd, took notice that the *Loadstone* would cleave to the *Iron* on his sandals ; and this discovery being improved, prepared the way for the use of the Magnet ; a knowledge in which enables the skilful *mariner* to traverse the pathless ocean, without the danger of missing his point of destination, or of running heedlessly into sure and inevitable destruction; either by running into *Qicksands,* or splitting his bark on *Rocks.—*

16

And it is now every where certainly known, that by applying the loadstone to a bar of steel of a certain given temperature, and then if the bar is suspended on a pivot or centre pin, the ends of the bar will never rest, until they have settled themselves down, in coincidence with the poles of the earth. This important fact, although now universally known, yet the cause of its existance has never been clearly understood. For although the immortal Sir Isaac Newton, with all his philosophical, and astronomical discovery, labored hard and employed his enlarged powers of mind, with indefatigable zeal, to discover the true cause of this phenomena, and also why it should so happen, that although the needle or bar of steel, thus impregnated with magnetism, would settle down nearly parallel with the axis of the earth, yet it would not exactly coincide therewith, but would have some variation therefrom; and why this variation should not at all times remain the same, but be found at some times to the East; at others to the west of a true meredian; at some times increasing; at other times decreasing; and again at other periods be found in an exact coincidence with a true meredian, were at once phenomena, the procuring cause of which he left to the world as a profound secret—a secret which all the philosophers that the world has ever known, have not been able to develope, and bring out of mystery, darkness and deep obscurity.

If then, there does exist one description of magnetism known to, and acknowledged by all men; and if in this magnetism there does exist, a secret, unknown, and inexplicable cause, which does produce the effect, which all will acknowledge to be the fact; why may not another description of magnetism exist, equally certain in its operation, and equally involved in mystery; and the denial of which, would, perhaps in half a century from the present day, be as contemptible and ridiculous, as it would now be, to deny the polarity of the Magnet.

"THAT such a magnetism is just now escaping from that profound obscurity, secrecy and darkness, in which it has remained from the commencement of time, to the present era, to me, it seems there is no doubt. I mean the attractive power, by which a tender forked rod, in the hands of a practitioner, will vibrate, and tend to the object of the search, or enquiry of the practitioner.

"To prove that a tender rod in the hands of a practitioner, will tend to or respond to the enquiry of the practitioner, suffer me to recite a few undeniable facts; facts which have been proven to a demonstration, perhaps in one hundred instances, viz: Take one of those practitioners to a vein of salt water, and although the vein is far below the surface of the earth, and the surface there puts on the same appearance that it does elsewhere, yet the practitioner will follow all the *zig-zag* meanderings of the stream, to any assignable or given distance. This would seem no how strange for the first attempt, for who could say whether the practitioner was right or wrong, the surface of the earth appearing all alike.

"But how will our astonishment appear, and how will our philosophy be shaken to the centre, when we see any given number of other practitioners, each being brought to the same ground, one by one, at different periods of time, and each of the latter, total and entire *strangers* to all that had formerly been said or done here; to see them one by one, join in unison, to mark out the very same spot for the vein to pass under; follow the very same *zig-zag* course—showing all the points, and passing directly over all the secret marks which might have been made here at the first shewing.

"HERE our reason fails us—here our philosophy is smitten—we become dumb—we see the act achieved before our eyes, and we cannot deny it—we cannot get over it—we are compelled in silence to

C

yeild our assent to the fact, whilst our reason is lost in profound mystery.

"Permit me to relate one simple matter of fact, which came within my own inspection, and I will be no further tedious on this subject, but will submit it to the candid mind; that is to say.—About the year 1803, being at that time a resident of the state of Kentucky, I was well acquainted with a blacksmith in the town of Paris, who labored hard, and drank much water; he complained that the spring was far from him, and that water got warm in the vessel before it reached him ; that he would give any reasonable sum for a Well on his own lot. He accordingly sent for a *Water-witch*, to make search for water on his own lot. The experimnet was made, a place was marked and the following advices given by the practitioner: Dig here, and after sinking a certain number of feet, (by him given) you will come to the rock, then after blowing down another given number of feet, you will strike a stream of excellent spring water. The advices were immediately put in practice, and all things succeeded precisely as foretold; for the owner himself told me, that he could not give a more minute account of the distances, after finishing his well, than he had received from the practitioner before the soil was broken.

"If then these proofs are thought conclusive, how shall we account for the cause which produces this effect? Shall we say that the effect is produced without a cause, and is the effect of mere chance? If so, would not another difficulty equally important arise, to wit: how mere chance should happen exactly alike to so many different persons, all in quest of the same object, and at the same place, but at different times, the one not knowing of the shewings of the other? But would it not confound the principles of sound philosophy, to assert, that any effect was ever yet produced, without a procuring, or producing cause. If this assertion would be in direct contradiction to the strict laws of nature, and it should be believed that every effect proceeds from some producing cause, would it be thought ridiculous and fantastical, if we should attempt to hazard an oppinion, touching the cause which produces this phenomenon.

"But before we enter upon the discussion of this point, we beg leave to premise a few plain truths, or simple matters of fact. And first, it is a fact acknowledged by all the practitioners of this art, that the mind must be strongly impressed with, and in a constant state of enquiry after the substance or thing sought for. Secondly—the forked rod must be of a young, quick, and tender growth, being porous and lively; the bark being fresh and green, and the outside rind thin as paper, so as to be susceptible of easy penetration; for a rough barked one will not do. Thirdly—It is required to be granted, that like substances, qualities, or properties, have an attractive influence one upon the other.

"The premises being laid, we will now risk an opinion, on the secret and mysterious cause which produces this effect, which is the subject under consideration.

"Of what then does the the animal frame consist; how has it been reared up; whence has it derived its support and growth; what its diet; from whence arose this diet; has not all been from the bowels of the earth, without a single exception? If so, how many different or various qualities, or properties, has our daily food been impregnated with; and if we have been reared up, upon food strongly impregnated with all the various qualities or properties which are combined in the bowels of the earth, what then may be the composition of qualities, or properties, of which all the fluids and juices which compose the animal system are impregnated with, or do partake of?

"And if all vegitable matter, as well as animal, is the immediate growth and offspring of the earth, which is the common parent of all, is it not fair to conclude that all vegitable matter is also composed, some in a greater and some in a less degree, with the same qualities or properties, that the earth itself possesses? If so, the forked rod made use of in this process, is also vegitable, and consequently, in some good degree, partakes of the same qualites or properties, that the human or animal system does, to wit: of Nitre, Salt, Sulpher, Metalics, &c.

"It has been premised, that when this process is performing, the mind of the practitioner must be strongly impressed with, and in a constant state of enquiry after the substance, or thing sought for.——This constant and earnest pressure upon the mind, it would seem, spreads through and effects the whole system; operates on the nerves, on the juices, and extends to the extremities; thereby strongly impregnating the effluvia, which passes through the pores of the body by common perspiration; and as our system is composed of various qualities or properties, as has already been shewn, it would seem that the quality of the same kind, with that on which the mind labors, now becoms warm, is roused into action, and for the present, govern all the rest; it being the only quality which is congenial with the strong agitations of the mind.

"It has also been premised that the forked Rod must be young, tender, green, porous, and susceptible of easy penetration, and that a stiff rugged, rough-barked rod will not do.——Shall we conclude therefore, that a practitioner having a suitable rod in his hand, sets out in quest of *Salt water;* his mind is bent down to the object; the effects of the mind flow to the extremities; the nerves, the juices, the effluvia which is perspired, all are strongly impregnated with the same enquiry; the saline qualities which compose the system, are now warmed and heightened; the hands of the practitioner, now grasping the rod closely, the warmth and dampness of the palms, strike through the tender bark of the rod, and into the soft and flexible pores of the wood ; and the same saline qualities being in the rod, they are now roused, made quick and active ; and the same enquiry seems by these means, to be communicated to the rod.—The practitioner equipped, with a mind thus impressed, it is said, may pass over fresh water, over Lead, over Nitre, or other minerals, and the rod will not be affected ; but he can no sooner arrive at a vein of *salt water*, than the attraction of the vein seizes the rod, and it will directly respond to the enquiry of the pactitioner.   And in like manner will it act, in unison with the mind, when in quest of fresh water, minerals of any description, or other metalic substances.

" I shall prosecute this head no further, but will close by repeating,—Can an effect be produced without a cause?

" 2ndly, If it cannot, has any thing like the probable cause, been advanced, or is there some other secret cause?

" 3rdly, If something like what has been advanvanced, is not the probable cause, to me it would seem hard to account for in any other way.

" ANOTHER branch of this secret intelligence given by the rod to the. practitioner, is to determine the depth of the stream beneath the surface of the earth. How this can be performed when standing perpendicular over the object, or what might be taken as a clue, to lead to this discovery, seems at once to baffle all conception, and leave us without any ground, upon which we might form an opinion ; for how, or by what rule can a rod know the depth of a stream, better than the man in whose hand it is ?—Can attraction determine distances, or show how far one object is from another, by the force or power, with which the one attracts, or operates on the other ?— Can an observer determine the latitude of the place of observation, by the degree of power, with which the Northern Pole attracts, or operates on the Magnet ?—Can we by the laws of gravitation, determine the height of a declivity, by the power, or force, with which a Globe, or other solid body would incline to descend it ?—If none of these examples will give a clue to the discovery of this mystery, I know not where to resort, or how to make the attempt at finding one.

"A man standing perpendicularly over an object, may exercise his judgment on the subject of its depth, and may hazard an opinion ; but I cannot yet believe, that a rod can afford any aid to a practitioner in determing depths in a perpendicular situation. The rod cannot derive any knowledge of depths, by any rule or law of nature, nor can I believe that by any means, a rod could be inspired with such discriminating faculties, as to discern the difference between feet and inches ; and even if it could be inspired with that knowledge, yet the difficulty would remain, as to how it could acquire a knowledge of the depth, better than the man who inspired it.—I conclude this mode of practice by saying it is performed by *guess*, and not by art, or of necessity ; we therefore find, that although all the practitioners will agree as to the *place* where those veins of water are, yet no two who practice in this way, will agree about the depth.

If then we can find no rational rule, by which depth may be determined, in a perpendicular direction above an object, let us resort to some other mode, and try how far the rule actually resorted to by the better practitioners of this art or mystery, will comport with the fixed laws of nature.

"It is said that when a point is ascertained, perpendicularly to the object in quest, and the depth of the object is required, the practitioner with his rod elevated, turns his face from the point thus marked, and walks cautiously, at right angles from the object ;—and that at a certain distance from the object, the rod will again operate, turning directy towards the breast of the practitioner, and consequently, tending towards the object : at this point they make a second mark;—the distance then of those points one from the other, being let fall perpendicularly from the first, or vertical point, will just extend to the object, and determine the depth beneath the surface.

"Before we enter into the investigation of this rule, we will premise, that by the laws or powers of exhalation, all rarified vapour, or effluvia, are caused to *ascend*.

"And that by the laws or powers of gravitation, all substances are caused to *descend*, or at least so to expand as to form a level, and be in equillibrio.

"If then the distance between the two points found as above stated, is equal to the distance from the vertical point to the object, it follows, that those dimensions form a right angled plain triangle, whose legs are equal, and consequently, whose accute, and opposite angles, will also be equal ; for equal lines subtend equal angles.   See the figure.

"In the triangle, A. B. C. let C. be the object, A. the verticle point, B. the point whence the attraction will cease to operate on the rod, and return towards the practitioner, C. D. a level, being parallel to A. B.

"It is proven to a clear demonstration in the first book of Euclid, that the sum of the angles in every plain triangle as A B C is equal to a semicircle, or to 180 degrees ; and also that every right angle as is the angle A contains 90 of those degrees ; it therefore follows, that the sum of the other two angles, B and C, must also be 90 degrees ; for if the three contain 180 degrees, of which the angle A contains 90, degrees, it follows that the other two, B and C must contain the other 90.   But if the line A B is equal to the line A C, it will also follow, that their opposite angles B and C will also be equal to each other ;

that is each being the equal half of 90 to wit, 45 degrees.

"It is also clearly proven in the book above cited, that if two lines as A B and C D be drawn parallel to each other, and if a line as B C be drawn to insercect them, the acute and opposite angles A B C, and D C B will be equal to each other.— Hence we infer, that the line C. B. inclines exactly as much to the level C D as it does to the perpendicular C A, and no more so, but a splitting line between the two, dividing the right angle A C D into two equal halves of 45 degrees each.

"If then as has been premised, the exhaling power would cause the attractive influence of all substances to ascend, and rise in the direction of the perpendicular line A C; and if as has also been premised, the power of gravitation would cause all attractive influences to expand and form a level, in the direction of the dotted line C D. It follows with irresistible force, that those contrary or opposing laws of nature, operating at once on the attractive influence of substances beneath the surface, with equal force and power, will have a direct tendency to direct the rays of attraction which pass from the object to take a middle course, and ascend directly with the splitting line C B, forming angles with the level and perpendicular of 45 degrees each.

"This rule would admit of mathematical demonstration, and is founded on such just principles, that if it is admitted at all, that a substance beneath the surface can attract a rod in the hands of a practitioner, it ought also to be admitted, that by the foregoing rule, the depth may also be pretty nearly ascertained. Ludicrous and simple as the foregoing pages may appear, to a person possessing your strength of mind, the impressions of mind which have for some time past pervaded me, are therein respectfully submitted."

Fourthly—*Of its Petrifactions,* **Volcanic Forma-**
tions, Ores and Poisonous Tracts

Petrifactions are of animal substances, or of vegetable ones, or argillaceous.

First, *Of the Petrifactions of Animal Substances.*
Three or four miles on the south side of Cumberland river, and as near Nashville, **Dr. Roane,** in
1818, found a petrified fish, adhering to a rock on
the side of a hill. It was probably carried to that
place, by waters which withdrew, leaving it dead
in the mud; which some time afterward was converted into stone.

In Davidson county, in the state of Tennessee,
on the plantation of Captain Coleman; at the bottom of his spring-house, from which the earth had
been removed, in searching for the foundation; is
a rock, on which the house is placed. On the surface of this rock, are petrified snakes, partly incorporated with the stone. It seems as if the snakes
had lain upon it; and had sunk, in part, into the
substance, which is now stone; giving the idea of
a petrifaction, at the same time, both of that substance and of the snakes which lay upon it. Petrified shells are found in parts of the county, south of
Nashville, just below the surface. Petrified turkey eggs have been found many feet under the
ground, and will be more particularly described in
another chapter.

Of Vegetable Petrifactions.

Eight miles south of Nashville, was found a
petrified mushroom; with a small stem at the bottom, which connected it with the ground on which
it grew. The tuberous top is divided by small
fissures; and upon the outward surface are many
small adjoining circles, with small circles within
to the centre, where is the smallest circle of
all, with a small excrescence in the centre. And
almost every day, we see petrified hickory nuts,
walnuts and cane roots. Petrified leaves we find,

D

in the interior of the rocks on the banks of the Cumberland at Nashville; and also nuts.

In May 1819, about seven miles from the town of Franklin, iu the county of Williamson, passing westwardly from the Fayetteville road to the Cumberland road, near to a small path leading through unsettled heavy timbered woods, was found by Mr. Pugh, a piece of petrified wood, which appeared to have been a stump dug up, with the roots cut off, one side hewed, and the upper end cut off. Two very plain chops are on the face of the hewed part, seeming to have been first chopped, and then hewed. The piece would weigh at least twenty pounds, and appears to have been ash, before it was petrified, from the coarseness of the grain.

Of Argillaceous Petrifactions.

In the county of Davidson, in West Tennessee, nine miles south of Nashville, on the plantation lately occupied by John Mayfield, is a stone hearth, and upon it are the tracts of crows of different sizes.

On the Cumberland road, which was opened in the year 1787, there is about halfway between Drowning creek and where Mr. Terril lives, and Obed's river where Mr. Graham lives, the impression of a horse's foot shod, all converted into solid stone; and near it, is the impression of a man's foot, upon the rock, also converted into solid stone.

In the county of White, on Cane creek, which runs into the Cany Fork northwest from Sparta fourteen miles, or two and a quarter miles below the road from Sparta to Carthage, is a flat rock, running from the bank into the water, where is a small stream of salt water running into the creek, on the north side of which are impressed three tracks of a horse, which seem to have been made as he went down the rock to the creek. When he came to the lower rock, near the water, he turned to the left, and made other tracks, also impressed into it. The tracks of his hinder feet being on the lower rock, and those of his fore feet upon another rock a little higher, in going down the rock, his feet appear to have slipped forward, and where he stood upon the lower rock, the track is so plain, that the impression made by the frog of his foot is as apparent as it would have been if made upon common clay. The tracks are so natural, that no one would take them for sculptured representations. The rock at the fore part of the tracks, seems to have been clay, raised by the foot as it slipped forward. The country in which this rock is, was ceded by the Indians in 1805, and first began to be settled by the whites in 1806. The Cherokees first had horses in 1700, or a little later. The French first settled Canada in 1608. Some of their hunters may have travelled on horseback through this country before 1700; otherwise it must be considered, that this petrifaction took place within a few years past. *See note A.*

Of Volcanic Formations in Tennessee.

In the country within the limits of this state, called the Chickasaw purchase, between the Tennessee river and the Mississippi, and near the latter river, are found in many places, balls which at first sight seem to be cannon balls, to which their resemblance is very striking. They are round and of a dark colour, but are composed of sand within, and in the centre is a small cavity, containing fine particles of very white sand. The shape is like that which is given to the vitrified, round and hollow substances, which are found in the vicinity of the Cumberland river, where it most nearly approaches the Tennessee, in the lower parts of Stuart county. The latter are supposed to have been thrown up in the times of earthquakes, from subterraneous fires, through apertures of a rounded form, which were opened in many parts of the country, giving

vent to the passages of sand, and fused materials.
The motion by which they ascended, was such as
produced rotundity in the rolled or upheaved mass,
and met the external air something like that, perhaps, which in a kettle of boiling water fixes watery globules on the surface. After crossing the
Tennessee river from east to west, and progressing
forty miles in that direction, everywhere in the
country, down to the Mississippi, are small longitudinal ponds of water, sometimes sixty poles long
and twenty-five or thirty poles wide. The water
within, is generally about six inches deep. The
water runs off in small drains or necks, to the lower lands. Near to the entrance into those necks,
are found balls with clear white sand in the centre.
The balls are perfectly round, the larger ones having the appearance of cannon balls. They are
from the size of a nine pound cannon ball to that
of a partridge egg. The materials which compose
them have internally the appearance of white clay,
and not more than one third heavier than pumice.
They may have been ejected from the bowels of
the earth, in the time of earthquakes; when also,
the ponds in which they are, may have sunk.
When broken, they make angular edges, and have
evident signs of gas confined within them. In the
neighbouring county of Stuart, on the east side of
Tennessee, are round pieces of vitrified matter,
with something that rattles in the inside. The
bottom of these ponds is a tough marl, of a white
consistence. The country near to the Mississippi
is somewhat defaced, by the earthquake of 1811;
and on the side of one of the rivers, a lake has
been formed, of ten or fifteen miles in length, and
eight or ten in breadth, with dead trees standing in
it, having their bodies immersed halfway up in
water.

In the same way, many have been formed in
more ancient times. That these balls have been

formed by the action of fire, and by the motion which prevails in the times of earthquakes, is rendered probable by another fact. A few miles from the town of Columbia, in the county of Maury, in West Tennessee, on the south side of Duck river, a digging was commenced in 1822, for the purpose of discovering a silver mine, supposed to be there. The diggers, after descending one hundred and fifty feet, came to a cavity, through which the well passed, having part of the cavity on both sides. Near it, the rocks had evident marks of fire having acted upon them. In the cavity, they found several balls, perfectly round, of the size of pound swivel balls; as heavy as cannon balls of the same size, or nearly so. The exterior parts of the ball were made a little uneven, by small square protuberances lying flat in some places, and by the projection of the edges, or ends of them, in others. One of them was broken, and contained, through all the interior, from the surface to the centre, a bright substance, of a cast inclining to sulphureous, and seemingly of a fusile quality. They found also on digging, a white, solid and semitransparent substance, which seemed to have shot like ice, longitudinally, and adhering together laterally, nearly of the colour of those stalactical substances, which cover the bottoms of our caves, and which are white, solid and heavy; sometimes three or four inches thick, and which have been formed of what fell from the dripping of the cave above. The substance now spoken of, as found near Columbia, is of the same colour but brighter, and is distinguished from the other by its longitudinal shoots, which that has not. The Columbia substance resembles alum in colour, but is more transparent, light and bright. The balls must have been formed when in a state of fusion, and also in such sort of melting as communicated a perfectly round form, such as gave the same form to the vitrified balls in

Stuart county, and to those which were found between the Tennessee ridge and the Mississippi.
The latter, it is true, were not heavy in proportion
to their size, and were of sandy materials in part.
It may be here mentioned, as possibly proceeding
from the same cause, that soon after the earthquake
in 1811, several pumice stones were found floating
in the waters of Cumberland river, and seemed to
have been discharged, by fire and fusion, of the
heavier particles which formerly made a part of
their composition. The earthquakes of 1811,
commenced on the 16th of December, half-past two
o'clock in the morning; and have been felt at intervals up to 1819, and as late as July 1822. The first
shocks which were the most violent, had these effects.
The water in the Mississippi, near New-Madrid,
rose in a few minutes twelve or fourteen feet, and
again fell like a tide. Some lakes were elevated,
and the bottom raised above the common surface of
the earth in the neighbourhood, and still remains so.
The country near New-Madrid, was everywhere
broken up in furrows, six or eight feet wide, and as
many deep. The streams of water in Tennessee
have ever since been more copious than before. In
many places in West Tennessee, old sulphur springs
have commenced running again, which some years
before were dried up. And in some places, new
springs of sulphureous water have broken out of
the earth, and still continue to run. The earth in
the western parts of West Tennessee, opened in
several places, and white sand issued from the
apertures. Near New-Madrid, hot water issued
from the holes, of a dark colour, and of a strong
sulphureous smell. Where the white sand was
thrown up, it lay around the hole in a circular
form. In some places, there issued from the earth
something like wind from the tube of a bellows,
passing through burning coal. In the Chickasaw
country, it cast up hillocks of white sand, of the

size of potatoe hills. These are all through the Chickasaw country. In some places west of the Mississippi, a troublesome warmth of the earth was perceptible to the naked feet. The next day but one before the first earthquake, was darkened from morning to night, by thick fog; and divers persons perceived a sulphureous scent. The wind ceased, and there was a dead calm, without the least breath of air, on the day of the earthquake. The like calm preceded all the shocks. The motions of the earth were undulating. The parts agitated quivered like the flesh of a beef just killed. They began just about the time the comet disappeared. The motions progressed from west to east; and these earthquakes have travelled progressively in that direction, agitating and alarming in succession, the countries of America, Europe and Asia, till they have gone into the ocean, east of Asia. The motions in Tennessee were sometimes, but seldom, perpendicular; resembling a house raised, and suddenly let fall to the ground. Explosions like the discharge of a cannon at a few miles' distance, were heard; and at night, flashes of lightning seemed sometimes to break from the earth. For two or three months the shocks were frequent; almost every day. Then they gradually decreased in frequency, and took place at longer intervals, which continued to lengthen till they finally ceased. In May 1817, in Tennessee, they had come to be several months apart, and were but just perceptible. The last of them was in 1822. When the shocks came on, the stones on the surface of the earth were agitated by a tremulous motion, like eggs in a frying-pan, and altogether made a noise similar to that of the wheels of a wagon in a pebbly road. The frightened horses ran snorting in the field; the hogs squealed; the dogs barked; and the fowls descended from their roosts. The ponds of water, where there was no wind, had a troubled surface, the whole day preceding any great shock. A deep gloom prevailed. In the time of the earthquake, a murmuring noise, like that of fire disturbed by the blowing of a bellows, issued from the pores of the earth. A distant rumbling was heard, almost without intermission, and sometimes seemed to be in the air. Bricks fell from the tops of chimneys. The agitations about, exceeded those immediately upon the surface. On the west side of the Mississippi, trees were in many places split from the root upwards, the roots themselves being divided. In some instances, the tree was wholly split to pieces, and in others a vacuum was left between the different parts. In some instances, the trees were broken off; the tops fell to the ground, and the trunks were left standing. Spouts of water, of three or four inches in diameter, sprang from the Mississippi, and ascended to a great height. In some parts of the Mississippi, the river was swallowed up, for some minutes, by the seeming descent of the water, into some great opening of the earth at the bottom of the river. Boats with their crews were ingulfed, and never more heard of. For six months before the earthquakes at least, and indeed for a longer time, the weather was unusually warm, little or no motion of the air was perceptible, and no lightning was seen or thunder heard. A dread calm brooded over futurity. In the time of the earthquakes, the fountains received muddy water into their beds, too thick to be drank. The watery passages seemed to be repairing, and the choaked avenues to be cleansing. A dull and heavy obscuration of the atmosphere usually preceded the shocks. The effluvia which caused the dimness of the day, seemed to be neither cloud or smoke, yet resembling both. It was too light for clouds, and too thin for common smoke; and was of a lighter cast. It seldom terminated in condensation, as Tennessee vapours usually do. In the time of the shocks, many persons experienced a nauseating sickness at the stomach, and a trembling of the knees. These earthquakes were followed by an epidemic complaint, in the years 1815 and 1816, which was very mortal. In the time of the earth-quakes, lights were seen in the night, sometimes westwardly like the light of the sun, before it is closed by the darkness of the night; but shooting much further, toward the east, and continuing much longer, than the light of the sun after setting. And sometimes in the night, the heavens would seem to be tinged with a reddish colour, supposed to be the effect of invisible effluvia, issuing through the pores of the earth; and collecting above us, like smoke in the spring, which rises from log heaps, and brush heaps; and shows itself like light at a distance. The water near New-Madrid, which was spurted from the bowels of the earth, was black, having the appearance of an intermixture with coal. Ever since the commencement of these earthquakes, in 1811 and from thence up to 1819, and afterwards, tremblings of the earth have occurred there almost every day, and in West Tennessee at intervals up to July 1822.

Of the Geodes found in Tennessee.

Beside the globular masses before described, there are others in Tennessee, which seem to have a different origin, which should also be described. After passing the Cany Fork, at Trousdale's, six or eight miles above Carthage, on the road from Nashville to Knoxville, the traveller ascends a hill, on the right and left of which are low grounds; far below the road on which he is; the waters descend-ing on the one side into the Cany Fork, and on the other into the Cumberland. The summit of the ridge is two hundred or two hundred and fifty feet above the low grounds on either side. In many places, the summit of the ridge is not more than ten or fifteen feet across. The ridge continues for

E

fifteen miles, before the hollows and low grounds disappear. Upon the summit of these ridges, as well as on the ridge in Roan county, before described as being three hundred and fifty feet high, are found in clusters, masses in rounded forms, inclining to eliptical, with tuberous excrescences, like those of large Irish potatoes. They are of a dark colour on the outside, and of the size generally of large cymblings, in some other countries called squashes. The centre is hollow, with loose particles in it, of the like sort as those which occupy the interval between the hollow and the exterior. This hollow is lined with a thin crust, or lamina of red dirt, of a deep tinge. The interval between this and the interior, is occupied by small chrystallized pieces, of the form of diamonds, with angular points, which pieces are incorporated and run into each other, no one being wholly separated and distinct from its neighbour. The whole mass has the appearance, and suggests the idea, of matter conglomerated, whilst in a plastic state, by rolling up the hill, till it reached the summit, where the waters were not of depth and force sufficient to move them any further. After which, petrifaction and chrystallization took place, the materials contracting toward the surface, and of course leaving the centre hollow. The angular pieces, in the shape of diamonds, will scratch glass. Many of these geodes, of the size of pumpkins, and of eliptical figures, are said to lie on the surface, between Murfreesborough and McMinnville. The groups in which they lie seem never to have been disordered by the misplacings of man.

Of the Ores of Tennessee.

Lead ore is found in small veins, in the county of Claiborne. Little search has as yet been made, to ascertain the fact of a lead mine being there.

A mine of lead has been worked in Jefferson county.

No part of the world produces better iron ore, than the county of Claiborne; nor in greater abundance. Twenty sets of iron-works in this small county, are generally kept in operation.

Iron ore abounds also in the county of Dickson, which contains within its limits, the Yellow-creek iron-works, those of Mr. Bell on Barton's creek, and those of Mr. Napier on the same stream, in the lower part of Davidson; also, near the Big Harpeth river, iron ore is very abundant. It is in the greatest profusion in the counties of Lincoln and Bedford.

Of Poisonous Tracts of Country in Tennessee.

On the confines of Sumner and Smith counties, in West Tennessee, and on the waters of Goose creek, two miles north of Mr. Donoho's plantation, on the road leading from Gallatin to Carthage, is a tract of country, in which, when cattle graze, their milk becomes poisonous : and when taken into the stomach, produces sickness which usually terminates in death. If the cow be killed for beef, the flesh taken into the stomach, produces the same symptoms and results. The crows, dogs and buzzards, which are fed on the flesh of cattle, which die shortly after grazing there, soon after die themselves. A deer which has been killed soon after feeding there, produces the sickness and death of those who eat the venison. The cause of this extraordinary mortality has not hitherto been discovered, but is supposed to lurk in the succulent parts of some vegetable which grows there. The researches of some experienced botanist, might be usefully employed in this spot; and might save many lives in future, by pointing out the cause, which once detected, would make known the antidote to be opposed to its deleterious powers. Information hath not made it known to the writer, whether the honey extracted from the plants which grow there, is equally or at all poisonous. The cow or deer itself is not poisoned, by the food it eats there, and yet its milk and flesh are poisonous. The fact is unaccountable though it is real. Whenever the real cause comes to be discovered, the wonder may be greatly abated, as well as the effects obviated or prevented, by the application of the appropriate medicaments. The only one now resorted to, is that of keeping the cattle confined in pens, so that they do not range upon this tract of country. Those who live upon the lands which are exceedingly fertile and productive, can neither eat the meat nor use the milk of the cattle. In other respects, there is no inconvenience to which the inhabitants are subjected, more than those who live upon the adjacent or more distant lands, in this section of country. In Bledsoe county in Sequatchie valley, is a tract of land, the grazing of which is followed by similar effects. This valley commences a few miles south of the Crab orchard, two and a half miles east of Spencer's hill, and extends in length to the Tennessee river, in a southwardly direction. Where it first commences, it is narrower, but where it joins the river, is the width of four or five miles. It is bounded on the west by the Cumberland mountain, and on the east by Walker's ridge, in which Spencer's hill is. The lands in the valley also are very fertile.

With respect to the symptoms of the disorder in affected animals, observed principally in the poisonous tract on Goose creek, in the county of Sumner. If the cow can get to water, it hastens the appearance of the symptoms, *tremour and the constipation* of the intestines. Her head is tossed from side to side, in agony; and if it remain in any one position for some time, the muscles cannot be acted on, so as to bring the head to any other posture. All the muscles have a peculiar rigidity. If milk be now drawn, it emits an odour known to those conversant with such milk. It is said not to froth so much as good milk, when flying from th₃ dug into a vessel. At boiling heat it quickly curdles. The cream has a greenish hue, and the butter made from it highly pernicious qualities. If the calf suck the milk, it trembles, staggers, and often falls, whilst sucking, and dies immediately. By abstracting the milk, the animal is somewhat relieved. At length, her abdomenal muscles are much contracted, presenting a meagre appearance of the body. Her breathing is laborious, and very offensive if inhaled by the by-standers. On dissection, the stench arising from the internal parts is almost insupportable. The several apartments of the stomach, and parts of the intestines are gangrenous. The retained contents are dry fœted matter. Other animals are similarly affected in the violent forms of the disease. The first suspicion of the cow being diseased, often arises from nausea at the stomach of those who for some days may have used the milk. Perhaps the calf is by this time affected. If under these circumstances the milk be regularly drawn, the cow may exhibit no symptoms of disease, eating and drinking as usual. Should she be made to undergo severe exercise, the complaint will appear in its customary form, and perhaps terminate in death, or in a slow recovery of six or twelve months' duration. Indeed, it is stated that animals once under the influence of this poison, never are so completely recovered as not to feel its effects in any future violent exertion, or what is vulgularly called healing the blood. At all stages of the disease, ardent spirits, and spirits of turpentine, are attended with salutary effects when freely administered. When the intestinal canal is freely purged, the danger is slight, with proper care.

In Sequatchie valley some sheep laboured under the poison: they vomited without much apparent effort, and were also purged without having taken any medicine. The owner thought if his cattle and sheep had remained on the hills, they would not have shown any marks of disease. The fatigue of being driven home, and then drinking water, produced the active form of the disease.

In the dormant state of the disease, the milk of a cow is not so deleterious, as when the complaint has assumed its more distinctive character.

That dogs, cats, hogs, turkeys, chickens, crows and buzzards die by using the flesh of animals which perished under this disease, can be attested by the oaths of hundreds. Sometimes buzzards are unable to fly from the carcase; and on a branch of Goose creek, called Hicherson's fork, sixty or seventy buzzards have been seen dead at one time near the water.

In driving fourteen steers from the hills to a farm two miles from them, seven sickened and died at the first branch of water they crossed: two only could be driven home, and they also died some time afterwards. Dogs have been unable to get home, after eating the flesh of dead animals. One of the neighbours of the late Colonel Benjamin Seawell, who stated these facts, when removing his family to a distant part of the country, had six or seven horses to die on the road, with the common symptoms of this disorder, although these horses were apparently well when setting off on the journey.

Mr. Elisha Henry, when fox hunting, found two of his dogs at a carcase he supposed to be poisoned. The same dogs, after running half a mile in a fox chase, came to water and drank, and died immediately.

The cows of Mrs. Britton were neglected, and ranged out of the pasture, whilst her husband was sick. She suspected the milk, from the greenish colour of the cream; and ordered some to be given to a pig. The servant believing the milk to be good, eat some of it, and was immediately attacked, but recovered. At the sale of her husband's estate shortly afterwards, she purchased a mare known to be affected by the poison, and this mare soon died. It being inconvenient to burn or bury the carcase, as is customary, a pen of wood was placed around. Into this inclosure none but small animals could find a passage. In the course of a day or two, one racoon and two opossums were found dead by the carcase.

So far as this sickness affects human beings, it can be invariably traced to taking into the stomach the milk, butter or flesh of animals which laboured under the same disease. With respect to both men and other animals, the violence of an attack is modified by the quantity and quality of milk, butter or flesh taken into the stomach, and the time it is retained.

A great many horses and cows die quite fat, within the limits of that section of country in which the disease exists : and a vast number of hogs and dogs die very soon after using the flesh of such animals, of a disease similar to that of which those animals themselves died.

The stomach and bowels of these animals are highly inflamed, and the intestines are filled with hardened, round, smooth lumps of excrements. Stock confined to an old, well cultivated pasture, never are affected with this disease; nor is their flesh or milk noxious. If a new piece of woodland be added to the farm the disorder often appears, but by separating those woodlands from the old lots, it will soon disappear. Vegetation here is the same as elsewhere. The country is rich and considerably broken with small mountains; the Millstone mountain, the Sandstone mountain, &c. Sulphur is intermixed with the rocks of the Millstone mountain. In human patients a burning sensation in the stomach is first perceived, which for a day or two is moderate, and not attended with any vomiting or pain. On the third day the burning in the stomach is severe, and the patient sometimes vomits every half hour: obstinate constipation takes place, with some pain in the stomach. The pulse is small, threaded and a little accelerated; and the heat of the extremities considerably below the common temperature. Restlessness and great anxiety prevails in the early part of the disease; a constant and an ungovernable desire for water, which when given allays the burning for a moment, but the fluid is soon rejected, and then vomiting and pain resume their usual violence. There is no soreness or pain in the regions of the liver, spleen, back or head. The disease is seated in the stomach and bowels, and there is great and immediate prostration of the whole system. These symptoms continue with great violence about twenty-four hours after the vomiting commences, with now and then a hickup. The vomiting, burning and pain then begin to subside, and the hickup becomes more and more frequent. Difficulty of breathing supervenes, especially as the patient inspires, which is performed slowly and with considerable difficulty: and as he becomes less restless, and his anxiety abates, stupor prevails, in the same ratio, till its subject is rendered completely insensible The pulse intermits, the eyes become fixed, and the palpibræ remain open. With these symptoms death closes the scene, in about sixty hours from the time the vomiting commences. The matter thrown off the stomach is nearly transparent, now and then a little bilious, generally tasteless; not acrid, having a very peculiar smell, conceit makes it sometimes resemble the smell that is frequently emitted from new milk just taken from cows which have recently fed on young wild vegetation and buds, and sometimes the smell of young bruised garlick. This is one of the most prominent diagnostics of the complaint. It occurs at every time of the year, but is most common in March, April, May, September, October and November. Cows giving milk, it is believed, labour for months under the influence of this disorder, without showing evident signs of it. The calves of cows apparently well, frequently die with a complaint, evidenced by the same train of symptoms, which other animals show, that are supposed to be poisoned.

There are hills separating the two principal branches of Goose creek from each other, towards their sources, and on the west from Bledsoe's creek. It is along these ridges and their bases, that animals contract the disease. The chain running between the upper and middle fork of Goose creek, is most remarkable for the poison. This high land runs in peaks and hills, to the height of two or three hundred feet above the level of the river. Of these hills, the Millstone knob is the most remarkable. From its summit, a country beautifully variegated with hills and dales, in a state of high cultivation, presents itself. The mill stone quarry, whence it has its name, is about two thirds the way from its base to the summit. Viewing the face of the quarry, it will be found that only a few feet of earth covers a loose flaky bed of slate, which extends to the depth of five or ten feet, and rests on the mill stone rock. This last seems composed of flint of different colours, the secondary limestone, with a small portion of sulphur, and a bituminous substance in combination. It is said, that when the hot bonds are applied around the mill stone, an oily substance with some sulphur exudes. The slate stone will blaze in the fire for some time, and emit an unpleasant smell. There is no discoverable mineral substance in this hill, except some coarse pyrites.

To one passing through the adjacent country, and Goose creek lands, the latter would present no

F

peculiarity, either in regard to the face of the country, its mineralogy, its water, or its vegetation.

This disease occurs in other places. Many of its peculiarities have been observed in Stokes county, North-Carolina, on the low lands, on both margins of the Yadkin river. In that part of the country it was called the river sickness, and could always be eradicated by cultivating the soil, as was proved on Poindexter's and Kirby's farms. It was there thought to be produced by the wild parsnip root, or by the numerous spiders with their webs, which adhered to the mulberry leaves.

On the Little Yadkin river, where there was a fulling mill and furnace, it was ascribed to mineral exhalations raised by the heat and their subsiding on the vegetables.

In the same state it occurs in Guilford and Burk counties, in North-Carolina. Also in some parts of South-Carolina. It occurs in the mountainous and flat lands of Kentucky, in the plains of Indiana, of Missouri, of Illinois, Michigan, and in Ohio. It is also met with in Bedford county, in the state of Tennessee, in Smith county, on the waters of Frenchbroad river, and on Emery's river. In Sequatchie valley, in Bledsoe county, it is very destructive. This valley is about seventy miles in length, about five and twelve miles wide. The Cumberland mountain is on one side, and its auxiliary chain, the Walnut ridge. From these two lofty mountains, in the summer time, is presented a delightful prospect of finely cultivated farms. The atmosphere in these mountains is singularly serene; the foggy valley below looks to the morning traveller like a lengthened lake below. Even in this peaceful valley, lurks the undiscovered cause of so much pain and misery. Inquiry for the cause puts on its eager hue, whenever a human being becomes the subject of its operation, and many and various are the conjectures which spring into view before it.

But the cause is yet undiscovered, not because it is beyond the reach of human investigation, but because those whose learning and qualifications for accurate research have not yet bestowed upon the subject the requisite pains for its elucidation.

For the latter statement in relation to the poisonous tract on Goose creek, the topography of that section, and the symptoms of the disorder, the author is indebted to communications made by Doctor McCall, who with all liberality, that everywhere marks the conduct of enlightened men, has furnished the requisite information, founded upon his own observations, and those of Doctor Sharp, who have both examined the phenomena with a scientific curiosity, suitable to the importance and novelty of the subject. And from whose continued pursuits there is ground to hope for the most beneficial results.

Here let a remark be indulged, that can do no harm, and may do some good. If this disorder were caused by mineral effluvia, it would prevail as much in winter as in the other seasons of the year, and not in alluvial soils, where there is no rock or mineral substance in the whole country, as in Indiana, Illinois, and on the Yadkin, in North-Carolina. Nor would its sources be reached and destroyed by the plough or other agricultural instrument.

If caused by some plant, it would cease to act in November and December; unless, indeed, the seeds of the disorder were taken into the stomach before. Nor would it begin to operate as early as March. It would, moreover, be discernable amongst the herbs of the forest: nor would it be eradicated by culture; but like other plants, would spring up again, when culture was discontinued.

But if some spider or small poisonous insect, or worm, it would be torpid in the winter months, when other animals became so, and begin to move again in March, when other torpid animals begin to move. Its residence would be just below the surface, and would be broken up and destroyed by the plough. From March to December, it would ascend to the surface, especially in the warmer months of the year, to enjoy the cool temperature of the evening and the morning; and fly from the rays of the sun, when too hot to be comfortable. This hypothesis, being not in collision with any of the observations hitherto made, is recommended to the consideration of the literate, when making their further researches.

Adjacent to Alabama, on the west of the Cumberland mountains, the same disorder occurs. These mountains run through the state obliquely, from northeast to southwest, dividing it into East and West Tennessee. East Tennessee is a rough, mountainous country, extremely healthy. Here the milk sickness is unknown, except as is before mentioned, and in Blount county. The part of West Tennessee adjoining to Kentucky, is also broken, and hilly; more to the south and west, the country is less so; the soil very fertile, and vegetation exceedingly luxuriant. The forests abound in large trees and thick undergrowth, which excludes the rays of the sun from the soil; and in wet weather, noxious effluvia rise in great exuberance. In some places the water runs off slowly, and in others are stagnant. Franklin county lies along the foot of the Cumberland mountain, thirty or thirty-five miles, and is watered by Elk river. On the north and west of Franklin lies Bedford county, watered by Duck river and its tributaries. As soon as the settlements commenced in these counties, in the year 1807, near the mountains, many cattle were lost, from some unknown poison, the nature of which has not yet been discovered. Sometimes whole herds were found dead, in some sequestered cove of the mountain. The poison is confined to certain spots, at or near the foot of the mountain, in those coves, as some imagine, which have a western or northwestern aspect; but as others say, in those coves, and others likewise, which have a different aspect. Those which look to the south, are supposed by some to be free from poison, but Sequatchie valley must be excepted. The existence of the poison is here periodical, from June to October, and is most virulent in August and September. If cattle remain in a poisonous tract during the night, or feed there, early in the morning, they invariably suffer more or less from the poison. But after the sun has risen so as to dissipate the dews, they may feed there with perfect safety. Some of the farmers pen their cattle in the night, and at nine or ten o'clock turn them out to range, without fear of the consequence. Within a few years, a fence has been extended for many miles along the foot of the mountain, so as to exclude this nuisance; in consequence of which precaution, cases of this disorder much more rarely occur than formerly. In 1820, the legislature interposed, and by an act passed for the purpose, directed to be fenced certain coves of the Cumberland mountain, to prevent, as it states, animals from eating an unknown vegetable, imparting to their milk and flesh, when used for diet, deleterious qualities. And it contained very strict provisions, obliging overseers to keep up these fences. Many of the inhabitants in this section of country have died of the disorder, as well as the cattle, supposed to have been poisoned by the flesh, milk or butter of animals, which had previously taken the poison into the stomach, and before it had manifested itself with sufficient violence to attract notice. Hence the popular name of the disease. Men, it is said, may be affected as other animals, by lying on the ground, on the poisonous tracts, or by remaining there for several hours during the night. In men, the disease thus induced is gastritious, with some modifications of the usual symptoms accompanying this affection, as supposed to be induced by miasmata generally. The stomach is extremely irritable; the bowels torpid, and obstinately costive, with great febrile excitement, and determination to the head. A peculiar odour emanates from the patient, especially as death approaches, which is perhaps the most striking diagnostic. But for this, it might be difficult to distinguish it from the most violent attacks of bilious remittent fever. The remedies adopted by the people, and by physicians, are active purgatives. To open the bowels is indispensable, but frequently difficult. The most operative medicines have frequently failed of success. In general, relief is the immediate consequence of evacuation. Convalescence is generally tedious, and relapses frequent, even at the distance of twelve months. The hair, epidermis, and nails, sometimes fall off; and some constitutions never recover from the shock. The stomachs of brutes have been opened after death, by dissection, and have shown in places the marks of inflammation, and some of the ventrils are said to have exhibited the appearances of having been broiled or contracted by heat. This poison is supposed by some to be vegetable; by others, mineral. In the poison fields of Chatham county, North-Carolina, hemlock is said to grow. In West Tennessee, mushrooms, and also a species of weed bearing a black berry, and other vegetable subtances have been suspected. The waters have been accused of mineral impregnation. Mineral exhalations, from imbedded ores, imbibed by the dew as it ascends, have been cited to the bar of examination. Some think, that it is a miasmatic exhalation. In the summer time they say, from 89 to 90 of Farenheit, that the nights are cool, and that oftentimes in twenty-four hours, there is a difference of the temperature from 20 to 30 degrees. Copious exhalations are produced by the heat of the day, of effluvia, from the ponds, rivers, marshes, and forests, so rarified as to be but little capable of injury. Night condenses them by a colder atmosphere, and from increased gravity they begin to subside. Vapours visible and invisible, this theory considers as attracted by mountains, and other elevated objects. There is commonly at this season of the year, a breeze from the west, by which the mists and vapours are gently wafted towards the neighbouring mountains, where they are intercepted and driven into the valleys. Becoming still more dense, the more ponderous particles gradually roll down the declivities, and settle in condensed bodies, in the low grounds and hollows, and confined coves, which become the hotbeds of the poison. Here, it is supposed, are generated, by concentration of the most noxious particles, disorders more virulent than even this called *the milk sickness*. And the miasmata, when received into the stomach, with the dews deposited on the herbage, are supposed to be adequate to the destruction which is produced. This theory, as well as others, has its difficulties to encounter; for the disorder prevails in East Tennessee, where there are no mountains to intercept the western breezes, nor cavities to receive their more ponderous particles, nor swamps and stagnant waters to generate the poison; where the winds blow directly from the Cumberland mountain, and from the high and broken lands near its eastern side; and where the air is as highly salubrious as in any part of the world.

Poisonous tracts are also on the east side of the Alleghenies, in Haywood county, to which the same remarks exactly apply.

In West Tennessee, for several years past, white clover, when eaten by horses and other animals, early in the morning, before nine or ten o'clock, produces profuse salivation, which sometimes ter-

minates in death. Formerly such effects were unknown: the cause is yet undiscovered: but as in
one circumstance it is very much like the poison
taken into the stomach by cattle, early in the morning, in the poison fields, it may in time become as
hurtful as the poison now in discussion. A perfect
discovery of the one cause, might shed a great deal
of light upon the other.

In the county of Blount, in East Tennessee, is
another of these poisonous tracts: A farmer, whose
plantation adjoins, extended his field over a part of
it. The ground yielded abundantly; and it has
not been perceived that the grain raised there, has
contracted any virulent quality. But he is assured
of the fact, that when using the land as pasture,
the disease of the cattle is contracted, although
there is nothing visible, but what in appearance
are the sweetest and most nutritive grasses. He
has observed, in gathering fodder from the corn
stock, that by suspending the blades, and keeping
them from the ground, while cutting, the fodder
receives no poisonous infusion, as it does invariably
when placed to dry in contact with the soil.

More to the east, but nearly in the same degree of
latitude, amongst the Alleghenies, on the west side of
the Blue ridge, forty miles from the southern boundary of North-Carolina, which is in the thirty-fifth
degree of north latitude, in three or four coves of the
mountain, where the lands are fertile, is the same
disorder. The animal that feeds upon them, when
heated by motion, loses the use of its limbs, and
dies in a short time. But if not heated by exercise,
very often escapes being disordered. That they
are poisoned, is hardly ever discoverable, till they
become fatigued by exercise. Their milk and flesh
is poisonous, and the butter likewise. The sickness from eating any of these, commences by puking
and a violent pain in the stomach. The breath of
the patient is very offensive, and the sweat from

his body may be smelled eight or ten steps from him: the scent is cadaverous. The poisonous effects are seen here in the months of August and September. There are four of these poisonous tracts in the county of Haywood, not far from the centre and the town of Waynesville. No ponds or stagnant waters are near them. The coves in which they are, bear to the southeast. There are some of these poisonous tracts also, in the county of Buncomb; nearly in the same degree of latitude, but rather more to the south.

Of the Indian Summer in Tennessee.

In Tennessee and in North-Carolina, and Virginia, a part of the year is distinguished by the name of the Indian summer; which is said not to be known in other parts of the world. About the middle of October, or a few days sooner or later, it commences. The weather is fair and warm, with a hazy or smoky appearance of the atmosphere, and causes agreeable sensations. It continues two or three weeks, and sometimes more, and is immediately succeeded by cold weather. Advantage is taken of its continuance, to gather in the cotton and other fruits of the earth. It is generally dispelled by a brisk current of wind from the south, followed in a few hours by clouds and rain, which are driven off by wind from the west or northwest. The cold season then advances, and through the winter to the beginning of April, whenever the wind is from the south, the temperature is warm, and the animal spirits depressed; which state of the atmosphere is soon followed by a brisk wind with clouds and rain in the rear. When their direction is changed by a wind from the west or from the northwest, the rain is oftentimes changed into snow before the horizon is cleared of them. The animal spirits are exhilarated by a wind from the west, and much more so by one from the northwest. In any part

G

of the winter, the wind is seldom from any point
beyond the south or northwest. When from the
west, the weather is cold; but more so when the
wind is from the northwest; and still more so when
it is from the north. When from the northeast, it
is in nearly the same degree of temperature as when
from a point between the south and west; but generally the weather is cloudy, and the clouds lower-
ing and charged with snow. The old remains of the
roots and bodies of trees blown up by winds, show
that there have been within a century past, very
strong gusts and currents of wind from the southeast.
Tornados are frequent in the summer, from the
clouds which frequently blow up in the evening,
and within the limits of their extent, are often very
destructive. When the atmosphere is cleared of
vapour, by a west or northwest wind, the weather
in winter becomes clear and cold; but each succeeding day becomes milder for three or four days;
whilst the wind creeps to the south, when it again
becomes warm, and frequently so much so, that it
is not agreeable to set by the fire. In a short time
afterwards, the wind springs up, and the clouds
follow as before mentioned. The nights in summer
time are much cooler than in North-Carolina.
There is seldom a night in Tennessee, when just
before daybreak, and thence to sunrise, a blanket
would not be comfortable. That part of the night
is so cool, as to indicate with certainty the near
approach of light. And indeed every part of the
night is cooler than in North-Carolina.

When the spring begins to advance, the air in
Tennessee is unequally warmed. In some places,
we enter into tepid columns, through which we pass
in eight or ten yards. The sensation they create,
is rather oppressive than otherwise.

There is much more rain and snow in the winters
in Tennessee, than in those of North-Carolina; the
sky is seldom clear in December and January, and

to the middle of February. The soil is diluted into mud, which reaches in many places to the knees of a horse travelling on the road. This constant humidity is the parent of consumptions to those whose constitutions are predisposed to that disorder. The summer nights are much cooler than those in North-Carolina. There is seldom, if ever, a summer night in Tennessee, where an hour before daybreak the cover of a blanket is not necessary for defence against the cold. One cause may be, that the numerous large trees which grow in the forests, exclude the rays of the sun in the day time, from the soil on which they stand; whereby it retains its moisture and coolness, which the falling of the dews increases: but this, if any cause, is not the only one, or perhaps even the most efficient; for a similar coolness is experienced in the barrens and wilderness, where there are no such forests, but possibly not in the same degree.

CHAPTER II.

WITHIN the limits of Tennessee are some geological phenomena, both upon the surface of the earth and below it, which ought to be recorded for the benefit of naturalists. And at the same time, there are numerous aboriginal vestiges; which added to those already preserved, may at some future day, help to elucidate what we so much desire to know, the history of the primitive settlers in this continent, with that of their exterminators, whom we in succession have exterminated. We will consider then in the first place, of marine appearances found upon or near the surface; secondly, of marine appearances under the surface; thirdly, of the productions of the surface found below it.

Sec. 1. First then, *Of Marine Appearances on the surface.* Shells are found in the limestone rock, in various parts of East Tennessee, particularly about the junction of the north and south forks of Holston. The volute of the conch is distinctly marked. Some of them are six inches in diameter. In many places, they may be seen in the road, by the observing traveller. The like appearances are discernable, at a few places near Bays mountain. The shells at the mouth of the north fork, are distant fifty miles from the summit of the Alleghenies. Similar appearances are abundant at Mr. Bradley's, fourteen miles east of Rogersville, and indeed through all the adjacent parts of the country.

Small shells of the same form as those commonly called *conch shells* of the ocean, are found upon the surface of the earth, in many places in West Tennessee. Upon the shells is an apex, and from it winding ridges, downwards, till the body of the shell is enlarged, where the animal once was enclosed. Thence it tapers and decreases, till it comes to a point at the bottom, with a part of the involuted shell covered by an upper one, with a space between, which the animal occupied whilst living. The colour of the inside is white with a mixture of red.

In many places amongst the rocks are found madripores, which are mistaken for petrified wasp-nests. These petrifactions exhibit a thousand cells in which animals once resided.

At a plantation in Davidson county, eight miles south- from Nashville, on the road leading to Huntsville, and through the whole neighbourhood of it, are limestone rocks on the surface; in which, through all parts of them, are intermixed bivalve shells, some of them of the size of the thumb nail of a middle sized man; others of the size of Spanish coined quarters of dollars. They are not quite as long as broad. Similar appearances are found in very great abundance, near Williamsburg, in Jackson county. Other petrified substances on the above mentioned plantation, are composed of small bivalve shells, of the same form, but two thirds less. These are found in masses, two or three feet under the surface, which are concretions formed of countless numbers of such shells; which are grooved on the outside, with radii all diverging from a point, near the upper end of the shell. The masses are easily broken into pieces, and seem to be in a state of decay. The shells are cemented together by mud converted into stone; in which mud they were embedded together, and were all of the same age when the animal functions were suspended, which must have been also at the same instant.

In Maury county, in the suburbs of Columbia, which stands on the south side of Duck river, are limestone rocks, in which are visible, numerous shells of the same species with those above described in the county of Davidson. And in the same suburbs, are madripores, and upon one of the rocks there, and forming a part of it, is a petrified crab fish. Similar shells are on Richland creek, and on Elk river. Marine appearances in short, are exhibited in all the counties within the limits of Tennessee, from the dividing ridge between the Tennessee and Mississippi rivers, to the Alleghenies, which divide this state from North-Carolina.

Between the Tennessee and Mississippi rivers, is a ridge of oyster shells, running in a northwardly and southwardly direction, and extending as far northwardly as the head waters of Forked-deer river; thirty or forty miles north of the southern boundary of the state of Tennessee. The Forked-deer being there nearly parallel with the boundary. How much further north the bank extends, at present is unknown to the writer. The ridge, or bank, is above the head of the rivers which run into the Tennessee on the one side, and into the Mississippi on the other. It extends southwardly, to the junction of the Blackwarrior river with the Tombeckbe; and in its course, is sometimes on the one side and sometimes on the other side of the Tombeckbe. In the state of Mississippi, in the lands occupied by the Chickasaw settlements, are several parallel ridges of oyster shells, three or four miles apart, dividing the head waters of Tombeckbe from each other. Some of these ridges are thirty or forty feet above the level of the water in the adjacent streams, and from half a mile to three quarters in width: others are of smaller dimensions. Some of them are wholly composed of oyster shells; and have the appearance of lime compacted, after it has been dissolved by slacking. It will crumble between the thumb and finger, like rotten dirt; and may be rubbed into the smallest particles, like lime from reduced shells.

Sec. 2. *Of Marine Appearances below the surface.*

Between the towns of Sparta and Carthage, and four miles from the former, is a mountain or ridge, through a gap of which the traveller passes, in going from the one town to the other. It continues circuitously, till it passes the Cany Fork, three miles below the Rock landing, and runs in a direction to join the main Cumberland mountain, on the north of Sparta. Its southwardly course is between Stone's river and Duck river, dividing the waters of the Cumberland and Tennessee rivers. This seems to be a similar circular chain within that which is twelve or eighteen miles beyond Nashville westwardly, which also is within an exterior one, more westwardly still, between the Tennessee and Mississippi, and to the ridge on the south, between the waters of the Mississippi and those of the Alabama. The smaller of these segments, in the shape of a rainbow, passes on the south of Sparta, three miles from it. Near the base, in a southwardly course from Sparta three miles, is the appearance of an old well, around which lie promiscuously a great number of conchs, from the size of a hen's egg to that of a thimble. Here the water below, it is said, affords a *strong salt-water attraction.* The ground around the old well, is firm and high. The well is five or six feet deep; and near its mouth is a small hillock of earth, made of the materials taken from the inside. There is no river in the country which at this day produces such shells. They were brought to the well, or taken from it by digging.

Mr. Spear sunk three wells in search of salt water, three miles from the town of Franklin, in Williamson county, and in a northwardly direction from the town, and near the road leading to Nashville. In one of them, at the depth of twenty feet, he struck limestone; on which he found periwinkles, one inch and a half in length, and two or three cockle shells, fluted on the outside. He dug up divers pieces of charcoal, of burnt white oak, at the depth of ten or fifteen feet. Fire and water, so hostile to each other, seem by all the subterranean phenomena which have been hitherto discovered in Tennessee, or in the neighbouring state of Missouri, to have joined their powers at the awful period when all these deposites were made in the bowels of the earth. Wherever we see trees, and *equatorial* plants heaped together under the surface, we never fail to find charcoal also. The fire seems to have exerted itself upon every combustible subject, which the waves did not conceal from its fury. *See D.*

Sec. 3. *Of the Productions of the Surface found below it;* first, *artificial;* secondly, *natural.*

First, *Of Artificial Productions of the Surface found below it.*

On Goose creek, on the Redbird fork of Kentucky river, not far from the bank of the creek, a well was sunk, to the depth of a hundred feet, and at the bottom was found a piece of an iron pot, and coal and ashes. General White, of Abingdon, related the fact to Colonel Ackland, the latter of whom stated it to the writer.

At Mr. Ready's, twelve miles southeast from Murfreesborough, ten feet from the bank of the east fork of Stone's river, and ten feet below the surface, he dug up a quantity of charcoal, in making an opening in which to fix his millhouse.—*See E.*

Secondly, *Of Natural Productions of the Surface found below it.*

The town of Sparta, in the county of White, in West Tennessee, is situated, at the foot of the Cumberland mountain, about one hundred yards east of a spring of the Cany Fork, called the Calfkiller, which runs by it from northeast to southwest.

H

The site of the town is an eminence, from the brow of which to the river on the west, is a declivity of twenty-five or thirty degrees, somewhat broken by the extremities of strata terminating one below another, and with a more western projection than the one next above, till the valley is arrived at, in which the river rolls. Between the brow and the river, in digging, was lately found, twenty feet under ground, five or six turkey eggs, all petrified. The end of one of them being broken off, the white and yolk were as plainly discernable as they were when the egg was in its primitive state. Thirty or forty yards below the spot where the well was sunk, is a sink-hole, now nearly filled up, which may have once extended to the place where the well was sunk. Part of the well caved in, and the clay which composed it fell to the bottom. The eggs found at the bottom may have come from this cavity, which was only twelve feet below the surface. The eggs looked like boiled eggs, but the colours of the yolk and white were not changed. Salt water is abundant through all this neighbourhood, and many nitrous caves are in the neighbouring mountains. These may have promoted and accellerated petrifaction. But how was the covering superinduced? Water mixed with sediment would have floated and separated the eggs. Dirt or clay torn off and thrown upon them, would have crushed them. The nest must have been in a cavity extending eastwardly, and under the covering over which the water glided, and from it fell below the nest, depositing sediments, which finally covered the mouth towards the west. Afterwards, the sediments were deposited equally over the covering of the cavity, and the alluvial accretion below. Most certainly, this covering to the depth of twenty feet, having been formed neither by inundation nor earthquake, shows evidently, that all other things under the same depth of covering, such as bones, metals and the like, may have been buried by progressive accretion. The hollows constantly fill up from the mountain to the plane; and Nature incessantly exerts herself to smooth the unevenness of the surface, which the deluge produced.

On the south side of Tennessee river, near the southern boundary of the state of Tennessee, are three trees entirely petrified. One a cypress, about four feet through; another a sycamore; and the last a hickory, but not as large. The roots, bark and limbs were still remaining in the year eighteen hundred and twenty-one, except parts which have been recenty broken off. They lie obliquely from the river, with the roots up stream, and are about five feet below low-water mark. About fifteen feet of the trees are exposed by the caving in of the bluff, and the residue of the trees is covered by the bluff, which at that place is estimated to be three hundred feet high, and is nearly perpendicular. The bluff is about a mile in length, and gently descends from the river. It consists of sand and white clay, and is by some called the Chalk bluff. Immediately over these trees, is a small spring, the water of which is strongly impregnated with iron and copperas. Similar petrifactions of wood, are to be found on Big Harpeth river; and also at the Chickasaw bluff, on the Mississippi. At the latter place, are several copperas springs, near to which are to be seen parts of trees, which have been lodged in the bank, in a state of petrifaction. The beach also over which the water passes, is for many yards incrusted with a petrifaction of clay or gravel. Part of a tree is also to be seen at this place, at low-water mark, some of which is petrified, and the balance has the appearance of stone coal, and from experiments made, no doubt is so. For several rods the coal is to be found, and when broken to pieces, exhibits the appearance of part having been once wood, and other parts clay.

The coal is stated by the settlers at the bluff, to have been formed within a few years. At Fort Pickering, which is about a mile below, Mr. Irvin, in digging a well, found about thirty feet below the surface, what he at first supposed to be a stone. There being none in the country, he had the curiosity to break it, and discovered that it was a petrifaction of clay and gravel, and that it enclosed a frog, which after being exposed to the sun, hopped off.

At William Young's, fifteen miles east of Rogersville, in digging a millrace in the side of a hill, at a point forty or fifty yards from the creek, at the depth of six feet below the surface, was found the upper part of *a goat's horn*, completely petrified, the length was an inch and a half.

Sec. 4, *Of the Ancient Animals of Tennessee.*

That every thing might appear wonderful to him who comes to explore the footsteps of past ages in this country of extraordinary spectacles, are left for the speculations of curiosity, a number of large bones, which belonged to animals of the brute creation, that have for ages disappeared, and at this time are not known to exist in any part of the globe. Some of them need only to be described, to give an idea of the size of these huge animals. They are distinguishable by the great claw, or megalinix, and the mammoth.

And first, *Of the Great Claw.*

In White county, on the west side of the Cumberland mountain, in West Tennessee, near the line of Warren county, and about eight miles south or southwest of the spot where were found the two human bodies which will be hereafter described, is *a cave,* in the spur of the mountain, having a small entry on one side, but on the other a mouth of much larger size. Half a mile from the small entry, the bones of some large animal were found, lying all together. Some of the teeth were taken up, and weighed seven or eight pounds. A horn, of much larger size, it is said, than the horn of the largest buffalo, but resembling it in shape, was taken from amongst or near to these large bones. In the cave, was a *prodigious claw, with very long nails,* but it does not appear, whether found with the bones above-mentioned or not. Many bones also of smaller beasts, were found in this cave. The tooth had the form of a dog's upper tooth, not at all in the shape of a grinder. This must have belonged to a carnivorous animal, of immense size, which preyed upon the buffalo, as well as animals of less bulk, and was probably of the feline genus. Another account of the same bones, has some particulars not stated in the former. It states, that the Big-bone and Arch caves are on the dividing line between White and Warren counties, and on the Cumberland mountain. They are six or eight hundred yards apart, or rather their mouths are, for they unite. They were discovered in eighteen hundred and six, and were sold out in shares, to forty or fifty persons, for sixty thousand dollars. They are now owned by Colonel Randolph Ross, of Rockbridge county, in Virginia. About twenty thousand pounds of saltpetre were made from the smallest cave, called the Arch cave. There are several branches to the Big-bone cave; from one of which, the dirt has been collected for upwards of half a mile. This branch of the cave has been explored upwards of half a mile. Three men were three days and nights in the cave, and represented that they went in it to the distance of ten or twelve miles. The proprietors think that they were mistaken as to the distance. The bones of a large animal were found when the Big-bone cave was discovered. The animal they belonged to was of the cat species. The ribs were placed on the back bone, the lower end in the ground. Jacob Drake, who is five feet nine inches high, walked erect in the hollow. The width of the ribs was between four and five inches. The hollow of the back bone was between two and three inches in diameter. The socket of the bone working in the shoulder blade, six inches. The tusk, between four and five inches in diameter, similar to a dog's. The claw, twelve inches in the round from point to point; straight, nine inches; hollow, one inch in diameter; weight, one pound and three quarters. There was also a scoop net, made of bark thread; a mockasin made of the like materials; a mat of the same materials, enveloping human bones, were found in saltpetre dirt, six feet below the surface. The net and other things mouldered on being exposed to the sun.

A claw was lately taken from a cave, in Perry county, in the Chickasaw purchase, which is apparently above five inches long. The upper part covered, about two inches down, with a brownish filament one eighth of an inch thick, with many little holes in the surface. In the inner or lower side of the claw, are two large holes, equidistant from the edge, and parallel to each other transversely; which seem to have received some tendon, that joined the upper ligaments, about the higher and hinder part of the foot. The upper part was in diameter about one half of an inch, and thence to the point about three inches.

At a lick, on Lick creek of Tennessee river, on the south side, was lately found, by Jeremiah Brown, Esquire, a large tusk or tooth, measuring eight feet in length. It was crooked like a horn, and round; and where it entered into the jaw, it was eight inches broad, and flat. He supposed it to be the tooth of a sea animal. But at the same place, some small distance under ground, have been found the bones of different land animals. The socket of the bone of one of them was so

large, that one man could hardly lift it. The petrified part of the hip bone was eight inches in
diameter. Some of these were probably the bones
of the animal to which the tusk belonged.

Secondly, *Of the Mammoth.*

In a lick in Sullivan county, was found a tooth,
now in the possession of Mr. Pemberton, who considers it a family relick, and will not part with it.
The lick is a large one, about eighteen miles due
east of Blountsville, near Holston river, which hath
the appearance of having been much used and fre-
quented by wild animals in former times. A person, in clearing out a spring near the lick, found the
under jaw bone of some large animal, which contained three grinders, the largest of which is now
in the possession of Mr. Pemberton, which weighed, at the time it was extracted from the bone, three
pounds and three quarters. The root or lower part
of the tooth, to the edge of the jaw bone, or
perhaps to the gum, was decayed, and in part
gone, at the time the tooth was found, and the
balance to the solid part of the tooth mouldered
away on being exposed to the atmosphere. There
were three jaw-teeth in the bone, and probably
never more. The tooth in the possession of Mr.
Pemberton, was the hindermost tooth, and measured about four inches from the cheek side to that of
the tongue, four inches from the upper edge to that
part next the root, and eight or nine inches from the
front part to the hinder. The socket in which the
grinder sat in the jaw bone, was fifteen inches long
and five wide. The jaw bone when laid on the
ground, exhibited a size equal to that of a large
dog's body. Between the grinder and the place
where the four teeth were, the bone was solid, similar to that of a horse or cow. At the end next the
fore teeth, was a cavity in the bone, a small part of
which remained large enough to receive a man's

arm. There the front teeth may have been. The ends of the jaw bone were decayed. From the curve, the jaw bone was estimated to be equal to that of a large man's thigh. The ribs were nine feet long, both ends being decayed some distance. Where the bones are, many small *pine knots* are found, perfectly sound. The bones when laid in water, will remain entire; but would dissolve, if exposed to the corroding atmosphere.

At Bledsoe's lick, in the county of Sumner, in making way by digging into the earth, to sink a gum for the collection of the water, and to separate it from the black mud at the lick, after digging some distance, the workmen came to the tusk of some huge animal, between two and three feet in length. Also grinders, eight or nine inches wide at least. The tusk was bent, like that of a hog, but not as much so, in proportion to its size.

At Mansker's station, where is a salt lick, and Mansker's creek, a well was sunk for salt water. After digging some distance, the diggers came to large bones, as thick as a man's thigh, and two, three or more feet long.

In the county of Maury, a few miles from Columbia, and on the south side of Duck river, on the lands of the late Mr. Williamson, is a spring of excellent water; near which, some years ago, were found under the surface, two teeth, or tusks, of a curved form, and two or three feet in length; the teeth tapering to a point, from that part of them which joined the socket to the end of the tooth which is pointed.

At a sulphur spring, ten or twelve miles from Reynoldsburg, on the south side of the Tennessee river, on a creek that discharges itself into the river, is a spring breaking out in the bed of the creek. In the water near the spout of the spring, was found in the year eighteen hundred and twenty, the tusk of a huge animal, curved inwards considerably, so as to form the segment of a circle. The end, which had grown in the socket of the jaw bone, was decayed. The tooth was eight feet six inches in length, and is supposed to weigh from one to two hundred weight. It is of a yellowish cast. Also was found there, the thigh bone. The part that turned in the socket is decayed. It was six feet in length, and three feet in circumference. Also were found, several parts of the back bone. The hollow, which enclosed the spinal marrow, measured six inches in diameter. Also was found there, a part of the scull, which contained the cavity in which the eye rolled. It was eight inches in diameter. Also was found there, a hip bone, the hollow of which that the thigh bone turned in, is capacious enough to receive a fifteen-gallon kettle. The bones were covered with mud. The spring is in about 35,45 north latitude. It is calculated from the appearance and size of the bones, that the animal when living must have been twenty feet high.

That the cold seasons are now advancing, and have been for twenty years and more, is proved by the observation of many persons; that the winters are now longer and more severe than they were twenty or thirty years ago. And very recently a phenomenon has occurred, which, though common in high northern latitudes, has never like been observed in Tennessee, by the white people who have settled there. On Friday morning, the 15th of February, 1723, the wind in Cumberland mountain from the south, with moderate rain; about 9 o'clock the wind shifted more to the west, and shortly after blew a strong gale from the northwest, with snow. The cold increased during the whole day. In the night, the heavens became clear; a strong gale still blowing from the northwest. The morning of the 16th was the coldest weather ever witnessed in Tennessee, by the oldest inhabitants.

I

The sun rose bright, but was not felt, a mist being in the atmosphere, which was perfectly congealed, and with every gale was drifted *a fine frost*. At times the whole atmosphere was filled with it. The sun was still visible, with a silver brightness, as through a curtain, not more oppressive to the eye than the moon in a clear night. The cold must have been at least four degrees more intense than in the valley below.

The same falling of frost through the whole day prevailed over all the country around Nashville.

On the mountain, the trees everywhere resounded, from the excessive freeze, with sounds frequently as loud as the report of discharged pistols. The cold subsided gradually, and the temperature became tolerable in the course of the two following days.—*See note ZB, at the end of this volume.*

CHAPTER III.

BEFORE entering upon the aboriginal history of Tennessee, a short comparison of the Mexicans with the Hindoos and Persians, and of the Natchez with the Mexicans, will, it is conceived, very much contribute to the understanding of many aboriginal relics, with which we meet in this country. This comparison therefore will be made: First, between the political institutions of the Mexicans and Peruvians on the one hand, with those of the Hindoos and Persians on the other: Secondly, between the religious practices of the Hindoos and Persians on the one hand, and of the Mexicans and Peruvians on the other: Thirdly, between the cosmical history of the latter, and that of the Hindoos and Persians: Fourthly, between the vernacular customs of the Hindoos and Persians, and those of the Mexicans and Peruvians.

First—Between the Political Institutions of the Mexicans and Peruvians on the one hand, and those of the Hindoos and Persians on the other.

Ancient authors consider the Hindoos and Egyptians as the same people; and believe that the one was a colony from the other, because of the sameness which was found in their religion, government, customs, sciences and arts. A similitude with one is therefore equally so with the other.

The Mexicans and Peruvians, like the Hindoos, invested their princes with despotic power; and like the Hindoos, Persians, Chinese and Ceylonese, denominated them children of the sun. The Persians called their princes brothers of the sun. The Mexicans, like the Hindoos, divided the people into five, or rather four, casts. The Mexicans had post-roads and couriers through all parts of the empire:[139] an institution first invented in Persia, by Cyrus, or soon after his time; and which was not introduced into Europe before the time of Augustus, and not into the states of modern Europe till very lately.

The lands in Peru were appropriated one third to the sun, the god whom they adored; to be applied to the erection of temples, and to the furnishing of requisites, for celebrating the rites of religion; another third, to the inea, or sovereign, and the other third was divided amongst the people; and at the end of every year a new division was made. The lands were cultivated jointly. The people were summoned by an officer, and worked with songs and musical instruments to cheer them. In Egypt, all the lands were divided into three classes, one for the king, one for the priests, and the other to the soldiers.[140] The husbandmen took these lands to farm, for a moderate portion of their produce. Joseph, in his time, acquired all the lands for the king; and returned them to the people, they paying to the king one fifth of their produce annually; and this law continued to the time of Moses.[141] The same law was carried into India in ancient times, probably after the time of Joseph, or in his time and possibly in the reign of Sesostris. There the monarch was the sole proprietor, and the people paid a land tax to their kings. Such also was the state of property in ancient times in Persia.[142] In Mexico, some of the people held lands as *inheritances*, some as annexed to the offices they held. The residue of the lands were divided into portions suited to the numbers of families who were to cultivate them. The product was deposited in a common storehouse, and divided amongst them according to their wants.

139 4 Herod. 222*; 2 R. H. Am. 265; 2 Rollins, 326.
140 D. Siculus, b. 1. p. 85.
141 Genesis, ch. 47, v. 18, 20, 22, 24.
142 Rob. Ind. 330; D. Seculus, b. 2, p. 153.

Sec. 2. Secondly—*Between the Religious Practices of the Hindoos and Persians on the one hand, and of the Mexicans and Peruvians on the other.*

The religious notions of the Mexicans conformed in a great variety of instances to those of the Hindoos. And in some instances, a conformity is discovered in the antiquities of Tennessee, which has not been mentioned by writers, as existing amongst the Mexicans, but which without doubt did exist, if those who formerly resided here were colonists from Mexico. The Hindoos have a *Trimurti,* or three principal divinities in one: *Brahma, Vishnu and Seva.* This union is intended to denote, that existence cannot be produced, without the combination of the threefold power of creation, preservation and destruction.[143] Originally, by the representation of three divine powers in one body, the ancient Hindoos intended the three great powers of nature, the earth, water and fire. This notion gradually vanished after images came into use; and the ignorant populace converted these representations by images into three distinct godheads. Thence came the notion into Egypt, and thence into Greece, of the mysterious virtue contained in the number three. But why or wherefore, they could not tell. Some said it was the representation of time, and that the three eyes in the image of Jupiter, one in the middle between the other two, was intended for time past, present and to come. Some said it meant three eternals, God, matter and form.[144] The Platonic system united three grand principles into one. In order to be the better understood, it considered one of them as the son of an eternal father, the creator and governor of the world. Having proceeded thus far, the lively imagination and active ingenuity of the Greeks soon branched these ideas into a thousand others.

[143] 1 Dub. 113.   [144] 3 Anach.

Jupiter, in his lifetime, supposed the three gods to be the sun, the earth and heavens ; and to them he accordingly sacrificed.[146] As soon as the sun became one of the three, his emblem, the serpent with one body and three heads, was twisted around a statue. The Romans thought the three gods were Jupiter, Mars and Quirinus.[147] Afterwards they deemed Pluto, Jupiter and Neptune the three supremes, as did the Trojans in the time of the Trojan war,[148] or the world below, the air and sea.[149] At Alexandria was the image of Serapis ; on his right hand was the body and head of a serpent branching into three tails, which were again terminated by the triple head of a dog, a lion and a wolf. From this origin, in short, the belief of a sacred virtue in the number three has spread over the whole earth. In many countries it hath been received without examination into the causes of its mystic qualities. Amongst others, the Hebrews, from a long residence with the Egyptians, adopted it likewise.[150] It originated from the Trimurte of India, and the religion of the Hindoos is founded upon books of the highest antiquity. Like the books themselves, it hath remained the same through a long succession of ages. It is one of the religious duties of the Brahman's, to bathe three times every day. The Hindoos celebrate a festival in honour of their ancestors three days ; and on those days make various offerings to their ancestors, of food and raiment. If we meet in America with the same deified *triplicity*, with the same reverence for this mysterious number, we may refer it to this Hindoo origin, until some better shall be assigned for it.

146 1 D Siculus, 5.   147 5 Gib, 3.
148 1 Iliad, 200,   149 15 Iliad.
150 Exodus, ch. 23, v. 14, 17 ; Numb. ch. 22, v. 13, 28, ch. 24, v, 10 ; Deut. ch. 16, v. 16 ; 1 Samuel, ch. 20, v. 41 ; 1 Kings, ch. 9, v. 25, ch. 17, v. 21 ; Daniel, ch. 1, v. 5, ch. 10, v. 13.

The Mexicans believe in a transmigration of souls; a doctrine first taught in India and Persia, and afterwards adopted by the Egyptians.

Two of the Mexican deities were the sun and moon. These were worshipped in ancient times by far the greater part of the nations of Asia, and by the Persians and Hindoos particularly.

The Mexicans had their penates or household gods. So had the people of Mesipotamia, 1600 years before Christ,[151] which probably they borrowed from the eastern countries, whence they emigrated.[152]

The Hindoos and the Egyptians worshipped animals: the dog and the cat were sacred animals. The Mexicans erected little chapels, in which they buried the wolf, the tiger, the eagle and the snake or adder.

The Hindoos worshipped the *garude*, or bird of prey, with a strong hooked bill; particularly those Hindoos who were of the sect of Vishnu. They pay it adoration every morning immediately after ablution. On the 25th of May, 1538, De Soto landed in Florida. " *The Lord's house stood near the shore, upon a very high mount, made by hand for strength. At another end of the town, stood a fowl made of wood, with gilded eyes.*" In one of the mounds of Ohio, the beak of a bird of prey, like that of the eagle, was found.

The representation of the Mexican god Huel-zettu-poçli, and the Hindoo god Crishna, very strikingly resemble each other.

The Mexican gods or idols were for the most part painted with red, and blue shirts. Blue vestments and decorations are usually met with in the statues of the Hindoo and Egyptian deities. Vermilion also was a common colour with the deities of the two nations. The Romans painted Jupiter's face red, and Vulcan was sometimes represented with a blue hat.

151 Genesis, ch. 31, v. 30.   152 Genesis, ch. 11, v. 2.

In Mexico, as well as in Egypt, the noses of their gods, or idols, were ornamented with gold rings, formed into the shape of a serpent, the emblem of the sun.[152]

The Mexicans celebrate the festivals which the Hindoos call Rama, and which the Peruvians also celebrated by the name of Rama-satea.

In Mexico, infants were passed through the fire: it was done by making a movement as if passing the child through a flame, kindled for the occasion. No doubt this practice was common to the Hindoos, with all the other worshippers of the sun.[152]

The Mexicans adore the sun by waving the hand towards him, and perhaps putting it towards the mouth. This also was a practice no doubt common to the Hindoos, with all his other worshippers.[153]

The masque of a Mexican priest is represented in Mexico. He is drawn as sacrificing a human victim; a sacrifice which all the worshippers of the sun everywhere made.[154] The masque represents an elephant's trunk, similar to the head so often portrayed in Indostan. As no elephants exist in America, it is reasonable to conclude that the designment was brought from Asia.

Vishnu, one of the principal divinities of the Hindoos, is with them the preserver of all things. And in this office, has been obliged, upon ten important occasions, to metamorphose himself, in order to effect his purposes. Once into a fish, to dive into the abyss of the sea, and to pluck the four books called the *Vedas*, from the bowels of a giant, who had stolen and swallowed them, and took refuge in the middle of the ocean. In the time of

152 Genesis, ch. 35, v. 4.
152 Leviticus, ch. 18, v. 21; Deuteronomy, ch. 18. v. 10; 2 Kings, ch. 16, v. 3, ch. 21, v. 6, ch. 23, v. 10, ch. 17, v. 17; 2 Chron. ch. 33, v. 6; 2 Dub. 171.
153 Job, ch. 31, v. 27.   154 2 Dub. 171.

the war between the gods and the giants, the celestials being vanquished, and praying to Vishnu, he ordered them to pull up the mountain Mandara-Parvata, and cast it into the sea. They made a ship of this mountain, with which to navigate the ocean. It began to sink, and the gods being in it, and like to perish, he metamorphosed himself into a *tortoise*, plunged into the ocean, and supported the sinking mountain on his solid back. He had, in short, perpetual war with the giants: often changed his form and appearance, and conquered. The island of Ceylon, with his ape auxiliaries, he conquered, and overcame the army of giants there. The Vishnu of the Hindoos resembles, in his attributes, the Neptune of the Greeks and Romans. Neptune lives in the waters, and rules over the ocean, armed with a *trident*. The tritons accompany him, sounding their *conch shells*. Vishnu is called Nara-yana, or one of the sojourners in the waters. He sleeps in the bottom of the wide ocean. His devotees bear on their foreheads *the symbol of the trident*. They blow the *sea horn*, and represent its figure, with hot iron on the shoulders.[154] When a universal deluge swept off all mankind, the *seven penitents* were saved, by means of a ship; into which Vishnu made them embark, and in which he acted as the pilot. This account is given in the Bagha-veta, one of the most ancient books which the Hindoos acknowledge. Extravagant as are these fundamentals of Hindoo mythology, they are contained in the most ancient writings of the world. Stripped of the fabulous covering which Hindoo imagination hath given them, we can discover, that Vishnu the dweller in the ocean, is signified by the symbolical representation of the *tortoise or the conch shell*. For this or some other cause, *shells and conch shells* were considered amongst the valuables of India, in the most ancient

154 1 Dub. 118.

J

times. And the law provided, that double the principal shall be the limited accumulation of interest, *in shells borrowed.* *"It is the same in respect of conchs or the like."*[155] His large statue on the island of Elephanta, is represented with his toes of *conch shells*, to signify his marine journeys. *Conch shells* were probably used for sounding his praises, convoking his worshippers, and in their ablutions. As it is presumable, that the followers of Vishnu everywhere practised the same ceremonies, we must expect to find wherever they have been, the relics of their rites and ceremonies. Such relics, when discovered, will be as good, if not better evidence of such rites, than if they had been simply mentioned by some writer. The truth is, that many such indicia may have been seen and not observed by writers, who had no suspicion of the former connexion between the Hindoos and Mexicans. And though not mentioned as existing amongst the Mexicans, must now be taken to have been in use amongst them, as well as amongst the Hindoos. Mr. Clifford said, in his lifetime, that conch shells reversed had been found at springs in Kentucky. Nine were found in digging out one spring; five or six in a spring near Williamsville, in Woodford county; fifteen others at a spring on General Kennedy's farm; eighteen large and twelve smaller ones, in like situations, at Mr. Jones's farm, two miles from Lexington, in Garard county: all in circumvallatory temples. In the temples in Garard county, where found, the entrances into the open area are directly opposite to the fountains. *These conchs* are perfect, and in as good preservation as shells usually are which are found upon the sea-beach. We can see from the imperfect lights before noticed, that *navigation* in India was cultivated and practiced, from times at least but shortly subsequent to the *Deluge. Their marine interest, al-*

[155] Colebrook's Hindoo Laws, 51, 61.

lowed of in the book called *Menu*, who lived, it is said, at as early a period of the world as Moses shows it. "*Whatever interest shall be settled, between the parties, by men well acquainted with sea voyages, or journeys by land, such interest shall have legal force.*"[156] Sea voyages then were performed in the time of Menu, by the people of India. For this reason they adored *Vishnu*. And now comes the important fact, which the preceding observations are intended to make appear in its true light. *In Mexico*, this deity, or god of the ocean, was adored equally with the sun, their greatest deity. And why did the Mexicans adore him? Did they derive from India the knowledge they had of his properties? did they, in imitation of the Hindoos, use *conch shells* as religious symbols of that deity? did they make their purifying ablutions with them at the springs, before they entered into the temple, to offer up prayer and thanksgiving? With the Hindoos, bathing is the proper remedy for sin and impurity. There are certain places of bathing, to which are attributed complete efficacy. Those who wash in certain sacred rivers, restore the soul and body from all sins and corruptions which they may have contracted. To think of these rivers in the performance of purifying ablutions is sufficient. There are also many *springs* and pools consecrated, and much renowned for the spiritual effects they communicate[157] to those who bathe in them. Some have the virtue every twelfth year; and there are others which have it periodically. When the year and day arrive for bathing in those sacred waters, a crowd of people almost without number, men, women and children, arrange themselves around the water, and as soon as the astrologer announces the favourable hour and, moment of the day, all, men, women and children, plunge into the

156 1 Hindoo Laws, p. 48, sec. 36.
157 1 Dub. 181, 182.

water at once, and with a mighty uproar. Vestiges of the same practices in America, in the use of *conch shells*, and of *multitudinous ablutions*, which will occur in the further progress of these inquiries, may assist in leading to the conclusion, that the Mexicans, who had many other traits of the Hindoo character, had also the rites of which we are now speaking. The same acts and circumstances produced defilement amongst the Hindoos, as are stated to produce it in Leviticus. And though in many instances, ablution is prescribed, both by the law of Moses and the Hindoos, yet *multitudinous ablutions* were not prescribed by the latter.[158] The use of this remark will be perceived in the sequel. The affinities between certain practices pointed out by the antiquities of this country, with those of the Hindoos, are so striking, that one who makes the comparison, cannot well abstain from the belief, that so many coincidences are not merely fortuitous. He cannot forbear to suspect, that the ancient inhabitants, who were probably colonists from Mexico, and by consequence the Mexicans themselves, had not only the religious ceremonies of India, but that even some of the *materials* which they used were actually exported from the shores of the Indian ocean. He will be inclined to think, that the *little conch shells* in the small graves which will be hereafter described, were used as religious emblems. That the adoration, which is paid by the Mexicans, to the *god of the ocean*, is founded upon the protection he is supposed to give to *navigation*, which being of course precedent to the power created for its protection, must have been used in India from periods long prior to European navigation as practised at the pressnt time, since the discovery of the navigator's needle, or in ancient times by the Mexicans themselves.

158 Leviticus, ch. 11, v. 25, 28, 32, 40, ch. 13, v. 6, 54, 58, ch. 14, v. 8, 9, 47, ch. 15, v. 5, 6, 7, 8, 10, 11, 12, 13, 16, 17, 18, 21, 22, 27.

The sacred buildings of the Mexicans were constructed upon the same principles with those of the old world: the pyramids of Egypt, the temple of Belus, and the pyramids of India.

The great temple of Mexico seemed to be composed of fine pieces or bodies, one above another, the larger below, and gradually diminishing in each successive piece to the top. The upper body was paved with smooth flat stones; and at the eastern extremity of the pavement, stood two towers, of the height of 56 feet. Each of these towers was divided into *three* bodies; the lowest of which was stone and lime; the two upper ones were of wood, well wrought, and painted. The stone part of each of these towers, was properly *the sanctuary*. Before each of them was a stove, in which was kept *a constant fire.*[159]

The tower of Babel was at its base a square of half a mile in circumference, consisting of eight towers, as they appeared to be, one above the other. The ascent to the top was by stairs on the outside; formed by a sloping line from the bottom to the top, eight times around it, so as to exhibit the appearance of eight towers, the uppermost of which is the most sacred. In this temple of Belus there seemed to be two deities worshipped; one the supreme God of heaven, while Belus was at least the delegated God upon earth. The two towers which stood in the Mexican temple, were each dedicated to a different deity.

In India are ancient pyradmids of large dimensions. They are rude structures, but of such a magnitude as must have required the power of some considerable state to have raised them.[160]

The Pagoda of Seringham is situated about a mile from the western extremity of the island of

159 2 Dub. 48; Plut. 79, 165, 166; 2 Dub. 34; 1 Joseph, 134; 2 Rol. 369, 370; 8 Gib. 239,
160 Rob. Ind. 270.

Seringham, formed by the division of the great river Caveri into the two channels. "It is composed of seven square inclosures, one within the other; the walls of which are twenty-five feet high, and four thick. These inclosures are 350 feet distant from one another; and each has four large gates, with a high tower, which are placed one in the middle of each side of the enclosure, *and opposite to the four cardinal points.* The outer wall is nearly four miles in circumference; and its gateway to the south is ornamented with pillars, several of which are of single stones, thirty-three feet long and nearly five in diameter, and those which form the roof are still larger. In the inmost inclosures are the chapels."

The largest of the pyramids of Egypt was built of rock, having a square base, cut on the inside as so many steps, and decreasing gradually quite to the summit. It was built of stones of a prodigious size, the least of which was thirty feet long, wrought with wonderful art, and covered with hieroglyphics. The summit of the pyramid, which to those who viewed it from below seemed like a point, was *a fine platform* composed of ten or twelve massy stones, and each side of the platform from sixteen to eighteen feet long. The four sides of this pyramid were turned exactly *to the four quarters of the world,* and showed the true meridian of that place.[160] This pyramid is so constructed, that an observer placed at its foot on the day of the equinox, could have seen the sun at noon seated as it were upon the summit. The inclined plane of the side of the pyramid, forms an angle with the plane of the horizon, equal to the meridianal height of the sun at that period. The pyramid being placed exactly in the latitude of 30 north, the angle ought to be 60. All the sides being equally inclined, the profile of the pyramid cut perpendicularly from the summit to the base, through the middle of two of

160 1 Rollins, 8, 11.

Its opposite sides ought to present an equilateral triangle.[161]

With these models let us now compare the American pyramids.

In the Mexican valley are the remains of two pyramids of San Juan de Teotihuacan, situated to the northeast of the lake Tezcuco, consecrated to the sun and moon; which the Indians call Tonituah-Ytzaqual, house of the sun, and Metzle-Itzaqual, house of the moon. Its base is 682 English feet; its height 171 feet. *They are within 52 seconds placed to the north and south and from east to west.* Their interior is clay mixed with small stones. The covering is with a thick wall of porous amygdaloid. *A stair of large hewn stones* formerly led to their tops, where, as the first travellers say, *were statues* covered with thin lamina of gold. Each was composed of four principal layers, subdivided into small gradations, of three feet three inches; of which the edges are still distinguishable, which were formerly covered with fragments of obsidion, that were the edges of instruments with which the priests opened the chests of human victims.[161] Around the houses of the sun and moon, of Teotihuacan, is a group of pyramids, not more than 29 or 32 feet high. There are several hundreds of these monuments, disposed in very large streets, which follow exactly the direction of the parallels and of the meridians, and terminate on the four faces of the two great pyramids. The lesser pyramids are more frequent towards the southern side of the temple of the moon, than towards the temple of the sun; and according to the tradition of the country, they were dedicated to the stars.

The great pyramid of Cholula, in Mexico, consists of four stages. It is 177 feet high at present. The base is 1423 feet. *Its sides are in the direction* of the parallels and meridians, and construct-

161 Ali Bey, 23.   161 2 Humb. 48.

ed of alternate strata of brick and clay. *The platform for the truncated pyramid* of Cholula, has a
surface of 45,208 square feet English. The pyramid of Cholula is exactly of the same height as
the Tonituah-Itzaqual of Teotihuacan. It is nine
feet eight inches higher than the Mycerinus, or the
third of the great Egyptian pyramids of the group
of Gheze. The apparent length of the base is almost the double of the great pyramid in Egypt
known by the name of Cheops. Around the Egyptian pyramid of Cheops, are regular depositions of
small pyramids, similar to those around the houses
of the sun and moon, or the pyramidal monuments
of Teotihucan, northeast from Mexico. Other pyramids in Mexico and its neighbourhood might be
described; but these will be enough to compare
with the like edifices in India, with those made by
the Natchez, and with those found in Tennessee.

The morais of the Pacific islands are upon the
same plan. That of Obera is 267 feet long and 87
wide at the base. It is raised by flights of steps
to the height of 44 feet. These steps are four feet
high, narrowing gradually till they end in a small
entabliture, in which, near the middle, stands the
figure *of a bird* carved in wood, and at some distance the broken fragments of a fish cut in stone.
It makes a considerable part of one side of a square
court, 360 by 354, with a stone wall and pavement,
with the same materials through its whole extent.
This *work is solid*, and without a cavity.

In the island of Owhyhee is a morai, 40 by 20,
and 14 high. *The top was flat*, and was surrounded by a wooden railing. A ruinous wooden building was situated in the centre of the area, connected with the railing by a stone wall dividing the
whole space into two parts. Altars were anciently
built on mounds.—The greater part of the foregoing statements are made from the writings of Mr.
McCulloch, of Baltimore.

*Thirdly—The Cosmical History of the Mexicans
compared with that of the Hindoos.*

In their ages of the world, the Mexicans very
nearly agreed with the Hindoos. The Mexicans
had four ages of the world. The first was that of
the sun, or the age of water, which continued from
the creation, till all mankind perished with the sun
by a great inundation. The second was the age
of the earth, from the time of the inundation, until
the ruin of the giants, and the great earthquakes
which concluded the second sun. The third was
the age of the air, from the destruction of the giants, until the great whirlwinds, in which all mankind perished with the third sun. The fourth is
the age of fire, beginning with the last restoration
of the human race, and to continue till the fourth
sun and the earth shall be consumed by fire.

The first age of the Hindoos was ended by a
mighty flood; the second, by a great whirlwind;
the third, by a great earthquake; and the fourth is
to be terminated by a general conflagration. All
the southeastern countries of Asia have this belief,
and they have transmitted it to America. No
doubt, mankind have derived it from the prophecy
of Noah,[171] which hath ever since been delivered
from one generation to another down to the present
day.

*Of the Vernacular Customs of the Hindoos, and
those of the Mexicans and Peruvians: first, of those
relative to Religion ; secondly, of those relative to
the Common Concerns of Life.*

First—Of those relative to Religion.

The religionists of Vishnu wore a plate of copper on the breast.[172] The Brahmans put on their
dead, necklaces made of beads, which are nearly
of the size and shape of a nut.[173] They place

171 Genesis, ch. 9. v. 11, 14, 15, ch. 8, v. 22.
172 1 Dub. 90. 173 2 Dub. 25, 108.

K

them in a hole about six feet deep, one half filled
with salt: the body is covered to the neck with salt.
Then more salt is added, till the head is covered,
and then earth is accumulated over the trench to
the height of several feet.[174] The Hindoos anciently sacrificed their prisoners taken in war; and
both in ancient and modern times, on very solemn
occasions, they sacrifice human beings.[175]

The sect of Vishnu wore necklaces of black
beads of the size of a nut, and particoloured garments. They travel to beg with a round plate of
brass, about a foot in diameter, and a large shell
called *sankha*, shaped like a *sea conch*, with either
of which they can make a noise to announce their
approach.[176] Answerable to these customs, and
seeming to be the effects of them, are divers discoveries made in this state, and in the neighbouring
state of Kentucky, and Ohio, which if taken to
have been colonized from Mexico and Peru, may
be presumed to have been equally practised there.
In Virginia, near Wheeling, on Grave creek, is a
mound 75 feet high, with many smaller ones around
it. In the interior parts of this mound, are found
human bones of large size, and mixed with them
are two or three *plates of brass*, with *characters*
inscribed resembling letters. A mound near Chillicothe being removed, discovered near the bottom,
in a cavity, the remains of some chieftain. A string
of *ivory* beads was around his neck, and on his
breast a stone about three inches long, with a hole
near each end, in order to fasten it to the wearer's
neck, rather thicker in the centre than at the extremities, flat on the side next the breast, remainder
of it round, and made of a species of black *marble*.
The latter may have been produced in America,
but the *ivory beads* most probably came from India
or the country in its vicinity, where the elephant is
raised, and the ivory worked. The sculls which

174 2 Dub. 25.   175 2 Dub. 172, 272.   176 1 Dub. 70.

will be hereafter mentioned, as found in caves near Bledsoe's lick, in Grainger county, will indicate the sacrifice of prisoners, or of human beings on solemn religious occasions. And the presumption is, that these are parts of the general system which prevailed in Mexico and amongst the Natchez; which is made out by the accumulation of all the evidences which are to be ascribed to worshippers of the sun.

Another kindred custom is, not only the worship of the sun by the Mexicans and Peruvians, *but the perpetual fire kept up in the temples.*[177] So also was it in the temple of Solomon, from his time to that of the Babylonish captivity. When this fire happened to be extinguished in those countries of the old world, it was restored by glasses of refraction, or by flint, or attrition or friction. The fire for the sacrifice of the Hamam in India is extracted from flint.

The bones of a wolf have been found in a Mexican grave. The Egyptians buried their deified animals; and no doubt the same practice was common to the Hindoos.

Secondly—*Of those relative to the Common Concerns of Life.*

The Mexican celebration of the rights of marriage, was a close imitation of that of the Hindoos. The priest tied the mantle of the bridegroom to the gown of the bride. The new married pair never stirred from the chamber for five days. These they passed in prayer and fasting; dressed in new habits, and adorned with the insignia of the gods of their devotion; and drawing blood from the different parts of the body. These austerities were observed with the greatest exactness; for they feared the heaviest punishments of the gods if the marriage were consummated before the end of the four days.

177 Boud. 57, 218, 220, 221, 247; 1 Plutarch, 79, 161, 166; 2 Plutarch, 70; 1 Dub. 143, 144; 2 Dub. 34, 48, 125, 414.

In Indostan, on the day when the skirts are tied together, the bridegroom shows to the bride the polar star, as au emblem or figure of constancy. During the three following days, the married couple must live chastly and austerely; on the fourth from the marriage, the bridegroom conducts the bride to his own house.

The sun, or brother of the sun, or children of the sun, the titles given to the princes of Peru and Mexico, and the Natchez, are the same which were anciently given to the princes of Persia, India, Ceylon and China.

The Hindoos, as well as the people of Japan, China, Siam, Tartary, the Curds and Laplanders, and the negroes on the banks of the Senegal, believe that the eclipses of the moon are occasioned by a *dragon,* which would devour that star. The fear they are in, brings them to make the greatest noise they can, to frighten the monster, and make him quit his prey. Mr. Goguet[178] thinks, this practice may be derived from the ancient astronomy of the orientals. To design the periodical cycle of the moon, they used the emblem of a dragon, whose head was placed at the point where the circle cuts the ecliptic, because it is always at that point, or its opposite, that the eclipses of the sun are made. The same practices obtains in Peru, and the people there must have brought it from the old world.

The Mexicans, like the Persians[179] and Jews, and other orientals, rend their garments for grief.

Of the Biblical Representations and Traditions of the Mexicans and Peruvians.

There is a Mexican painting which contains the tradition of the mother of mankind having fallen

178 2 O. L. 413, Mc. 172.
179 Herod. Urania, 100; 2 Samuel, ch. 13, v. 31, ch. 15, v. 32, ch. 13, v. 19; Job, ch. 1, v. 20, ch. 2, v. 12.

from her first state of happiness; and she is resented as accompanied by a serpent. Also is foun l the idea of a great inundation overwhelming the earth, from which a single family escaped on a raft. There is a history of a pyramidal edifice raised by the pride of man, and destroyed by the anger of the gods. The ceremony of ablution is practised at the birth of children. Similar traditions of high antiquity are found amongst the followers of Brahma, and amongst the Shamas of the eastern Steppes of Tartary.

The nations of Cuba had an account of the flood. An old man, they say, foresaw the intention of God, to cover the world with a deluge. He built a canoe, and embarked with his family and a great number of animals. When the flood subsided, he sent out a raven, which finding carrion, did not return. A pigeon was then sent out, and soon returned with a sprig of *hoba* in its mouth. At last the ground became dry. The old man quitted his canoe, and making some wine of the wood grape, drank till he was intoxicated. And falling asleep, one of his sons mocked him; but the other covered his nakedness. He blessed one, and cursed the other. In Indostan, in a book of the Hindoos, called Pudnam-Param, Sir William Jones found, and transcribed verbatim, nine sections where the same story is told with all its circumstances. It states the intoxication of the king of the whole earth, his three sons, and the undutiful behaviour of one of them, for which his father pronounced a curse against him. And it is added, that he gave to one of them, Sher-ma, the whole dominion on the south of the Snowy mountain, and to *Jugpeli* he gave all on the north of the Snowy mountain.

The Chiapanese say, that a certain Votan, nephew of the one who attempted to erect a building that should reach heaven, and which is the place where man received his different languages, went by express command of the Deity to people South-America. Baron Humboldt has seen the hieroglyphical representation of these traditions, and gives his opinion, that they were the actual belief of the Mexicans.

These traditions relate to events which preceded the time of Abraham, and could not have been learned from the mosaic writings, but from the more ancient history of the world, which was preserved in India. And being at this day in the traditional possession of the people of America, bears evidence of a genuine original, from which came both the writings of Moses and these traditions.

CHAPTER IV.

Some and indeed considerable insight may be acquired into the history of the American aborigines, by some additional comparisons. Particularly, first, of the astronomical learning of the Mexicans, with that of the Hindoos. Secondly, of the practises of the worshippers of the sun in general, with the phenomena which are seen in Tennessee and its vicinity. Thirdly, of the lingual and nominal coincidences between the southern Americans and people of the old world. And fourthly, by a statement of some of the indigenous practices of the Mexicans, to be compared with certain appearances in Tennessee and its vicinity.

First then—*Of the Astronomical Learning of the Mexicans, to be compared with that of the Hindoos.*

The Mexicans knew of the solar year of 365 days and 6 hours. They lost a day in every four years, and added 13 to every 52 years, to make up the defalcation. Like the Egytians, they placed the five days at the end of the year as thrown away. The beginning of the Mexican day was at sunrising; so was that of the Persians, Egyptians, Babylonians, and the greater part of the nations of Asia, except the Chinese. And it was divided into eight intervals, as was also the day of the Hindoos and Romans. The Chilian year consisted of 12 months of 30 days, and they intercalated 12. Their year commenced on the 22d of September. It was divided into four seasons. Their day was divided into 12 equal parts, and commenced at midnight. The year of 365 days was not known in Egypt in the time of Moses. In describing the deluge, he calls 150 days five months. In times prior to the days of Moses, they had calculated the year at 354 days; and not at 365 till

1322 before Christ. But still by degrees getting more light upon the subject, the Egyptians had discovered in the time of Plato, 384 before Christ, that the solar year consisted of 365 days and nearly 6 hours. The Chaldeans had discovered that it was of longer duration than 365 days, before the return of the Israelites, from the Babylonish captivity, in the year 458 before Christ. About this time it was that they discovered it to be of the length of 365 days, 5 hours, 51 minutes and 36 seconds. Berosus, a Chaldean historian, who wrote in the third century before Christ, made use of a period composed of these years.[180] After this period the Mexicans learned it. Not from the ten tribes who had been removed for nearly 300 years, into the northern parts of Asia, and never did know it at all; but from some of the enlightened nations to which it had been communicated from Chaldea. The Mexicans divided their year into eighteen months of 20 days to the month. And several names by which they designated these days of their month, are those of the signs of the zodiac, which have been in use from the remotest antiquity, among the nations of eastern Asia. Baron Humboldt compares the names of the Mexican symbols for these days with the Tartarean, Japanese and Thibetan names of the twelve signs, and also with the names of the Noschatras, or lunar houses of the Hindoos. In eight of the hieroglyphics the analogy is very striking. Alt, the name of the first day, as also of water, is indicated by a hieroglyphic, the parallel or undulating lines of which remind us of the sign Aquarius. In the Thibetan zodiac, the sign is marked by a rat, an emblem of water. The rat is likewise an asterism in the Chinese zodiac. The ape is a character used in the Mexican calendar, as it is in the Thibetan zodiac, and in the lunar houses of the Hindoos, though

180 3 O. L. 265.

this animal does not exist in the high countries of the Andes. The people of America called the constellation which we call the Great Bear, by a name which also signifies bear. The Egyptians and then the Asiatics first gave it the name of the Great Bear. Before alphabetic writing was in use it is probable that constellation was represented by the image of a bear,[181] and when afterwards it came to be written, instead of being represented by an image, it was called by the name of the image. These latter evidences afford full proof that the astronomy of the Mexicans was not invented by them, but learned from the countries whence they emigrated. And united with the Biblical traditions before stated, raise a question of very difficult solution. The traditions came no lower down than to the building of the tower of Babel. Had the Mexicans learned them from the writings of Moses, they would have known of the history of Abraham and of the Israelites, as well of the facts to which the traditions relate. Either they left the old world before the writings of Moses came into existence; or must have lived in some part of Asia where the prevalence of idolatry excluded the writings of Moses so hostile to it, in all its precepts; and in some country too where the people had access to the astronomical learning of the Chaldeans after the period of 384 years before Christ. If the Mexicans came into this country over a continent now sunk into the ocean, why have not the large animals of Asia reached America over the same continent? If they came in early times, before those animals had time by propagation and emigration to reach America, and before the days of Abraham and of the Exodus, then they could only learn the length of the year, and the astronomical discoveries of the Chaldeans, from an intercourse

181 Job, ch. 9, v. 9, ch. 38, v. 31; 1 O. L. 231, 241; 2 O. L. 398, 405.

L

with Asia, kept up by navigation subsequently to the year 384 before Christ. This latter idea receives countenance not only from the great devotion of the Mexicans to the god of the ocean, but also from a very curious fact related by Pliny the elder, after Cornelius Nepos, who, in an account of a voyage to the north, says that in the year 60 before Christ, certain *Indians* who had embarked in a commercial voyage, were cast away on the coast of Germany, and were given as a present by the king of the Survians, to Metellus, at that time proconsular governor of Gaul.[182] About the year 1770, a set of navigators from Japan, were driven by a storm to the northern coasts of Siberia, and having landed at Kamtschatka, were conveyed to Petersburg, and were there received by the empress of Russia, who treated them with great humanity. The Indians given to Metellus either came through Bhering's straits, or were shipwrecked between them and Kamtschatka, (for all the seas north of the Baltic were then called the German ocean,) and were conveyed by land to the Baltic; or otherwise, the Northern ocean being then unobstructed by ice, or more so than in late ages, (as it probably was before the sea between Iceland and Greenland was covered with ice in the tenth century,) they passed through Bhering's straits to the coast of Lapland and Norway. The latter supposition is very improbable. If trading vessels from India, 60 years before Christ, visited the ocean south and east of Bhering's straits, and adjoining to them, and there suffered shipwreck, could other vessels from the same country, or from Japan, as readily and as easily have sailed to the neighbouring shore of America? We cannot see in Mexico the science of astronomy in operation, or any of its principles in the learning of the people; but we can see the product itself of this science, the true length of the

182 Tacitus upon Agricola, sec. 28, notis.

solar year in complete perfection. Either the science of astronomy has perished in Mexico, or it was left by the Mexicans in Asia. We cannot see in Chili the metallurgic art in being which taught the smelting of iron from the ore; but we hear the Chilians pronounce the name of iron and the names of iron tools in contradistinction to all others.

Either then the art has been lost in Chili, or was left by the people of Chili in those countries of Asia whence they emigrated. If for some time an intercourse was kept up by navigation, the emigrants had iron tools upon their first arrival, and until that intercourse was discontinued. The gold, the emeralds[182] which are not the production of Europe or Asia,[183] and the algum tree, for musical instruments, which is probably mahogany, and which were imported from the golden Chersonesus into the Red sea, in the time of Solomon,[184] and which must have been brought from countries as far beyond the Chersonesus as the Red sea is on this side of it, were very probably the productions of South America.

The Mexicans, like the Hebrews, reckon their ecclesiastical year by nights and moons, commencing with the new moon of the vernal equinox.

Some bits of ivory seen by Captain Cook in some of the Pacific islands,[185] which had never before been visited by European navigators, must have been brought thither by Asiatic navigators.

Secondly—*Of the Practices of the Worshippers of the Sun in general, to be compared with the Phenomena in Tennessee and its vicinity.*

In the time of Moses, all the civilized nations of Asia worshipped the sun. Cities and countries

182 Genesis, ch. 9, v. 12; Job, ch. 28, v. 6; Ezekiel, ch. 28.
183 2 O. L. 120; 3 Raynol, 8, 22, 49.
184 Jos. Ant. 398, b. 8, ch. 6, sec. 4.
185 1 Cook's Voyages, 397; 2 Cook's Voyages, 232.

were everywhere named after him. Heliopolis in Egypt and Syria, Baalbeck, or the city of the sun, Apollonea, or the country of Apollo, and all the places in scripture called Baal, with an addition, are plain indications of it. It had subsisted for ages before the time of Moses; and so far were his many and earnest injunctions[186] from subduing a disposition for the same worship, in the minds of the Hebrews, that 500 years after his time, Solomon, the wisest of princes, and a great part of Samaria and Judea, embraced the idolatrous worship of the sun. It is fair to suppose, that the customs of his worshippers at one place were the same with those in all other places. And happily we are furnished with a detailed account of their customs and practices in Judea and Samaria, by the most authentic history in the world. The various passages in the Bible respecting the worship of the sun and the usages of his votaries, will furnish this history. It shall now be briefly stated for comparison with the aboriginal antiquities of this country; and we shall receive much better assistance for the investigation, than can be furnished from any other source. These various passages embodied form this history.

The worshippers of the sun built high places, inclosed them in open courts, erected houses for their idols upon them, and placed their idols within the houses. Upon these high places they burnt incense, unto Baal, which was an image, to the sun, and to the moon, and to the planets and to the host of heaven. Upon those high places they sacrificed human beings, and there made offerings to the sun of horses and chariots. To those high places they retired to grieve and to make lamentation. Their idols they decorated with silver and gold, and clothed them in blue and purple, and embroidered

186 Deut. ch. 4, v. 19. ch. 17, v. 3; Judges, ch. 2, v. 13, ch. 10, v. 6; 1 K. ch. 11, v. 5, ch. 18, v. 19; 2 K. ch. 23, v. 5; Jer. ch. 44.

garments. The images of beasts, and of creeping things which were deified, and of their idols, were painted upon the walls of their temples with vermilion. Upon these high places they sacrificed their sons and their daughters to their gods. In worshipping, they were placed towards the east. They stretched forth the hand toward the sun, and drawing it back, they kissed it. They made their children to pass through the fire to their idols; and when the sun at the summer solstice began to recede to the south, they kept the festival of Tammuz or Adonis, in which they bitterly wept and lamented for his departure. In doing so, they sat on the north side of the temple. We shall presently see by the aboriginal relics, which are yet found in the country, whether in ancient times similar religious notions and customs once prevailed here.

Profane writings inform us also, that the revolution of the sun has been known and celebrated in Persia, ever since the time of Zoroaster, 600 years before Christ, and probably was at the summer solstice, or in June, the same time that our southern Indians celebrate the green corn dance.

In ancient times, when the mysteries of religion were expressed in hieroglyphics, the serpent was the hieroglyphic symbol to signify the obloquy of the ecliptic or the winding course of the sun, from one solstice to the other.[187] The serpent twisted around the figure it entwines, represents the spirals which result from the combination of the diurnal motion of the sun, with his motion of declination.

To those who worshipped the sun, the moon and the planets, and host of heaven, astronomy, which taught the motions, revolutions and relations of the heavenly bodies to each other, from time to time, and the supposed influences of these relations, so much relied on by the astrologers of those days, was a science of infinite importance. These

187 10 Gib. 367; 2 O. L. 407.

who studied it, were in the pursuit of wisdom;
those who became proficients were wise men; to
excel in the understanding of it, was pre-eminence.
As new discoveries were made from time to time,
they were exhibited by some token in their temples:
the motion of the sun; the constellations; the
months of the year; the days of the year; the
animals to which divine honours were paid. Sa-
bianism, says Mr. Gibbon,[189] was diffused in Asia
by the science of the Chaldeans and the arms of
the Assyrians. From the observations of 2000
years, the priests and astronomers of Babylon deduced the eternal laws of nature and providence.
They adored the seven gods, who directed the
course of the seven planets, and shed their irresistible influence upon the earth. The attributes of
the seven planets, with the 12 signs of the zodiac,
and the 24 constellations of the northern and southern hemispheres, were represented by images and
talismans. The seven days of the week were dedicated to their respective deities. The Sabeans
prayed thrice each day, and the temple of the moon
at Haran was the term of their pilgrimage. They
held a singular agreement with their Jewish captives, in the tradition of the creation, the deluge
and the patriarchs, and they practised the right of
circumcision. They lived in a remote period of
antiquity. How near a resemblance to this representation is discovered in the pyramid of Papantla
in Mexico! In the middle of a thick forest it stands.
Enormous stones are used in the structure, which
are covered with hieroglyphics. The only materials employed are immense stones, of porphyritical
shape, and mortar is in the seams. The edifice is
remarkable for its symmetry, the polish of the
stones, and the great regularity of their cut. The
base is an exact square, each side 82 feet in length:
the height, from 52 to 65 feet. It is composed of

189 9 Gib. 249.

several stages; six are distinguishable, and the *seventh* is concealed by the vegetation with which the sides of the pyramid are covered. A *great stair* of 57 steps conducts to *the truncated top*, where the *human victims* were sacrificed. On each side of the great stair, is a small one. The facings of the stones are adorned with hieroglyphics, in which *serpents* and crocodiles carved in relievo are discernible. Each story contains a great number of square niches symmetrically distributed. In the first story, 24 on each side; in the second, 20; in the third, 16. The number of these niches in the body of the pyramid is 366, and there are 12 in the stair toward the east. Did the seven stages of the pyramid represent the seven planets? and the seven days of the week? and the 366 niches, all the days that could be in any year? Did the 12 niches in the stair toward the east, represent the 12 months in the year? and the 24 niches, the 24 constellations?

Thirdly—*Of the Lingual and Nominal Coincidences between the southern Americans and people of the old world.*

The Hebrews, who spake a dialect of the Sanscrit, anciently the language used in India, called the sugar cane *kaniche;* so did the Caribs when discovered by the Spaniards. This indicates another fact besides: that the sugar cane of the continent, like that of Otaheite and of the Pacific islands, grew in America before the arrival of the Spaniards. They could not have had name for a thing they knew not of. *Tona,* in Japanese, signifies sun, moon, governor, king, prince. The Mexicans called the sun *tonticus,* and the moon *tona.* In Hispaniola, all persons of noble or princely blood were called *taino. Montezuma* is the general appellation of a Japanese monarch: Montezuma in Mexico, was the title of their monarch. Canaan is called by the Creeks, Kenaa. A Roman is called in Carib, Ishto: the same in Hebrew. They had known of Rome and of Canaan, otherwise they could not have had names for them.

Fourthly—*Of the Indigenous Practices and Characteristics of the Mexicans and southern Indians.*

The Mexicans had a god, called the god of the shining mirror. In his left hand was a golden fan, set around with beautiful feathers, and polished like a mirror, in which they imagined he saw all that passed in the world. His image was made of a black strong stone.

The Mexicans were addicted to war. The use of money was unknown to them. They had watchmen in ther towns. They made *feathered mantles, of variegated and changeable colours.* They had ornaments of gold and silver; *and utensils* also. When the king died, his attendants were sacrificed to wait on him in the next world.[189]

The Mexicans had pikes, pointed with copper, which appears to have been hardened by an amalgam of tin. They had when the Spaniards first arrived amongst them, carpenters, masons, weavers, and founders. And if it be true, as stated by some of the writers in the southern parts of America, that the Peruvians did not worship idols; but carried them to their temple of Cusco, from the countries they conquered, and placed them there as trophies; then, all the mounds upon which images have been placed, found in Tennessee or its vicinity, are ascribable neither to the Peruvians nor the Chilians, whatever they may be to the Mexicans or Natchez. Nor were human sacrifices ascribable to either of them, for many centuries before the arrival of the Spaniards; for one of the legislators of the Peruvians had abolished the practice. It remained with the Mexicans and Natchez.

189 2 Herod. 370.

The Peruvians used mattocs of hardened wood, and bricks hardened in the sun. They had the art of smelting ore; of refining silver, and sometimes made domestic utensils of it. They buried the bodies of their dead, and vessels of value with them, in mounds. They have also mirrors of various dimensions, made of hard shining stones, highly polished, such as the people of India used both in ancient and modern times.[189] *And they had hatchets of copper made as hard as iron.* They had tools also, with which they could exercise the sculptural art. In the Peruvian city of Tehuanac, were two giants, cut from stone, with *bonnets* upon their heads, and *garments* which reached to the ground.[190]

In Chili are rich copper mines, amongst the mountains of the Cordilleras, as well as of other metals, which yield greater quantities of it, than any others in the world were ever known to furnish. Also *native brass.* These mines of copper are dispersed through the whole country. And upon the Andes in Chili, are very rich silver mines. Mountains of marble are found in the Cordilleras of Copeapo, and in the marshes of Maule, in zones of various cetors. The Chilians, in the time of the Spanish invasion, worked in marble, and made polished vessels of it. They had gold, silver, copper, lead and tin, and made of the copper, bell metal, which they fashioned into axes, hatchets and other edged tools, but in small quantities. They had a specific name for iron, which distinguished tools made of it from other metals. They had the art of smithery, and smiths amongst them. Those of the Chilians who live in the valleys of the mountains, and on the east side of them, are of lofty stature, but generally not much exceeding six

189 1 O. L. 352, 353; Guth. Gram. 719.
190 Ex. ch. 28, v. 40, ch. 29, v. 19, ch. 39, v. 28; Leviticus, ch. 8, v. 13; Judges, ch. 4. v. 18; 1 Samuel, ch. 28, v. 14.

M

feet. The Araucanians, a part of them, are of a reddish brown colour; their hair dark and black, but rather coarse. The Baroans of Chili, in the 89th degree of south latitude, are *white* and as well formed as the northern Europeans. They worship a spiritual God only. They have from time immemorial made *dies and paints,* the colour of which never fades. They believe as the Persians did, in two spirits, good' and evil. They obtain fire by friction, as the Kamtschatkadales do. They pay parents for their wives. They have words of Greek and Latin pronunciation, and signifying the same as in those languages. But there are many Latin words clearly assimilated in sound and signification, to words of the Hindoo language.[191] In Chili, as at Rome, the axe is a badge of supreme authority. To these standards we shall have occasion frequently to recur in travelling through the antiquities of Tennessee, and of the countries in its vicinity.

191 1 Dubois, 68, 148.

CHAPTER V.

HAVING compared the Mexicans and Peruvians with the Hindoos and Persians, we will now compare the Natchez with the Mexicans; and afterwards, the ancient inhabitants of Tennessee with both.

All those nations which lived on the west side of the Mississippi, when they first became known to the Europeans, between the years 1682 and 1697, were worshippers of the sun, and were governed by despotic princes; two prominent circumstances of distinction between them, and the Indians who lived on the lakes, and on those rivers which flow into the Atlantic, on the eastern side of the Alleghenies.[191]

The Natchez at this time extended from the river Manches, or Iberville, which is about 50 leagues from the sea, to the Wabash, which is about 450 leagues from the sea; and it is probable, that they extended laterally up all the rivers which fall into Mississippi between these two extremes. The mounds are perhaps within the limits of their settlements, and not beyond them. They had at this time 500 sachems of the nation. They were under the sovereignty of one man, who styled himself *the sun*, and bore upon his breast the image of that luminary, of which he professed to be the descendant. He regulated war, religion and politics, at his will and pleasure. His wife was called the wife of the sun, and was also clothed with absolute authority. They had the arbitrary disposal of the lives of all their subjects. They all laboured in common for his benefit. When he or his wife died, the guards killed themselves, to attend their sovereign in the other world. Their religious ceremonies were multifarious. They had one temple for the whole na-

191 5 Raynol, 181.

tion. When it caught fire upon a certain occasion, some mothers present threw their children into the fire to stop the progress of the flames, and on the next day were extolled in a public discourse by their despotic pontiff. Some families were reputed noble, and enjoyed hereditary dignity. The body of the people was considered as vile. The former were called *respectables :* the latter, *stenkards.* Their great chief, the brother of the sun, the sole object of their worship, they approach with religious veneration, and honour him as the representative of their deity.[192] Their temples were constructed with some magnificence, and were decorated with various ornaments. In them they *kept up a perpetual fire,* as the purest emblem of their divinity. The first function of the great chief every morning, is an act of obeisance to the sun.[193] The people of Bagota worshipped the sun and moon. They had temples, altars, priests, and sacrifices of human victims. They, like the Mexicans, painted the forms of dei- fied beasts on their temples, and sacrificed human beings for the propitiation of their deities. Their captives taken in war, like those of the Mexicans, were slain, and their hearts and heads were conse- crated to their deities. The body was eaten by the warrior who had made the victim his prisoner. If we meet in Tennessee with appearances which nothing but these facts can account for, we shall know how to refer them to their proper cause.

The nation of the Natchez mouldered away, and their decline seemed to keep pace with the wasting away of the Mexican empire. But whilst a part of their former splendour and power still remained, the French who had come from Canada, and sailed down the Mississippi to the gulf of Mexico in the year 1682, began to be acquainted with their coun- try. In the year 1697, Iberville attempted to make

192 2 R. H. America, 140.
193 2 R. H. Am. 192, 39 ; 1 Plut. 79, 165, 166.

settlements on the Mississippi; but failing there, actually made an establishment at the Mobile, on Dauphin island. Fort Mobile was afterwards placed on the bank of the Mobile river. This settlement was ruined by a storm in 1717. *Some went in quest of better settlements;* some staid behind and lived upon vegetables; till their company was reduced to 28 families. French settlers at various times, before the year 1723, planted themselves in the country of the Natchez; who supplied them with provisions, assisted them in their tillage, and in building their houses, and indeed saved them from famine and death. The Natchez possessed the strongest disposition to oblige them, and would have continued eminently useful to the French settlers, if the commandant had not treated them with indignity and injustice. The first dispute was in 1723; when an old warrior owed a soldier a debt in corn. Payment being demanded, the warrior alleged that the corn was not ripe, but that it should be delivered as soon as possible. They quarrelled, and the soldier cried *murder*. When the warrior left him to go to the village, a soldier of the guard fired at and shot him. The commandant would not punish the offender. Revenge drew them to arms. They attacked the French in all quarters; but by the influence of a noted chief, peace was restored, which prevented the utter extermination of the French settlers. Peace was made, and duly ratified, by Monsieur Branville; yet he took advantage of it, to inflict a dreadful and sudden blow upon the Natchez. He privately brought 700 men. fell upon and slaughtered them in their huts, and demanded the head of their chief, which they were obliged to surrender. The slaughter lasted four days. A peace was then made, but confidence was destroyed. A sachem soon afterwards, in an indignant reply to the solicitation and address of a French officer, upbraided them with their ingratitude, perfidy and rapacity. In

1729, being greatly ill treated by the commandant, they caused him to be summoned before the governor of New-Orleans, to answer their complaints. They were overjoyed at the 'attention paid to their remonstrances. But the commandant was dismissed without removal from office, and returned, more inimical to the Natchez than he had been before. He resolved to gratify his revengeful spirit. He selected for the site of a town, which was to be immediately built, a village belonging to one of the sachems, which covered a square of three miles in extent. He sent for *the sun*, or chief, and directed him to clear the huts and to remove to some other place. The chief replied, that their ancestors had lived there for *so many ages*, and that it was good for their descendants to occupy the same ground. The commandant was offended at the answer, and threatened punishment for disobedience, in case of pertinacity a few days longer. The Indians secretly prepared for a conflict. By various excuses they attempted to defer the execution of his plan. He rejected their excuses, and reiterated the menaces. They obtained permission to wait till their harvest was in. In this interval their scheme was perfected. They determined in concert to make one grand effort, in defending the tombs of their ancestors. A woman of their nation betrayed the secret. The commandant disbelieved and punished her. On the close of the last day of 1729, the *grand sun*, with several warriors, repaired to the fort, with their tribute of corn and fowls, which had been agreed on. They secured the gate and other passages, and cut off the soldiers from the means of defence. All opposition was vain. They massacred the men generally through the whole of the French settlements. The women, and some of the slaves, they spared. The commandant, too ignoble in their estimation to be slain by the hands of a chief, was committed to the charge of one of the lowest of the tribe, and from his hands received an ignominious fate. The whole settlement of 700 men was broken up. The settlements at Yazoo and Westatu were extirpated.[192] The governor of Orleans being implacably bent on the destruction of the *Natchez*, they fled beyond the Mississippi, and settled 180 miles up the Red river, where they built a fort for their protection. Thither he pursued them, besieged the fort, and compelled them to surrender at discretion. The women and children were reduced to slavery, and were scattered amongst the plantations. The men were sent as slaves to St. Domingo. Their villages at first consisted of 1200 souls. Of all the Indians, they were the most polished and civilized. The probability is, that they had all the arts of the Mexicans, as well as their form of government and religion. They had an established religion, and a regular priesthood. They had kings, or chiefs, and a kind of subordinate nobility. The usual distinctions created by rank were understood and preserved. In all which instances there were not any affinities between them and the Indians east of the Mississippi and north of the Ohio, and also east of the Alleghenies and north of the Savannah. The Natchez were skilled in the knowledge of medicinal plants, and their properties. The cures they performed, particularly amongst the French, were almost incredible. They did not deem it glorious to destroy the human species. They were seldom engaged in any other wars than defensive ones. They were just, generous, and humane, and greatly attentive to the wants and necessities of those who needed assistance. It is extremely probable, that this nation, when in the days of its prosperity, extended to the Wabash, extended up all the rivers from the Mississippi southwardly and eastwardly, the waters of which fall into that river. And it

192 Boudinot, 306.

may be that their settlements were at all the places upon those rivers and their branches, where we now see the *high places*, which at the present day are attractive of so much notice. The Mexican empire, with its dependent provinces and kingdoms, before the arrival of the Europeans, in all likelihood, presented to those nations which were on the west and north, too formidable a front to encourage their hopes, or flatter their cupidity. Thus the stream of emigration may have been turned to countries less inviting, and to climates less suitable to savages, which being less populous, and more distant from the centre of Mexican grandeur, furnished more sanguine prospects of success. Then perhaps, countless hosts of embattled adventurers, grown too numerous to be sustained in their own country, left the first settlements which they had made in America, and made their appearance upon the branches of the Missouri and Mississippi, and like the mighty torrent of the latter river, deposited the tokens of their awful inundations over all the prostrate countries on the east of that great river. We shall see presently, there is reason to believe that this was actually the fact. The Natchez, in the time of De Soto, seemed to participate in the afflictions which embittered the last moments of the Mexican empire. The numerous towns which he passed in his march, replete with inhabitants, on both sides the Mississippi, in less than a century afterwards, had disappeared, and in the places where they once stood, were seated men, the most ignorant and the most savage of human beings. The Mexican empire crumbled into ruins; the defence of the frontier was gradually weakened; new encroachments may have been made, till finally the cemented parts of this mighty empire falling asunder, the inhabitants either wholly perished, fled for safety to remote regions, or united with other tribes as chance offered or the occasion dictated. The neglected arts began to languish, as their troubles arose; the comforts and conveniences of life which these supplied, disappeared; and in a few years, except to the eye of the inquisitive antiquarian, no sign remained to announce their former existence. If the chief ruler of the Natchez did not govern the country over which he provided, as a viceroyalty, forming a part of the Mexican empire, at least; his people received from thence, the religion they professed; the form of government; the titles and dignities, both in church and state; the arts, sciences and degree of civilization which distinguished them. Their customs, habits, manners, and permanent institutions, point to the same origin. When we first knew them, they were great in ruins, but hastening through the last stages of a tragic scene. Like thousands of rocks in their country, broken in the age of earthquakes, into numerous pieces, which nature had once conjoined, the throes and convulsions they experienced, were attested by the many and distant fragments of their scattered tribes. Whatever religious practices were sanctioned at Natchez, the same it may be presumed took place on Tennessee, the Cumberland, and the Frenchbroad, when the inhabitants lived upon those rivers, in the undisturbed enjoyment of all their institutions, supported by the veneration of ages, and by the solidity of a government, which like all other mighty nations, they imagined to be of eternal duration.

A remnant of the Natchez lived within the present bounds of this state, as late as the year 1750, and were even then numerous. They were extirpated in a war which they carried on against the French and Choctaws; at the end of which, such of them as were not roasted in the fire, were sold into slavery. But in 1758, when all the French forces were called to the aid of fort Du Quesne, the enslaved Natchez rose in their absence, and de-

N

stroyed all the French of every description, who had been left behind. Intelligence of the fall of fort Du Quesne, met the advancing troops of the French at the falls of the Ohio; and they were ordered back to their respective stations. When those of the Natchez country returned home, they found the women and children all dead, and the Natchez Indians, their late slaves, all fled. A French soldier, tired of the service, deserted, and went for safety from pursuit into the Cherokee nation, with six other deserters. Unfortunately for the poor Frenchmen, the Cherokees and Chickasaws were then at war. The deserters had travelled in a path that led towards the Cherokee nation, and camped in it for the night. The Chickasaws came upon them, and killed them all but one; who pursuing his path, came to the great island in Tennessee. To his great surprise, there were those Natchez whom he had driven as slaves for four years. He quickly departed from this place, and lived in the towns amongst the mountains. These Natchez, though incorporated with the Cherokees, continued for a long time a separate tribe; not marrying or mixing with the other tribes; still having their own chiefs and holding their own councils. When first driven by the French from their own country, many of them took refuge with the Chickasaws, and received from them the *rites of hospitality*. The French for a long time dared not demand them, because of the well known courage and integrity of the Chickasaws. At length, however, they had the temerity to make a demand of them; and met with a refusal, which led to a rupture in the year 1736; when one division of the French army was repulsed with loss, and the other totally defeated. Four years afterwards, in 1740 and 1741, the French renewed the attack with fresh troops from Europe, and met with no better success. A part of this people remained with the Chickasaws ever since; a part incorporated with the Creeks. This powerful nation has yielded to the canker of time, and at this day hardly any thing is known of their history but the name, and whatever is gleaned from the relics of ancient times. It is probable, that they continued to erect *high places*, to the last period of their national existence. At Sultzertown, in the state of Mississippi, six miles from Washington, is a mound or *high place*. It is a parallelogram. Its sides bear the proportion of two to three, measured at the outside of the *ditch*, and contains more than six acres. The first elevation is 40 feet, the area 4 acres. On the west side, about the middle, is a circular mound, diameter 50 feet, from the base 85 feet. Opposite to it on the east end, is a similar mound 50 feet high, but seems to have been much higher. The north and south sides are the longest, have three or four lesser elevations considerably washed down, the whole having been frequently ploughed, supposed to have been formerly ten feet above the first elevation. The whole surrounded by a deep ditch, which on the east and west side is very perceptible. On the *north* and *south* sides are the passages out and in. Twenty or thirty years ago, the country was timbered, and covered with cane brakes. There was *then* no timber upon the fortification, of more than *a foot* diameter. The growth of the timber 30 years ago, shows that the place had been recently deserted before that time, corresponding with the time when the Natchez were expelled from the country by the French.

The people who inhabited the countries now covered by East Florida, Alabama and the state of Mississippi, are supposed to have been of the same lineage with the Natchez, except as to the Chickasaws, in the years 1538 and 1540, when De Soto marched through those countries. There was a glaring discordance between their institutions and manners, compared with those of the Indians between the Alleghenies and the Atlantic; which showed them to be distinct races; and therefore, before we take leave of the Natchez, it will not be amiss to take a short view of these inhabitants, to be compared with the Natchez and Mexicans, and with the Indians of North-Carolina, in the year 1730; of the latter of whose laws, customs and manners, a short view will also be taken.

We have already spoken of the *mounds* which the Spaniards saw upon their landing, and of the bird upon one of them. Thence they marched to *Appalaches;* and in the direction from thence to the *Chiaha,* the houses began to be covered *with reeds like tiles.* Those they had passed were thatched with straw, some had walls daubed with clay. Every Indian had a house for the winter, daubed with clay within and without, and the door was small. They shut it at night, and made a fire within; and it was as warm as a stove. They had others for summer; and their kitchens near them, where they made their fire and baked their bread. And they had *barbacoas* in which they kept their grain: which were houses set upon four *sticks, boarded* like a chamber, and the floor was of cane hurdles. Great men's houses had galleries in their fronts; and under them, seats made of cane like benches. And around them they had lofts, in which they deposited *the tribute paid them :* which tribute was paid in corn, deer skins, *and mantles of the country, which were like blankets.* They made them of the inner rind of the barks of trees, and some kind of grass nettles, which when beaten was like flax. The women cover themselves with the mantles. They place one from the waist downwards; and another over the shoulders, with their right arm out, like the Egyptians. The men wear but one mantle upon their shoulders, after the same manner. The private parts were covered with deer skin, made like a linen breech sometimes used in Spain,

The skins were well curried, and they gave them what colour they pleased. If red, it resembled a very fine cloth in grain; and the bleach is most fine. Of the same sort of leather they make shoes, and they die their mantles in the same colours; and cover them all over with exquisite paintings of wild beasts, and devises representing antiquity. Passing by *Achese* and *Altamaca,* De Soto arrived at *Ocute* on the 10th of April, 1540, having landed at Spirito Santo on the 25th of May, 1539. The king of *Ocute* sent him a present of *conies, partridges, corn bread,* two *hens,* and many *dogs.* He travelled till he came to a forest of pines. With great difficulty they discovered a town, in which was a storehouse full of flour *ground* from parched maize. He then set off for Catufachiqui, governed by *a queen,* which no northern tribe of Indians ever was. She came to the river in a chaise, where certain of the principal Indians brought her to the river, where she embarked into a barge which had the stern lettered over; and on the floor a *mat* was laid, with two cushions upon it, upon which she sat down. And with her came the principal Indians in other barges, attending her. She took from her own neck a cordon of *pearls,* and threw it around the neck of the governor. In the storehouses were great quantities of clothes, *mantles of yarn* made of the barks of trees, and others made of *feathers, white, green and yellow.* De Soto and his troops travelled on through many towns to *Chiaha,* where the soldiers found *gourds* full of *honey,* and a great quantity of *the oil of walnuts.* At another place the people would not obey the young king in his *minority, because* his uncle was the *regent* during his minority. From *Chiaha* he marched to *Coca.* The king met him in a chaise borne upon the shoulders of his nobility; like Montezuma when he met Cortez. He sat upon a cushion covered with a garment of masterns, of the fashion and bigness of a woman's huke. On his head a *diadem* of feathers; and many Indians playing upon flutes, and singing. At length, as the governor passed towards the Mississippi, he went through many towns which were *walled*, a circumstance unknown among the northern Indians, and came near the Tuscaluca king. He was seated on a *high place*. They spread a mat and two cushions, one upon another, for him to sit on; and *around* him the Indians placed themselves, at some distance from him, his chiefest men near him; and one with a *shadow* of deer skin, which kept the sun from him, being round, and of the bigness of a target, quartered with black and white, and far off it seemed to be of taffeta, for the colours were very perfect. It was set in a small staff stretched wide out. When De Soto came to *Movilla*, he found it to be a walled town; where the Indians stood ready to defend themselves, through their loopholes, and from the tops of their battlements. He proceeded thence to Chicaca, where being roughly treated, he marched to *Alimama*, where the Indians were seen walking with their weapons upon the top of the strong fort. At Movilla they marched out in squads, in regular order, and each rank discharging his arrows, gave place to another, which advanced to the front and discharged also. We shall by-and-by see whether there be any coincidence at all between these people and the Indians east of the Alleghenies, when first known to the Europeans.

We shall now proceed to consult those fragments of ancient days, which alone are able to instruct us in the history of the aboriginal settlers of Tennessee. After it shall have been finished, we shall be enabled to say, that the primitive inhabitants of the countries watered by the Ohio and its branches, like the Peruvians, Mexicans and Natchez, and the Hindoos and Persians, were worshippers of the sun, and built *high places,* facing to the *cardinal* points, with *flattened tops*, and *steps on the outside* to ascend to those tops. That they erected *houses* upon them *for their idols*, and placed those idols within them. That they enclosed those *high places in open courts* and *intrenchments*; and burnt incense upon them, unto the image, to the sun and to the moon, and to the planets, and to the host of heaven. They placed altars upon them, and on those altars they sacrificed human beings. That in worshipping they stood towards the east, and lifted up their hands and eyes towards heaven and towards their idols. That they venerated the number three, and worshipped *triune idols*. That they deemed the cross a sacred symbol, and worshipped idols, as did the Phenicians, Hindoos and other nations of Asia. That some of them were lingomites, as some of the Hindoo sectaries are, and as were the Phenicians. That they used the conch shell as emblematic of the properties of their god of the ocean, as the Hindoos did, and like them and the Peruvians and Mexicans, made deep, and wide, and long intrenchments. That, like the people of India, Arabia, Phenicia and Mesopotamia, they made *tanks*, in which water is perpetually preserved in abundance, and in a pure state. They made wells also, walled up with stone from the bottom. They had swords of iron and steel, and steel bows, and mirrors with iron backs, knives of iron, with ferules of silver: tools also of iron and steel, and chisels with which they neatly sculptured stone, and made engravings upon it; and spades, with which they sunk their wide and deep ditches. With unfading dies they painted the sun and moon, upon high rocks, in handsome style, and in some instances we perceive that they, or *their exterminators*, had stone axes, stone balls, and other lapideous instruments. They had marble, and copper, and excellent dies. Like the Mexicans and people of the Sandwich islands in the

Pacific, they made feathered mantles and caps, and fans of various colours. Like the Mexicans and Hindoos, they buried their sacred animals, and placed their dead under mounds raised over the body and over the remains not consumed on the funeral pile. Like the Mexicans, they made bricks and burnt them, and used both them and stone in their buildings. Their complexion, hair and eyes were like those of the Baroans of Chili, their stature was of the common size, but that of their exterminators, a new and modern race, like the Gauls in the time of Lucullus, was frightfully gigantic. These and many other instances of conformity, we shall perceive enough, it is believed, to prove that the aborigines of Kentucky and Tennessee came from the south, and had intimate connexions with the people of Mexico, and some intercourse with the Peruvians and people of Chili. But at length came a chilling frost, from the frozen regions of the north, and nipped the blossoms of prosperity. Those same marauders, who from the 7th to the 11th century of the Christian era converted the cultivated fields of Italy into a wilderness, and filled it with lakes and stagnant ponds, and made the dark ages to reign in gloomy ignorance, came hither also searching through all the corners of the world, for plunder and subsistence; and acted over again the same scenes which had formerly been acted in Palastine, between the worshippers of a spiritual God on the one hand, and the idolatrous adorers of the sun and moon on the other. The new comers into America worshipped a spiritual God, without mounds, idols, or human sacrifices, or any of those peculiarities which characterized the southern people, and which have just now passed in review before us. If at present the reader may look upon this as conjecture, it will soon be converted into the shape of real history.

CHAPTER VI.

Of the Religion of the Aborigines of Tennessee.

LET us first take a view of the aboriginal religion of Tennessee, so far as it is to be collected from the ancient signs which have been left us, and which are fairly referable to this topic.

These are suns and moons painted upon rocks; marks or tokens of triplicity; the cross; mounds; images; human sacrifices; the lingam; the dress of the images; conch shells; and vestiges of the sanctity of the number seven.

First—*Of the Sun and Moon painted upon rocks.*

About two miles below the road, which crosses Harpeth river, from Nashville to Charlotte, is a bend of the river, and in the bend is a large mound, 30 or 40 feet high, and a number of smaller ones near it which will be particularly described hereafter. About six miles from it is a large rock, on the side of the river, with a perpendicular face of 70 or 80 feet altitude. On it below the top some distance, and on the side, are painted the sun and moon in yellow colours, which have not faded since the white people first knew it. The figure of the sun is six feet in diameter: that of the moon, is of the old moon. The sun and moon are also painted on a high rock, on the side of the Cumberland river, in a spot which several ladders placed upon each other could not reach; and which is also inaccessible except by ropes let down the summit of the rock to the place where the painting was performed. This is near the residence of Mr. Dozun; and it is affirmed by a person of good credit, that by climbing from tree to tree, he once got near enough to take a near view of this painting, and that with it, on the rock, were literal characters which did not belong to the Roman alphabet, but at this time,

O

1822; for he looked again lately, the paint has so-far faded as to make the form of these characters undistinguishable. The sun is also painted on a high rock, on the side of the Cumberland river, six or seven miles below Clarksville; and it is said to be painted also at the junction of the Holstein and Frenchbroad rivers, above Knoxville, in East Tennessee. Also on Duck river, below the bend called the Devil's Elbow, on the west side of the river, on a bluff: and on a perpendicular flat rock facing the river, 20 feet below the top of the bluff, and 60 above the water out of which the rock rises, is the painted representation of the sun in red and yellow colours, six feet in circumference, yellow on the upper side and a yellowish red on the lower. The colours are very fresh and unfaded. The rays both yellow and red are represented as darting from the centre. It has been spoken of ever since the river was navigated, and has been there from time immemorial. No one has been able since the white people knew it, to approach the circle, either from above or below. The circle is a perfect one. The painting is done in the most neat and elegant style. It can be seen at the distance of half a mile.

The painting on Big Harpeth, before spoken of, is more than 80 feet from the water, and 30 or 40 below the summit. All these paintings are in unfading colours, and on parts of the rock inaccessible to animals of every description except the fowls of the air. The painting is neatly executed, and was performed at an immense hazard of the operator. It must have been for a sacred purpose, and as an object of adoration. What other motive was capable of inciting to a work so perilous, laborious and expensive, as those paintings must have been? Whence came the unfading dies? the skilled artist capable to execute the work? By what means was he let down, and placed near enough to operate? and for what reward did he undertake so danger-

ous a work? When executed, of what use could
it be to any one, unless to see and to worship?
Taken in connexion with the mounds which are in
the vicinity, *the high places* upon which, in the old
world, the worshippers of the sun performed their
devotional exercises, there can be but little difficulty
in perceiving that these paintings had some relation
to the adoration of that luminary, the god of the
Egyptians, Hindoos and Phenicians, and the great
god of the Mexicans and Natchez, and of the ancient inhabitants west of the Mississippi.—*See G.*

Secondly—*Of Triplicity.*

In White county, in West Tennessee, was dug
up a few years ago, in an open temple, situated on
the Cany Fork of Cumberland river, *a flagon,*
formed into the shape of three distinct and hollow
heads, joined to the central neck of the vessel, by
short thick tubes, leading from each respective occiput. It was made of a light, yellow and compact
clay, intimately intermixed with small broken fragments, and dust of powdered carbon of lime, and
in a state of chrystallization. This vessel held a
quart. Its workmanship is well executed. The
heads are perfectly natural, and display a striking
resemblance of the Asiatic countenance. None of
the minor parts have been attended to, though a
small oval prominence somewhat towards the top of
each head, is probably meant to represent a knot of
hair. In other respects they appear bold. Each
face is painted in a different manner, and strongly
resembles the modes by which the Hindoos designate their different casts. One of the faces is slightly covered all over with red ochre, having deep
blotches of the same paint on the central part of
each cheek. The second face has a broad streak
of brown ochre across the forehead, and another
running parallel with the same, enveloping the eyes,
and extending as far as the ears. The third face

has a streak of yellow ochre, which surrounds and
extends across the eyes, running from the centre at
right angles, down the nose, to the upper lip; whilst
another broad streak passes from each ear, along
the lower jaw and chin. Upon this image the following remarks suggest themselves: The Hindoos
have various marks, by which they paint their faces
to designate the different casts,[195] and to distinguish
amongst the same casts those who are the peculiar
votaries of certain gods. Mr. Dubois says they use
only three colours, red, black and yellow. Probably the face which now seems to be covered with
brown ochre, was originally black, says Mr. Clifford. If it was, says the latter, a metallic paint, as
the other colours certainly are, the black having an
admixture of iron, would certainly change from the
lapse of time, and become what to all appearance
it now is, a dark brown ochre. The other two colours, being native minerals, usually found in the
earth, are not subject to change. If so, these colours were originally the same as those used in In-
doštan. Mr. Dubois mentions, that the Hindoos
draw three or four horizontal lines between the
eyebrows, whilst others describe a perpendicular
line from the top of the forehead to the root of the
nose. Some northern Brahmans *apply the marks
to either jaw*, meaning probably the same sort of
line above described in the face painted with yellow
ochre, as extending from the ears, along the lower
jaw, to the chin. He says further, that the Brahmans draw a horizontal line around the forehead,
to denote that they have bathed, and are pure. The
vessel described, Mr. Clifford thought, was intended for sacred uses. It being found within one of
the circumvallatory temples, is an evidence in favour of this supposition. It would certainly not
have been a convenient vessel for any domestic
purpose. The angular position of the heads, with

195 1 Dub. 295, 296.

respect to the neck of the flagon, must have prevented its being emptied of any liquid, by other means than a complete inversion. The contents of two of the heads might be discharged by an inclined position, with some difficulty and much gargling. But to empty the other, the neck must become vertical. The ancients were unacquainted with goblets, pitchers and decanters, as intermediate vessels. They used large jars or vases, to hold their liquors for safe keeping or carriage, and poured the contents into bowls or horns, from which they drank. Our aborigines were hardly more refined. And whilst the small size of the flagon precludes the idea of its being a vessel for deposite of liquids, its shape plainly indicates that it could not have been used for a drinking vessel. As the ancients always completely inverted the vessel from which they poured their libations, it is reasonable to suppose that this flagon was intended for the same purpose; and that the *three* heads, with the different marks of casts, might designate the various orders of men for which such libations were made. If so, the evidence is almost direct of the identity of religion professed by the Hindoos, and the aborigines of Tennessee. No fabulous circumstance or train of thought, could have occasioned such striking similarity in the paints and modes of applying them, in order to distinguish the different orders of men in their respective nations. If, however, the flagon is not a vessel of libation, the fact of its having *three* heads, possessing Asiatic features, and painted as before is stated, is certainly a strong evidence of Asiatic origination. *Brama,* one of the three principal gods of the Hindoos, was represented with a *triple head,* from the remotest antiquity, as is proved from his colossal statue in the cave of Elephanta. Numerous Hindoo idols in the island of Java, have *three heads.* This character in the image of their gods was very common, as is proved by a number of them delineated by Mr. Raffle, in the second volume of his history.

Some of the Hebrew cherubims are represented with *three* faces.

Baal Shalisha, or the god of triplicity,—or the deity whose image is divided into *three* distinctions, yet remaining combined in one whole,—was a common emblem, and still maintains itself in India.

In the same temple of Elephanta before mentioned, is another triple-formed divinity, with *three* faces, and *three* arms ; in one hand holding a *globe ;* a proof that the ancients of India, as well as the Indians of Carolina, knew that the world was round.

On a medal of Syracuse, is a figure with *three* heads, extremely like the symbols adopted by the Hindoos, and resembling much the Indian figures.

The famous Siberian medal hath *three* heads, and *three* pair of arms. The resemblance of the heads, to the deities of India, leaves no doubt of the origin of the emblem. It is seated on a flower. The heads hold various symbolic articles, among which the ring is clearly distinguishable.

The Hindoos celebrate the first day of the year for *three* days.[196] At the winter solstice they keep a festival for three days. *Three* prostrations are made in presence of distinguished persons. When a child is named by the Brahmans, and the mantras or prayers are made, the father calls him three times by the name he has received.[197] The Brahmans wear a cord over the shoulders, of *three* thick twists of cotton, called the *triple* cord. The threads are not twisted together, but are separate from one another. On the third day of the cere- monies for investing with the triple cord, the young Brahman, his father and mother seat themselves upon three little stools.[198] When carrying a body

196 2 Dub. 134.   197 1 Dub. 131.
198 1 Dub. 77, 143, 149.

to the funeral pile, they stop with it three times on the way.[199] The chief of the funeral goes *three* times around the funeral pile ; and when the body is consumed, the four attending Brahmans go around it *three* times. When a *sannyasi* is made, he takes with him three articles ; a cane of a bamboo with *seven* knots, a gourd filled with water, and an antelope's skin. He drinks of the water in the pitcher.[197] The sacredness of this number was recognised in Chaldea, for the Hebrew children were to be instructed *three* years.[198] Daniel kneeled upon his knees three times a day.

Amongst the Hebrews themselves, it was received, and had as firmly grown into a custom with them, as it was established in India.[200]

Other Tennessee instances of triplicity are seen in the chapter 6, sec. 4, part 1. See ch. 6, sec. 4, part 1, part 2, part 6, part 13, sec. 5.—*See note H.*

Thirdly—*Of the Cross.*

It is not recollected that the cross has been found in Tennessee, except upon the small vessels buried with the pigmy skeletons, in White county, which will hereafter be adverted to

The ring or cross, in ancient Persian medals, were represented as sacred symbols, and had a commemorative intention. In one place the circle is surrounded by 19 points resembling jewels, and unites in a cross. There are figures cut on rocks at Persepolis, of Baal and Moloch, on horseback. Moloch has a club in his left hand, holding a large ring in his right hand. The *ring*, in this instance, is the symbol of unity. Amonea, Baal and Moloch, reconciled, united. The family of Noah was

199 1 Dub. 13, 344.   197 2 Dub. 95.
198 Daniel, ch. 1, v. 5.   199 Daniel, ch. 6, v. 10, 13.
200 Numb. ch. 22, v. 28, 33 ; Exod. ch. 23, v. 14, 17 ; Deut. ch. 16, v. 16 ; Numb. ch. 24, v. 10 ; 1 Sam. ch. 20, v. 41 ; 1 Kings, ch. 9, v. 25, ch. 17, v. 21.

early divided into two parties; one called of the sun, the other of the moon. They boasted of their divinity each to the other; and to prove their superiority, each fought the other's divinity. This shows their reconciliation. These are the most ancient idols.

A medal of Demetrius the second, dated in the 168th year of the Leleucida, has on it the representation of a goddess, a Tyrian and Sidonian Venus, standing giving directions. Her right hand and arm extended: in her left, she holds a *cross* with a long stem to it. These without any further multiplication of instances, prove sufficiently, that in ancient times, in Asia Minor, Persia and India, the ring was emblematical of union, and the cross a sacred symbol. If the *ring and the cross* represented upon the vessel found in the pigmy graves, which will be hereafter described, be also emblematical, and not merely accidental and without meaning, then we are referred for their meaning and origin to the western countries of Asia, from whence they may have come. See I.

Sec. 4.—*Of the Mounds in Tennessee.*

Part 1. It would be an endless labour to give a particular description of all the mounds in Tennessee. They are numerous upon the rivers which empty into the Mississippi, running from the dividing ridge between that river and Tennessee. They are found upon Duck river, the Cumberland, upon the Little Tennessee and its waters, and upon the Big Tennessee, upon Frenchbroad and upon Elk river. The trees are of more recent growth which are upon the mounds that are found in the last settlements of the Natchez; for instance, near the town of Natchez, and on the waters of the Mississippi within the present limits of Tennessee; than those are which grow upon the mounds in other parts of the country: a circumstance which furnishes the presumption, that the ancient builders of the latter were expelled from the other parts of Tennessee, at a period corresponding with the ages of the trees which the whites found growing upon them.

A careful description of a few of these mounds in West and East Tennessee, will put us in possession of the properties belonging to them generally.

In the county of Sumner, at Bledsoe's lick, eight miles northeast from Gallatin, about 200 yards from the lick, in a circular enclosure, between Bledsoe's lick creek and Bledsoe's spring branch, upon level ground, is a wall 15 or 18 inches in height, with projecting angular elevations of the same height as the wall: and within it, are about 16 acres of land. In the interior is a raised platform, from 13 to 15 feet above the common surface, about 200 yards from the wall to the south, and about 50 from the northern part of it. This platform is 60 yards in length and breadth, and is level on the top. And is to the east of a mound to which it joins, of 7 or 8 feet higher elevation, or 18 feet from the common surface to the summit, about 20 feet square. On the eastern side of the latter mound, is a small cavity, indicating that steps were once there, for the purpose of ascending from the platform to the top of the mound. In the year 1785, there grew on the top of the mound a black oak three feet through. There is no water within the circular enclosure or court. Upon the top of the mound was ploughed up some years ago, an *image* made of sandstone. On one cheek was a mark resembling a wrinkle, passing perpendicularly up and *down the cheek.* On the *other cheek were two similar marks.* The breast was that of a female, and prominent. The face was turned obliquely up, towards the heavens. The palms of the hands were turned upwards before the face, and at some distance from it, in the same direction that the face was. The knees were

P

drawn near together; and the feet, with the toes towards the ground, were separated wide enough to admit of the body being seated between them. The attitude seemed to be that of adoration. The head, and upper part of the forehead, was represented *as* covered *with a cap, or mitre, or bonnet*, from the lower part of which came horizontally a brim, from the extremities of which the cap extended upwards conically. The colour of the image was that of a dark infusion of coffee. If the front of the image were placed to the east, the countenance obliquely elevated, and *the uplifted hands*, in the same direction, would be towards the meridian sun. Near to this mound is a cave, which contained, at the time of the first settlements by the whites, a great number of human sculls, without any other appearance of human bones near them.

Baal and Ashteroth, spoken of in scripture, were the sun and moon. The latter being a female, was also called the Queen of Heaven, Venus, Urania, Succothbemoth, Diana, Hecate, Lucena, Cœlestes; and was represented with breasts, sometimes all over, to signify that she is the supplier of the juices which are essential to animal and vegetable existence.

Mr. Earle has lately made another and more scrutinizing examination of this mound, by which have been brought to light several particulars of great consequence in this discussion. His report follows: "This mound is situated in a plane, and is surrounded by hills, which enclose from 75 to 80 acres of flat land, with *three* fine sulphur springs, and at the junction of four roads leading to different parts of the state, and considerably travelled, and about two miles from Cragfont, the residence of General Winchester. This is the place where Spencer and his friend Mr. Drake spent the winter of 1779 and 1780. The trunk of the tree which they inhabited during this hard winter, is just visible above the ground. The diameter is 12 feet. The mound measures, beginning at the northwest corner, running *east*, four and a half poles to the *northeast corner;* then the horizontal projection from the principal mound, north one pole; then *east* 11 poles, to the southeast corner; then *west* 11 poles, to the original mound; thence with the original mound west $4\frac{1}{2}$ poles; thence north $4\frac{1}{2}$ poles, to the northwest corner before mentioned. The elevation to the top of the chief mound is $2\frac{1}{2}$ poles; its diameter 2 poles, in the centre, and from three to four feet. The declivity of the mound is an angle of about 45 degrees. A tree of considerable size is yet growing on the mound, and a decayed stump of $2\frac{1}{2}$ feet in diameter, but too much decayed to count the annual rings or circles in it. An intrenchment and circumvallation encloses 40 acres, encircles this mound and others of lesser size. There is also a circumvallatory parapet, five feet high. On the parapet are small tumuli like watch-towers, about 95 feet distant from one to the other. In the line of circumvallation, and from each *fifth* tumulus, there is an average distance of 45 or—from thence to 180 feet to the next one. It thus continues around the whole breastwork. Mr. Earle dug into the parapet in several places, from two to three feet in depth, and found ashes, pottery ware, flint, muscle shells, coal, &c. On the outside of the intrenchment are a number of graves. In several different places, flat stones are set up, edge-wise, enclosing skeletons buried from 12 to 18 inches under the surface. Three hundred yards distant from the great mound, on the southwest side of the intrenchment, is a mound of 50 yards in circumference, and six in height. In the opposite direction from this to the *northeast*, stands another smaller mound, and of the same dimensions as the one last mentioned. So that the *three* stand upon a line, from northeast to southwest, in the same

order as the trimurti are placed even to this day in
the temple of Jugernaut.[201] The next principal
mound in size, within the intrenchment, in a southeast course from the great mound, and about 170
yards distant, circumference 90 yards, elevation 10
feet. Thirty-five yards distant, in a southwest
course, is a small tumulus, two thirds as large as
the one last mentioned. At the same distance, on the
northeast corner of the great mound, is another of the
same size as that last mentioned. Each of these tumuli hath a small one of about half its size in the
centre between them and the great mound. The earth
in which this mound was constructed, appears to
have been taken, not from one place, leaving a cavity
in the earth, but evenly from all the surface around
the mound. In about 200 yards distant, extending
from the mound, the soil hath been taken off to a
considerable depth. The corn which is planted
within this place, yields but a small increase. The
tumuli upon the parapet project beyond it, both inwards and outwards; the summit of these being 3
feet above the summit of the parapet, and 5 feet
above the surface of the common earth. They are
10 or 12 feet in diameter at the base. Between
every *fifth* tumulus, and the next tumulus, which
is the first of the next five, there is a large interstice.
One of the intervals to the north, is 180 feet wide.
The next towards the west, 145. The summit of
each tumulus diverges from the base towards a point,
but at the top is flat and wide enough for two or
three men to stand on. The common distance between the tumuli is 95 feet, without any variation.
The intrenchment is on the inside of the parapet,
all round. From it the parapet has been made.
Mr. Earle commenced his excavation on the north
side of the principal mound, ten feet above the common surface of the earth, and penetrated to the
centre of the mound, in a cavity of about 7 feet in

[201] Buch. 15, 18.

breadth. Two feet from the summit, was found a stratum of ashes 14 inches through, to a stratum of earth. On the east side of the cavity the same stratum of ashes was only from three to four inches in depth. The diggers then came to the common earth, which was only two feet through to the same substance, *ashes*. Then again commenced the layers of ashes, from one to two inches through to the earth. Then again to ashes; and so the layers continued alternately, as far as they proceeded. The layers of ashes were counted as far as the excavation descended, and amounted to 28. The earth between the layers of ashes, was of a peculiar description, yellow and grey. The ashes were of a *blackish* colour. The yellow earth was of a saponaceous and flexible nature. The grey was of a similar kind to that of the common earth. At eight feet from the top of the mound, they came to a grave, which had the appearance of having once been an ancient sepulchre. The earth caved in as the diggers sunk the cavity. The cause of this was soon ascertained to be, the skeleton of a child in quite a decayed state, but sufficiently preserved to ascertain the size. Doctor Green and Doctor Saunders, of Cairo, examined the bones, and pronounced them to be the bones of a child. This skeleton was lying on *three* cedar piles, five feet and a half in length, and considerably decayed, but sound at the heart. The head of the child lay towards the east, facing the west, with a jug made of sandstone, lying at its feet. This jug or bottle was of the ordinary size of modern gallon bottles, such as are commonly manufactured at Pittsburgh, with the exception that the neck is longer, and there is an indentation upon its side, indicating that a strap was used to carry it. The grave was on the east side of the cavity, eight feet from the centre of the mound north. The excavation from the top of the mound, perpendicularly into the earth, was

22 feet. At the time they found the grave above mentioned, they also found other graves, and small pieces of decayed human bones, and *bones of animals,* amongst which was the jaw bone with the *tusk* attached to it, of some unknown animal. The jaw bone is about a foot long, having at the extremity a tusk one inch and a half in length. The tusk is in the same form as that of Cuviers mastaden, but has more curvature. Having been accidentally broken, it was found to be hollow. The jaw bone has in it at this time, two grinders, like those of ruminating animals, with an empty socket for one other of the same size, and one large single tooth. Towards the extremity of the jaw and near to the tusk, is another small socket, calculated for a tooth of minor magnitude. This jaw bone was found at the depth of 18 feet from the surface of the earth. They also found the bones of birds, arrow points of flint, pottery ware, some of which was *glazed,* muscle shells and winkle, coal, isinglass, burnt corncobs. The further they penetrated downwards, the greater were the quantities of flat stone, found all standing edgewise, promiscuously placed, with the appearance of once having underwent the action of fire. And finding at every few inches, a thin stratum of ashes and small pieces of human bones. At 19 feet they dug up part of a corncob, and small pieces of cedar completely rotted. We will now make a few remarks. This mound was built precisely to the cardinal points, as were the mounds of Mexico, the pyramids of Egypt and the Chaldean tower of Babel. Like them, its top was flattened. The image which once stood on its top, was similar to that of Ashteroth, or the moon. Those who worshipped, stood on the east of the image on the platform, and held their heads towards her. The ditch was probably dug with metallic tools. That and the parapet perhaps represented the year. The five tumuli represented

the five days into which the Mexicans divided time. The interstices, the four quarters into which each Mexican month was divided. The whole composing the 72 quintals that made up the year, or 360 days. The wider passages to the north and south, east and west, like the Hindoo temple of *Seringham*, which is before described, represented the four quarters or seasons of the year. The walls around the ancient temples of India are passed by passages precisely to the cardinal points.[202] The three mounds in a line, the larger being in the middle, represent the trimurti, or three great deities of India, upon all three of which idols were probably once placed, as they are now placed in the temple of Jugernaut; and are intended to represent EOA, or Ye-Ho-Wah: whence in every country in Asia, including the Hebrews, came the sacred reverence for the number *three*, which is so apparent in all their solemnities. Part of this name, the A and O, or the alpha and omega, yet signify with us, the beginning and end of all things;[203] with three attributes, *which is, which was, and which is to come*. This was a part of the description which belonged to the triune *great one*, whom idolatry caused mankind to lose sight of, whilst those who only worshipped a spiritual God, preserved it in its original purity. But in every country, whether corrupted by idolatry or not, proceeds from the great, original and uncorrupted religion, which emanated immediately and directly from EOA, or the great good spirit. It cannot be conceived for a moment, that here was a fortification for military purposes. For when did ever any such work have so many passages, so regularly and equally placed. The worshippers of the *heavenly hosts* were the greatest cultivators of astronomy, whilst the only religion of the world opposed to

202 Robertson's India, 270.
203 Rev. ch. 1, v. 8, 11, ch. 21, v. 6, ch. 22, v. 13.

them, discouraged the contemplation of those ob.
jects of her heathenish adoration. They involved
in the circle of their adorables, all the constellations and planets. In some places we see a mound
and five or six smaller ones around, which seem to
represent the *Pleiades*, and sometimes other luminaries seem to be represented. These layers of
ashes are unlike those in the time of the Trojan
war, over which were raised mounds of earth, after
the bodies of Patroclus and Hector were consumed
in them, and their bones taken away and put into
an *urn*. But the strata of ashes, at intervals from
top to bottom, with human bones intermixed, show
that here *were human victims* committed to the
flames, after decapitation and removal of the scull
to the neighbouring cave, where it was laid up in
darkness for the use of the deity. The black ashes
denote the consumption of *tobacco*, the only incense
in America which they could offer, in which also
was consumed the *consecrated victim*. A heated
fire of solid wood would have consumed bone and
all. The great number of graves on the outside,
show that the people neither usually buried in
mounds, nor usually consumed dead bodies on the
funeral pile. The skeleton of the child found
within, shows that it was a privilege peculiar to his
family to be buried there, whilst the other ranks of
men were buried without the circumvallation. He
was very probably one of the children of the sun.
The earth taken from the surface, within the circumvallation, was holy and consecrated; it was
earth impregnated by the beams of the sun, and
must have been removed by a great number of
hands, compelled by despotic power to obedience,
when placed on the expiring embers of sacrificial
fire. The enclosures of all such mounds are circular, or for the most part are so, to represent possibly
the course of the revolving year, and to make upon
them the divisions of time which the sun describes

in his progress. It is easy to compare what is found in this mound and about it, with the collection of scriptural passages, before stated, and to see how far there is an accordance between them or not. See chapter IV. sec. 2. And therefore it is needless for the writer any further to pursue the subject.

Part 2. On the Big Harpeth river, in a bend of the river, below the road which crosses near the mouth of Dog creek, from Nashville to Charlotte, is a square mound, 47 by 47 at the base, twenty-five feet high, *and two others in a row with it,* of inferior size, from 5 to 10 feet high. At some distance from them and near to the eastern extremity of the bend, are *three* others in a parallel row, with a space like a public square between the rows. Near these mounds are other small ones, to the amount of 12 in all. All around the bend, except at the place of entrance, is a wall on the margin of the river. The mounds are upon the area enclosed by the wall. Within them also, and not far from the entrance, is a *reservoir of water.* Its mouth is square, and it is 15 feet over. The water in it is nearly even with the surface. There are besides the entrance, two gateways; from thence to the river is the distance of 40 yards. The wall is upon the second bank. On the top of the large mound, *an image* was found some years ago, eighteen inches long from the feet to the head. Soapstone was the material of which it was composed. The arms were slipped into the socket, and there retained with hooks. They hung downwards, when not lifted up. The trees standing upon the mounds were very old. A poplar stood on one of them, 5 or 6 feet through. A large road leads through the entrance, which is at the point where the river turns off to make the bend, and after making it, returns to an opposite point near it. Into the river at this latter point, runs a branch,

Q

from near the first mentioned point; between which and the branch is an interval wide enough for a road, and from this point to the branches, is a deep gulley, which is filled up as wide as the road, till made level with the adjoining land on the other side. Over this filled up interval, passes a road from the great mound, between the point where is a high bluff, and the branch in a southwardly direction. It is at this time two or three feet deep and six or seven wide. It crosses the river in less than half a mile. On the north side of the bend and wall, is a gateway, and also on the south. On parts of this wall, at the distance of about 40 yards apart, are projected banks, like redoubts, (See ch. 6, s. 4, part 1.) on which persons might have stood. On the east side of the first large mound, is a way to ascend it, wide enough for two men to walk abreast, and sloping to the top. Steps were no doubt once there, though not now visible. From the gateway on the south side of the bend and wall, are the traces of two old roads, one leading to the other works, within a mile of these, in another bend of the creek, and over an intervening bottom of rich land, made by the winding of the river between the two bends, and in fact forming a middle or intermediate bend on the opposite side; so that there are three bends, the two outer and the middle. The other road leading to the mouth of Dog creek, and traceable for several miles beyond it. The first of these roads passes from the gateway into the public square, between the mounds first described, to the other gateway on the north side. Higher up the river, and within a mile of the above-described enclosures, and above the road leading by the mouth of Dog creek to Charlotte, is another bend of the river, so formed as to leave a bend and bottom on the north or opposite side of the river, and between the two bends on the south side. In the other bend on the south, above the road, is a square wall, abutting on the south side upon the river, on a high bluff of the river, upon the bank of which a wall is also built, as it is on the three other sides. On the outside of it is a ditch, five or six feet wide, with large trees on it. In the eastern wall are two gateways. About the centre of this enclosure, is a mound of the same dimensions as was the large mound in the other enclosure. On the east, north and south sides of it, is a raised platform, 10 or 12 feet high on the east side, but less as the hill ascends on the north and south. The top is level; from it to the top of the mound itself, is 10 or 12 feet or more. The top of this mound was ascended to from the west, where the height is not more than 5 or 6 feet. The platform is 60 feet over. Two large gateways are in the eastern wall. From the most southwardly of them, a road leads to the river and across it in a northwardly direction, near the mouth of Dog creek. And from the most northwardly gateway, a road leads to the river and across it, in a northwardly direction, or a little east of north. It then passes over the intermediate bend, or bottom, on the east side of the river, and into the enclosures first described. The bottom on which the second enclosures stand, and also the bottom on the opposite side of the river below this, and that on which stand the enclosures first described, is full of *pine knots*, which are ploughed up daily. There are no piny woods nearer to these bottoms than 5 or 6 miles. These knots are the most abundant in the intermediate bottom, and but few in the first described enclosures. Mr. Spears supposes, that these are the remains of old field pines, grown to full size after the desertion of cultivation, and the total exhaustion of the lands by long continued tillage. That after allowing their full growth, and after the soil had been restored by long rest, the pines fell down, and were succeeded by the growth we now see standing upon the bottom; large oaks, poplars and sugar trees. One large sugar tree stands there with its roots shooting through the upper part of a large decayed pine stump. Allow 250 years for the growth of the pines to maturity, and 300 for the present growth, and the cultivation must have been relinquished at least 550 years ago: that is, as early as the year 1272, or earlier.

The remarks which offer themselves upon these mounds, are not only that the doctrine of triplicity is here very prominent, but also that the well, or *tank*, for holding of water, must have been constructed with *peculiar art*, probably upon the plan that the Hindoo tanks were, and those of Mesopotamia and Judea were in ancient times. But the most material consideration is, the uses to which the waters of the *tank* were applied. Is it probable that the inhabitants of the country lived upon this consecrated ground, upon which stood their temples and gods? If not, the waters of the tank were for sacred uses; for ablutions and purifications; another great symptom of the Hindoo ritual. It is a remarkable truth, that the same law of defilement and ablutions has actually existed amongst the Hindoos, from times of the remotest antiquity, which Moses delivered to the Hebrews.[203] What the Mosaic law was, is stated in various scriptural passages,[204] and retains only such rites observed by the Hindoos and Egyptians as were proper for the Hebrews, in the new countries and climates, in which they were about to settle.

Part 3. Not far from the residence of Colonel Ward, in Davidson county, 14 miles above Nashville, on the south side of the Cumberland river, is a mound; the elevation of which, above the common

203 1 Dub. 160, 166, 168, 178, 185.
204 Lev. ch. 2, v. 32, 33, ch. 5, v. 11, 12, 13, 14, ch. 11, v. 13, 24; Numb. ch. 9, v. 6, 7, 10, ch. 19, v. 8, 11; Deut. ch. 23, v. 11.

surface, is from 12 to 13 feet; the circumference about 75 yards. The dirt of which it was constructed, was brought about 90 yards. Stumps of trees are standing on the hollow whence it was taken, containing 155 rings or circles. The dirt from the commencement of the digging into it, in April, 1820, was a red gravel, and continued so for the depth of 9 feet from the summit, when the diggers came to a very light earth, resembling that of ashes mixed with a common earth, and as dry as if it had been exposed to a hot summer's sun for several weeks. A few inches above these light ashes and common earth, was found another stratum of clay. These light ashes and common earth continued so far downward in the centre as the diggers penetrated, which was about 18 feet from the summit. At the distance of 12 feet they found coal; at 16 feet, leaves; and 17 feet, pure ashes, with mixtures of lime, and substances having a perfect resemblance to human bones after having been burnt. These substances when exposed to the air, crumbled into dust, with the exact appearance of the ashes of a human body after having been consumed by fire. Trees are upon this mound, which must be from 100 to 130 years old. At 20 yards distance is another mound, about half the size of the one above described, with a stump in it counting 130 annulars. Also a decayed stump, half as large again as the one just mentioned. The coal 12 feet below the summit, and of course only one foot above the surface of the earth, is where we could expect to find it, let the fire have been kindled for whatever purpose it may. But finding leaves 16 feet below the summit, and 3 feet below the surface, or 4 below the coals, indicates a deposition of the leaf after the coal was made and the fire extinguished; and that below the coal at the time of its deposition, was a hollow. Ashes one foot lower than the leaf, or 17 feet from the summit, prove the same fact. The) dryness of the ashes continued from 9 feet below the summit to 18 feet below it, shows that the mound was a receptacle prepared for them before they were placed in it. The covering of the interior with an outward coat of red gravel, contrived for the absorption of rain water, and for preventing its access to the ashes, shows the sacred estimation in which they were held. The thin stratum of clay was the inner covering used because of its attractive property, and to make the outer covering the more readily and closely attach to it. Why so much labour bestowed to ensure the object to be accomplished? If the materials of which the outward covering was composed were removed from the hollow the distance of 90 yards, how many hands must have been employed in the removal, wagons and carts not being in use? And if the wheel was unknown to the people who built the mounds, what sort of a government must there have been which was able to command the services of so many persons at one and the same time, who must have contributed their joint efforts for this erection? Any where near to this mound there is not any species of earth of the crumbling property and unadhesiveness of particles, that would when dried by a fire of the most intense heat, assume so much the appearance of ashes as the interior substances above described do. Much less had water ever been intermixed with it. There is much reason to believe that the substance supposed to be ashes is really so. And why does ashes occupy the whole interior? If ever used for a habitation, the ashes would have been removed from time to time. There must have been a crater at the summit. From the coal and the ashes must have been received into the inner parts of the mound and into the hollow below the surface. The leaf must have fallen through the crater, after one burning and falling in of the ashes, and must have been covered before the next took place, or the ashes must have been made at another place, and must have been brought from it to this mound. And in passing from one place to another must have received the leaf. The substance to which the leaf adhered is now petrified, or ossified, for it has the latter appearance at least as much as the other. It hath the impressions of the stem of the leaf clearly apparent upon it, so that no one can mistake it. In India some sectaries burn and others inter the bodies of the dead. The followers of Vishnu burned. When a Brahman dies, his body, with fire in a vessel, is carried to the pile. A trench six or seven feet long is dug. A pile is erected of dry wood, on which the body is laid at full length, and fire is put to the pile. Perhaps the reddish coat which incrusted the ashes, may have been caused by the the action of fire in the interior of the mound, the outer covering of which may not have been added till after the fire had reduced the pile to ashes. And the leaf may have been introduced before the opening on the top of the mound was closed. The leaf being of full growth, shows the time of the year when it fell into the mound. There is no circumstance in nature which would lead men everywhere to raise mounds over the dead, for the purposes of religious adoration. We see in this age, and in all ages, many nations which have not any such custom, still less is there a cause in nature for taking the dirt of which the mound is composed at a considerable distance from the mound itself, a circumstance in which evidently our mounds agree with those of England and Scotland, and perhaps other northern countries of Europe, which were first settled by the Goths and Fins from the borders of India and China. This latter circumstance must have been deduced from a common origin. Burning of the dead also, so far from being the result of a natural cause, hath been practised but by few nations. All these customs are imitative. If we can discover who buried under mounds, and who burnt, and especially if we can discover who did both, we get possession of a clue which is very important in this investigation. The interment alone of dead bodies was practised by the Ethiopeans, Egyptians, Sybeans, Hebrews, the Parthians, the Phenicians,[204] Thraceans, Sarmatians, and all the Scythian tribes. Burning on funeral piles was practised very generally, but not universally, in India. The Trojans, Greeks and Romans burned as well as buried. Burning ceased amongst the Romans, and probably amongst the Greeks, in the time of Theodosius, the Roman emperor, in the fourth century of the Christian era. The funeral of Patroclus in Homer, and of the father of Eneas in Virgil, show the custom that prevailed 1000 years before Christ in Asia Minor. The Hindoos burn the wife on the funeral pile of the husband. Their philosophers frequently burned themselves. It is pretty certain that the Greeks and Romans had no intercourse with America; and if so, we can look nowhere else but to the southern and southeastern parts of Asia for this custom, to those countries where the dead are both burned and buried. Whether, like the high places for worship, these customs have a connexion with the religious tenets of the people who practised them, must be submitted to the judgment of the learned.

Part 4. On the 21st of July, 1821, Mr. Earl proceeded to the mound near Nashville, on the field of David McGavock, Esquire, with workmen furnished with spades and pickaxes to cut into it. This is the mound upon which Monsieur Charleville, a French trader, had his store in the year 1714, when the Shawanese were driven from Cumberland by the Cherokees and Chickasaws. It stands on the west side of the river, and on the

204 Genesis, ch. 23, v. 6.

north side of French lick creek, and about 70 yards from each. It is round at the base. About 30 yards in diameter, and about 10 feet in height, at this time. The workmen opened a circular hole about the centre of the summit, and a ditch from thence to the western extremity. They found pottery, of Indian fabrication, everywhere within the mound; and two or three feet under the summit, the jaw bone of an animal not human, of the carnivorous species; and small fragments of bones, whether human or not, could not be determined. About 4 feet below, they came to a layer of charcoal, or rather of black cinders, about two inches through, and extending from the central hole towards the west 8 or 10 feet, and exhibiting an appearance which made it probable, that the dirt in which it lay was once the top of the mound, and had been flattened, and a large fire made upon it, which had consumed to cinders the fuel which had been placed on it and set on fire; and that afterwards the mound had been raised higher, by the accumulation of fresh dirt thrown upon it, of the same sort as that which composed all the rest of the mound. This dirt was black, rich and very fine, and seemed to have been brought to it in pots, the fragments of which were seen through every part of the mound. Below the layer of cinders, they frequently came to detached pieces of coal, as they descended towards the base. About 4 feet below this layer of coal, they took up the tooth of a carnivorous animal, and an arrow head of flint, very neatly shaped into an acute angled triangle, sharp on the sides, which had been cut by the application of other stones to it. When they began the central hole they saw some flat rocks, partly covered and in part not. After raising them and digging about a foot below, they came to a piece of metal of an oval form, of the size of a ninepenny piece of silver, but more than twice as thick, with an indented representation of

R

the head of a woman on one side. It is supposed to be of European manufacture, and resembled a watch seal. And as it was found below where the House of Mr. Charleville formerly stood, in 1714, and for many years before.. The mound also had been stockaded by the Cherokees between the years 1758 and 1769. The metal was remarkably heavy for its size. Very large burying grounds once lay between the mounds and the river, thence westwardly, thence to the creek. Vast numbers of bodies had been interred. The great extent of the burying ground and the vast number of interments, induce the belief, that a population once resided here, which more than 20 times exceeded that of the present day: and suggested also another idea, that the cemetery was in the vicinity of the mound, because the latter was an erection consecrated to religious purposes. The layer of cinders had been made from fuel very combustible; and soon reduced to ashes. It seemed to have been pounded hemp reduced to cinders, or the pounded bark of the poppaw tree. Upon reflection, it is now thought to have been tobacco, the only plant in the country of which incense could have been made. From hence arose the conclusion, that the object in kindling the fire was to have a flame of no long continuance, and that thousands of jars of dirt had been poured upon it as soon as the fuel was reduced to embers. That the jars themselves had been broken to pieces, and the remnants left intermixed with the dirt which had been emptied from them. That fire had been employed as an agent at different periods of the mound's growth, and that the matter consumed, whatever it was, had been preserved with sacred veneration, by strata of dirt thrown over it, before the rains had washed it away, or the winds had scattered it. The stratum of cinders was remarkably black, suggesting the idea that rains had not fallen upon it for any time so as to change its colour in any degree before it was covered over with fine black mould. The fragments of pottery were composed of clay, and pounded cockle shells, many of which unpounded and unimpaired were found in parts of the mound not far removed from the surface. These were used probably for scooping the dirt, and for getting it into the pots and jars in which it was carried to the mound.

By the opening of this mound, there is not any thing discovered in its structure which denotes civilization. But to raise the mound, was in the estimation of the builders, a duty of immense importance. For it must have been formed by a succession of deposites, and by contributions from thousands of hands, at different and perhaps distant periods. The principle, whatever it was, that impelled them to action, was not only of irresistible force, but also permanent and perpetual in point of duration. It could not have been raised for the monarch of the nation to be seated on, in view of the assembled people; savages do not possess such devotion to their leaders. If the government was old and despotic, they would not have placed the mound for such a purpose on a burying ground. The intermixed articles repel this idea. It could not be for any purpose relative to war; for to be placed on the mound would only be a greater exposure to the arrows of an enemy. It could not have been a tower, for there is no narrow pass near it to be guarded. It could not be for a fortress, for there is no water nearer to it than the river and creek. The only use which could have been made of it, was that of adoration. When standing upon this *high place*, the hand of the worshipper might pass from his mouth, and from thence be stretched forth towards the bright luminary, which is at once the source of life, of pleasure, and the nourisher of all that grows in the animal or vegetable king-

dom.[205] The worshippers of the sun performed
their religious exercises on *high places*, and made
their sons and daughters to pass through the fire to
Moloch, or the image of the sun.[206] They burnt
human victims in magnification of his powers.[207]
Fire, the purest of the elements, emanated, as they
supposed, directly from their deity. It purified
their victims, and was itself adored as a divine es-
sence, proceeding directly from the source of light
and life—the deity which was the principle of all
animation. It was perpetually preserved in the
temples of his worshippers, both in Persia and in
Natchez; by the vestals of Rome, and in the Grecian temple of Apollo. The fires kindled upon this
mound, before the summit rose to the elevation it
now hath, may have been an object of adoration for
the assembled multitude, or may have been made
for the initiated worshippers of the sun to pass
through, or in which human victims were consumed,
or for incense to their deity. When the sun returned to the summer solstice, they had a feast of
joy, in which they offered the first fruits, and kindled new fires, which had been extracted by glasses
from the sun, or by the friction of two pieces of
wood. And such is yet the practice at the green
corn dance of the Creeks. The sacrifice of human
beings was practised, as may be inferred from appearances, by those who lived on the Ohio, Cumberland and Tennessee, and on the Mississippi below the mouths of these rivers. Here too, as in
India, the priests of the sun wore on their breasts
the sign of the cross. And here too are placed the

205 Job, ch. 31, v. 27; 1 Sam. ch. 9, v. 12; 1 Kings, ch. 3,
v. 4; 1 Chron. ch. 16, v. 39, ch. 11, v. 7; 2 Kings, ch. 23, v.
15; 2 Chron. ch. 1, v. 3; Ezekiel, ch. 16, v. 24, ch. 25, v. 31.
206 Lev. ch. 18, v. 21, ch. 20, v. 2, ch. 2, v. 4; Jer. ch. 32,
v. 35.
207 2 K. ch. 16, v. 3, ch. 21, v. 3, 4; Jeremiah, ch. 19, v. 5,
6; 2 Chron. ch. 28, v. 3; Jeremiah, ch. 7, v. 31, ch. 32, v. 35,
ch. 19, v. 5; Psalm 106, v. 37, 38; Ezekiel, ch. 16, v. 20, 21.

images of Baal and Chemosh upon their *high pla-ces.*[208] They also, both in India and Egypt, dei-fied animals of the canine species; and here their bones are found, both in this mound and in the dwarf graves near Sparta. This mound was erect-ed before the coming of the Shawanese to settle on Cumberland river. They did not reckon it among places consecrated to religion, otherwise they would not have suffered a trader to live on it. This also proves that they, for any purpose, had not been at the pains bestowed upon its erection. For had they been the builders, they would more carefully have preserved it for the intended uses. It was a *high place* appropriated to the performance of the religious rites; incense was burnt upon it, and hu-man victims sacrificed there—and this long prior to the time when the ravages of war or of pesti-lence had thinned the population of the country. Wherever the worshippers of the sun have dwelt, through the whole earth, *high places* attest the fact. The same evidences give also unerring proof of their having come into America. Their customs, in general have been everywhere the same, and whenever they are conquered they melt into disso-lution. The maledictions of Providence seemed to have followed them for their atrocities; and through the whole world, the religion which adores a spiritual God, seems always to have triumphed over the idolatrous worshippers of matter and ima-ges.

Par. 5. On the south side of Big Harpeth river, on a high impassable bluff, about three miles from Franklin, in Williamson county, is an ancient *in-trenchment,* nearly in the form of a *semicircle,* sup-

208 1 Kings, ch. 14, v. 23; 2 Kings, ch. 17, v. 10, ch. 23, v. 24; 2 Chron. ch. 14, v. 3, ch. 28, v. 2, ch. 33, v. 22, ch. 34, v. 3; Isaiah, ch. 17, v. 8, ch. 27, v. 9; Jeremiah, ch. 43, v. 13; Ezekiel, ch. 6, v. 6, 7, 20, ch. 21, v. 21, ch. 30, v. 15; Hos. ch. 10, v. 2.

posed to contain 20 acres or more. Within the enclosure made by the intrenchment and the bluff, are several mounds of different forms and sizes, from six to ten feet high, and from ten to twelve yards wide. Others nearly round, about ten yards in diameter. The largest of these mounds, is is nearly in an oblong, with rounding corners, 68 feet wide by 148 long; about ten feet higher than the surface of the surrounding earth. In another part of the enclosure are small mounds, or rather hillocs, from two to three feet high, and perhaps five or six yards in diameter. One of these is also considerably larger than the rest. The soil within the intrenchment is very rich, and the trees in it, as also those in and upon the edge of the ditch, as large as the trees generally in that part of the woods. A few yards within the intrenchment is a small lasting spring, which runs into the river bottom between where the ditch strikes it and the commencement of the bluff. There are seven passways over the ditch, at convenient distances from each other, about eight feet wide, where the earth remains in its original state. From the great length of time that must have elapsed since the making of the ditch, it is impossible to say with certainty, on which side the earth was thrown, and although the greater part was on the outside, it is probable that some was thrown on both. For the same reason, it is difficult to ascertain its depth or width. In some places it appears to be five or six feet wide, and three or four deep. At others it is wider and more shallow; and so much altered by time, that it hath almost disappeared. A white oak stands in the ditch, four feet in diameter.

Par. 6. In the county of Williamson, on the north side of Little Harpeth, in the lands owned by Captain Stocket, northwardly from Franklin, are walls of dirt running north from the river, and east and west. In 1821 they were four or five feet high; and are in length, from the river, between 400 and 500 yards. There is a ditch on the outside, all around, four or five feet in width, partly filled up; and upon the soil which has partly filled it up, are black oaks two feet or more in diameter. A spring of excellent water is in the inside of the enclosure, and a branch from it into the river through the interval left by the wall for its passage. The enclosure contains 40 or 50 acres. Three mounds are in the inside, standing in a row from north to south, and near to the wall and ditch, on the north side of the area. All of these mounds are nearly of the same size. Within the enclosure is a vast number of graves, all of them enclosed within rocks, and the bones very large. James McGlaughlin, who is seven feet high, applied one of the thigh bones found there to his thigh, and it was three or four inches longer than his thigh. The area is in low grounds, which are never overflowed by freshets in the river. The mounds are not more than three or four feet high. They are the relics, in all likelihood, of oval houses which have there fallen; not mounds over dead bodies, or the ashes of dead bodies near mounds for temples in places of worship. Springs are seldom in the inside of enclosures dedicated to religious purposes; for ablutions were to be made before entering the holy place.

7. At the junction of Piny river with Duck river, into which it falls on the north side, after coming near to Duck it turns off and makes a large bend, and then discharges itself into Duck. Before reaching the point where it turns off, it runs parallel with Duck river for some distance. From the upper end of this parallel, is a deep ditch to the river. It is now 10 or 12, and in some places 6 feet deep. Trees of large size grow upon it. There is a high bluff of rocks on each river; and at the point where the bend commences, a ditch is drawn from one river to the other, which encloses not only the bend,

but also the lands between the two rivers. In the latter enclosure are 25 or 30 mounds, and amongst them a large one 15 feet high, round, and rather rising on the top, but flat enough to build a house on. At the base it is 30 or 40 yards across. There are mounds in all the bottoms of Duck river. The caves in this neighbourhood are numerous, and for the most part contain human bones.

8. On Powell's river, in Warren county, in West Tennessee, at the plantation of Mr. Hill, is an old ditch extending from a mound in the bend of the river, to the river. It was five or six feet wide, and appears to have been of considerable depth. This ditch led from the mounds southwardly to the river, from the eastern extremity of the mound. The space below the mound and the river westwardly, is about 100 paces. No appearance of a ditch was here. The mound was 15 feet high.

9. Near Fayetteville, and within half a mile of it on Elk river, below the mouth of Norris's creek, and not more than a hundred yards from it, is a wall and ditch proceeding from a point on the river circularly, till it comes to one other point on the river, forming with the river an enclosure of 9 or 10 acres. The river from one point to the other, defends the enclosure by a high bluff. North from the bluff, and within the enclosure, is a mound not more than 50 yards from the river, six or eight feet high. The ditch is about two feet in depth at this time, and four feet wide; but is filled up from the bottom to within two feet from the surface. On the outside of the wall, but joining to it, are angular projections at the distance of about 60 yards from each other. These projections extend 8 or 10 feet from the wall. The interior of the angles is solid. A black-oak tree stood on one of them, and was cut down, and the annulars counted 260; so as to show that its growth commenced in the year of our Lord 1561. Very large poplars also stand on the

wall. On the mound was the stump of a mulberry tree almost decayed, two feet in diameter. There was no appearance of the trunk. The stump was older than our first settlements of the country. There is no spring in the interior of the circle. The diameter of the mound is about 15 yards. There are no gateways observable.

10. Eight miles south from McMinnville, on Collins's river, on the east side of the river, 150 yards from the bank, and in the bend of the river, is a mound 30 feet high, with a flattened top, which contains an area of an acre and a half of land at least. On either side of the mound to the north or south, is a broad ditch, 18 or 20 feet wide, and four deep at this time. Both intrenchments abut on the river at both ends on a high clift of rocks, and each intrenchment is parallel to the other; so that the two ends of the enclosure in which the mound is, are defended by two high bluffs of the river, and on the sides two wide intrenchments, which were no doubt once too deep to admit of an ascent from the bottom of the intrenchment without great difficulty, and exposure to danger. A wall was made on the exterior side of each ditch by the dirt thrown from the cavity. The timber upon the ditch is very old. Very large stumps are upon the mound itself, the remains of trees which had grown upon it of great age.—*D.*

11. Ten miles above Southwest Point, in Roane county, in East Tennessee, on the south side of the Tennessee river, and about 20 poles from the bank of the river, stands a mound about 30 feet high, with a flattened top, which contains upwards of one fourth of an acre, with a regular ascent from the bottom to the top on each side. Immediately at the end of the ascent is a stone wall, which is continued all around the summit, and is at this time about two feet high. On the north side of the river is a high bluff jutting over the western end, and

fronting the mound, on the face of which are cut three images, painted with black and red colours from the waist upwards, one of which figures is the representation of a female. About six miles below Southwest Point, on the south side of the Tennessee, are five large mounds in the bend of the river, all of which stand in one acre of ground nearly. One of them is much larger than the rest, and the top flat, with a stone wall like the one before mentioned, and to the east from the other four. The whole are enclosed with a wall raised up, composed of dirt, two or three feet high. Many carvings of rocks are in the vicinity, and lately human bones have been found here.

12. There is a mound on the Frenchbroad river, one mile above the mouth of Nolichucky, on the east side of Frenchbroad, 30 feet high. There is an acre of ground upon the top. Many similar ones are upon Frenchbroad. Old trees stand upon them. There are mounds also on the upper parts of Cumberland river in Kentucky, and many near the head of Kentucky river.

13. In the 10th district, 4th range, and 3d section of the Chickasaw purchase, are seven mounds, one of them 17 feet high, and 47 yards across, with an intrenchment 40 yards in circumference. The trees on it are two feet in diameter.

14. Seven miles southwest of Hatchy river, 50 miles east of the Mississippi, in a fertile part of the country, are three mounds enclosed by an intrenchment 10 feet deep and 30 feet wide. Two miles south of the south fork of Forkeddeer, 50 miles west of the Mississippi, is a mound 57 feet high, and 70 yards over.

15. On the south fork of the Forkeddeer river, in that part of the state of Tennessee which is between the Tennessee and Mississippi rivers, is the appearance of what the people there call an ancient fortification. It is 250 yards square. The wall is

made of clay, and is now 8 feet above the common surface. Trees as large as any in the country, are growing on the sides and top of the wall. There is no appearance of any intrenchment. Within this wall is an ancient mound, 87 feet high by actual measurement. It is circular except the top, which is square at the sides, and level at the top. The top is 50 feet square. It is accessible only on one side. On the sides and edges of the mounds, are trees as high and as large as any in the surrounding country; but no trees are immediately on the top. This mound is, on the area within the wall, near the south side. Other small mounds of different sizes and descriptions, are also within the enclosure. Without the enclosure, and within a quarter of a mile, is a group of small mounds, one of which is of an oblong figure, about 50 feet in length, 15 or 20 in width, and from 12 to 15 in height. Two or three miles from this place is another walled enclosure, more spacious than the former, within which are mounds of different descriptions. There is no water within any of these enclosures; but some fine springs are near the first, and the Forkeddeer is within 200 yards, where is a beautiful bluff.

16. Eight or ten miles above these walls, at the place where Mr. Ellis lives, are many mounds. Two of them are of singular figures. One of these at its base and at its top is square, about 30 feet in diameter, and about 8 feet high. The other is about the same height, and has the form of an oblong, with a bastion, thus, and is 25 feet by 40; near to which are other mounds, of a circular form, and of different sizes. There is no spring near them; but the mounds themselves are within two or three hundred yards of a creek. Another group is to be seen about half the distance between the enclosure and Mr. Ellis's house. These mounds are all in first rate lands for that country, and beautifully situated, generally on a plane or level.

17. In Overton county, on Obed's river, which
runs into Cumberland river, and 16 miles above the
mouth of Obed's river. is a creek, which runs
into Obed on the east side, and with the river forms
an acute angle of some considerable length. There
is a bluff both on the creek and on the river, from
the upper part of which on the creek to the river, is
a ditch about 50 yards long, 8 or 10 feet wide, and
considerably filled up. Trees as large as those of
the adjoining forest, are upon it, and on the point
are many mounds.

Mounds are on the waters of Holston, but none
very large. There are many on the waters of
Frenchbroad.

18. West 36 or 40 miles from the Tennessee
river, on the south side of Forkeddeer, which runs
into the Mississippi 60 or 70 miles above the mouth
of that fork, is a mound on the north side of the
fork, and about two miles from it. The diameter
of the base is about 100 poles. There is a plain
ascent from the base to the summit, on the east side.
The summit is flat, and contains three or four acres
or more. The trees which stand upon it are of
small growth of willow and oak, to which there is
no other like growth except in the small ponds.
On the east side adjoing it, and reaching nearly
around it, is a raised platform about four feet above
the surface, like that at Bledsoe's lick, and extending a considerable distance from east and northeast
to southeast. There is a great number of mounds
in this part of the country, more than in any other
part of Tennessee.

19. On the north bank of Holston, five miles
above the mouth of Frenchbroad, are six mounds
on half an acre of ground, placed without any apparent regularity. Their form is pyramidal, or
rather the section of a pyramid. The bases are
from 10 to 30 feet in diameter. The summits of
the largest are ten feet above the ground. The

figure is remarkably regular. One of them was cut into perpendicularly, in which was discovered a good deal of charcoal and ashes. These mounds are surrounded by an old ditch, which can at this time be distinctly traced on the sides, and encloses several acres of lands besides the mounds. At every angle of the ditch is a sweep, forming a semicircle. On the south bank is a bluff of limestone opposite the mounds, and a cave in it. The bluff is 100 feet in height. On it are faintly painted in red colours, like those on the Paint Rock, the sun and moon, a man, birds, fishes, &c. The paintings have in part faded within a few years. Tradition says, these paintings were made by the Cherokees, who were accustomed in their journeys to rest at this place. Whether such a tradition be entitled to credit, is for the judicious reader to determine. Wherever on the rivers of Tennessee are perpendicular bluffs, on the sides, and especially if caves be near, are often found mounds near them, enclosed in intrenchments, with the sun and moon painted on the rocks, and charcoal and ashes in the smaller mounds. These tokens seem to be evincive of a connexion between the mounds, the charcoal and ashes, the paintings, and the caves. The latter frequently contain the skulls of human beings, supposed to have been sacrificed by fire, on the mounds. The paintings are supposed to have represented the deities, whom the people adored. And the ditches are supposed to have pointed out the consecrated ground, which was not to be polluted by the tread of unhallowed feet. The larger mound with a flattened top, having below the surface of the summit an image of stone, which is supposed formerly to have stood upon the summit, and sometimes having the image at the margin of its base covered with soil a few inches, as if it had tumbled from the top, is supposed to have been the high place, around which the people assembled to offer up their adorations.—*See note K.*

Section 5.—*Of Images.*

Besides 'the mounds in Tennessee, images are frequently found upon them, or near them. We have already met with instances in chap. 6. sec. 4. par. 1, 2, 19. These images were, without doubt, placed upon the mounds, and received adoration from their worshippers. The evidences upon this subject are so numerous and cogent, as cannot fail to convince those of their mistake, who suppose that the Indians in America generally had no knowledge of image worship.

Many years ago, at Nashville, was found a clay vessel about 20 feet under the surface of the earth, in digging a well in a narrow valley between hills liable to wash. The diggers came to a natural spring issuing from a rock, on which this piece of pottery was placed. Its capacity was nearly a gallon. The base was a flat circle, from which rises a somewhat globose form, terminating at the top with the figure of a female head. There is no aperture except a round hole, situated toward the summit of the globular part of the vessel. The features of the face are Asiatic. The crown of the head is covered with a cap or ornaments, shaped into a pyramidical figure, with a flattened, circular summit ending at the apex in a round button. The ears are very large, extending down in a line with the chin, which is a Hindoo custom,[206] and an Indian and Egyptian hieroglyphical emblem of wisdom and supernatural knowledge. This head resembles many of those engraved for Mr. Raffin's history. A certain general resemblance may also be observed, as respects the crown or cap, the Asiatic headdress being somewhat conical, or else pyramidical, with a round or square apex. See chap. 6. sec. 4. par. 1. Had this vessel been sent to Mr. Raffle, says Mr. Clifford, he would have taken it to be of the same origin as the Hindoo

206 1 Dub. 135

statues of the island of Java. The small hole in the vessel is round, though in other respects there is no designation of its having been intended as an opening by the fabricator. There is no raised margin, or other means of showing it was thus originally designed, whilst its awkward position must have rendered it unfit either for the ready reception or escape of liquids. There are some marks of paint having formerly existed on the head, though too much worn off to admit of any definite description. Those acquainted with the paintings and statues of the Hindoos, Mr. Clifford believed, will be of opinion, on seeing this vessel, that our aborigines possessed the same religious notions, and formed the models of their divinities upon a similar plan, and with the same expressions of countenance, as the nations of Hindostan and their colonists. The Hindoo family has branched into the Egyptians, Celts, Goths, Peruvians and Mexicans; whence came the builders of the mounds, and the worshippers of these images, which are found in Tennessee. We have already spoken under the head of triplicity, of the three-faced image found in White county, and of those others already referred to in chap. 6. Besides these, an image was found near the base of a mound at Mayfield's station, 12 miles southwardly from Nashville, one near the base of a mound near Clarksville, and another in the neighbourhood of the Rev. Mr. Craighead. The first of these images, that found at Mayfield's station, in the county of Davidson, 20 years ago, was of sculptured stone, representing a woman sitting upon her hams, with both hands under her chin, and her elbows upon her knees. It was neatly formed, and well polished and proportioned. Mr. Boyd took and kept it at his tavern in Nashville a long time. Dr. Brown had two images, found by ploughing the ground near a very large mound below Clarksville. These also were sculptured. One represented an old man with his body bent forward, and head inclined downwards, exceedingly well executed. The other represented an old woman. The fact cannot perhaps be doubted, that these sculptured images were idols made for the worship of those who built the mounds, upon which were placed houses that sunk a little into the mounds, and when consumed by time left a small cavity on the top. Another idol was found near Nashville. It was of clay peculiar for its fineness and its use, which is quite abundant in some parts of Kentucky. With this clay was mixed a small portion of gypsum and sulphate of lime. It represents in three views a woman in a state of nudity, whose arms have been cut off close to the body, and whose nose and chin have been mutilated. In all these respects, as well as in the peculiar manner of plaiting the hair, it was exactly such an idol as was found in the southern part of the Russian empire. This idol near Nashville had a fillet and cake upon his head. It seems to have been the fabrication of some tribe once near Hindostan, where the authors of the triune idol originated. When the Greeks sacrificed, the sacred fillets were bound upon the head of the idol, the victim, and the priest. The sacred fillet and the salted cake were upon the head of this idol. The Greeks borrowed many of their customs from the Persians and Hindoos. At the same time this looks exceedingly like the sacrifice of the ancient Scythians, spoken of by Herodotus. They selected, he says, every hundreth one of their captives, poured libations upon his head, cut his throat, and poured the blood into a vessel. From the human victims they cut off the right arms close to the shoulders, and throw them up into the air. They then depart, the arms remaining where they happened to fall, and the bodies elsewhere.[208] This sacrifice was made to their god of war.

208 Herodotus Melp. sec. 62.

On Cherry creek, in the county of White, in a northwest direction from Sparta, are the remains of a large town, in the field of Mr. Howard. Several mounds are there from 12 to 14 feet high, and higher, say 20 feet above the ground before it was cultivated. These mounds in the inside are hollow. A horse in ploughing fell into one of them, and some of them have sunk into a basin since the clearing of the ground. In this field was found an image, or bust, from the waist upwards. The head was well carved, with the mouth, nose, and eyes, &c. all in perfect symmetrical proportion. The polish was very smooth. The substance of which it is made, is white on the inside, glittering, with specks, and the outside of a greyish colour. There are also plates of the same substance, with Indian pots in the form of soup plates, carved on the edges, and sculptured. Half a mile from this place, at the foot of the mountain, is a large cave full of human bones, perhaps several wagon loads; some of which are small, and others very large. The under jaw of some of them, Mr. Howard could have put over his face, and he is six feet high. He says, they must have been much larger than he is. These, I suspect, are the remains of those gigantic men of the north, who overran and depopulated Tennessee and Kentucky, and partly expelled, and partly extirpated, the aborigines. And if so, very probably this bust was not an idol, but a mere representation in sculpture of the human figure. What are here called mounds, are but the round houses in which the inhabitants lived, which in a fallen state are not more than two or three feet high. *See note L.*

Section 6.—*Of Human Sacrifices.*

Besides the sculls found in great numbers in the cave near Bledsoe's lick, without any other part of the human frame attached, or near to them, a large number of sculls in the like situation and circum-

T

stances, was found in a cave not far from Rutledge, in East Tennessee. These indicia, with parts of bones of human beings in and near the layers of cinders, found in the mound at Nashville, suggest the opinion that the immolation of human victims was practised by the builders of the mounds, as well in Tennessee, as by the people of Mexico and Bagota. Not more than two hundred yards from the great mound at Bledsoe's lick, is a cave in which, when first discovered, was a great number of human sculls. In the Sandwich islands, after the bodies of human sacrifices have lain some time interred, the sculls are taken up to be deposited, as may be presumed, in some sacred place.—*See M.*

Section 7.—*Of the Lingam.*

The Lingam is an idol which is spread all over India. It is generally enclosed in a little box of silver, which all the votaries of Siva wear suspended at their necks. It represents the sexual organs of a man, sometimes alone, and sometimes accompanied. It is represented in the temples, on the highways, and in other public situations. But it is worn by the votaries of Siva, one of the principal divinities of India, as a most precious relic, hung at their necks, or fastened to their arms or hair, and receives from them sacrifices and adoration. The worship of the Lingam more particularly prevails in the west of the peninsula, where many districts are composed chiefly of this population. The original worship was paid to the procreative power of nature, represented by this emblem, to which at length, instead of the thing represented, the people offered up their adoration. From the same origin came the Phallus of the Greeks, the Priapus of the Romans, the Baol Peor of the Moabites and Midianites,[209] as also the obscene idols in the Sandwich islands.

209 2 Dub. 207, 208; 3 R. India, 306; Star in the East, 16; 3 Cook's Voyages, 160.

A stone of a green colour, passing into a greenish white, semi-transparent, and extremely tough, is regarded in India as a specific for the nephritic cholic, and is fashioned into forms of great delicacy. The Hindoos and Chinese form it into talismans and idols.

There was found on the farm of Turner Lane, Esq. in White county, in West Tennessee, five or six miles from Sparta, a piece of stone 11 inches long, and about 12 inches in diameter. At one end it was sloped off to a sharp edge, terminating in the middle in a sharp point. It was highly polished, and showed great skill in the workmanship. It was variegated with green and yellow spots, the general body of the stone being of a deep grey colour. No doubt can be entertained in the mind of a careful observer, that it is not the production of this country.

Another stone of similar shape, of very high polish, and of variegated colours, was since found 10 or 12 miles from Sparta, near a mound. It is now before the writer. It is about 18 inches in length, and one and a half in diameter, rather broader than thick, though circular. A conical hebetated termination is at each end. It is very smooth and heavy, and neatly polished. On part of one side it seems to have received from paint a reddish hue, and the other parts of it seem to have been variegated with some colouring now dark, but probably brown formerly. It may have been used for pounding in a mortar; but it greatly resembles a Phallus. See, for colours, ch. 6, sec. 2, sec. 4, par. 11, sec. 7.— *See note N.*

Section 8.—*Of the Dress of Idols.*

The dress of the idols of Tennessee in ancient times, and of course of the people in the same times, is to be collected from the representation of one found upon the mound at Bledsoe's lick, Ch. 6, sec. 4, par. 1, sec. 5, of the image found under ground near Nashville, Sec. 5. and of the one with its arms cut off, found in a tumulus near Nashville. Sec. 5. The dress consisted of a cap, or bonnet, on the head, with a narrow brim, from the extremity of which the cap or bonnet rises in a pyramidal form to the top, which is flat, and circular, and ending at the apex in a round button. The human victim had its arms cut off, its nose and chin mutilated, and a fillet and cake upon its head.

Section 9.—*Of Conch Shells.*

For proof of the supposition that these were anciently used in Tennessee for sacred purposes, reference must be had to the description of small skeletons, which have been found near Sparta, where at least a ground will be had for such conjecture. Ch. 9, sec. 2. This taken in conjunction with what has been already stated to have been discovered in Kentucky, in respect of the numerous conchs there found, will render such conjecture, if not supported by evidence, at least a subject worthy of earnest inquiry. Our southern Indians, at the annual feast of harvest, send to those who are sick at home, or unable to come out, one of the old consecrated shells full of the sanctified bitter cassena.[210] The Creeks used it in 1778, in one of their evening entertainments at Altassé, where, after the assembly were seated in the council-house, illuminated by their mystical cane fire in the middle, two middle aged men came in together, each having a very large conch shell full of black drink, advancing with slow, uniform and steady steps, their eyes and countenances lifted up, and singing very low, but sweetly, till they came within six or eight steps of the king's and white people's seats, when they stopped, and each rested his shell upon a little table; but soon taking it up again, advanced, and each presented his shell, one to the king, and the

[210] Boud. 233, 260.

other to the chief of the white people. And as soon as he raised it to his mouth, they uttered or sung two notes, each of which continued as long as he had breath, and as long as these notes continued so long must the person drink, or at least keep the shell to his mouth. The notes were solemn, and inspired a religious awe. All these tokens united are sufficient to induce the belief, that conchs in Tennessee and Kentucky, as well as in India, were consecrated to religious solemnities.—*See note O.*

Section 10.—*Of the Vestiges of the Sanctity of the Number Seven.*

Upon this head there is nothing further to refer to in this state, but the seven passages through the semicircular ditch and intrenchment on Big Harpeth, three miles above Franklin. Ch. 6, sec. 4, par. 5. which could not be necessary as passages for any inhabitants who ever lived within the enclosure. They have probably a relation to some division of time, which their god of the sun made in his course, or to the planets which were there worshipped, or to the tenets of that ancient religion in Asia, which spread the sanctity of this number into all the southern and western nations of Asia, imparting to it a mysterious virtue, which no other number possessed. In the Bible itself, we find as many instances of it as in any other book, which ever was written. A great number of instances are to be found among the Hindoos, to this day. If the example now referred to has the relation supposed, it is a great evidence that the builders of the mounds also had the same Asiatic religious notions.—*See note P.*

Section 11.—*Of the Incense which they burned.*

See ch. 6, sec. 4, par. 1, 4.

CHAPTER VII.

We will next take a view of the sciences of the aborigines of Tennessee, of their letters, of their sculptures, of their paintings, of their manufactures, of their fortifications, of their coins and other metals, of their ornaments, of their mirrors, of their tanks, of their mechanic arts, of their games and pastimes, of their colour, and of their Mexican coincidences.

Section 1.—*Of their Sciences.*

The mounds are sometimes laid off in perfect squares, with their sides precisely to the cardinal points, Ch. 6, sec. 4, par. 1, 6. which evinces a considerable share of both astronomical and geometrical knowledge.—*See note Q.*

Sec. 2.—*Of their Letters and Literal Inscriptions.*

Upwards of 80 miles below the Lookout mountain, on the Tennessee river, boatmen, as they descend the river, see painted characters on what is called the Paint Rock, in the neighbourhood of Fort Deposite, not far from John Thompson's. These paintings are of difficult access, owing to the extraordinary height of the rock on which they appear. The characters are said to have stood there for ages. It is said, that below the Harpeth shoals, on a bluff on the side of the Cumberland river, are painted characters resembling letters. See ch. 6, sec. 1.

On a rock on the Frenchbroad river, about six miles below the warm springs, is a great number of painted characters, apparently regular, but not resembling the letters of any known alphabet. The rock is on the north branch of Frenchbroad, immediately on the margin of the great road leading to the west, and is one of the largest rocks to be found. It is about 200 or 250 feet at the base, and 150 perpendicular. The paintings are scattered over the vast surface of the rock, disposed in groups, commencing about 20 or 30 feet from the ground, and extending to the top. The characters look too much, it is said, like artificial painting, to admit the idea, that they are natural; and their position almost forbids the idea, that they were made by human hands. The operator must have been suspended from the top of the rock. They are too high, many of them at least, to have been reached by a ladder. The rock is well known by the name of the Paint Rock. Some, however, who have seen the rock, say, that these supposed literal characters are nothing more than the oozing through the rock of water, impregnated in the interior with some mineral, which makes a deep and indelible dve.

It is stated to have been affirmed by Captain Daniel Williams, a man of undoubted truth, that several years ago, in a cave five or six miles above Carthage, on Cumberland river, in which cave workmen were collecting dirt for saltpetre, were many human skeletons, one of which was a female in a state of preservation, with yellow hair, and the flesh shrivelled. Around the wrist was a silver clasp, with letters resembling those of the Greek alphabet. The body was replaced in the spot whence they had taken it.

At a gap of the mountain, through which the Indians pass, and near the head of Brasstown creek, which is towards the head of the Hiwassee, and among the high lands, is a large horizontal rock, on which are engraved the tracks of deer, bears, horses, wolves, turkeys, and barefooted human beings of all sizes. Some of the horses' tracks appear to have slipped forward. The direction of them is westward. Near them are signs of graves. Star, an intelligent white man, who has lived in the Cherokee nation 30 or 40 years, says, there are on this rock apparently marks or characters, made in horizontal lines, which he believes to be letters of some unknown alphabet. These impressions or inscriptions have been ever since the Indians knew the country. Star, however, only conjectured that these are literal characters, having no evidence to induce a settled belief that they are. A road is now opened to Georgia, passing within 16 miles of this rock, which is itself 60 or 80 miles from the settlements of the whites. Here is higher land than within the limits of North-Carolina, Virginia, Tennessee or Georgia, or east of the Mississippi. Here rise the large water courses that go in different directions—the head springs of New river, which runs into the Ohio; of the Watauga and Frenchbroad, which fall into Holston; of the Hiwassee; of the Tugalo, or head waters of the Savannah; of the Apalachicola, or Chatahoochee, so called towards the head; and the Coosa, which by its junction with the Talapoosa, makes the Alabama. The parallel and small ridges supply the head waters of the small streams. Every where springs are abundant at the bases of these ridges, and become less so as the distance towards the west increases, and in proportion to the distance, unless in instance of knobs or single hills, which furnish springs in the neighbourhood. Near this engraved rock are numerous heaps of stones, which are doubtless monumental memorials of some great event, which forced both men and animals, whether wild or domesticated, to take refuge here from some incommoding cause, which drove them from their former abodes in the east. The horses' tracks would seem to indicate the time of this occurrence to have been after European accession to the eastern shores of this continent. But the letters indicate a time long prior to that event, and may signify the deluge of which the North-Carolina Indians had a tradition, which once happened, they said,

U

by the overflowing of the Atlantic ocean; a fact, which there are some circumstances besides the tradition, to render probable as having taken place in modern times, compared with the epoch of the general flood. Coin in the bowels of the earth, coal also, trees in the bank of the Tennessee, a piece of iron pot 100 feet below the surface, the trees found in digging for wells, the glass bottle and old walls in North-Carolina covered over with soil, all at considerable depths below the surface, together with the numerous cemetrial tumuli upon the tops of the hills west of the Harpeth, are signs which give a specious aspect to this hypothesis, and may hereafter lead to more satisfactory conclusions than can be attained at present. Such supposition, however, well accounts for the disappearance of population since the days in which those fragments are left where we now see them.—*See note R.*

Section 3.—*Of their Sculptures.*

In March, 1823, a rude piece of sculpture was dug up on the farm of Mr. McGilliam. The farm lies on Fall creek, near Quarle's, in Wilson county. The figure is cut out of a hard rock, of what kind Mr. Rucker could not determine. It was designed for a female statue. The legs were not drawn. It only extends a little below the hips. It is fifteen inches long, and thick in proportion. It has a flat head, broad face, a disproportionately long aquiline nose, low forehead, thick lips, and short neck. The chin and cheek bones are not prominent, but far otherwise. On the back part of the head is a large projection, so shaped as to show, perhaps, the manner of tying and wearing the hair. The nipples are well represented; though the breasts are not sufficiently elevated for a female of maturity. The hands are resting on the hips, the fingers in front, and the arms akimbo. Around the back, and above the hips, are two parallel lines cut, as is supposed, to represent a zone or belt. The ears project at right angles from the head, with holes through them. The head and face very much resemble the paintings and images of the Mexicans, the engravings which Mr. Rucker has seen in Humboldt's New Spain, and also those of the Chinese, which he has seen in several works. It was found a few inches beneath the surface of the earth. No mounds are near, but an extensive burying ground of apparently great antiquity. Two miles farther east, on a ridge, there is another of large dimensions occupying an area of three hundred yards in length, and two hundred in width. The graves are in straight lines, close by the side of each other, and raised above the surface a foot or upwards.

Under this head, too, may fall the following discovery: In the bed of Fall creek is a large flat rock, on which are the tracks of various animals—human tracks of all ages, those of the horse, and the impressions of wheel carriages on the rock, lines and indentations equidistant from each other, similar to those made by wheel carriages. They were much more distinctly marked 12 years ago than at present, being now in some degree effaced by the passage of animals, and possibly by the attrition of the waters since the white settlements, and the consequent increase of cattle.

For the progress they had made in the sculptural art, reference must be had also to the chapter on images, and to the statues cut in stone, with bonnets on their heads, and garments reaching to the ground. See S.

Section 4.—*Of their Paintings.*

For the paintings of the aborigines, see chapter 6, sec. 1.—*See T.*

Section 5.—*Of their Manufactures.*

In the spring of the year 1811, was found in a copperas cave in Warren county, in West Tennessee, about 15 miles southwest from Sparta, and 20 from McMinnville, the bodies of two human beings, which had been covered by the dirt or ore from which copperas was made. One of these persons was a male, the other a female. They were interred in baskets, made of cane, curiously wrought, and evidencing great mechanic skill. They were both dislocated at the hip joint, and were placed erect in the baskets, with a covering made of cane to fit the baskets in which they were placed. The flesh of these persons was entire and undecayed, of a brown dryish colour, produced by time, the flesh having adhered closely to the bones and sinews. Around the female, next her body, was placed a well dressed deer skin. Next to this was placed a rug, very curiously wrought, of the bark of a tree and feathers. The bark seemed to have been formed of small strands well twisted. Around each of these strands, feathers were rolled, and the whole woven into a cloth of firm texture, after the manner of our common coarse fabrics. This rug was about three feet wide, and between six and seven feet in length. The whole of the ligaments thus framed of bark, were completely covered by the feathers, forming a body of about one eighth of an inch in thickness, the feathers extending about one quarter of an inch in length from the strand to which they were confined. The appearance was highly diversified by green, blue, yellow and black, presenting different shades of colour when reflected upon by the light in different positions. The next covering was an undressed deer skin, around which was rolled, in good order, a plain shroud manufactured after the same order as the one ornamented with feathers. This article resembled very much in its texture the bags generally used for the purpose of holding coffee exported from the Havanna to the United States. The female had in her hand a fan formed of the tail feathers of a turkey. The points of these feathers were curiously bound by a buckskin string well dressed, and were thus closely bound for about one inch from the points. About three inches from the point they were again bound, by another deer skin string, in such a manner that the fan might be closed and expanded at pleasure. Between the feathers and this last binding by the string, were placed around each feather, hairs which seem to have been taken from the tail of a deer. This hair was dyed of a deep scarlet red, and was one third at least longer than the hairs of deer's tail in this climate generally are.

The male was interred sitting in a basket, after the same manner as the former, with this exception, that he had no feathered rug, neither had he a fan in his hand. The hair which still remained on their heads was entire. That of the female was of a yellow cast, *and of a very fine texture.* Both male and female, by their hair, afforded incontrovertible evidence, as some of those who saw them supposed, of European or Asiatic extraction. The female was, when she deceased, of about the age of 14. The male was somewhat younger. The cave in which they were found, abounded in nitre, copperas, alum and salts. The whole of this covering, with the baskets, was perfectly sound, without any marks of decay. The eyes of those persons seemed perfectly sound, only somewhat sunk below the ordinary position in the socket, caused by their dry state. De Soto, in his march in 1539, 1540, saw great numbers of these mantles. See, in chapter 5, where his march is described. After crossing the Mississippi, and arriving at the Indian towns on the west side of it, which the inhabitants abandoned at his approach, he found there great numbers of mantles. See also ch. 4, sec. 4, where it is stated that the Mexicans made such feathered mantles.

In the island of O-why-hee, in the Pacific ocean, in the year 1777, when Captain Cook visited them,

the king and his chiefs were dressed in red feathered cloaks, which in point of beauty and magnificence were nearly equal to that of any nation in the
world.[39] Fans were made there also, of the fibres
of the cocoa nut, the tail feathers of the *cock* and of
the tropic bird, and also feathered caps. In 1730,
the Indians of North-Carolina used feathered match
coats, exceedingly pretty, says Dr. Brickell; some
of which, he also remarks, are beautifully wrought
with a variety of colours and figures, which seem
at a distance like a fine flowered silk shag. When
new and fresh, he continues, they serve for a bed,
instead of a quilt. Some match-coats, he says, were
made of hair, or racoon, beaver or squirrel skins;
others again were made of the green part of the
skin of the mallard's head, or other fowls, which
they stitch or sew perfectly well together; their
thread being the sinews of a deer divided very
small, or silk grass. When these were finished
they looked very beautiful. Did not these skeletons belong to persons of the same race with those
white people, who were extirpated in part, and in
part driven from Kentucky, and probably also from
West Tennessee, as Indian tradition reports?

At the place where old John Curry formerly
lived, in the county of Williamson, on the banks of
Mill creek, not far below the head, is a cave, in
length 20 or 30 feet from the mouth to the back, and
six or eight feet wide. The cave forked. In the
right fork, which was the largest, was a well or
shaft sunk 14 feet deep and four feet wide, from the
bottom of which the digging had been extended in
one direction more than 20 or 30 feet, to which it
had been followed. Here it is supposed ore was
once dug. One piece of ore was found near the
mouth of the cave, containing lead and silver. The
cave was at the foot of a hill. Upon the hill had
been a large town and burying place. On the top

of the hill, too, were several piles of rocks, which being opened, discovered human bones of the *common size*, and with them was found an *ivory button*, an inch wide and perfectly round, well executed, with a hole in the middle, and about the eighth of an inch thick, very smoothly polished, and cut with some iron tool. The bones are very ancient, and the trees near them as large as any in the forest. Ivory, it is well known, is made of the tooth of the elephant, which lives in the southern part of Asia and in Africa. It has been sometimes made in Russia, of the tooth of the mammoth.—*V.*

Section 6.—*Of their Fortifications.*

In the time of Sesostris, 1650 before Christ, when he invaded and overran India, there were no cities or fortresses in that country. They had before his time no enemies to overrun and plunder them. The earth was an unpeopled wilderness, with a few patches of population upon the face of it. Fortifications, and particularly intrenchments, are the effects of dense population, of iron tools and of architecture.[40] The fortifications of Troy were walls and towers, but no ditch. They had no machines nor circumvallation. The seige of Thebes, in Bœotia, was the first in Grecian history; and at that time the besiegers did not know how to draw lines of circumvallation, nor were they acquainted with escalades. They *intrenched* only before the city, and formed a blockade. The first fortifications in Greece were only 1390 before Christ. The art of besieging and defending places came into use only a short time before the days of Pericles and Alcibeades, the former of whom died 429, and the latter 404, before Christ.[41] After that period, walls and towers, and ditches, came to be in general and common

40 3 O. L. 329, 336; Joshua, ch. 8, v. 12, ch. 20, v. 29; Numb. ch. I, v. 45, 46.

41 3 O. L. 181.

use.[42] Ninevah was taken 601 before Christ. It is described by Djoderes Siculus. It had high walls and towers around it, but no ditch. Babylon was taken 538 before Christ. The fate of Ninevah possibly had made the inhabitants of Babylon surround it with a ditch. Jerusalem was rebuilt 467 before Christ; it was then surrounded by a wall, but no ditch. Somewhere about the beginning of the sixth century before Christ we may date the application of intrenchments to the defence of fortified places. It was probably after this art came into general practice, that the knowledge and use of it was imported into America, together with the year of 365 days and 6 hours, and perhaps together with the Roman coin uttered in the time of Antoninus Pius, and of Commodus, the latter of whose reign ended about 190 after Christ, and probably after the time of the three emperors, in the year of our Lord 337, in whose time, it may be rationally conjectured, was issued the copper coin, having on it the representation of an eagle with three heads, which will be presently stated. The time when intrenchments first came into general use, may furnish a datum to be compared with others in searching for the time when this art first came into America. We shall soon see that it was in very general use with the aborigines of Tennessee and the adjacent countries.

Near the head of Wells's creek, in Stuart county, and near the bank of the creek, and within one hundred yards of the fortification, there is a lasting spring, the branch from which runs within five feet of what appears to have been the entrance or gate into the fort. The fort is about 80 or 100 feet square, exclusive of the bastions at the corners; which bastions are about twelve feet square. The walls, which are of dirt, and must have sunk considerably, are now about twelve feet high. Large white oaks and hickories grow on them. And there is still a flight of steps visible, which were once used to ascend the walls and bastions, which are near the corners where the bastions and walls join. A great number of flint spikes, or spears for arrows, are to be found in or about the fortification. It is near to a fertile tract of land, bearing evident marks of having been in cultivation.

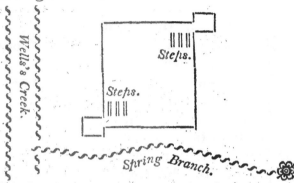

Twelve miles below Carthage, on the Cumberland river, is a cave in which are human bones, of all sizes, about a mile from the river. There is a burying ground near to the fortification. In this burying ground, 15 years ago, were many skeletons, and with many of them were found pipes and water vessels of earthen ware. Near to the burying ground is a deep creek running into the river, forming an acute angle. At some distance from the junction, is a ditch from the creek to the river, and the remains of a parapet. Opposite to the entrance way and about six feet from it, is the appearance of a wall in the inside, so formed as to turn those who entered to the right or left. In the interior were several mounds.

The Stone Fort lies in Bedford county, in the two most northern of the three forks of Duck river, in the state of Tennessee. The walls of this are composed of stone, whence the name of *Stone Fort.* Its antiquity is indubitable. At the first settlement of this country, the oldest Indians had heard their

V

fathers speak of it. At its northern extremity, on the front of the wall, are two mounds of stone, about six feet in height, and circular. Directly in the rear is the north wall, which extends from the river, and is situated exactly at the foot of falls of about 15 feet. This wall has one gateway, and is about 10 feet in height on the inner side. In the rear of the gate is a stone building of about sixteen feet square, with a smaller one by its side. Running south with the wall, it still maintains the same height, until you arrive again at the foot of falls of about 20 feet, where this part of the wall terminates, and is discontinued for some distance, in consequence of a bold rising bluff of solid limestone rock, at about midway of which there has been excavated a footh path to the river. The like also occurs at the foot of the falls on the opposite side of the fort. On passing this bluff, the stone wall is again continued to its most southern angles. On the south side the wall is again continued from river to river, having but one gateway. On the west side the wall is continued, with the same interposition of falls, bluff and foot path, as on the east, until it joins the western extremity of the north wall. On the south wall there appears to have been *an excavation of the earth from* 80 *to* 100 *feet in breadth, and about* 40 *feet in depth,* at the bottom of which, and next to the stone wall, is a ditch of about 20 feet in width. Both the excavation and the ditch extend from river to river. The form of the fort is nearly triangular, the north wall being but a few yards in length. The whole ground contained within the wall of the fort, is from 30 to 32 acres. It appears probable, that the earth taken from the cavity on the south, has been spread over the face of the *fort,* and over the narrow strip of land which is south and next to the river, as both the fort and this piece of land are higher than the neighbourhood. These walls are about 16 or 20 feet in thickness at the base, and on top from four to five. The present appearance of the walls is, as might be expected, quite rough; the whole area, as well as the excavation, being covered with heavy forest trees, as large any in the neighbouring country. On the north of the fort, and near the public road leading from Nashville to Georgia, there is a mound of considerable magnitude, being of an oval form from 20 to 25 feet in height, 100 in length, 40 in width, and covered with very heavy timber. About half a mile west of this, is another of similar form. Captain Eastland attempted to cultivate a part of the ground within the *fort*, and on the first time in running a deep furrow, he ploughed up a piece of flint glass, about one inch thick, and remarkably transparent: it appeared to be a piece of a bowl, very neatly fluted on its sides. There was also found, a stone very beautifully carved and ornamented, much superior to any known art of the Indians. On the outward appearance of the fort are the strongest evidences of the hammer. On the 7th of August, 1819, Col. Andrew Erwin, on whose land the Stone Fort is, caused to be cut down, a white oak tree which grew on the top of the wall. Major Murray and himself counted 357 annulars. He observes, that he could not say how long after the building of the wall the tree commenced growing; it may, said he, have been within 100, or not within 1000 years thereafter. The wall, said he, is mouldered down so as to be at present about 16 feet wide on the surface of the earth, about six feet high. The rocks are covered with earth, and appear like a hedge along an old ditch. One half or more of the rock, he says, is a slate copperas ore, taken out of the bottom of the creek on each side of the *fort*. The fort contains 33 acres of land within its walls. The age of the tree was 78 years when De Soto landed in Florida, and 30 years when Columbus discovered America. By some, this description of the fort is said to be inaccurate, and that there is no sign of the hammer upon the stone, and that indeed there is no wall of stone at all, the rocks being only heaped up together with the dirt and intermixed with it. Be this as it may, it is not disputed, as I understand, but that the large excavation and deep ditch are there, which is before described. And that is enough for my present purpose. The writer is not convinced, however, that any part of the preceding description is inaccurate.

On the south side of Forkeddeer river, 60 miles above its mouth, is a dirt wall parallel to the river, and distant three or four rods from it, where is in the river a deep and steep precipice or bluff, at least 50 feet from the surface to the water. The wall itself is a mile long, and is at present 18 inches or 2 feet high, and 10 in width, with poplars growing upon it five feet through. Opposite to this is another wall of the same size and length, distant one quarter of a mile, and in some places 59 poles from the other. At the lower end they approach each other till they come within four poles. Between the walls are 75 acres of exceedingly rich lands. At the interval where the walls approach within four poles of each other, and between the walls, there is, in the inside of the passage, a mound 8 or 10 feet high, which commands the passage, so that all who came in must on the inside turn to the left or right, between the mound and the wall. On the outside of the entrance is a steep bluff of a swamp, winding round the southern wall, and passing in a northwardly direction, near the entrance to the river, with a wide swamp on the eastern side of the bluff. On the inside of the walls are square ones, 40 or 50 feet in diameter, at different places, which probably were once covered, when the ancient inhabitants lived there. There are square mounds on the inside, which are not hollow, 14 or 15 feet high. Poplar trees are upon them, 5 feet through at least.

The wall next to the river, at a point equidistant from its end, turns to the river; and from the river, by another short parallel wall, runs to a point in the direction of the wall prior to the diversion, and thence is continued in 'that direction. The two short walls to the river, leave an opening from it into the interior of the enclosure, and doubtless was once a covered way for the protection of those who went to the river for water.

At the distance of about four miles southwest of Sparta, on the waters of the Cany Fork, are the remains of an ancient fortification, containing about five acres, perfectly square. The walls being composed entirely of dirt, as appears from the present state of its ruins. Here is a great burying place. The human skeletons discovered here, are remarkable for their gigantic stature. From all that can now be discovered, this must have been a race of men averaging at least 7 feet in height. Such men, it is probable, never grew in the tropical climates. No instance is recollected, of giants between the tropics. Some were planted by the Scythians in Palestine, when in a very distant age they penetrated as far as to the confines of Egypt, and built the city of Scythopolis. But such men never came from between the tropics. The skeletons now under consideration, were some of the ancient Scythians, who, down to the Christian era, terrified the nations which they invaded, by their enormous bulk.—*W.*

Section 7.—*Of their Coins and other Metals.*

About the year 1819, in digging a cellar at Mr. Norris's, in Fayetteville, on Elk river, which falls into Tennessee, and about two hundred yards from a creek which empties into Elk, and not far from the ruins of a very ancient fortification on the creek, was found a small piece of silver coin of the size of a ninepenny piece. On the one side of this coin, is the image of an old man, projected considerably from the superficies, with a large Roman nose, his head covered apparently with a cap of curled hair; and on this side, on the edge, in old Roman letters, not so neat by far as on our modern coins, are the words *Antoninus Aug: Pius.* PP. RI. III cos. On the other side, the projected image of a young man, apparenty 18 or 20 years of age; and on the edge, *Aurelius Cæsar. AUGP.* III. cos. The U is made V. PP. perhaps are the initials of princeps pontifar: RI. Romanorum Imperator. It was coined in the third year of the reign of Antoninus, which was in the year of our Lord 137, and must in a few years afterwards have been deposited where it was lately found. The prominent images are not in the least impaired, nor in any way defaced, nor made dim or dull by rubbing with other money; neither are the letters on the edges. It must have lain in the place where lately found, 1500 or 1600 years. For had it first circulated a century, before it was laid up, the worn-off parts of the letters and images would be observable. It was found five feet below the surface. The people living upon Elk river when it was brought into the country, had some production of art, or of agriculture, for which this coin was brought to the place, to be exchanged. It could not have been brought by De Soto, for long before his time it would have been defaced and made smooth by circulation; and, besides, the crust of the earth would not have been increased to the depth of five feet in 277 years, the time elapsed since De Soto passed between the Alabama and the Tennessee, to the Mississippi. This coin furnishes irrefragable proof of one very important fact; namely, that there was an intercourse, either by sea or land, between the ancient inhabitants of Elk river, and the Roman empire, in the time of Antoninus, or soon afterwards; or between the ancient Elkites, and some other nation, who had such intercourse with it. Had a Roman fleet been driven by a storm, in the time of Antoninus, on the American shores, the crews, even if they came to land all at the same place, would not have been able to penetrate to Elk river, nor would any discoverable motive have engaged them to do so. And again: Roman vessels, the very largest in the Roman fleet of that day, were not of structure and strength sufficient to have lived in a storm of such violence and long continuance in the Atlantic ocean, as was necessary to have driven them from Europe to America. Nor are storms in such directions and of such continuance at all usual. Indeed, there is no instance of any such, which has occurred since the European settlements in America. The people of Elk, in ancient times, did probably extend their commerce down the rivers which Elk communicates with; or if directly over land to the ocean, they were not impeded by small independent tribes between them and the ocean, but were part of an empire extended to it. A thick forest of trees, not more than 6 or 8 years ago, grew upon the surface where the coin was found, many of which could not be of more recent commencement than 300 or 400 years; a plain proof that the coin was not of Spanish or French importation.

Besides this coin impressed with the figures of Antoninus and Aurelius, another was also found in a gully washed by torrents, about two and a half miles from Fayetteville, where the other coin was found. It was about four feet below the surface. The silver very pure, as was also the silver of the other piece; evidently much more so than the silver coins of the present day. The letters are rough, Some of them seem worn. On the one side is the image of a man, in high relief, apparently of the age of 25 or 30. And on the coin, near the edge, were these words and letters: *Commodus.* The C is defaced, and hardly visible. AVG. HEREL. On the other side, TR. IMP. III. cos. II. PP. On this latter side also, is the figure of a woman, with a horn in her right hand. She is seated in a square box; on the inside of which, touching each side, and resting on the ground, is *a wheel.* Her left arm, from the shoulder to the elbow, lies on her side, but from the elbow is raised a little above the top; and across a small distaff, proceeding from the hand, is a handle, to which is added a trident, with the teeth or prongs parallel to each other. It is supposed, that Faustina, the mother of Commodus, who was deified after her death, by her husband Marcus Aurelius, with the attributes of Venus, Juno and Ceres, is represented by this figure. The neck of Commodus is bare, with the upper part of his robes flowing in gatherings from the lower part of the neck. His head seemed to be covered with a cap of hair curled into many small knots, with a white fillet around it, near its edges, and the temples and forehead, with two ends falling some distance from the knot. Commodus reigned with his father, Marcus Aurelius, from the time he was 14 or 15 years of age, till the latter died, in the year of our Lord 180. From that time he reigned alone, till the 31st of December, 192, when he was put to death. Counting from his final elevation, he was a second time emperor in the year of our Lord 181, and the third time in the year of our Lord 186, and a fourth time in the year of our Lord 191. But computing from the time he began to reign alone, he was a second time emperor in the year of our Lord 190. And he was a second time consul under the last emperorship, in the beginning of the year of our Lord 191. He at one time assumed the title of the *Roman Hercules;* and at another, of *Paulus,* a celebrated gladiator. Perhaps the letters *HEREL.* PV. may be the initials of these titles. This piece of money was probably coined in the year of our Lord 191. That these coins were not brought hither since the discovery of America by

Columbus, is proved by the several large trees standing in the ground below the surface of which the coins were found, the greater part of which were of an age commencing before that period. A French settlement was made about 130 years ago, or somewhat later, in the present state of Alabama; but, for the reasons before given, these coins could not have been brought into the country by those who made that settlement. If the coins with the figure of Antoninus upon them were used by the Romans in the provinces, as talismans and holy relics, and for that reason have been renewed in later times, did the Christians continue the same usage? and did either pagans or Christians entertain any reverence for the odious Commodus, so as to be induced by it to renew his image in remembrance of the qualities he possessed? There seems to be no just grounds for referring the date of these coins to any other period than that which they purport to bear. Being in the vicinity where burnt bricks and the short sword, and also of the Stone Fort, and of the silver buttons having the representation of a deer in front of a dog which is in pursuit of him, it is but reasonable to conclude that a civilized race of men once lived on Elk and Duck rivers, who carried on commerce, used coined money, and forged iron into tools. And, moreover, had intercourse with nations who had at least commercial connexions, mediately or immediately, with the Roman empire. If, for instance, these coins were paid to the Chinese, who in the time of Antoninus supplied the people of Rome with silks, which were carried down the Oxus, into the Caspian sea, through which and the Euxine, and the Egean sea, they were carried into the Mediterranean and to Rome, how easy was then the passage from China to Japan, thence to Mexico, and up the Mississippi, to Elk and Duck rivers? where the makers of bricks, swords and intrenchments lived, and could not fail

W

to have some surplus commodities to exchange for those foreign coins which navigation had brought from distant countries, as the most precious articles for which they could be exchanged. If we can once believe in the early navigation of the Hindoos, Malayese and Chinese, precedent to the completion of that science in Europe, the whole difficulty is removed, and the practicability of its arrival in America anterior to the time of Columbus ceases to be any longer problematical. That the Hindoos, as early as the days of Moses, were extensive navigators of the ocean, and the Chinese in early times, may be collected from chapter 7, sec. 9, and the passages there referred to, which treat of conchs, and of the uses which the Hindoos made of them. That these coins came hither long before the age of Columbus, is almost certain; and to say that they came in the course of navigation, is as probable as to say that they came in a shipwrecked vessel. Savages who had neither agriculture or commerce, or the mechanic arts, would not have traded them as curiosities worth preserving, much less would they have removed them carfully from the ocean to their places of residence on Elk river. Why should a savage be at this trouble, when amongst his countrymen he could not have purchased, with it, a pipe of tobacco. These reflections go far to induce the belief, that the coins in question were not the importations of European navigation. When to these are added the considerations inseparable from other like instances, in the neighbourhood of Tennessee, where strange coins have been found, some with superscriptions in unknown characters, and others with dates anterior to the discovery of America, if such dates relate to the Christian era, then we are driven as it were *with force and arms*, from the beloved prejudices of youthful days. We have believed, that our ancestors, the Europeans, were the inventors, and first practisers of transmarine navigation—how unacceptable is the information, that this is a mistake! We profess devoted submission to truth; but we are really unwilling to find it and to recognize it as it is. This is prejudice, an obstinate heretic, which is seldom completely vanquished.

Between the years 1802 and 1809, in the state of Kentucky, Jefferson county, on Big Grass creek, which runs into the Ohio at Louisville, at the upper end of the falls, about 10 miles above the mouth, near Middletown, Mr. Spear found under the roots of a beech tree which had been blown up, two pieces of copper coin, of the size of our old copper pence. On one side was represented an eagle, with three heads united to one neck. The sovereign princes of Greece wore on their sceptres the figure of a bird, and often that of an eagle. The monarchs of Asia had that custom.[42] But possibly this may have been a coin uttered in the time of the three Roman emperors. It cannot be a Hindoo or Chinese coin, because they did not make coined money till modern times.

Lately a Cherokee Indian delivered to Mr. Dwyer, in the year 1822, who delivered to Mr. Earl, a copper medal, nearly or quite of the size of a dollar. All around it, on both sides, was a raised rim. On the one side is the robust figure of a man apparently of the age of 40, with a crown upon his head; buttons upon his coat, and a garment flowing from a knot on his shoulder, towards and over the lower part of his breast; his hair short and curled; his face full; his nose acquiline, very prominent and long, the tip descending very considerably below the nostril; his mouth wide; the chin long, and the lower part very much curved, and projected outwards. Within the rim which is on the margin, and just below it, in Roman letters, are the words and figures *Richardus III.* DG. ANG. FR. et

42 1 Herodotus, 245, notes.

HIB. Rex. The letters are none of them at all worn. Both the letters and figures protuberated from the surface. On the other side is a monument, with a female figure reclined on it, her knees a little raised, with a crown upon them, and in her left hand a sharp pointed sword. Underneath the monument are the words " Coronat 6h Jul, 1483." And under that line this other, " Mort, 22 Aug. 1485." From 1785, when this medal was made, to 1616, when the English first settled on this continent, were 131 years. It must have been the greater part of that time, and ever since, in a quiescent state. All the letters and figures upon it, are in perfect preservation.

A singular silver button was lately ploughed up, in a field on Elk river, in Lincoln county, in West Tennessee, eleven miles from Fayetteville, where the Roman coin above mentioned was found, and near to the mouth of Coldwater creek, and about 600 yards distant from the river. The button is about the size of a half dollar in circumference, and is of the intrinsic value of little more than $37\frac{1}{2}$ cents. The silver is very pure. The button is convex, with the representation of a deer engraved on it, and a hound in pursuit. The eye of the button appears to be as well soldered as though it had been effected by some of our modern silversmiths. It was in the spring of 1819, when the first discovery of this button was made. On the opposite side of the river is an intrenchment, including a number of mounds. Mr. Oliver Williams lives within three miles of this place; and says, that during the year 1819, one dozen of the like buttons were ploughed up; and that for every year since, more or fewer of them have been found; the whole amounting to about three dozen. Upon all of them the device is that above stated. These buttons have been found promiscuously, at the depth to which the plough generally penetrates into the earth, or from 9 to 12 'inches. The field in which the buttons were found contains from 60 to 70 acres of land. Trees lately grew upon it, before the laud was cleared, from 4 to 5 feet in diameter. The country around is rather hilly than otherwise.

As to other metals found in Tennessee, there is this fact: In the month of June, in the year 1794, in the county of Davidson, on Manscoe's creek, at Manscoe's lick, on the creek which runs through the lick, a hole or well was dug by Mr. Caffrey, who, at the distance of 5 or 6 feet through black mud and lose rocks, found the end of a bar of iron, which had been cut off by a cleaving iron, and had also been split lengthwise. A small distance from that, in yellow clay, 18 inches under the surface, was a furnace full of coals and ashes.

Another fact evinces most clearly, the residence of man in West Tennessee in very ancient times, who knew how to forge metals, make axes and other metallic tools and implements, and probably also the art of fusing ore and of making iron or hardened copper, such as have been long used in Chili by the natives. It also fixes such residence to a period long preceding that at which Columbus discovered America. In the county of Bedford, in West Tennessee, northeast from Shelbyville, and seventeen miles from it, on the waters of the Garrison fork, one of the three forks of Duck river, on McBride's branch, in the year 1812, was cut down a poplar tree five feet some inches in diameter. It was felled by Samuel Pearse, Andrew Jones, and David Dobbs, who found within two or three inches of the heart, in the curve made by the axe which cut into the tree, the old chop of an axe, which of course must have been made when the tree was a sapling not more than three inches in diameter. If 400 years of age when cut down, it must have been 70 when Columbus discovered America, and 118 when De Soto marched through Alabama. If the

chop was made by an axe which the natives obtained from him, it must have been made since the
commencement of 282 years from this time; and a
poplar sapling of three inches in diameter could
not be more than 8 or 10 years of age; making the
whole age of the tree, to the time it was cut down,
about 300 years: in which time a tree of that size
could not probably have grown.

Two pieces of brass coin were found in the first
part of the year 1823, two miles and a half from
Murfreesborough, in an easterly direction from
thence. Each of them had a hole near the edge.
Their size was about that of a ninepenny silver
piece of the present time. The rim projected beyond the circle, as if it had been intended to clip it.
On the obverse, was the figure in relief of a female,
full faced, steady countenance, rather stern than
otherwise; with a cap or helmet on the head, upon
the top of which was a crescent extending from the
forehead backwards. In the legend was the word
Minerva; on the reverse was a slim female figure,
with a ribbon in her left hand, which was tied to
the neck of a slim, neatly formed dog that goes before her, and in the other a bow. The legend is
given below. Amongst the letters of the legend in
the reverse, are SL. After the ground which covered this coin had been for some years cleared and
ploughed, it was enclosed in a garden on the summit of a small hill; and in digging there, these
pieces were found eighteen inches under the surface.
There are no Assyrian or Babylonean coins; nor
is there any Phenician one till 400 before Christ.
Sydon and Tyre used weights. Coinage was unknown in Egypt in early times. The Lydian coins
are the oldest. The Persian coins began 570 before
Christ. The darics were issued by Darius Hys-
taspes 518 or 521 before Christ. Roman coins have
been found in the Orkneys, and in the remotest parts
of Europe, Asia and Africa. Some of the small

brass coins of the Romans have three heads upon the side, as that of Valerian and his two sons, Galliences and Valerian. On the Roman coins are figures of deities and personifications, which are commonly attended with their names; Minerva, for instance, with her helmet and name inscribed in the legend, sometimes a spear in her right hand, and shield, with Medusa's head, in the other, and an owl standing by her, and sometimes a cock and sometimes the olive. Diana is manifest by her crescent, by her bow and quiver on one side, and often by her hounds. The Roman brass coins have SC. for senatus consultum, till the time of Galliences, about the year of our Lord 260. The small brass coins ceased to be issued for a time in the reign of Pertinax, A. D. 192, and from thence to the time of Valerian. Small brass coins continued from the latter period till A. D. 640. Some coins are found with holes pierced through them, and sometimes with small bass strings fastened. Such were worn as ornaments of the head, neck and wrist, either by the ancients themselves, as bearing images of favorite deities, or in modern times, when the Greek girls thus decorated themselves. From these criteria it may be determined, that these metals are not counters, but coins. Of all the Roman coins that have been found in Tennessee and Kentucky, the earliest bears date in the time of Antoninus, the next in the time of Commodus, the next before the elevation of Pertinax, and the last in the time of Valerian. Coins prior or subsequent to the space embraced in these periods, are not found; and from hence the conclusion seems to be furnished, that they were brought into America within one or two centuries at furthest, after the latter period, which is about the year of our Lord 254, and thence to 260; and by a people who had not afterwards any intercourse with the countries in which the Roman coin circulated. The medium of difference between 260 and 640, is 190, which added to 260, makes 450, for the period of their arrival in Tennessee. One of these pieces was stained all over with a dark colour resembling that of pale ink, which possibly is the erugo peculiar to that metal, which issued from it after lying in a dormant state for a great length of time, and which thus preserved it from decay. The legend on the reverse, on the lower part, below a line across, are the letters EL. SL. RECHP. a hole—ENN.

The author, since writing the above, has seen another coin of the same metal precisely, which seems to be a mixture of silver and brass. Upon it, on one side, is the figure of a man's face; and in the legend, LEOPOL. DG. IMP. On the other, under a mark or cross, EL. SL.; also, the sun at the top; and in the legend, only a contraction of those in the larger piece, namely, RL. C. PERNN. This, then, is a German coin of modern date.—*X.*

Section 8.—*Of their Ornaments.*

About the month of April, 1823, on the Cany Fork of Cumberland, 13 or 14 miles from Sparta, in a southwestwardly direction, Mr. Tilford observed a stone standing erect, the top being about a foot above the ground, the width a foot, and extending to the depth of a foot in the ground. He moved it from its position, and dug in, and discovered, about twelve inches under the surface, some bones of a human skeleton. He took up several. They were larger than those of men of common stature, indicating that the whole skeleton would be six feet three or four inches in length. They were thicker than bones of the same denomination ordinarily are. The teeth were in a state of preservation as far as the enamel reached, but those parts which entered the socket were in a state of decay. The teeth were longer than those of ordinary men. The scull was larger in the same proportion, and by the operations of time had become thinner than sculls usually are. Hence was inferred the great antiquity of the grave ; though, perhaps, as correct an inference would be, the northern formation and growth of the scull, far from the vertical rays of the sun, which usually thicken the scull, when not defended by hats or bonnets, or mitres. A vast number of periwinkles lay near the grave and around it, spread over two or three acres of ground. They are supposed to have been brought from the Cany Fork, which is about half a mile from the spot, but are of much larger size than any which are found at this time on that river. The thigh bone, when there was an attempt made to move it, fell into, dust. These latter circumstances are taken as concurrent evidences of great antiquity. The grave was upon the summit of a high bluff, rising from the river to the spot; the trees near it were of as large size as any in the adjacent forest, and at a small distance were some mounds on which the timber was of equal size. A part of the scull, when exposed to the air, was quickly dissolved into dust. In this grave, Mr. Tilford found, near where the neck of the skeleton was, a great number of beads, some of them adhering closely together in a circular shape, which showed that they once encircled the neck. Others were separated. He took up 260 of them, and left a considerable number more, which he did not remove. One was larger than all the rest, in the shape of a barrel; bored through the centre, from one end to the other; one half of an inch in length, and about one half of that length in diameter; supposed to have been placed in a string which connected the whole, at the lower part, so as to divide one half of the beads above, from the other half above. This bead, when cut on the surface, is very smooth, of a whitish colour, inclining by a small shade towards a pale yellow, and very much resembles ivory. Fine longitudinal grains are visible

X

on the surface; and it is the opinion of good judges, that they are made of a species of ivory. The other beads are circular, all of the like materials which compose the large bead. Some of them are of greater diameter than others, and of greater width from the one side to the other. The diameter of the larger ones is about one fourth of an inch; the width on the exterior of the circle, about a third of the length of the diameter. The side of the one adjoining the side of its neighbour, when connected by a string, appears to have been made smoother by friction, than when first formed. It is as smooth and ungranulated as an ivory comb; in some instances, however, showing the unevenness of the cut made by the tool which originally separated the bead from the mass it was taken from. In some instances, the bead, from the hole in the centre to the exterior of the circle, appears by friction to have reduced the width of the exterior from one side to the other, so as to make it unequal to the opposite exterior of the circle; whence is inferred the long time it had been used before the death of the wearer. From these appearances the inference is, that some of the strands encircled the neck, whilst others hung from the neck upon the breast. The sound which is made by handling or striking the beads, is dull and heavy; not the sharp and tinkling sounds of metals or flint. The materials of which they are composed, were probably not the product of Tennessee; though it is possible, they may have been taken from the tooth of the mammoth or of the alligator. The workmanship is rude. The holes were not made by a screw, but by incisions made from the centre of each side, towards the other. They were probably of Tartarean fabrication; or may have been made in America, by some of those who expelled the aborigines. The principal deduction to be made from them is, that the style of the dress and ornaments with which the wearer was decorated, was the same which the ancients of Asia used, and which the Hindoos to this day[1] accustom themselves to wear. The originals which this chain imitated was, in all likelihood, the fashion when Joseph was decorated with a chain of gold;[2] and Daniel, in the time of Nebuchadnezzar; when in the time of Isaiah, about 700 years before Christ, the women of Jerusalem had bells on their feet, and, amongst other things, chains, and bracelets, and mufflers.[3] The writer, after giving the above description, with the cordon of beads before him, in order to avoid the possibility of mistake, caused them to be submitted to the inspection and experiments of Doctor Throchmorlin, of Sparta, whose literary acquirements, good experience, and uncommon intelligence, have made him peculiarly well qualified to decide upon the question, whether the materials be of stone or other substance. His decision, that unquestionably they are of *ivory*, of the finest and best quality. The dingy coating which obscured the beads, was cleared, by his experiments, from one of them, and it then appeared to be a beautiful white, with the degree of shade which characterizes and softens the ivory colour. The whole chain thus brightened, must have formerly exhibited a very superb appearance. Upon the contemplation of this discovery, the inquisitive mind is impelled irresistibly, to ask, whence came this gigantic skeleton, the chain which he wore, and the ivory beads which compose it. His size and the thinness of his scull prove that he was from the north, and probably of that race of huge stature which, in the time of the Roman empire, so much excited the wonder of their writers; and which, in the decline of the empire, spread desolation, ruin and darkness over its whole extent. He came

[1] 1 Dubois, 295.
[2] Gen. ch. 41, v. 42; Daniel, ch. 5. v. 7, 29.
[3] Isaiah, ch. 3, v. 17, 18, 19, 20, 21, 22, 23.

hither in quest of new adventures, and to act, in presence of the aborigines of America, the same scenes which had been so successfully acted in the Roman theatre. His notions of dress he received from his ancestors, who once lived in Egypt, then in Palestine, next on the heads of the Oxus and the Indus, having intercourse with the Persians and Hindoos; thence they were transplanted to the Irtish, thence to the Volga, and next into Siberia; whence in time they took a wider flight, and passing the Esquimaux, rested awhile in Canada, and within the western limits of New-York, where leaving upon rocks the memorials of themselves, they advanced to the plunder and the extermination of the nerveless aborigines of Tennessee and Kentucky. The beads were acquired by a commercial intercourse with traders, from India who transplanted them by successive removals into the wilds of Siberia. And all this was done after the period when the latest coins were uttered, that are found in Tennessee and Kentucky—which see under coins. And it was done before the last periods in which history speaks of the huge stature of the northern inhabitants.

For more upon this article, reference must be had to the dress of the idols, and to the cross found on the heart of a skeleton, and to the clasps on the arms of a female skeleton near Carthage, and to those similar to the ivory ones from Indostan, and to the marble ornament found on the beach near the mouth of the Muskingum.—*Y.*

Section 9.—*Of their Mirrors.*

For this article, reference must be had to the plate of isinglass, found at the bottom of a mound at Circleville, in the state of Ohio, which will be described in the appropriate note.—*Z.*

Section 10.—*Of their Tanks, or Wells.*

For this article, reference must be had to the one in the enclosures in the bend of Big Harpeth, near

Dog creek, and to one on the cave near to which the ivory button was found. Chap. 8, sec. 5.—*A.A.*

Section 11.—*Of their Mechanic Arts.*

It cannot be supposed, that the many deep and wide intrenchments of which we have already spoken, could be made without the aid of metallic tools, such as the spade and the pickaxe; nor could bricks be of any use to the ancient inhabitants, without the trowel and the masonic art, not to mention the building of stone walls. And this presupposes a great number of other arts; the fusing of ore, the forging of metals, and smithing or the forging of metallic utensils to the various ends they are intended for. The mark of the axe near the heart of a poplar 400 or 500 years old, and the water pond in the enclosures in the bend of Big Harpeth, which could not have been made without hoes and spades, are evidences of the use of iron or copper tools.

A few miles from the town of Columbia, in Maury county, in West Tennessee, and on Duck river, are a number of fortifications, as they are called, and mounds, into some of which some young men dug a small distance; and found several well burnt bricks, about nine inches square, and three inches thick; also, several fragments of earthen ware, and a sword about two feet long, differing from any in use since the white people visited the country, apparently once highly polished, but now much eaten with rust. Those who buried these articles there, could fashion the sword, and could make bricks, and use them by the masonic art.—*BB.*

Section 12.—*Of their Games and Pastimes.*

The following articles are supposed to be used in their games, for rolling on a level surface, and perhaps through balls, as no other use for them can be conceived of, and as they appear to have been provided and prepared with great care, labour and expense.

In the possession of General Cocke, of Grainger county, and in the town of Rutledge, is a circular stone, found in the woods there, of three inches in diameter, resembling in colour dark yellow barber's soap. In the centre, on each side, is a small circular excavation about an inch in diameter or a little more, scooped out as far as to its circumference, extending not quite half way from the centre to the circumference of the stone itself. On both sides there is a declivity from the centre to the edge, making the extremity not more than half as thick as the stone is at the centre. It is very smoothly cut. It seems as if on both sides it had filled some insertion opposite to one on the other side. It must have been cut by some very hard and sharp instrument. It is of a polish extremely smooth. The stone itself approaches in fineness to marble. In the museum of a lady at Nashville is one of a similar shape; it is made of stone very white, like snow, some transparent and glittering; very hard and heavy. It is about three inches in diameter, or perhaps a little less; the excavation in the centre on each side, seems adapted to the thumb and finger, and at the extremity it is wider in proportion than the one before described. And lately was taken from a mound in Maury county, a stone perfectly globular, very hard and heavy, of a variegated exterior, and exceedingly well polished. It probably belonged to some employment that the other circular stones did. They were all of them cut by some iron or steel instrument. It was two or three inches in diameter. The variety of colours with which its exterior is diversified, seems to have been painted. Dyes of very unfading quality must have been employed in making the colours. The materials of which it is made are different from any of the natural productions of the country, and were probably brought from abroad.

Section 13.—*Of the Colour of the Aborigines of
of Tennessee.*

The section upon the literal inscriptions of Tennessee, gives one instance of a skeleton in a cave
near Carthage, the hair of which was yellow. The
hair of the female covered with the curious mantle
of feathers, in the section of manufactures, which
was found in a cave in White county, was of a yellow cast, and very fine. It is evident, that these
did not belong to Indians of the same races with
those of the present day.

Near the confines of Smith and Wilson counties,
on the south side of Cumberland river, about 22
miles above Cairo, on the waters of Smith's Fork
of Cany Fork, is a cave, the aperture into which is
very small. The workmen in the cave enlarged
the entrance and went in; and digging in the apart-
ment, next the entrance, after removing the dirt and
using it, they came, upon the same level with the
entrance, to another small aperture, which also they
entered, and went through, when they came into a
narrow room, 25 feet square. Every thing here
was neat and smooth. The room seemed to have
been carefully preserved for the reception and
keeping of the dead. In this room, near about the
centre, were found sitting in baskets made of cane,
three human bodies; the flesh entire, but a little
shrivelled, and not much so. The bodies were those
of a man, a female and a small child. The complexion of all was very fair, and white, without
any intermixture of the copper colour. Their eyes
were blue; their hair auburn, and fine. The teeth
were very white, their stature was delicate, about
the size of the whites of the present day. The
man was wrapped in 14 dressed deer skins. The
14 deer skins were wrapped in what those present
called blankets. They were made of bark, like
those found in the cave in White county. The
form of the baskets which enclosed them, was

pyramidal, being larger at the bottom, and declining to the top. The heads of the skeletons, from the neck, were above the summits of the blankets. *See CC.*

Section 14.—*Of their Mexican Coincidences.*

On the side of the road leading from Nashville to Charlottte, one mile east of Big Harpeth, near the lower part of Mr. Lake's plantation, was a grave, with rocks set up at the feet and head, and containing the bones of a dog. The bones in another grave near it, were human.

The Mexicans killed a little dog, around whose neck they tied a string, for the purpose of guiding the deceased master, and buried this animal with him, or burned it, if the master was burned.[43]

43 McCullough, 167.

CHAPTER VIII.

THOUGH what is said in this chapter, is made to relate to the aborigines, as the preceding chapters have, yet one opinion, if not the better one, refers the articles of this chapter to those northern conquerors, who overran the old world, and who seem also to have passed over to this continent, in pursuit of their chief business, the trade of war and desolation. But whether more appropriate to the primitive, or these secondary aborigines, will be submitted to the judgment of the learned reader.

We will examine first, into their size; secondly, into the history of their pigmies; thirdly, into their martial music.

First, then—*Of their Size.*

This is ascertained by the length and dimensions of the skeletons which are found in East and West Tennessee. These will prove demonstratively, that the ancient inhabitants of this country, either the primitive or secondary settlers, were of gigantic stature, compared with the present races of Indians.

On the farm of Mr. John Miller, of White county, are a number of small graves, and also many large ones, the bones in which show that the bodies to which they belonged, when alive, must have been seven feet high and upwards.

About the year 1814, Mr. Lawrence found, in Scarborough's cave, which is on the Calf-killer river, a branch of the Cany Fork, about 12 or 15 miles from Sparta, in a little room in the cave, many human bones of a monstrous size. He took a jaw bone and applied it to his own face, and when his chin touched the concave of the chin bone, the hinder ends of the jaw bone did not touch the skin of his face on either side. He took a thigh bone, and applied the upper end of it to his own hip joint, and the lower end reached four inches below the

Y

knee joint. Mr. Andrew Bryan saw a grave opened about 4 miles northwardly from Sparta, on the Calf-killer fork. He took a thigh bone, and raising up his knee, he applied the knee joint of the bone to the extreme length of his own knee, and the upper end of the bone passed out behind him, as far as the full width of his body. Mr. Lawrence is about 5 feet, 10 inches, high, and Mr. Bryan about 5 feet, 9. Mr. Sharp Whitley was in a cave near the place, where Mr. Bryan saw the graves opened. In it were many of these bones. The sculls lie plentifully in it, and all the other bones of the human body; all in proportion, and of monstrous size. Human bones were taken out of a mound on Tennessee river, below Kingston, which Mr. Brown saw measured, by Mr. Simms. The thigh bones of those skeletons, when applied to Mr. Simms's thigh, were an inch and a half longer than his, from the point of his hip to his knee: supposing the whole frame to have been in the same proportion, the body it belonged to must have been seven feet high or upwards. Many bones in the mounds there, are of equal size. Suppose a man seven or eight feet high, that is from 18 inches to 2 feet taller than men of the common size; suppose the body broader in the same proportion, also his arms and legs; would he not be entitled to the name of giant? Col. William Sheppard, late of North-Carolina, in the year 1807, dug up, on the plantation of Col. Joel Lewis, 2 miles from Nashville, the jaw bones of a man, which easily covered the whole chin and jaw of Col. Lewis, a man of large size. Some years afterwards, Mr. Cassady dug up a skeleton from under a small mound near the large one at Bledsoe's lick, in Sumner county, which measured little short of seven feet in length. Human bones have been dug up at the plantation where Judge Overton now lives, in Davidson county, four miles southwestwardly from Nashville, in making a cellar. These bones were of extraordinary size. The under jaw bone of one skeleton very easily slipped over the jaw of Mr. Childress, a stout man, full fleshed, very robust and considerably over the common size. These bones were dug up within the traces of ancient walls, in the form of a square of two or three hundred yards in length, situated near an excellent, never failing spring of pure and well tasted water. The spring was enclosed within the walls. A great number of skeletons was found within the enclosure, a few feet below the surface of the earth. On the outer side were the traces of an old ditch and rampart, thrown up on the inside. Some small mounds were also within the enclosure.

At the plantation of Mr. William Sheppard, in the county of Giles, seven and a half miles north of Pulaski, on the east side of the creek, is a cave, with several rooms. The first 15 feet wide, and 27 long; 4 feet deep; the upper part of solid and even rock. Into this cave was a passage, which had been so artfully covered, that it escaped detection till lately. A flat stone, three feet wide and four feet long, rested upon the ground, and inclining against the cave, closed part of the mouth. At the end of this, and on the side of the mouth left open, is another stone rolled, which filling this also, closed the whole mouth. When these rocks were removed, and the cave opened, on the inside of the cave were found several bones—the jaw bone of a child, the arm bone of a man, the sculls and thigh bones of men. The whole bottom of the cave was covered with flat stones of a bluish hue, being closely joined together, and of different forms and sizes. They formed the floor of the cave. Upon the floor the bones were laid. The hat of Mr. Egbert Sheppard, seven inches wide and eight inches long, but just covered and slipped over one of the sculls.

At the mouth of Obed's river, on the point between it and the Cumberland river, which is high ground, certain persons, in digging, struck, a little below the surface, four stones standing upright, and so placed in relation to each other, as to form a square or box, which enclosed a skeleton, placed on its feet in an erect posture. The scull was large enough to go over the head of a man of common size. The thigh bones applied to those of a man of ordinary stature, reached from the joint of his hip to the calf of his leg.

About ten miles from Sparta, in White county, a *conical* mound was lately opened, and in the centre of it was found a skeleton eight feet (*See DD.*) in length. With it was found a stone of the flint kind, very hard, with two flat sides, having in the centre circular hollows exactly accommodated to the balls of the thumb and fore finger. This stone was an inch and a half in diameter, the form exactly circular. It was about one third of an inch thick, and made smooth and flat, for rolling, like a grindstone, to the form of which, indeed, the whole stone was assimilated. When placed upon the floor, it would roll for a considerable time without falling. The whole surface was smooth and well polished, and must have been cut and made smooth by some hard metallic instrument. No doubt it was buried with the deceased, because for some reason he had set a great value on it in his life time, and had excelled in some accomplishment to which it related. The colour of the stone was a dingy white, inclining to a darkish yellow. At the side of this skeleton were also found two flat stones, about six inches long, two and a half wide at the lower part, and about one and a half at the upper end, widening in the shape of an axe or hatchet from the upper to the lower end. The thickness of the stone, about one tenth of an inch. An inch below the upper end, exactly equidistant from the lateral edges, a small hole is neatly bored through each stone, so that by a string run through, the stone might be suspended on the sides or from the neck as ornaments. One of these stones is the common limestone. The other is semitransparent, so as to be darkened by the hand placed behind it; and resembles in texture those stalactical formations, like white stone, which are made in the bottoms of caves by the dripping of water. When broken, there appears a grain running from one flat side to the other, like the shootings of ice or saltpetre, of a whitish colour inclining to yellow. The latter stones are too thin and slender, for any operation upon other substances, and must have been purely ornamental. The first described stone must have been intended for rolling. For why take so much pains to make it circular, if to be used in flinging? or why, if for the latter purpose, so much pains taken to make excavations adapted to the thumb and finger. The conjecture seems to be a probable one, that it was used in some game played upon the same principles as that called ninepins; and the little round balls, like marbles, but of a larger size, were so disposed as that the rolling stone should pass through them. Such globular stone, it is already stated, was found in a mound in Maury county. With this large skeleton were also found eight beads and a human tooth. The beads were circular, and of a bulbous form. The largest about one fourth of an inch in diameter; the others smaller. The greater part of them tumescent from the edge to the centre, at which a hole was perforated for a string to pass through and to connect them. The inner sides were hard and white, like lime indurated by some chemical process. The outside was a thin coal of black crust, very much resembling japan. When we reflect, that the Scythian nations between the Danube and the Tonais, as late as within one century of the Christian era, were of a size which as-

tonished the southern inhabitants of Europe and
Asia; that they scalped their enemy; that they
buried their dead in heaps of earth thrown over
them, with such articles as were deemed by the
deceased most valuable in his lifetime; and that
their tumuli, or barrows, are yet to be seen in the
plains towards the upper part of the Irtish and
Jenesee, and from the banks of the Wolga to the
lake Baikal; we cannot refrain from the conclusion,
that this skeleton belonged to a human body of the
same race, education and notions with those who
lived on the Volga, Tonais and Obey. The same
unknown cause which, in the course of 2000 years,
has reduced the size of the ancient Scythians and
their tribes, the Gauls, and Germans, and Sarmatians, has produced the same effects here. The
descendants of these giants, both in the old and
new world, agree with each other in bulk, as their
ancestors did with each other, which proves a uniform cause operating equally both in the old and
new world. The decrease in bulk seems to have
kept pace everywhere with the increase of warm
temperature, and with the abbreviation of longevity.
The giants of Hebron and Gath, and those of Laco-
nia and Italy, whose large skeletons to this day
attest that there they formerly dwelt, compared with
those now found in West Tennessee, demonstrate
that a change of climate, or of some other cause,
has worked a remarkable change in the human
system; and with respect to the mammoth, the
megalonix, and other animals, has either extinguished or driven them into other and far distant
latitudes. Nature, as it grows in age, is less vigo-
rous than at the beginning, and in its early age it
was; its productions correspond with its debility,
and the time must come, when she, like all her
productions, will give up the ghost and work no
more. But the principal use we have to make of
the skeleton before us, is to discover, first, that he

came from a cold or northern climate, and not from the south, as the primitive aborigines did, for men of large stature were never found within the tropics. Secondly, that he must have come from the north of Europe or of Asia, because of the similarity of customs already remarked: and thirdly, that he probably belonged to those northern tribes, which some centuries ago exterminated the nations which had come from the south, and were settled upon the Cumberland and its waters.

With this skeleton was found another nearly of the same size, with the top of his head flat, and his eyes placed apparently in the upper part of his forehead. The Aztecs or Mexicans represent their principal divinities, as their hieroglyphical manuscripts prove, with a head much more flattened than any which have been seen amongst the Caribs, and they never disfigured the heads of their children. But many of the southern tribes have adopted the barbarous custom of pressing the heads of their children between two boards, in imitation, no doubt, of the Mexican form, which, in their estimation, was beautiful, or in some way advantageous. And here it may not be amiss to mention, that the Chilians, who lived as far to the south of the equator, as formerly did the Scythians, Goths, Vandals, Gauls and Germans, so remarkable in ancient times for their stature, did on the other side of it,[44] were men of large stature.

One remark may be of some use in the drawing of inferences from the preceding facts. The skeletons, we find, are entire under conical mounds, or in part consumed by fire, and under such mounds, or entire in shallow graves, with flat rocks placed on the edges, at the sides, and at the head and feet, or are entire, above the common surface, and in the conical mounds enclosed in rocks placed together

44 1 Molina, 233, 234, 236, 237; 2 Molina, 111, 114, 197, 502.

in the form of a box, or stand erect in such boxes, with the head some depth below the surface. To burn and cover with a mound, is Hindooic, Grecian, and belonging to the ancient countries of Asia Minor, and probably belonged to the aborigines of America, properly so called. To cover the entire body, is Scythic. To bury in graves, or in boxes, is Ethiopic, Egyptian, and in part Hebraic, the Hebrews having learned it during their residence in Egypt, though they did not generally adopt it.[k] It may be concluded, that the mounds over entire bodies, are Scythic; graves and boxes, Hebraic; and boxes in the mounds, Hebraic and Scythic; and of course, that the unconsumed skeletons, we see here, are either pure Scythians or Hebrew Scythians, whilst all others are Hindooic, or in other words aboriginal. The large men of the world have always been found in the north, and they have often invaded and broken up the people of the south. They have never been found in the south; nor have the people of the south ever broken up their settlements there, and marched upon those of the north, to expel them from their possessions, to make room for themselves. The men who deposited the skeletons we are now contemplating, were of northern growth, and they came to the south to drive away the inhabitants whom they found there, and to seat themselves in their possessions.

Section 2.—*Of their Pigmies.*

Certain small tombs, and skeletons in them, having been discovered a few miles from Sparta, in the county of White, and a publication having been made concerning them, in the Nashville Whig, of June, 1820, Mr. Lane, from whom the information first came, was written to, all his feelings were

[k] Genesis, ch. 50, v. 36 ; Luke, ch. 7, v. 14; Matt. ch. 27, v. 60; Mark, ch. 6, v. 29; John, ch. 11, v. 44 ; 2 K. ch. 13, v. 21.

alive, and all his exertions were roused. The result was a communication, some time afterwards, from him, carefully reduced to writing; which, with the materials referred to, were submitted to the examination of medical gentlemen at Nashville. The written communication from Mr. Lane, was dated on the 26th of July, 1820; and stated, that he had undertaken to make some further discoveries amongst the little *tombs* which seemed to be peculiar to the settlement in which he lived, a few miles from Sparta. He found in one of the small graves (the package No. 1) the fractured part of a skeleton. The grave, as usual, was about two feet in length, and 14 inches broad, and 16 inches deep from the covering rock to the bottom, as nearly as could be ascertained, for the bottom of these graves is never covered with rock. The scull of this being, he said, was much larger than any he had before seen in these graves; but from the length of the thigh and arm bones, may be conjectured the height. He also sent the teeth, to the end that it might be decided whether they were canine, monkey or human. The scull, though fractured, in his opinion retained enough of its original form to determine to what class of beings it once belonged. The body to which this scull belonged, seemed not to have been interred in the usual form, but to have been set up in the grave, with his back against the head rock of the tomb. The scull was found uppermost, and directly beneath it, the ribs; but these were so decayed, that they crumbled with the slightest touch, and could not be preserved. Next were the arms and thigh bones, lying beside each other, with their upper ends near the head rock, and the scull directly on the upper end of these bones; hence it is supposed the body was not prostrate. With this personage were found some other singularities; three vessels and two conch shells, when one of each set is customary in these small graves. The

Z

size and figure of the furniture is noticeable, namely: A vessel that, from what of it remains, appears
to have holden a quantity between one and two
quarts, whilst the other graves have a vessel holding about one pint. This large vessel also being
carved and laced, whilst the others have their vessels entirely plain, is in this respect singular. The
basin, though otherwise plain, is laced round the
rim. The other vessel is so broken down, that no
observations can be made on it: further than this,
that from the strength which seems attached to the
bottom, it must have been intended for drudgery.
These vessels were found in the following order:
the large carved pot on the right, and the strong
bottomed vessel and two conchs on the left. These
things considered—the size of the head; the unusual largeness of the grave; the number, quantity
and size of the vessels; and the number of shells,
they being muscle instead of conch shells; the vessels being placed on the right and left, and the
body being set erect,—all indicated a difference
between the person to whom this skeleton belonged
and ordinary ones. On Saturday the 29th of July,
1820, Mr. Lane went to Captain Simon Doyles's,
the place where Mr. Anderson formerly lived, to
search there for further discoveries. He and those
who were with him, opened two small graves. The
first 18 inches long; about 12 inches broad. · It
contained the little bones, pieces of part of one
tooth, and other things contained in package No. 2.
The second grave was 2 feet long, 13 inches wide,
and 15 inches deep. It contained the bones, teeth,
vessel and shells enclosed in package No. 3. This
person was laid upon the right side, with his head
to the south, and his face to the east. The body
lay north and south, and the thigh bones east and
west. The legs were then laid back, so as to form
an angle with the thighs, of about 30 degrees. All
this could be clearly ascertained by a cautious and

careful examination of the bones, which, although plainly to be seen, yet nevertheless were so decayed, that they would crumble at the slightest touch. Nor could they possibly lift the bones, in any sounder condition than as they were presented to view in the package. The under side of the scull, as it was in the grave, was sounder and stronger than that which was uppermost. The scull which was in the grave last opened, could not possibly be raised, for the graves were all full of dirt, as closely bound together as any other ground outside the grave; and when the scull is discovered, the probability is, that a hole will break into it on the upper part. The concave is perfectly hollow, but the earth could not be removed from about it, without crumbling it down as fast as the earth was removed. The concave diameter Mr. Lane measured. It was about 5 inches. Some small scraps of it (No. 3) he sent. The socket of the eye was perceptible; the knettings of the head were visible. The chin, the size and strength of the teeth, and the size and curvature of the ribs, were all apparent. The graves lie promiscuously through the farm of Mr. Lane. But at Mr. Anderson's, where Captain Doyle now lives, there is a large and closely connected burying ground, all of the description already given; and there are others of the same description four miles south of Sparta. Mr. Anderson formerly opened many of them: Capt. Doyle, the present owner, has opened several of them; and they both say, they believe hundreds might be found there. There is no discernible rising on the surface of the earth by reason of these graves; but they are found by striking an iron tool into the ground so deep as to strike the covering rock. This rock being then removed, the grave can be easily discovered by the edges of the side and end rocks. On Tuesday the first of August, 1820, Mr. Lane, in company with his son, Jacob A. Lane, Esquire, made further searches in the burying ground at Capt. Doyles's, formerly Mr. Anderson's. They opened another small grave, just 22 inches long, made after the usual form, and took out of it the bones and little trinkets in package No. 4. This skeleton lay on its back, with its feet drawn up, so as to raise the knees about 4 inches above the bottom of the grave. The head was raised above the bottom of the grave also, so as to cause the chin to lie on the breast. They measured the skeleton carefully, as it lay in the grave, and found it to be, from a little below the ankle joints to the top of the scull, 2 feet, 10 inches, taking care to measure the limbs as they meandered, and making sufficient allowance for the reclining of the head; at any rate, it was not above three feet high. Its head was to the east, the face to the west. This grave was 4 feet from the one last mentioned. The little round shell found in this grave, with two little holes, a *cross and two circles* cut in it, is what was not seen in any other grave they had opened, that is to say the cross and circles were not. *Three* vessels were in the grave, but all broken down, so that they were not worth preserving. Five feet from the grave just opened, they opened another. It was large, constructed after the manner of a coffin, the head 14 inches broad, the elbows 22 inches, and the foot 10 inches. The sides and ends were lined with flag rock, after the manner of the small graves, but not quite so deep, it being only 12 inches. In this grave lay a person 5 feet, 5 inches, high; the head to the west, and the feet to the east. They uncovered the bones of this skeleton from head to foot, without moving any bone, until they had a full view of the entire skeleton. It was not shrouded, for its mouth was extended, wide open, and was full of teeth. The arms lay along the sides; the ribs were broad and flat, and more than double the size of those of the pigmies. The head was longer, the eyes much wider asunder, the forehead much higher above the eyebrows, and the under jaw measured just one inch longer, at each side, than the little one sent to Nashville. They laid them together, and ascertained the exact difference. The collar bone, the arm, thigh and leg bones, of this being, appeared strong, beyond what they expected from that size of human bones. The elbows, knee and ankle joints, were much larger than was expected. After they had measured it, and satisfied themselves of its true position, they raised many of the bones, particularly the head, all the limbs, some few joints of the back bone, some ribs, and the broad flat bones at the bottom of the lower chest. The scull had not a fracture, except the top of the right cheek bone, which they undesignedly struck off. The limbs were all lying in their proper posture, with joint to its joint, and bone to its socket. When they raised the scull, *a great* number of hairs were found sticking to it, which seemed to be the hairs of the head of the person interred. *They were fine and straight*, and of a *bright silver grey*. These bones they laid back in the grave, covered them with the former covering, rocks, and then with earth. No vessels or trinkets were found with this skeleton; and from the great dissimilarity in the shapes of their heads, the size and make of their ribs, the great disproportion between the size of the joints and the bones of their limbs, they seemed to belong to very different tribes of people. The heads of the pigmies appeared larger upon inspection, than they had supposed them to be; and upon finding the bones in package No. 1, no person in the neighbourhood, who had formerly seen the little graves opened, could believe that this was of the same kind, owing to its size; but in that they must have been mistaken, for the graves are the same in every particular, though when measured they seem to be a few inches longer in length and breadth than was at first imagined, for it had been five or six years since they had seen any of them. Nor could they have yet believed otherwise, had they not searched out new ones, and reduced them to actual measurement. They have attended to a circumstance now, which before had not been thought of, namely: that the body, as laid in the grave, with its limbs, particularly the legs and thighs, were laid crooked, so as to reduce the length; and being a person of two feet ten inches high, or perhaps as high as three feet, into a grave of two feet long. But, continues Mr. Lane, from the great number of graves of this description and size, which we found here, and amongst them all, but one of a larger size, it seems to be intimated, that there hath been a race of people here in ancient times, whose height was from two feet, ten inches, to three feet; and that they have addicted themselves to strong superstitions, is indubitable. As ancient as the hair of the large skeleton seemed to be, there was not a tooth lost, or unsound, in the whole head. But the pigmy head in No. 4, has in the upper jaw a decayed tooth; whence it is conjectured, that the person to whom this skeleton belonged was elder than the other. Mr. Lane sent also for examination, a small package No. 5. This contained two dozen small *conch shells*, and two other small shells, like a taper screw. In the small package, are the small pieces of old pots, picked up above ground at the old town at Mr. Wilson's. It remains sound, after lying above ground perhaps for several hundred years. The small *conchs* in this package, were found about 4 miles southwestwardly from Sparta, and about 8 miles west of Mr. Lane's farm, near where the large skeletons were found, of seven feet in length or upwards, which have been already mentioned. They were there shown a little mound, on the margin of one of their old towns, which was literally covered with them.

They got a hoe, and dug into it, and found that the shells lay mixed with the earth, about 4 feet deep, but none that they could find deeper. Amongst them were many of the *taper shells, terebratula*. They also found, just below the surface, some old decayed bones, which they believed to be human, and some pieces of fire coal. A quantity of those shells, to the amount of half a bushel, might be gotten at this place. Package No. 6 was also sent by Mr. Lane, in which is a small stone. This and many others of the same shape are found about the old towns. Some of them are of a bluish colour, some green and some black. They are of different sizes; but all appear to be of the same species or quality of rock, of which it is said there are none such, which are the natural productions of the country.

These packages and their contents were submitted to the gentlemen of the medical faculty at Nashville, and they examined them. Various opinions were entertained upon the maturity or infancy of the small skeletons. The prevailing opinion seemed to be, that these skeletons belonged to adult persons. One gentleman agreed, that one of the small sculls belonged to an adult, but thought that the size of the body could not be judged of from the *cranium;* but that the cylindrical bones in No. 1, and the tooth, belonged to some animal of the *canine species.* Another believed, and so the fact seems now to be taken, that the bones and tooth in No. 1, belonged to some carnivorous animal of the canine genus; but that the scull belonged to an adult person of small size, not much exceeding 3 feet in length. Another has given the same opinion upon inspection of the bones.

The small conchs, two dozen in number, might be accounted for by reference to the Hindoo customs, were it not for the neighbourhood of the large skeletons, which forbid the idea of emigration from the south. They were found in a small mound, on the margin of an old town, which mound was covered with them, and they were intermixed with the clay to the depth of four feet below the surface. One of them was placed in the water vessel, of the capacity of a pint, which was placed at the head of each pigmy skeleton. Had they not been deemed very sacred, the inhabitants of the town would have gradually removed them from the mound; for at least they were curiosities, not being of the growth of the country; and having been brought from the ocean, at least 500 or 600 miles, if they did not come from the northeastern shores of America. Yet they were left undisturbed, so long as the people remained who placed them in the crust of the mound. Beneath them were human bones, perhaps of some distinguished priest of Vishnu. And perhaps each grave in which was one of these skeletons, contained the bones of a worshipper of Vishnu. In ancient times, the worshippers of the sun from the confines of China and Thibit, emigrated to Sarmatia, and thence to Germany, and thence to Finland, and the country of the Samoiedes, which so much resemble the Esquimaux; and these latter also were worshippers of the sun, as well as the Greenlanders.[43] From the country of their primitive emigration, the Esquimaux may have brought with them to America, through many other ages and people, this branch of the most ancient religion of India and of the east. For an explanation upon the subject of the conchs, and bones of animals, reference may be had to chapter 3, sec. 2. With respect to those small conch shells found buried with the small skeletons, which conchs are about the size of pullets' eggs, we may conjecture with some degree of certainty, that these are relics of Hindoo superstition, which came mediately or immediately from India, where it originated. But as

43 Grotius de Rebus Religiocis, book 4, page 338.

it is admitted on all hands, that these skeletons be-longed to human beings, though some bones and teeth of the canine species are intermixed, we shall be at a loss to conjecture, where, in times of anti-quity, lived this diminutive race of human beings. That such a race of men once existed, is asserted by Homer and Herodotus, the most ancient profane writers that we know of; but the assertion has never received credit.[44] They were mentioned also by Pliny, Strabo, and Mela, as existing in India, as well as in Ethiopia, where Herodotus states them to have been. But Jovius says, they are found in the extremities of the northern regions; referring, no doubt, to the Samoiedes of Lapland, and those to the north of them. The best opinion advanced upon the subject, seems to be, that some of the northeastern inhabitants of America came in the train of the Scythians or Tartars, when the latter migrated to this country. Of the stones found about the old towns in White county, some of a bluish colour, some greenish, and some black; and all, as it is supposed, foreign to the country where found. It shall suffice to mention, that a stone about six inches long, half an inch thick, three inches wide, and still widening to the edge, and having an edge like an axe, was found in an old fortification in White county, five or six miles from Sparta. It seemed tinged on the edge and sides with blood which had been petrified on a part of the axe. The colour of green was intermixed with a few spots of lighter complexion. It is very hard, and smooth. Stone axes of exactly the same de-scription are brought from the Fejee or Friendly islands, in the Pacific, by navigators. The same species of stone is found on the banks of the Ama-zon. From the former of which places came also the art of making the feathered mantles before spo-ken of.—*See DD.*

44 Herodotus Euterpe, sec. 32.

AA

Thirdly—*Of their Martial Music.*

About 18 miles east from Rogersville, in the county of Hawkins, in East Tennessee, was ploughed up a stone trumpet. It tapers on the outside, from either end to the middle, and is there surrounded by two rings of raised stone. The inside, at each end, is a hollow, of an inch and a quarter in diameter; but at one end the orifice is not as large as at the other. Probably the sound is shrill and sharp when blown from one end, and more full and sonorous when blown from the other. The hollow continues throughout, from the one end to the other, but in the middle, under the rings, it is not as wide as at the ends. It seems to have been made of hard soapstone; and when blown through, makes a sound which may be heard perhaps two miles. It is very smooth on the outside, but rough within. Probably it was used for similar purposes to those for which the trumpet of the Israelites was used, namely—principally to convene assemblies, and to regulate the movements of the army.[45] On days of rejoicing, to make a part of the musical sounds with which the people were entertained. From it, perhaps, these deductions may be made. There were no large hollow horns in the country, which could have been used for the same purpose, and more effectually, too, as large steer horns are now used by hunters. Nor had they the use of metals; for gold or silver, or copper, might have been formed into trumpets of the same size and shape, with much less labour; and when made, would have been lighter and more sightly, and might have been used more effectually than the stone one. And the people who made it, had no intercourse with the Mexicans, as the aborigines on the waters of the Ohio had; for otherwise they could have been supplied with silver, or gold and copper, of which to make

45 Job, ch. 39, v. 24, 25; Numb. ch. 10, v. 2, ch. 31, v. 6.

their trumpets. It is difficult to conjecture how the hollow was made: it is furrowed within, as well as rough. But a more important question is, whence could those who made the trumpet have known its properties and use? They could not have attained that knowledge by blowing through the large horns of animals; there were none such here, or they never would have made this stone trumpet. Most evidently, it was conceived to be of great value; otherwise so much time, as must necessarily have been consumed in fashioning and hollowing it, would not have been spent for such purpose. The makers must have learnt its use from some nation that employed the trumpet in sounding charges, or for giving directions to march, or to stop the pursuit of an enemy. Prior to the departure of the Israelites from Egypt, there is no scriptural or other account of trumpets.

In Egypt, Pharoah followed the army of the Israelites with chariots and horsemen, but the trumpet is not spoken of. It was sounded on Mount Sinai, where God delivered the law to Moses; and it is intimated, that the people had never before heard the sound of the trumpet. "The voice of the trumpet was exceedingly loud, so that all the people that was in the camp trembled. And all the people saw the thunderings and the lightnings, and the noise of the trumpet, and the mountains smoking; and when the people saw it, they removed and stood afar off."46 Afterwards it was directed, that two trumpets should be made, for convening the elders, and for giving signals for the marching of the tribes. Some were to march at one signal, and some at another. A signal was appointed for convening the whole congregation. Some time afterwards, the Israelites made use of trumpets for various other purposes; but being separated by their natural institutions and religion, in a great

46 Exodus, ch. 14, v. 6, 7, ch. 19, v. 13, 16, ch. 20, v. 18.

measure, from all the other people of the world, did not soon communicate to them the use of this instrument. When Bacchus overran India with an army from the west, the use of the trumpet was not known.[47] In the time of the Trojan war, neither Greeks nor Trojans used the trumpet. The Trojans had in their camp the sound of flutes and of pipes.[48] Stentor, a man of mighty voice, proclaimed to the army the orders which were given by the general. In the year 514 before Christ, when Darius the Mede crossed the Danube and invaded the Scythians, on his return, finding the bridge broken down, which he had left, he caused an Egyptian, remarkable for the loudness of his voice, to pronounce, with all his strength, the name of the admiral of the fleet, who immediately answered and came to him, and made a new bridge of boats, for his transportation. A trumpet could have been much more effectually used, and could have sent the appointed signal to a much greater distance. When Xerxes invaded Greece, 478 years before Christ, no trumpet was then used; the signal for battle was given by torch-bearers.[49] In aftertimes it was given by drum or trumpet. Signals also announcing any important occurrence, were given by holding up a torch of fire.[50] Soon after the invasion of Greece by the Persians, trumpets were used in Greece for many purposes, as well as those relative to the motions of their armies. The Greeks probably learned it from the Phenicians. The dispersed Israelites, either those carried into captivity by the Assyrians, or those of the Chaldean captivity, have imparted the knowledge of the trumpet and its uses, to the people from whom it came, mediately or immediately, to the Americans,

47 Diodorus Siculus, b. 2, ch. 3.　　48 Iliad, b. 10, v. 13.
49 Herodotus Thalia, sec. 6.
50 Herodotus Calliope, section 2; 1 Anacharsis, 191, 283; 289; 2 Anacharsis, 31.

who made the trumpet in question. The communication must have been made in or subsequent to the 6th century before the Christian era, possibly several centuries afterwards. But still it furnishes an additional and strong evidence of the fact inferred, namely: that the trumpet and its uses came either mediately or immediately from the countries of the east, where the trumpet was first used. Thence they may have obtained the knowledge of it through various nations; or possibly were the descendants of the very Israelites, who were removed by the Assyrians to the east and north of the Caspian sea and of the Euxine; and who built on the east of the former, the city of Charazen, named after a city of the same name on the east of the river Jordan, and the city of Samarsand, originally, before the name was corrupted, called Samaria, after the city of that name from which the ten tribes were carried into captivity.

CHAPTER IX.

THIS chapter will speak of the Indians within the limits of the United States generally; secondly, of the Indians formerly within the limits of North-Carolina; thirdly, of Indian traditions.

First, then—*Of the Indians within the limits of the United States generally.*

The northern parts of the United States had a much more abundant population, when first known to the Europeans, than had the southern. The density seemed to increase as a travéller advanced to the north, and to diminish as he progressed to the south. North-Carolina contained but a few tribes, and those not very numerous, whilst Virginia was covered all over with small nations, which had been pressed from their more northern abodes by tribes from the north and northwest. Lenopes, a powerful nation from the north or northwest, had crossed the Mississippi, and were travelling to the eastward. Some settlements they made in their progress on the east side of the Mississippi; the rest in great numbers pressed forward till they came to the Delaware, then called the *Lenope Wehittuck*. Then called themselves the Lenni-Lenope, or the first people; meaning, probably, that they were the stock from which their colonies had been set out.[47] Another part of the same Indians went to the Hudson, and seated themselves in the country, having the Hudson to the east, and extending westward beyond the Susquehanna, north to the heads of the Susquehanna and Delaware, south to the hills in New-Jersey and Pennsylvania. From those settlements, some crossed the Hudson and settled the eastern states. Others went south, and settled in Delaware and in Maryland. Their claim

[47] Sand. 124.

of territory extended beyond the Mississippi, to the heads of the Hudson, south to the Potomac, and north beyond the St. Lawrence. The Iroquois, or Mangoacs, had come by force to the lakes, and settled in a part of the country which they now occupy. Their own preservation declared to them the policy and necessity of forming a confederacy against the overwhelming power of the Lenopes. And this they effected. The Mohawks, Gunlocks, Oneidas, Stone-pipe Makers, the Onondagoes, the Cayugas, and the Senacas, or Mountaineers. These were the members which composed the confederacy formed about the year 1650, or earlier, and were called the five nations. Sometimes they are called the Iroquois, sometimes the Senacas, and sometimes the Oneidas, or Mohawks. In 1730, some of the Iroquois were settled on the Allegheny mountains, between this state and North-Carolina. Of these nations, came the Manacons, who settled on James river, above the falls; a part of whom had gone into North-Carolina, and settled on Ta river, Trent and Neuse, and must have come originally from the head waters of the Susquehanna. In the year 1713, when the Tuscaroras had concerted a plan to destroy all the white settlers in North-Carolina, and had actually proceeded to put to death a great proportion of them. They expected assistance from the five nations, but did not receive it. Being severely chastised for this insidious behaviour, a great part of the Tuscaroras left the country, and joined the five nations, in the year 1713; by whom they were received and aided to the confederacy, *because they spoke the same language.* In 1603, the five nations were settled about the site of Montreal; and came, very probably, from the north and northwest. Most certainly they came travelling to the south, for they settled on James river, and on Ta and Neuse rivers, in North-Carolina. They could not have been long settled in North-Carolina, when the white settlers first came into that country. Their connexion with the parent stock was yet recent; they corresponded with it; were probably under its protection and government, and returned again when they could no longer live safely apart from them. Even 50 years' separation in an independent and unconnected state, would have effaced, amongst unlettered savages, all sense of a common origin, and in the third generation it would have had no influence upon them. The Tuscaroras, it would seem from this consideration, had come from the north, and had not been long settled in North-Carolina, in 1712. As they cannot be traced to the west or the northwest of the Mississippi, from whence the Lenopes came, it is probable they came to the lakes in a direction more to the north or northeast. There is nothing in the history of the Lenopes or of the five nations, or of any of their tribes, which can induce a belief, that they erected mounds, worshipped the sun or moon, or built fortifications, enclosing them in intrenchments, or that they sunk wells, which they walled up with stone, or that they had the knowledge of metals. In the year 1766, another part of the Tuscaroras removed to the Susquehanna, and leased out a part of their lands on the Roanoke, in Bertie county, to enable them to defray the expenses of removal. In the year 1806, the Tuscarora nation was said to be extinct in North-Carolina; and those who had old grants for their lands, began to bring forward their claims under them. The Potawatomies also came from some place north of the lakes. They came last, they say, from the country between lake Michigan and the Missouri.[48] The Chippewyans seen by Mr. McKenzie, in the countries northwest of the lakes, were extending their settlements from the northwest to the east and northeast.[49] The era of

48 Sand. 154.   49 1 McKenzie, 143.

BB

the Lenope migrations is nearly ascertainable, by the date of the confederacy of the five nations, and by the Indian traditions relative to the extirpation of the ancient settlers of Kentucky, which the Lenopes found there on their arrival, or which the Iroquois found there after their confederacy was formed. The tradition of the Indians northwest of the Ohio, is, that Kentucky had been settled by whites, and that they had been exterminated by war. They believe that the old fortifications now seen in Kentucky, on the Ohio, were constructed by those white inhabitants. An idea very much confirmed by the white skeletons, and the petrified female found in a cave in Kentucky; and by the colour of their eyes and hair, all which are wholly dissimilar to the Indian complexion, hair, and colour of the eyes. A very aged Shawanese chief on the Auglaise river, concurred in the truth of this tradition. He was 120 years of age, and must have been born some time about the year 1680. An old Indian informed Mr. Moore, that the western country, and particularly Kentucky, had been inhabited by white people, but that they were destroyed by the Indians; that the last battle was fought at the falls of the Ohio, and that the Indians drove the *aborigines* into a small island below the rapids. He stated it to be an undoubted fact, handed down by tradition. When the waters of the Ohio had fallen, a multitude of human bones were discovered on Sandy island, and the Indians told Gen. Clark, of Louisville, that the battle of Sandy island decided finally the fate of Kentucky with its ancient inhabitants. General Clark says, that *Kentuke*, in the language of the Indians, signifies river of blood. And in addition to the proof of a great battle near the falls, it is said by General Clark of Louisville, that there was at Clarksville a great burying ground, two or three hundred yards in length. Some of the Sacs, in 1800, told Colonel Joseph Daveess, that

Kentucky had been the scene of much blood, and was filled with the manes of its butchered inhabitants. The ancient inhabitants, they said, were white, and possessed arts unknown to the Indians. Cornstock told Col. McKee, that it was a current and assured condition, that Kentucky and Ohio had once been settled by white people, possessed of arts not understood by the Indians: that after many severe conflicts they were exterminated. He said, the Great Spirit had once given the Indians a bark, but that they lost it, and had never since regained the knowledge of the arts. He did not know who made the graves on the Ohio and at other places, but that it was not his nation, nor any he had been acquainted with: that it had been handed down from a *very long time ago*, that there had been a nation of white people inhabiting the country, who made the graves and forts. He said, that some Indians, who had travelled very far west and northwest, had found a nation of people who lived like Indians, although of a different complexion. We may judge of the antiquity or recency of the facts preserved by tradition, from the particularity of its details or its generality. After two centuries, it assumes the appearance of fable; but a particularity of detail bespeaks it to be a more recent occurrence. Going back two centuries, we come to 1620 or 1630, the time when the Lenopes spread devastation and the terror of their name through all the countries between the Mississippi and the St. Lawrence, and as far as to the head of Susquehanna. This, too, is not far from the time of the confederacy of the five nations, and not far from the period when the Tuscaroras must have settled on Ta river, Contentnea and Neuse, in North-Carolina. The Creeks were not then the inhabitants of the country now called East Florida and Alabama. In the year 1715, a war broke out between the Yamassee, Creeks and Appalaches on the one side, and the people of Carolina on the other. At a place called the Salt-catchers, they were completely routed and defeated by a body of 1200 men, who opposed their incursions. Fearing to reside where they had before done on the Savannah, they went southwardly and made new settlements in East Florida, which they afterwards extended to Alabama, and even as far as to the Tennessee. In 1731, the Creeks ceded to Governor Oglethorp, some of the Georgia lands, which he intended for the residence of a new colony then about to repair to that province. In 1712, they assisted Barnwell in his expedition against the Tuscaroras. He was joined, at the same time, by the Cherokees and Catawbas. We shall presently see, that the Shawanese also once dwelt on the Savannah, and probably came from the north; as, like the Tuscaroras, they returned to the northern tribes, and, indeed, put themselves under the protection of the five nations; when, like the Tuscaroras, they met with difficulties which they deemed themselves unable to overcome. The presumption is, that they originally came from the countries to which they finally retired, and where they remain to this day. *Savannah* signifies south, or south river. On removing northwardly, some seated themselves on the Ohio, some in Lancaster, some at the falls of Ohio, and some on the spot where Philadelphia now stands. What remains of all the tribe, is now united in a body on Stony creek, a tributary of the Big Miami, and at Wapochonata, on the Auglaise.[50] The Shawanese who settled on the Ohio, claimed the lands on the Cumberland, which was formerly called Shawanœ river, and by the French, Chauvanan, the name by which they denominated the Shawanese. The Cherokees asserted their claim to the same lands. For many years they maintained a most bloody contest; till at length both nations, fearing the consequence of

50 Sand. 151.

meeting each other, abstained from going upon it. This became known to the French and English hunters; and as they expected not to meet with molestation from Indians, and as moreover the game being not killed either by the Shawanese or Cherokees, had from that circumstance become plenteous on the abandoned tract, these hunters came hither as early as 1765 and 1769; and returning home, reported to the frontier settlements the fertility and natural advantages of the country, and soon roused by their animated representations a new spirit of emigration, which after some time broke out into action. Immense numbers of the ancient inhabitants are buried in all the caves, and at every lasting spring, on both sides of the Cumberland river, from the mouth to the head. This proves an ancient population far exceeding the numbers of the Shawanese at any period of their history. The mounds built by that ancient population have trees standing upon them as large as any in the forest, bearing invincible testimony that their burials and mounds preceded the arrival of the Shawanese, and that the people who made them were no portion either of the Shawanese or Cherokees, or any other tribe of Indians east of the Mississippi. The Savanners, or the Shawanese, or Shawanœs, or Chauvaṇans, so called from living on the Savannah or South river, must have received the name from those who lived in the north, not from those who lived in the east or west, for then it would have been called west or east river. This is another indication, that it was settled by persons from the north. General Robertson stated in his lifetime, in relation to the Shawanese, what he had learned of it from the Indians. They say, that about a century and a half ago, the Shawanese were settled in this country, and were scattered over it, from the Tennessee to the spot where Nashville now is, and even considerably north of the Cumberland. A little more than a century ago, or about the year 1700, they left this country, and went to the northern tribes, and were received by the six nations as a wandering tribe, but were *not allowed to have any claim to the soil,* further than to obtain temporary subsistence at the discretion of the six nations. In 1772, the Little Corn-planter, an intelligent Cherokee chief, who was then supposed to be 90 years of age, stated, in giving a history of his own nation, that the *Savannechers,* which was the name universally given by the Indians to those whom the English call Shawanese, removed from Savannah river, between Georgia and South-Carolina, by the permission of the Cherokees, to Cumberland; they having been fallen upon, and almost ruined, by a combination of several of the neighbouring tribes of Indians. That many years afterwards, a difference took place between the two nations, and the Cherokees, unexpectedly to the Shawanese, marched in a large body to the frontiers of the latter. There dividing into several small parties, they *treacherously,* as he expressed himself, fell upon them, and put to death a great number. The Shawanese then forted themselves, and maintained a long war, in defence of their possession of the country, even after the Chickasaws had joined the Cherokees. He observed, that when he was a small boy, which must have been about 1699, he remembered to have heard his father, who was a great chief, say, that he once took a large party against the Shawanese; and after taking several scalps, was returning home with his party, through a difficult pass in the mountain, where he met another large party of his own nation going to war, who took him for an enemy, and *fired* on him before they discovered their mistake, and killed five or six of his men. The Little Corn-planter distinctly recollected having seen Shawanese scalps brought into his nation:

In the year 1779, General Robertson was in the Illinois country, and heard Mr. Charleville, a very respectable man of the age of 84 years, say, that when he was about 15, which was about the year 1710, he had attended an old trader, who had long carried on a traffic with the Shawanese. His store at the time was kept in a *fort*, which stood in the mound, situated a short distance below the mouth of the lick branch, on what is now the Nashville side of the Cumberland river. The Shawanese then were, and for a long time had been, so much harassed by their enemies, that they had been going off in small parties for several years. Their numbers were then small, and they had come to a determination to leave the country entirely. That he (Charleville) was sent off by the trader, in *March*, with several loads of skins; and that the trader was to follow him in May or June, when the Indians should break up. The Chickasaws got notice of the intended removal of the Shawanese; and resolved to strike a decisive blow, and, if possible, to make themselves masters of the stores of the Shawanese. A large body of Chickasaws posted themselves on both sides of the Cumberland river, and just above the mouth of Harpeth river, provided with bark canoes to prevent escape by water. They attacked the Shawanese, killed all or the greater part of them, and the trader, and took all their property. This affair has been handed down, like all their other traditions, from one generation to another, and is yet repeated by many of the Chickasaws. It is well known, he remarked, that the Savannah river was called after the Shawanese, when they were known by the name of *Savannehers*; where also are to be seen, the same sort of artificial mounds that abound in this country. About the year 1710, this removal took place. The Shawanese had lived here as early as 1650, if not earlier. And as the hostilities of these tribes did

'not 'cease by any formal treaty of peace, they continued to destroy each other whenever an opportunity offered. And afraid of meeting each other,
wholly abstained from this country. French hunters came from Orleans and Illinois, to take game;
the skins and furs of which they carried to Orleans
and sold advantageously. From them the French
lick received its name; and so did Harpeth river.
After remaining unoccupied by any of the human
species for more than 60 years, the country which
they had left, began again to be settled under the
auspices of General Robertson. The Cherokees
were settled on the Tennessee; and claimed the
country, except as against the Iroquois, from thence
to the Cumberland river, as early as 1650. And
it was not without their permission, that the Shawanese settled on the Cumberland river. There was
in 1730, as related by Dr. Brickell, in his work
published in Dublin in 1737, a nation of Indians
called the Iroquois, or *Senegars;* which nation,
and that of the Cherokees, were in 1730, very powerful. They then lived near the Alleghenies, on
the east side, which were then called the *Cherahes*
mountains; and in 1730 had been a long time at
war with the Tuscaroras, and could not be per-
suaded by the whites to make peace with them.
For some years, however, before 1730, they had
not made any inroads upon the Tuscaroras, and for
that reason were supposed to be at war with some
nation west of the *Cherahes* mountains. The Iroquois then had the character of being an erratic
tribe, who *travelled* over all the countries *between*
the gulf of Mexico and the river St. Lawrence. A
part of them were, in the year 1730, at the foot of
the mountains which divide this state from North-
Carolina, 15 days' journey from the then frontier
settlements of North-Carolina.[51] The Indian town
in which the king lived, was in less than a day's

51 Brickell, 389.

journey from the foot of the mountains. The king's houses were in the centre of the town. The rest of the buildings were not arranged, like an ancient town in the county of White, where the buildings were in a cluster within the limits of a circle. Having passed one ridge of mountains, Mr. Brickell came to another, higher than the former, with large trees in several places, but little or no pasture. From it there was a beautiful prospect, of large trees and forests. The explorers returned from thence to the east. The war that raged for many years between the Cherokees and Shawanese prior to 1730, accounts for the reason why they had suffered the Tuscaroras to remain undisturbed, from 1712, when they, with the Creeks and Catawbas, aided Barnwell in the war which he waged with the Tuscaroras. They were neutrals in the war which the Tuscaroras commenced in 1715, in which, by an army commanded by Colonel Moore, their fort on Contentnea was taken; and after sustaining immense loss, they were compelled to sue for peace, and obtained it in 1717. The interval between these periods, is that spoken of by Doctor Brickell, in which no disturbance was given by the Cherokees to the Tuscaroras. The vigilant attention which their safety required to be employed in watching the movements of the Shawanese, and in penetrating and preventing their designs, left no time for the indulgence of their inveterate animosity against the humbled and dispirited Tuscaroras.

The Cherokees were firmly established on the Tennessee river, or Hogohege, before the year 1650, and had the dominion over all the country on the east side of the Allegheny mountains, which includes the head waters of the Yadkin, Catawba, Broad river, and the head waters of the Savannah. From thence westwardly, they set up a claim as far as the Ohio, and from thence to the head waters of the Catahouche and Alabama. One tradition which

they have amongst them, says, they came from the
west, and exterminated the former inhabitants; and
then says, they came from the upper parts of the
Ohio, where they erected the mounds on Grave
creek, and that they removed hither from the country where Monticello is situated. They are not
noticed by Mr. Jefferson, in his table of original
tribes which inhabited any part of Virginia at or
subsequent to the year 1606, and from thence up to
1669. They say themselves, that their nation did
not erect the mounds, nor paint the figures of the sun
and moon upon the rocks where they are now seen.
And they say, that their nation never paid adoration to those luminaries, nor to images of any sort.

Section 2.—*Of the Indians of North-Carolina
in* 1730 *and before.*

As the Cherokees came from a country east of
the Alleghenies, and are supposed to be a distinct
race from those who extended their settlements from
Mexico to the Alleghenies, it will be proper, as far
as possible, to state the laws, manners and religion
of other nations, who were the neighbours of the
Cherokees before their removal. Of this description were the Indians of North-Carolina in 1730
and before. These were, as Doctor Brickell informs us, the Iroquois, Pasquotanks, Tuteloes, Mo-
henens, Cherokees, Catawbas, Tuscaroras, Macha-
pungoes, Caroniues, Sapponies, Toleras, Keyawies,
Curratukes, Pamlicoes, Mattamuskeets, Chowan-
ches, Marattas, Mangoacs, Cores, Weapomeacs, and
Chesopians. They hold a great festival, at which
they give a traditional relation of what happened
amongst them for many ages past, to their young
men; having no other method of recording what
their ancestors have done; and which are known
by traditions from father to son, and by their hieroglyphics. Some of them said, that they were descended from an old man, who came hither in a
boat, which they called a canoe. They cannot de-

termine whether this were after or before the great deluge. ～ In general, the memory is preserved amongst them of a deluge; but whether to be understood of the universal deluge, or of the inundation of some particular provinces, Doctor Brickell will not determine. They deemed it very dishonourable to cut off their hair and sell it, which they sometimes do, when drunk; but when sober, considered it the greatest affront that could be offered, if a proposal were made to them to sell their hair.[52] The same sentiment prevailed amongst the nations of Asia.[53] When a young Indian wishes to have a certain girl for a wife, it is proposed to the father or mother, or nearest relations, who reply, that they will consider of it. An assembly is then held, to consider of the proposed match. The girl is spoken to, to know if she is willing; if she assents, the husband pays the stipulated price. The like custom is in Mexico, India, and amongst the Assyrians.[53] Or if he does not pay the price, he keeps the girl at his house, without consummating the marriage, till the price is paid. This custom came to America from the old world, where in ancient times it almost universally prevailed.[54] They never marry so near as a first cousin; but a man may marry two sisters, *or a brother's wife.*[55] They preferred marrying one of their own tribe: when that cannot be done, they marry strangers. An incestuous connexion with one's own sister, if she prove fruitful, is punished with burning the offender, and throwing his ashes into the river.[55] They separate when convenient; and whoever takes an abandoned

52 Brickell, 293.

53 1 Dub. 352; 2 Melena, 10; 1 Dufins, 208; 1 Her. 247.

53 Isaiah, ch. 7, v. 20; 1 Chron. ch. 19, v. 4; 3 Roll. 36; 2 Herodotus, 294; 1 Sam. ch. 18, v. 25.

54 1 O.L. 25; Gen. ch. 24, v. 10, 53, ch. 29, v. 28, ch. 34, v. 22.

55 Genesis, ch. 28; Deut. ch. 25; Numb. ch. 36; Genesis, ch. 49, v. 10; Leviticus, ch. 18, ch. 20.

55 Deuteronomy, ch. 27, v. 22.

228

wife, must pay the price of her to her former husband. If turned away without cause, she keeps the presents made to her before marriage. The widow of an indebted husband is not bound to pay his debts; but if another man takes her, he is; and for the shortest connexion, he becomes liable for all the dead husband's debts, but may indemnify himself by selling her to another for his own or less price. Women, after childbirth, absent themselves from the company of men for forty days.[56] They assume names, as fox, wolf, panther, &c. They have no sabbath. The months they name from the productions of the month, as honey month for March, strawberry month for April, mulberry month for May. Others name them by the trees that bud or blossom at particular seasons of the year, such as dogwood tree, &c. Others distinguish the time of the year from the flight of birds, and the gobling of turkey cocks. They shake hands and scratch the shoulders of those they esteem, which are looked upon as the greatest marks of sincerity and affection, which can be shown amongst them, not only to strangers, but to each other. When going to war, their hair is combed, and anointed with bear's grease and the red-root, and they adorn it with feathers of various beautiful colours, besides copper and iron rings, and sometimes wampum or peak in the ears. And they paint their faces all over, as red as vermilion, making a circle of black about one eye, and another circle of white about the other. When they go to war, they carry their idol with them, and ask counsel of it as the ancients used to do of the oracle of Apollo. They scalp their prisoners, and stick their bodies full of pitch pine, and burn them like torches, making them dance around the fire, buffeting and degrading them till they expire. The weapons they kill or wound their enemies with, are kept with the blood upon them as

56 Leviticus, ch. 12, v. 2, 4.

trophies of their victory. But after the English
colonists came into their neighbourhood, they sold
their prisoners to them as slaves. To encourage
the young men to be industrious in planting their
maize and pulse, they place a kind of idol in the
field, dressed up exactly like an Indian, with a great
quantity of wampum or money, that is made of
conch shells hanging about his neck. This image
none of the young men dared approach, the old
ones not suffering it; but telling them that it is a
former warrior, who died many years ago, and is
now come to see if they work well, and to report
their good conduct to the *good spirit*, to send them
plenty of corn, and to make them good hunters and
warriors. The old men sit around the image, paying
it the most profound respect, and maintaining invi-
olable silence. They sit on benches or mats. The
infliction of punishment for offences, is often left by
their kings to the nearest relation of the deceased,[57]
who prosecutes with great rage and fury; but his
revenge may be commuted for wampum, beads or
tobacco. When they live in the neighbourhood of
a river, they wash frequently every day. This
custom prevailed in India,[58] as well as amongst the
Israelites.[59] They will not walk over a tree that
lies across across their path. They get their fire
by friction.[60] They make an offering of their first
fruits, and they throw 'the first bit or spoonful of
every meal they sit down to into the ashes near the
fire;[61] and they say this ceremony is for the same
purpose with them, as what the Europeans do when
going to victuals they pull off their hats and talk
over it. They make fires and cast the powder of

57 2 Samuel, ch. 14, v. 7 ; Jos. Ant. b. 7, ch. 8, sec. 4.
58 1 Dub. 57, 95, 160, 210, 213, 218 ; 2 Dub. 12, 15, 16, 109.
59 Exodus, ch. 29, v. 4, ch. 30, v. 19, 20, 21, ch. 40, v. 12 ;
Leviticus. ch. 14, v. 8 ; Deut. ch. 23, v. 11 ; Leviticus, ch. 14,
v. 9. 15, 16, ch. 16, v. 4, 24, ch. 22, v. 6, ch. 17, v. 16 ; 2 Kings,
ch. 5, v. 10, 12, 13 ; 2 Chron. ch. 4. v. 6 ; Job, ch. 9, v. 30.
60 2 Dub. 48. 61 1 Dub. 144.

tobacco into them, as a sacrifice to the gods; and when overtaken by a storm upon the water, they cast some of it into the air or water.   This is performed with strange ceremonies, stamping, leaping, dancing, clapping of hands, and uttering of strange words.   Some of them, says Dr. Brickell, use the *Jewish custom of circumcision.*   He knew but two families who were circumcised, and could never induce them to give the reason why they did so.. Whenever he urged them upon the subject, they were silent,[62] which according to the Indian custom, is a refusal to answer.   When a person dies, the nearest relation is the principal mourner, and he is clad in moss.   He, with a stick in his hand, keeps up a mournful ditty three or four days, his face being made black with the smoke and soot of the pitch pine, mingled with bear's grease.   To all who pass, he tells the name of the deceased, and the feats he has done in his lifetime.   On the death of a king or great man, they place the nearest relations near the corpse, who mourn and weep with dishevelled hair.[63]   They sit upon mats at the funeral of a great man.   They consider many, wives and children as a great blessing.   In India, no number of children is too great.   It is a misfortune and disgrace not to have them.   One cannot there be happy, and not have them.[64]   The same sentiments had the Hebrews.[65]   The bones of their dead are carefully preserved, and removed with them in their migrations.[66]

62 The Hebrews were always silent as to the above name, and as to matters of religion, when interrogated by strangers. Jos. An. b, 1, ch. 13, b. 3, ch. 5, sec. 4.   The same silence was observed by the Greeks on similar occasions as may be seen by several passages of Herodotus.

63 2 Chron. ch. 25, v. 25; Amos, ch. 9, v. 16; Jeremiah, ch. 9, v. 17; Job. ch. 3, v. 8.

64 1 Dub. 301, 311; 2 Dub. 93, 119, 170, 172, 173, 174.

65 Genesis, ch. 30, v. 1, ch. 15, v. 2, ch. 30, v. 23; Leviticus, ch. 20, v. 20; Jeremiah, ch. 22, v. 30.

66 Genesis, ch. 50, v. 25; Exodus, ch. 13, v. 19; 1 Sam. ch. 13, v. 13; 1 Chron. ch. 10; 2 Samuel, ch. 21, v. 12, 13, 14.

CHAPTER X.

THE history of the Cherokees will now receive an undivided attention, not only because in all their principal customs, religious notions, and political institutions, they differ in all respects from the aborigines of Tennessee and Kentucky, but also, because they in the subsequent parts of this narra- tive, are the principal actors in the transactions which are to be detailed.

We will consider, first, of the countries from whence they came; secondly, of their military character; thirdly, of their traditions; fourthly, of their computation of time; fifthly, of their Hebraic rites; and sixthly, of their political government, laws, and civil customs.

First—Of the Countries from whence they came.

The truth is, that although they set up a claim for the country upon the Cumberland, and from thence to the Tennessee, they did not found it upon the expulsion of the aborigines; but on driving the Shawanese from the river Cumberland. Their claim to the country, was not a perfect one. It was only better in their own estimation, than that which the Shawanese had. This fact became very apparent in the year 1766, when a treaty was made at fort Stanwix, under the authority of the king of Great-Britain, by Sir William Johnson, the king's agent for Indian affairs, with the Iroquois, in the month of November in the same year. The latter there claimed all the lands south of the Ohio, as far as the Tennessee river. An incident which took place at the treaty, affords conclusive evidence of the sense entertained by the Cherokees, of the claim which the Iroquois were then about to surrender. Some of the visiting Cherokees on their route had killed game for their support; and on their arrival at fort Stanwix, tendered the skins to the Six Nations, saying, "They are yours, we killed them after passing the big river," the name by which they had always designated the Tennessee. By the treaty of fort Stanwix, the Six Nations ceded all their right southeast of the Ohio, down to the Cherokee river, which they stated to be their *just right,* and vested the soil and sovereignty thereof in the king of Great-Britain. By the treaty of 1783, he resigned his sovereignty and dominion, leaving the land to those states in whose limits they were. The Six Nations have a traditionary history which states them not to be the aborigines of the country; but conquerors of the first possessors. The abandonment of the conquered tribes, they relied on as the evidence necessary to perfect their title, the only one to be relied on in unlettered and savage negotiations. The right is that of conquest, acknowledged perfect amongst nations, when either a treaty at the end of the war confirmed it, or the conquered nation is wholly extinct, or flies to foreign countries, leaving theirs in the possession of their enemies. In the year 1781, Col. Croghan, who had lived thirty years amongst the Indians as deputy superintendent, deposed, that the Six Nations claim, by right of conquest, all the lands on the southeast side of the river Ohio, down to the Cherokee river, and on the west side down to the Big Miami, otherwise called Stony river; but that the lands on the west side of the Ohio, below Stony river, were always supposed to belong to the Indians of the western confederacy. That he has for thirty years been intimately acquainted with the above country, and the Indians, and their different claims to territory, and never heard the Six Nations claim, and knows they never did claim, beyond the above description; nor did they ever dispute the claims of the western confederacy. The aborigines then having been expelled by the western confederacy, and the Six

Nations, and the Cherokees being entitled to no part of those lands, it follows that the Cherokees did not belong to either of these confederacies. The settlement of the Cherokees on the south side of Holston and Big Tennessee, is an admission of the correctness of the claim set up by the Iroquois at fort Stanwix in 1766. If it be true, that the Natchez once possessed all the country between the Iberville and the Wabash, and from the Mississippi to the Alleghenies, the conquest must have been made of them by the Iroquois and Chickasaws; for the latter have claimed the land on the Mississippi, and as far as to the Tennessee, ever since they were known to us. The historical fact seems to be established, that the people from the north overran and exterminated the aborigines. Before the year 1690, the Cherokees, who were once settled on the Appomattox river, and in the neighbourhood of Monticello, left their former abodes and came to the west. The Powhatans are said by their descendants to have been once a part of this nation. The probability is, that migration took place about or soon after the year 1623, when the Virginians suddenly and unexpectedly fell upon the Indians, killing all they could find, cutting up and destroying their crops, and causing vast numbers to perish by famine. They came to New river and made a temporary settlement, and also on the head of Holston. But owing to the enmity of the *northern Indians,* they removed in a short time to the Little Tennessee, to a place now called the middle settlements. Cornelius Dogherty, a refugee of James the second's party, came to those settlements shortly after the accession of King William, probably about the year 1690. He died in 1788, at a very advanced age. He said that he was 120 years of age. He was a trader, and sent peltry, by the Indians packed to Charleston, who returned also packed with merchandise, which they received in exchange. He

Dd

afterwards taught the Indians to steal horses from Virginia, which were the first horses the Cherokees ever had. Another tribe of Indians came from the neighbourhood of Charleston, in South-Carolina, and settled themselves lower down the Tennessee. The Carolina tribe called themselves Ketawaugas, and came last into the country. The Cherokees found white people near the head of Little Tennessee, who had forts from thence down the Tennessee river to the mouth of Chicamauga. They had a fort at Pumpkintown, one at Fox Taylor's reserve near Hamilton courthouse, and one on Big Chicamauga, about twenty miles above its mouth. The Cherokees waged war against them, and drove them to the mouth of Big Chicamauga, where they entered into a treaty, by which they agreed to depart the country, if the Cherokees would permit them to do so in peace; which they did. Mr. Brown, a Scotchman, came into the Cherokee nation in the year 1761, and settled on the Hiwassee river, or near it. He saw on the Hiwassee and Tennessee, remains of old forts, about which were hoes, axes, guns, and other metallic utensils. The Indians of that time told him, that the French had formerly been there, and built those forts. When the Cherokees first came to the country, they found no Indians, but great appearance of the country having been once inhabited. The mounds, which are perhaps more numerous in the country they settled than in any other portion of the United States, exhibited the same appearances at the arrival of the Cherokees, as they now do. The former inhabitants appeared to have lived in houses, which on the outside seemed to be of the colour of a blacksmith's coal-pit. The houses were made by setting up poles, and then digging out the dirt, and covering the poles with it. They were round, and generally about ten feet in diameter. At the time the Cherokees came to this country, the Creeks were living on, and claimed all the southern waters; but did not occupy any place on the waters of the Tennessee. When the Cherokees settled on the waters of the Savannah, and on those of Coosa, a general war ensued between them and the Creeks, which ended by the Cherokees keeping the country of which they had taken possession. The war between them ended about the year 1710. The farthest extent of the Cherokee settlements was about the town of Seneca, in what is now called Pendleton district, in South-Carolina. From thence, at late periods, they carried on war against the whites to Long-cane, Ninety-six, and Saluda. When they first settled on the Little Tennessee they were numerous; but owing to the hostility of all the neighbouring nations, they were soon obliged to live all together in fortified towns. They were generally engaged in war, sometimes with the Creeks, sometimes with the Shawanese, and sometimes with the Indians west of the Mississippi. About the year 1730 or 1735, on an expedition against the western Indians, a party of Cherokees took, on the Mississippi, the crew of a French boat prisoners, amongst whom was Francis Budwine. He lived amongst them, and in the family into which Star married. Star has lived amongst them nearly forty years. He married a Harlin, a half breed, whose grandmother, Mrs. Ward, is now said to be 115 years of age. Star has always enjoyed the confidence of the Cherokee nation, and for some time officiated as priest amongst them, or as the white people call it, *conjurer*. He is a man of good natural sense, and a man of veracity; and from him has been received the foregoing statement.

The Cherokees have in their language, names for whales and sea serpents, and from thence it might reasonably be conjectured once lived on the shores of an ocean in the northern regions of America.

The names of places given by the Cherokees, and others of the northern tribes within the limits of the United States, east of the Mississippi, may be of some weight in the scale of evidence to show the countries from whence they originally came. Colonists and emigrants everywhere give to the countries in which they establish themselves, the names of places which they left in their own country. In the state of New-York, is a mountain in sight of Cohoe, which the Indians call Ararat. Oonolaskky is the Cherokee word for *near to.*

In New-England is a nation called Pequods, so much like the Pekoos of Ezekiel.[67] There are Indian towns on the south side of the Susquehanna called Konoa. The Jennessee, so like to the river Yenesee, which runs into the Frozen ocean in Europe. The river Taa after the river Taz, and sometimes Ta in the same country with the Yenesee. Niagara after the western point of the Euxine, which is called Nagara. The Tenare, as formerly written, but now corrupted into Tennessee, after the river Tanais. The White mountains towards Japan, one of the Tartarean boundaries, is the name applied to the Unaca near the Cherokee settlements, which in their language signifies *white.*

The Cherokees had an oration in which was contained the history of their migrations, which was lengthy, but now nearly lost. It says, towns of people in many nights' encampment removed. It is very certain, says Mr. Hicks, that the Cherokees came from the seacoast, where whales and sea snakes abounded. The names of monsters of the deep are still retained amongst them. Their traditions say, that they came from the rising sun, and were placed upon this land by the divine orders of the four councils sent from above. The memorial of their migrations had been kept up in the former part of his mother's time, by orations

67 Ezekiel, ch. 23, v. 23; Boudinot, 141.

delivered at the national festival of the green corn dance every year. The only settlements noticed by the Cherokees were near Nolichucky; but having been long settled there, they could not go farther back to others. But they have farther and more recent accounts of numerous settlements on the heads of Hiwassee, upwards of 170 years age, that is, prior to the year 1652, or as early as the period when Cornelius Dogherty came to the nation, Mr. Hicks says about the year 1697. His children by the first wife are all dead, and the eldest of his second wife's children are more than 70 years of age. Their grandmother died in 1774 or 1775. She was a girl 12 years of age when the first gun was introduced amongst the Cherokees. Supposing forty years between the birth of the grandmother, and the birth of these grandchildren, we shall be carried back 110 years, to the year 1665, for her birth, and to the year 1677 for the first introduction of fire-arms amongst the Cherokees. The country around Fortville and the Little Tennessee up to its head, he thinks has been settled very long; because Chola had claimed to be the eldest brother in the nation, and was acknowledged by all the red people to be such. They had no certain accounts of any nation of red people found living on the Tennessee, except the Creeks near the mouth of Hiwassee river, and some Shawanese on the Cumberland.

Section 2.—*Of their Military Character.*

When the white people in North-Carolina first became acquainted with the Cherokees in the year 1712, they placed their chief happiness in military glory. In the hazardous enterprises of war, they were animated by a restless spirit, which goaded them into new exploits, and to the acquisition of fresh stocks of martial renown. The white people for some years previous to 1730, interposed their good offices to bring about a pacification between the Tuscaroras, with whom they had long waged incessant war. Their reply was, "We cannot live without war. Should we make peace with the Tuscaroras with whom we are at war, we must immediately look out for some other, with whom we can be engaged in our beloved occupation." We must not be surprised at this statement; for what but the same sentiment impels the most enlightened members of civilized society, to leave the arms of a beloved wife, and the circle of endearing friends, to seek the onsets and the blasts of war in countries beyond the ocean, where not one being on either side in the hosts of combatants is known to him. There he takes side with one or the other, and rushes on the first opportunity that offers, with desperate determination into the thickest crowd of the embattled legions, which he has chosen for his foe. It is that he may enjoy the ravishing delight of mounting on the admiration of the world to military glory, in which is contained the keenest sensation of pleasure that is known to human sensibility. Man does not kill and tear in pieces like the eagle or the vulture, for the purpose of satisfying a hungered appetite; but for the acquisition of a fancied good, one which vanishes away for ever so soon as it comes within the reach of the eager wooer, to whom the delusive goddess has promised her favours. The thirst for military glory in individuals, is supposed to be of less utility than when it belongs to nations; for in the latter instance, it is oftentimes the parent of great national advantages. It is a defence against foreign invasion, or the interference of foreigners with our national rights. In this point of view it is of the highest utility. But whenever it leads a nation to disregard and trespass upon the rights of others, and to estimate physical power more than the natural duties it owes to other men, then immediately the country of its residence is transferred into a den of tigers, who take for the

law of their conduct the cupidity of bloodless desire. Actuated by the restless activity of this sentiment, there have been but few intervals in the history of the Cherokees, when they have permitted
themselves to sink into the inglorious arms of peace,
and be employed only in the less perilous slaughter
of the wild beasts of the wilderness. They have
hardly ever ceased to sigh for danger, and to aspire
to the rank which is attained by acts of heroic valor.
They could not abstain from acting a part in the
war of the whites, against the Tuscaroras, in 1713.
Soon afterwards they warred themselves against
the white people, and made peace with them in
1719. And from those days to the present, their
history is intimately connected and blended with
that of North-Carolina and Tennessee. In 1730
they were at war with the French. In 1756 they
were at war with the people of North-Carolina.
In 1755 they made a treaty with Governor Dobbs,
and were united in war with the colonists till 1758
or 1759. In the latter of these years they invested
fort Dobbs, situated on a creek of the Yadkin, above
Salisbury, in what is now the county of Iredell, and
made peace in the year 1760. Small incidents
sometimes show the genuine character of a people,
more clearly than it can be perceived through any
other medium. When in the last mentioned war
the Cherokees had pushed their inroads almost to
Salisbury in North-Carolina, in various dispersed
detachments, destined to fall upon the frontiers at
different points, as nearly as possible at the same
moment of time, one of those parties consisting of
six or eight men were discovered, watched, and
pursued till they entered into a deserted cabin to
sleep there for the night. Early in the morning
the whites were posted around the house, and so
placed behind a fodder stack, and some small out-
houses, as to be ready to shoot both at the top of
the chimney, and the door; and they had begun to

throw fire upon the roof of the house. One of the Indians within observed to his comrades, that it was better for one to die than that all should; and that if they would follow his directions, he would save all of the company but himself. He ordered them to stand ready, and to issue through the door as soon as he should have extracted the fire of the assailants, and then to go off as fast as they could. They agreed to obey his commands. He issued through the door, and skipped hither and thither, from one place to another, till all the whites had fired upon him. He feel and expired. His companions in arms, before the guns of the whites could be again charged, rushed through the space between them, and escaped unhurt. How greatly is it to be regretted that the name of this hero is not known to the writer, that it might be recorded with this specimen of Cherokee bravery and patriotism, firmness and presence of mind in the hour of danger!

The Cherokees, by the year 1761, had lost sight of their old enemies, the Tuscaroras, who by partial removals, in 1713, 1733, and 1766, had been reduced in North-Carolina to insignificance. They still kept at war with the Shawanese; and being unable to endure the unchequered scenes of peaceful indolence, they took umbrage at some alleged conduct of the unoffensive Chickasaws—that people who had formerly assisted them in driving the Shawanese from the Cumberland river. But they had not in the event the same cause for self-gratulation as the wolf had, who rejected all the arguments of the defenceless lamb. The Chickasaws, like the chafed rattlesnakes of their country, when forced into hostilities, are capable of dreadful resistance. They met the thunderbolts of war at the Chickasaw old fields, shortly before the year 1769, and gave them a most signal overthrow, compelling them to retreat by the way of Cumberland river and the Cany Fork, where as they marched they enclosed themselves in forts, as a safeguard against the assaults of their incensed enemy, by practising upon whom they expected to keep alive their own military spirit.

After they first came to the Little Tennessee, their traditions say, that there were some Creeks near the mouth of Hiwassee river. These were their nearest neighbours, and in the war which the Cherokees waged with the Shawanese on Cumberland river, pretended to be in friendship with the former; but at the same time secretly abetted the Shawanese. The Cherokees, at one of their national festivals at Chota, for their duplicity and treachery, fell upon them and cut them nearly all off. The consequence of this act was an immediate war between the Cherokees and Creeks, which after being sometime prosecuted, caused the Creeks to abandon their settlements, and the waters of the Tennessee: A large body of them went as low as the Creek path, and there went across over on the Coosa river, from which circumstance it has ever since retained the name. It is further stated in the traditionary history, that a large body of the Creeks once made settlements at the island on the Creek path, and that the Cherokees went thither, and by stratagem drew the Creeks from the island, with numbers of canoes, to the place where they formerly lay in ambush, who rose and had a severe battle with them, took their canoes, went into the island, and destroyed whatsoever they could find there. A chief of the name of Bullhead, had a command in this war. His bravery is greatly extolled by tradition, and he is supposed to have been the person who planned and conducted the measures put in practice against the Creeks.

Section 3.—*Of the Biblical Traditions of the Cherokees and other Indians on and east of the Mississippi, and of their Hebraic Customs.*

It is a tradition amongst the southern Indians of the United States, that their ancestors once had a

Ee

book, and that whilst they had it they prospered exceedingly; but that the white people bought it of them and learned many things, whilst the Indians lost their credit, offended the Great Spirit, and suffered greatly from the neighbouring nations. That the Great Spirit took pity on them, and directed them to this country. That on their way they came to a great river which they could not pass, when God dried up the waters and they passed dry shod. They say their forefathers had a divine spirit, by which they could foretel future events, and control the common course of nature; and this they transmitted to their children on condition of obeying the sacred laws. That they did by these means bring down showers of plenty on the beloved people. But that this power had for a long time ceased.

In 1764 an Indian from the west of the Mississippi, who had never before seen a white man, related to an intelligent clergyman as one of their traditions, that a great while ago they had a common father, who lived towards the rising sun, and governed. That all the white people's heads were under his feet. That he had twelve sons by whom he administered the government. That his authority was derived from the Great Spirit by some special gift from him. That the twelve sons tyrannized over the people, and greatly abused their power, and offended the Great Spirit, who suffered the white people to introduce spirituous liquors amongst them, which was followed by various consequences, and by their subjection to the white people. But that they had a tradition, that the time would come, when the Indians would regain the gift of the Great Spirit and their ancient power, when the white people would be in subjection to them.[68]

An old Indian on the Ohio, more than fifty years ago related to a clergyman, that an uncle of his,

68 Isaiah, ch. 11, v. 11, 15

who died in 1728, had stated to him several traditions and customs of former times, and amongst
others, that circumcision was practised amongst the
Indians in old times; but had been disused because
of the mockery the young men made of it. He also
mentioned the deluge, and that all mankind perished, except a few, who had been saved in a canoe.
He also mentioned the building of a high place,
and the loss of language that happened there, and
the great confusion and misunderstanding which
took place in consequence of it.

The Hurons and the Iroquois say, that the first
white man came from heaven, and had twins,
and that the elder killed the younger. The
Mohawks also had the mutilitated story of Cain
and Abel. The Conewauches say, that angels
in old times frequently visited the people, instructed them how to pray, and to appease the
Great Spirit when he was offended. They were
to offer sacrifice, burn tobacco,[69] and buffalo and
deer's bones.

On the way from the lakes of Canada by the
lakes of the Woods, between that and the South
sea, the Indians have a tradition, that they originally came from another country inhabited by wicked
people, and had traversed a great lake, where they
had suffered great hardships and much misery; it
being always winter, with ice and deep snows. At
a place they called Coppermine river, where they
made the first land, the ground was covered with
copper, over which a body of earth had since been
collected of a man's height. They believe that in
ancient times their ancestors had lived till their feet
were worn out with walking, and their throats with
eating. They described a deluge when the waters
overspread the whole earth except the highest
mountain, on the top of which they were preserved.
They believe in a future judgment.[70]

69 Exodus, ch. 30, v. 7, 8.   70 McKenzie, 113.

The Indians to the east of New-Jersey say, that their ancestors once used circumcision; but not being able to assign any good reason for its continuance, they abolished the practice. Mr. McKenzie says, that the appearance of circumcision was general among the Stone and Dogrib Indians, far to the northwest of the lakes of Canada. They live about 200 or 300 miles east of Kamschatka.

One of the ancient traditions of the Cherokees is, that once a whale swallowed a little boy, and after some time spewed him upon the land.[71]

Some of the Indian nations stoned to death for adultery.[72] Some of them employed hired mourners.[73] Some buried in caves.[74] Some assign semicircular positions for their chiefs in the congregational assemblies. Some do not eat of the hollow of the thigh. Some grieve by putting the hand to the mouth, and the mouth to the ground. Some collect and remove with them the bones of the dead. Some retained the observance of a jubilee. Some anointed their beloved men, when inducted into high offices.[75] They observed the purification and separation of women, on the occurrence of lunar impurity. They have clean and unclean animals, fastings and ablutions. Some worship towards the east, puffing the smoke of tobacco towards the sun, and towards the cardinal points. Some consecrate the conch shell to sacred uses. Some have a tradition of a good and evil spirit, the latter of whom was bound, and that the Great Spirit is *Abba*, father. One extraordinary feature of this people, which belongs to no other upon the earth but the Israelites, is the incapability to suffer commixture or consolidation with other nations, which makes them prefer in all instances extinction to it. Another peculiarity

71 Jonah, ch. 1, v. 17, ch. 2, v. 1, 10—626 before Christ.
72 Leviticus, ch. 20, v. 10.
73 Amos, ch. 9, v. 16; Jeremiah, ch. 9, v. 17; Job, ch. 8, v. 8.
74 Genesis, ch. 33, v. 19, ch. 49, v. 29; John, ch. 11, v. 38.
75 1 Samuel, ch. 10, v. 1, ch. 16, v. 13.

common to the Indians and the Israelites, is their aversion to *strange* women, with whom the Israelites thought it the greatest disgrace to have any connexion. These Indians were never known to violate, or even attempt the chastity of female captives.[76]

Section 4.—*Of their computation of Time.*

It is to be noticed as a singular mark of distinction between the northern and southern Indians, that the Mexicans, like the Chaldeans, Syrians, Persians, and Egyptians, begin their day from sunrising; because, being worshippers of the sun, that was the moment when they paid their adoration to him. The Hebrews counted in the same way till after the exodus; and then, Moses, to lead the Israelites as far as possible from any conformity or intercourse with the idolatrous nations which surrounded them, instituted a new year, to be counted by lunar revolutions, or mooneths, or months, and to begin at the first new moon in March, because in that month the Iraelites came from Egypt. In this month also, their festivals commenced, and their day began in the evening. This institution immediately removed the Israelites from all the festivals held by the sun's worshippers, from all computation of time made by his motion, from all want of the knowledge connected with his progress, and from all connexion or agreement with those who adored him. And it banished, as far as possible, the idea of dependence upon him, and precluded as far as possible, a relapse into the idolatrous worship of him.

The northern Indians also counted by moons and nights, and the year by moons, beginning the year at the first appearance of the new moon in March. Here is established a clear difference between the northern and southern tribes, and proves that they are not of the same extraction.

76 Josephus's Antiquities, book 12, ch. 4, sec. 6.

Section 5.—*Of their Hebraic Rites.* First, up to the year 1775; secondly, up to the year 1810; thirdly, since that period.

About the year 1730 or 1735, Mr. Adair came to the Cherokee nation as a trader, and continued to live amongst them and trade with them forty years, or till the year 1775. Whilst there, being a man of learning and observation, he carefully noted and reduced to writing all the circumstances which were calculated to give exact ideas of the countries they had formerly dwelt in, and of the nations with which in former times they had maintained an intercourse. What he has stated has been confirmed by a gentleman of the highest veracity, who resided amongst them soon after Mr. Adair left them. Mr. Adair's descendants are still in the Cherokee nation, in the most respectable stations which can be possessed amongst them. The practice of their ceremonies is far less perfect at this day than in the time of Mr. Adair; but enough of them still remains to show, that in ancient times the customs were generally such precisely as Mr. Adair represents. Their intercourse with the whites has filled their country with vicious habits, new diseases, and passions to which they were before strangers, and has made them less observant of the precepts, and mystical rites, which they received from their forefathers. From what he has written, are extracted the Indian peculiarities during the time of his residence amongst them. Many of their words are partly Hebraic. Their language is guttural, with strong aspirations. Their discourses abound in allegory and metaphors. They express themselves in their public orations with great vehemence, and in short pauses. They have long and many religious emblems of the divine name *Jehovah.* Rowah, which with them signifies *the rumbling of thunder,* seems to have been derived from the Hebrew word *Ruah,* or rushing wind.

Before they go to war, they have many preparatory ceremonies of purification and fasting. When the leader begins to beat up for volunteers, he goes *three* times around his dark winter house contrary to the course of the sun, sounding the war whoop, singing the war song, and beating a drum, which is a skin drawn over a large gourd, or frame of wood. When the people come around, he whoops again, and calls upon them to join him, and to sanctify themselves. A number soon joins him in his winter house, when they live separate from all others, and *purify* for *three* days and three *nights*, exclusive of the first broken day. On each day they fast until sunset. They watch the young men, and drink plentifully of their purifying *beloved* physic. During that time, they will not allow the best beloved trader to be amongst them on the ground appropriated to the duty of being sanctified for war, much less to associate with the camp in the woods at such a time, though united with them in the same war design. He must walk and encamp separately by himself, till the leader has purified him with the consecrated things of the *ark*, which is made of pieces of wood securely fastened together in the form of a square. The middle of three of the sides extends a little out, but the fourth is flat, for the convenience of the person's back who wears it, and is half the size of the Jewish *ark*, which was three feet nine inches long, two feet three inches broad, and two feet three inches deep. The Indian ark has a cover, and the whole is made close with hickory splinters. The leader and beloved waiter carry it by turns. It contains several consecrated vessels made by beloved superannuated old women, and of various antique forms. The two carriers are purified longer than the rest, that the first man may be fit to act in the religious office of a priest of war, and the other carry the awful sacred ark, all the while they are engaged in the act of fighting.

The beloved waiter feeds each of the warriors by an exact stated rate, giving them even the water they drink out of his own hands, lest by intemperance they should spoil the supposed communicative power of their holy things, and occasion disasters to the war camp. They never place the *ark* upon the ground, nor sit it upon the bare earth whilst they are carrying it against the enemy. On hilly ground, where stones are plenty, they place it on them; but on land where stones are not to be had, they use short logs, always resting themselves in like manner. They have a strong faith in the power and holiness of their *ark*, ascribing the success of a party to their stricter adherence to the law than the other. The *ark* is deemed so sacred, and dangerous to be touched, either by their own sanctified warriors, or the spoiling enemy, that they will not touch it on any account. It is not to be meddled with by any but the war chieftain and his waiter, who are consecrated for the purpose, under the penalty of incurring great evil. Nor would the most inveterate enemy amongst the nations touch it in the woods, for the same reason. On the Ohio, in the year 1756, was a stranger very importunate to view the inside of the Cherokee *ark*, which was covered with a dressed deer skin, and placed on a couple of short blocks of wood. An Indian sentinel watched it, armed with a hickory bow, and a brass barbed arrow. Finding the stranger obtruding with apparent determination to pollute the supposed sacred vehicle, he drew his arrow to the head, and would have shot him through the body, had he not suddenly withdrawn. They religiously abstain from all kind of intercourse even with their own wives, for the space of three days and nights before they go to war, and so after they return home; because they are to sanctify themselves. When they return home victorious over an enemy, they sing the triumphant song Yo-

He Wah, or Jehovah, or the *Great Good Spirit,* ascribing the victory to him. When an application for peace is made, and the applicants arrive near the town, they send a messenger ahead to inform the enemy of their amicable intentions. He carries a swan's wing in his hand, painted with specs of white clay, as an emblem of his peaceful embassy. The next day, when they have made their peaceable parade, by firing off their guns, and whooping, they enter the beloved square. The chief, who is ahead of the rest, is met by one of the beloved men of the town. They approach each other in a bowing posture. The former says, "Are you come a friend in the name of the Great Spirit?" The other replies, "The Great Spirit is with me. I am come a friend in his name." The beloved man then grasps the stranger with both hands around the wrist of his right hand, which holds some green branches, then again about the elbows, then about the arm close to the shoulder, as a near approach to the heart. Then he waves an eagle's tail, which is the strongest pledge of good faith. When they greet each other, the host says, "Are you a friend?" The guest replies, "I am come in the name of O E A, or Yohewah. The southern Indians, when any of their people die at home, wash and anoint the corpse, and soon bring it out of doors for fear of pollution. They place it before the door in a sitting posture. They then carry it three times around the house in which he is to be interred; for sometimes they bury him in his dwelling house, and under his bed. The religious man of the family of the deceased, in this procession, goes before the corpse, saying each time in a solemn tone, *Yah,* then *Ho,* which is sung by all the procession. Again he strikes up *He,* which is also sung by the rest. Then all of them suddenly strike off the solemn chorus, by saying *Wah,*—which constitutes the divine name Yohohewah. In the Choctaw nation

Ff

they often say *Hallelujah*, intermixed with their lamentations. They put the corpse in the tomb in a sitting posture, with his face towards the *east*, and his head anointed with bear's oil. He is dressed in his finest apparel, having his gun, pouch, and hickory bow, with a young panther's skin full of arrows, along side of him, and every other useful thing he had been possessed of. The tomb is made firm and clean inside. They cover it with thick logs so as to bear several tiers of cypress bark, and then a quantity of clay over it. They call their prophets *Loache*, men resembling the holy fire, or Elohim. Their traditions say, that their forefathers were possessed of an extraordinary divine spirit, by which they foretold things future; and this they transmitted to their offspring, provided they obeyed the sacred laws annexed to it. They believe, that by the communication of the same divine fire, working in the Loache, they can yet effect the like. But they say it is out of the reach of bad people either to comprehend or perform such things; because the holy spirit of fire will not cooperate or actuate the accursed people. They never mention the name *Y O He Wah* altogether in common speech, as neither did the Hebrews. The Indian prophets invoke Yo He Wah, and mediate with the supreme holy fire, that he may give seasonable rains. They have a transparent stone of supposed great power in assisting to bring down the rain, when it is put into a basin of water, agreeably to a reputed divine virtue impressed on one of the like sort in times of old, which communicate it circularly. This stone would suffer great injury, as they assert, were it even seen by their own laity; but if by foreigners, it would be utterly despoiled of its divine communicative power. All the Indian nations, and particularly the Muskogees, have a sanctum sanctorum, or most holy place, in their tabernacle and temple. It is partitioned off by a mud wall about breast high, between the white seat at which it always stands, and the left hand of the red painted war seat. There they deposite their consecrated vessels and supposed holy utensils, none of the laity daring to approach the sacred place, for fear of a particular damage to themselves, and a general hurt to the people, from the supposed divinity of the place. Among the Indians, as soon as their first spring produce comes in, on a day appointed, while the sanctified new fruits are dressing, six old beloved women come to the temple or sacred wigwam of worship, and dance the beloved dance with joyful hearts. They observe a solemn procession as they enter the holy ground or beloved square, carrying in one hand a bundle of small branches of various green trees, when they are joined by the same number of beloved old men, who carry a cane in one hand, adorned with white feathers, having green boughs in the other hand.[77] Their heads are dressed with white plumes, and the women in their finest clothes, and anointed with bear's grease or oil, having also tortoise shells, and white pebbles fastened to a piece of white dressed deer skin, which is tied to each of their legs.[78] The eldest of their beloved men leads the sacred dance,[79] at the head of the innermost row, which of course is next to the holy fire. He begins the dance. After going once around the holy fire in solémn and religious silence, he then in the next circle invokes *Yah*, after their usual manner, in a bass key, and with a short accent. In another circle he sings *Ho Ho*, which is repeated by all the religious procession, till they finish that circle. Then in another round they repeat *He He* in like manner, in regular notes, and keeping time in the dance. Another

77 Leviticus, ch. 23' v. 40.
78 Exodus, ch. 23, v. 32, 36; Isaiah, ch. 3, v. 16, 18.
79 Dancing was a religious ceremony with the Hebrews, of great solemnity. Psalms, ch. 149, v. 3, ch. 150, v. 4; 2 Samuel, ch. 6, v. 14.

circle is continued in like manner, repeating the words *Wah Wah*—making in the whole the divine and holy name Yah-Ho-He-Wah. A little after this is finished, which takes considerable time, they begin again, going fresh rounds, singing Hal Hal, Le Le, Lu Lu, Yah Yah. In like manner, and frequently the whole train, strike up Hallelu Hallelu, Hallelujah Hallelujah, with great earnestness, fervor and joy, while each strikes the ground with the right and left foot alternately, very quick, but well timed. Then a hollow sounding drum joins the sacred choir, which excites the old female singers to chaunt forth their grateful hymns and praises to the divine spirit, and to redouble their quick joyful steps in imitation of the beloved man at their head. On other occasions, and at their feast of love, they sing *Aleyo Aleyo*, which is the divine name by the attribute of omnipotence. They also sing *He Wah, He Wah*, which is the immortal soul drawn from the divine essential name, as deriving its faculties from *Yo He Wah*. These words of their religious dances, they never repeat at any other time. It is believed that they do not now understand either the spiritual or literal meaning of what they sing, any further than by allusion to the name of the *Great Spirit*. In these circuitous dances, they also frequently sing in a bass key *Aluhe Aluhe, Aluwah Aluwah*, also *Shiloyo Shiloyo, Shiluhe Shiluhe, Shiluwah Shiluwah*, and *Shiluhah Shiluhah*. They transpose them several ways also, but with the very same notes. Three terminations make up the four-lettered divine name Jehovah, or the *Great Good Spirit;* and the word Shilu preceding each syllable, means Shiloah sent, or he who is to be sent, making all together the *Great Good Spirit*, who is to be sent, or the Messiah, the redeemer of the world. They continue their grateful divine hymns for about fifteen minutes, and then break up. As they degenerate they lengthen their dances, and shorten the times of their fasts and purifications. They have so exceedingly corrupted their primitive rites and customs, within the space of ninety years, that at the same rate of declension, there will not long be a possibility of tracing their origin, but by their dialects and war customs. At the end of this notable religious dance, the old beloved women return home to hasten the feast of the new sanctified fruits. In the mean time, every one at the temple drinks plentifully of the *cassana*, and other bitter liquids,[80] to cleanse their sinful bodies, as they suppose. After which they go to some convenient deep water, and there they wash away their sins with water. They then return with great joy in solemn procession, singing their notes of praise till they again enter the holy ground, to eat of the new delicious fruits, which are brought to the outside of the square by the old beloved women! They all behave so modestly, and are possessed of such an extraordinary constancy and equanimity in pursuit of their religious mysteries, that they do not show the least outward emotion of pleasure at the first sight of the sanctified new fruits. If any of them should act in a contrary manner, they would say to him, chehaskel Kenoha, you resemble such as were beaten at Kenoha. Formerly, on the north side of the Susquehanna, in Pennsylvania, were some old Indian towns called Kanaa; and about ninety years ago, there was a remnant of a nation, or a subdivided tribe of Indians, called Kenaai. On the evening of the same day they have another public feast, when a great quantity of venison is provided, with other things dressed in the usual way, and distributed to all the guests, of which they eat freely that evening; but that which is left is thrown into the fire and burned, as none of it must remain until sunrise on the next day;[81]

80 Numbers, ch. 9, v. 11.
81 Leviticus, ch. 22; v. 30; Numbers, ch. 9, v. 12.

nor must a bone of the venison be broken.[82] The southern Indians offer a sacrifice of gratitude, if they have been successful, and have all returned safe home; but if they have lost any in war, they generally decline it; because they imagine, that by some neglect of duty, they are impure; and then they only mourn their vicious conduct, which defiled the *ark*, and thereby occasioned the loss. They believe that their sins are the procuring cause of all their evils, and that the divinity in the *ark* will always bless the more religious party with the best success. This is their invariable sentiment, and is the sole reason for mortifying themselves in so severe a manner whilst they are out at war, living very scantily, even in a buffalo range, under a strict rule, lest by luxury their hearts should grow evil, and give them occasion to mourn. The Muskogee Indians sacrifice a piece of every deer they kill, at hunting camps, or near home. If the latter, they dip the middle finger in the broth, and sprinkle over the domestic tombs of their dead, to keep them out of the power of evil spirits, according to their mythology.

They have one other most solemn feast and fast, similar to the Jewish feast of harvest, and day of expiation of sin.

The Indians formerly observed this great festival of the annual expiation of sin, and the offering of the first fruits of the harvest, at the beginning of the first new moon in which their corn became full eared; but for many years past, they are regulated by the season of their harvest. Yet they are skilful in observing the revolutions of the moon, as ever the Israelites were, at least till the end of the first temple. For during that period, instead of measuring time by astronomical calculations, they knew it only by the phases of the moon. In like manner the Indians annually observe their festivals, and

82 Exodus, ch. 12, v. 46; Numbers, ch. 9, v. 12.

days of afflicting themselves before the Great Spirit, at a prefixed time of a certain moon. The great chief fixes the day for the beginning of the festival of the harvest, which lasts *three* days, spent in sports and feasting. Each private person contributes something of his own hunting, his fishing, and his other provisions, as maize, beans, and melons. The great chief presides at the feast. All the sachems are around him in a respectful posture. The last day the chief makes a speech to the assembly. He exhorts every one to be exact in the performance of his duties, especially to have a great veneration for the spirit which resides in the temple, and to be careful in instructing their children. The fathers of families never fail to bring to the temple the first produce of the harvest, and of every thing they gather, and they do the same by all the presents made to their nation. They expose them at the door of the temple, the keeper of which, after presenting them to the spirit, carries them to the king, who distributes them to whom he pleases. The seeds are in like manner offered before the temple with great ceremony. But the offerings which are made of bread and flour every new moon, are for the use of the keepers of the temple. As the offering of the fruits of the harvest precede a long strict fast of two nights and a day, they gormandize such a prodigious quantity of strong food, as to enable them to keep inviolate the succeeding fast. The feast lasts only from morning until sunset. The feast being over, some of their people are carefully employed in putting their temple in proper order for the *annual expiation*, whilst others are painting the white cabin and the supposed holiest with white clay; for it is a sacred and peaceable place, and white is its emblem. Others, of an inferior order, are covering all the seats of the beloved square with new mattresses, made out of fine splinters of long cane tied together with flags. Several are busy in sweeping the temple, clearing it of every supposed polluted thing, and carrying out the ashes from the hearth, which has not perhaps been cleared but a few times since the last year's annual offering. Every thing being thus prepared, the chief beloved man or high priest orders some of his religious attendants to dig up the old hearth or altar, and to sweep out the remains that by chance might either be left, or dropped down. He then puts a few roots of the button snake root, with some green leaves of an uncommon small kind of tobacco, and a little of the new fruits at the bottom of the fire-place, which he orders to be covered up with a white marly clay, and wetted over with clear water. Immediately the magi or priests order a thick arbor to be made over the altar, with green branches of the various young trees, which the warriors had designedly chosen, and laid down on the outside of the supposed holy ground.[83] The women in the interim, are busy at home, cleaning out their houses, putting out all the old fire, renewing the old hearths, and cleaning all their culinary vessels, that they may be fit to receive the pretended holy fire, and the sanctified new fruits, according to the purity of the law; lest by an improper conduct they should incur damage in life, health, or future crops, and the like. Formerly none of the Indians would eat or even handle any part of the new harvest, till some of it had been offered up at the yearly festival of the beloved man or high priest, or those of his appointment, at their plantations, although the light harvest of the past year should almost have forced them to give their women and children of the ripening fruits to sustain life. Having every thing in order for the sacred solemnity, the religious waiters carry off the remains of the feast, and lay them on the outside of the square. Others, of an inferior order, sweep out the smallest

83 Leviticus, ch. 23, v. 40.

crumbs, for fear of polluting the first fruit offering; and before sunset the temple must be cleared, even of every kind of vessel or utensil that had contained any thing, or had been used for any kind of provision, during the past year. Now one of the waiters proclaims with a loud voice for all the warriors and beloved men, whom the purity of the law admits to come and enter the beloved square, and observe the fast. He also exhorts the women and children with those who have not been initiated in war, to keep apart according to the law. Four sentinels are now placed, one at each corner of the holy square, to keep out every living creature as impure, except the religious order and the warriors, who are not known to have violated the law of the first fruit offering, and that of marriage, since the last year's expiation. They observe the fast till the rising of the second sun; and be they ever so hungry in that sacred interval, the healthy warriors deem the duty so awful, and disobedience so inexpressibly vicious, that no temptation could induce them to violate it. They at the same time drink plentifully of the decoction of the button snake root, in order to vomit, and cleanse their sinful bodies. In the general fast, the children and men of weak constitutions are allowed to eat, as soon as they are certain that the sun has begun to decline from his meridian altitude. At the end of this solemn fast, the women, by the voice of a crier, bring to the outside of the holy square, a plentiful variety of the old year's food newly dressed, which they lay down and immediately return home. The waiters then go, and reaching their hands over the holy ground, they bring the provisions, and set them down before the famished multitude. They think it wholly out of order to show any joy or gladness, for the end of their religious duties. They are strict observers of their set forms. As soon as the sun is visibly declining from the meridian the *third* day of the fast, the chief beloved man orders a religious attendant to cry aloud to the crowded town, that the *holy fire* is to be brought out for the sacred altar, commanding every one to stay within the house, as becomes the beloved people, without doing the least bad thing, and to be sure to extinguish every spark of the old fire, otherwise the divine fire would bite them severely. Now every thing is hushed. Nothing but silence all around. The great beloved man and his beloved waiter rising up, with a reverend carriage, steady countenance, and composed behaviour, go into the beloved place, or holiest, to bring them out the beloved fire. The former takes a piece of dry poplar, willow, or white oak, and having cut a hole, but not so deep as to reach through it, he then sharpens another piece, and placing that on the hole, and both between his knees, he drills it busily for some moments, till it begins to smoke; or by rubbing two pieces together for a quarter of an hour, he collects, by friction, the hidden fire, which they all consider as proceeding from the *holy spirit of fire.* They then cherish it with fine chips till it glows to a flame, by using a fan of the unsullied wing of a swan. On this the beloved man brings out the fire in an old earthen vessel and lays it on the altar, which is under the arbor, thick woven at the top with green boughs. They rejoice exceedingly at this appearance of the holy fire, and it is supposed to atone for all their past crimes, except murder. Although the people without may well know what is doing within, yet by order a crier informs them of the glad tidings, and orders a beloved old woman to pull a basket full of the new ripened fruits, and bring them to the beloved square. As she is prepared for the occasion, she readily obeys, and soon lays it down at the corner thereof. Then the fire-maker rises from his white seat, and walks northward *three* times around the holy fire, with a slow pace, and in a sedate and grave manner, stopping now and then, and speaking some old ceremonial words with a low voice and rapidity of expression, which none know but a few of the beloved old men, who equally secrete their religious mysteries, that they may not be performed. He then takes a little of each sort of the new fruits, rubs some bear's oil over them, and offers them up, together with some flesh, to the bountiful spirit of fire, as a fruit offering, and an annual oblation for sin. He likewise pours a little of a strong decoction of the button snake root and of the cassana, into the pretended holy fire. He then purifies the red and white seats with these bitter liquids, and sets down. All culprits may now come forth from their hiding places, dressed in their finest clothes, to pay their thanks, at an awful distance, to the forgiving divine fire. Orders are now given to call the women to come for the sacred fire. They gladly obey. The great beloved man, or high priest, addresses the warriors and women, giving all the particular and positive injunctions, and negative precepts they yet retain of the ancient law. He uses very sharp language to the women. He then addresses the whole multitude. He enumerates the crimes they have committed, great and small, and bids them look at the holy fire, which has forgiven them. He presses on his audience by the great motives of temporal good, and the fear of temporal evil, the necessity of a careful observance of the ancient law, assuring them that the holy fire will enable their prophets, the rain-makers, to procure them plentiful harvests, and give their war leaders victory over their enemies. He then orders some of the fire to be laid down outside of the holy ground, for all the houses of the various associated towns, which sometimes lie several miles apart. If any are sick at home, and unable to come out, they are allowed one of the old consecrated *conch shells* full of their sanctifying bitter cassana, carried to them by a beloved old man. At the conclusion, the beloved man orders one of his religious waiters to proclaim to all the people, that the sacred annual solemnity is now ended, and every kind of evil averted from the beloved people, according to the old straight beloved speech. They are then ordered to paint themselves, and go along with him, according to ancient custom. They immediately fly about to grapple up a kind of chalky clay, to paint themselves white. They soon appear all over as white as the clay can make them. The beloved man, or high priest, heads the holy train, his waiter next, the beloved men according to their seniority, and the warriors according to their reputed merit. The women follow in the same orderly manner, with all the children who can walk, ranged according to their height. The very little ones are carried in their mothers' arms. In this manner they move along, singing Hallelujah to Y O He Wah, till they get to the water, when the high priest jumps into it, and all the train follow him. Having thus purified themselves and washed away their sins, they consider themselves out of the reach of temporal evil. They now return to the centre of the holy ground, where having made a few circles dancing around the altar, they finish their annual great festival, and depart in joy and peace.

They have also a daily sacrifice. The women always throw a small piece of the fattest of the meat into the fire, before they begin to eat. At times they view it with pleasing attention, and pretend to draw omens from it. The Indian men observe the daily sacrifice, both at home and in the woods, with new killed venison. They also draw the new killed venison, before they dress it, several times through the smoke and flame of fire, both by way of offering as a sacrifice, and to consume the blood, which with them as with the Hebrews, would be a most horrid abomination to eat. Their annual sacrifice cannot be offered anywhere but in their temples, otherwise they would not atone for the people, but bring down the anger of the Great Spirit, and utterly spoil the power of their holy place and holy things. They who sacrificed in the woods do it only on important occasions, allowed by their laws and customs. Mr. Adair says, that in his time the Cherokees still observed the laws of refuge so inviolably, that they allowed the beloved town the privilege of protecting a wilful murderer, but they seldom allowed him to return home from it in safety. The town of refuge called Choota, or Chota, is situated on a large stream of the Mississippi, some miles above where fort Louden stood. Here, some time ago, a brave Englishman was protected after killing an Indian warrior in defence of his property. He told Adair, that after some months' stay there, he intended returning to his house in the neighbourhood, but the chiefs told him it would prove fatal to him; so he was obliged to continue there till he satisfied the friends of the deceased by presents to their full satisfaction. In the upper country of the Muskogees, there was an old beloved town called Koosah, now reduced to a small ruinous village, which is still a place of safety for those who kill undesignedly. They pay their religious worship to the great, beneficial, supreme, holy *spirit of fire*, who resides above the clouds, and on earth with unpolluted holy people. They were never known to pay the least perceivable adoration to images, or dead persons, or to celestial luminaries, or evil spirits, or to any created being whatever. None of the various nations from Hudson's Bay to the Mississippi, have ever been known to attempt the formation of any image of the Great Spirit, whom they devoutly worship. The Cherokees and Choctaws, in the time of Adair, had some representation of the cherubimical figures in their places of worship or beloved square, where, through a strong religious principle, they dance almost every winter's night, always in a bowing posture, and frequently singing Hallelujah, Yohewah. They have in their places of worship which Mr. Adair has seen, two white painted eagles, carved out of poplar wood, with their wings stretched out, and raised five feet from the ground, standing in the corner close to the red and white seats; and on the inner side of each of the notched pieces of wood where the eagles stand, the Indians frequently paint, with a white chalky clay, the figure of a man with buffalo's horns, and that of a panther (the nearest in America to that of a lion) in the same colour. The emblems of the congregational standards of the Hebrews were the bull, the lion, the man and the eagle. Their figures they paint afresh at the first fruit offering in the annual expiation of sin. None of these emblems, however, are the objects of divine adoration. They kill the eagle and panther wherever they find them. They believe in a future state, where the spirit exists, which they call the world of spirits, where they enjoy different degrees of tranquillity and comforts, agreeably to the life they have spent here. They hold their beloved man or priest in great respect, and pay a strict obedience to all he directs. These beloved men are supposed to be in great favor with the Deity, and able to procure rain when they please. The northern Indians of Canada, in the time of Charlevoix, would not, at their feasts, eat of the part under the lower joint of the thigh.[84] The Cherokees inflict punishment upon the members of that nation whose people have slain some of theirs; and when about to be put to death, are greatly comforted if inspired with a belief that revenge will be taken for them by their surviving friends. The tribes claim preeminence by seniority. They are exceedingly cruel to their prisoners of war. All these are traits of the Hebraic character. Liberty

84 Genesis, ch. 22, v. 25, 32.

is the ruling passion of these Indians, as it was of the Hebrews, who in all ages have been conspicuously impatient of foreign dominion and domestic tyranny.

Secondly. From 1775 to 1810, the religious notions and practises had considerably faded. In the latter part of this period, they say, the Great Spirit created the heavens and the earth, and all that is therein. That then he made a white and a red man, and set them upon the earth. To the red man the Great Spirit gave a book, who took and looked into it, but could not understand it. The Great Spirit then gave it to the white man, who read and understood it. To the red man the Great Spirit gave a tomahawk, and a bow and arrows, and taught him to subdue his enemies, love his friends, hate riches, and bear hunger and abstinence; hunt the buffalo and bear for skins to make him warm, and the deer and turkey for food. He taught him to love truth, to hate a lie, never to steal from his neighbour, nor kill any but his enemies. He taught him not to be afraid, though the winds blew, the lightning flashed, and the thunders rolled. The Great Spirit then gave him a wampum belt, which he fastened around his waist, that he might recollect all that he had taught him. From the book the white man learned a great many things—architecture, agriculture, fortification, and machinery of various sorts. From the wampum the Indian learned patience, abstemiousness, to suffer privation, hunger, thirst, and fatigue; to endure heat and cold, poverty, and misery, to bear pain without murmuring, to reverence the Great Spirit, love his friends, hate his enemies, and to seek revenge. The white man hath found out many inventions—society, metallurgy, commerce, politics. The Indian hath only one God, or Great Spirit. If we reverence him, love our friends, hate our enemies, and do justice to all, he will cause the corn to grow, the fruits to ripen, the game to be plentiful, and carry us to a good hunting place when we die. But if we are false to our friends, cowardly to our enemies, cheat, lie, or steal, the corn is blasted, the fruit withers and drops off, and the game hides where we cannot find it. They do not believe in a plurality of Gods, or spirits, but they believe that the *Good Spirit* will punish them when they do wrong. The Great Spirit they believe made the Indians, and gave them their hunting ground. But whenever they offend him he causes the game to be scarce, and their enemies to make war upon them, and to take away their hunting ground.[86] When the Great Spirit is offended, they try to appease him by good deeds. The chiefs assemble all the nation together, who build great fires, around which they all gather to sing and dance, to hear the wise men and doctors repeat the traditionary history of their wars, and great chiefs to talk of their courage and virtues, and to exhort the young men to be brave and good like their forefathers.

The green corn dance is an annual feast of thanksgiving. It is most splendid, and full of devotion. Here it is they sacrifice to the Great Spirit for giving them a good crop of corn and tobacco. Here it is that all injuries are forgiven, which have been done to one another. Vengeance and cruelty are forgotten in the sacrifice made to friendship. No one who has been guilty of unpardonable offences, can be partaker of this feast; and all who are permitted to partake of it, must be forgiven, no matter what may be the nature of the offence. This feast consigns to oblivion, and extinguishes all vengeance, and for ever banishes from the mind all the sentiments of displeasure, which before separated them from a close and friendly intercourse with each other.[87]

86 Leviticus, ch. 5, v. 1, ch. 26, v. 14, 39.
87 Leviticus, ch. 7, v. 12, 15, ch. 22, v. 29; Nehemiah, ch. 11, v. 17.

Thirdly. From 1810 to the present time. The statements next following have been collected in part from one of the native Cherokees, who has all his lifetime resided among them, and is a man of excellent understanding, and of considerable learning; and in part from a white man of good character and understanding, who has lived for forty years in the Cherokee country. The Cherokees believe, in a good and bad spirit, and that they are hostile to each other. They believe that after death the spirits of all mankind go on one road some distance, to a point where the road forks. When the spirit of the deceased comes to the point where the road forks, he is met by the messenger of the Great Spirit, who conducts those who have lead good lives, along the right-hand path,[88] into a pleasant country, which hath an eternal spring, where game and every thing else they want is plenteous; whilst those who have lived wicked lives are forced by the messenger of the Great Spirit to take the left-hand road, which leads to a cold, barren country, where there is no game, where they endure constant hunger, and where they are exposed to perpetual danger and frights of bad spirits, and the farther they travel the more their difficulties and torments increase. It is the opinion of a half-breed of the Cherokees, resident amongst them, and who is sensible, observing, and well educated, that the Cherokees, by their intermixture with the whites, have greatly descended from the high rank of their ancestors. The practice yet prevails, he says, of preparing new fire every spring, for sacrifices of the new growth of corn and beans.[89] These fires they

88 1 Kings, ch. 2, v. 19; Psalms, ch. 16, v. 11, ch. 45, v. 9, ch. 110, v. 1, ch. 12.
89 Gen. ch. 15, v. 7; Leviticus, ch. 2, v. 14, ch. 9, v. 24; 1 Kings, ch. 18, v 38; 2 Chron. ch. 7, v. 1; Lev. ch. 23, v. 10, 21; Exo. ch. 22, v. 29, ch. 23, v. 19; Numb. ch. 19, v. 20; 2 Cook's Voyages, 514; Plutarch, 79, 165, 166; 2 Plut. 40; 1 Dubois, 14, 143, 154, 344; 2 Dubois, 25, 34, 44, 48, 125.

consider as the agents of the great fire above. The sun they call the day moon, or female, and the night moon, the male. A custom once prevailed, that when the moon changed, they held the palms of their hands forward and stroked them over the face.[90] They had no idols, or images, or names for them. They would deem it as hideous and laughable, says Mr. Hicks, to see a man paying his adoration to an image, as it would impress them with awe and reverence to see one paying his devotions to an invisible creator, whom they acknowledge to be the master of breath.[91] The Cherokees are addicted to conjuration, to ascertain whether a sick person will recover. This custom arose after the destruction of their priests. Tradition states, that such persons lived amongst their ancestors, and were deemed superior to others; and were extirpated long ago, in consequence of the misconduct of one of the priests, who attempted to take the wife of a man who was the brother of the leading chief of the nation. An ancient custom is still in use in some parts of the nation, of making sacrifices when the green beans become eatable, and when the green corn becomes fully eared. At the former festival, the dance lasted four days; at the latter, one night, and in the morning sacrifices were offered.[92] There still is a festival called the green corn dance, which comes on some time in September. The strict observance of these customs is now fast wearing away, says Mr. Hicks. They have not, since his time, who was a half-breed, born in the nation, and now one of their judges, used the words Jehovah, Hallelujah, Shiloh.

Mr. Love, who was raised near that part of the Cherokees, which is nearest the white settlements

90 Job. ch. 31, v. 27.

91 Psalms, ch. 146, v. 4, ch. 33, v. 6; Isaiah, ch. 11, v. 4, ch. 30, v. 28, 33.

92 Leviticus, ch. 23, v. 10; Exodus, ch. 22, v. 29, ch. 23, v. 19; Num. ch. 15, v. 19, 20.

In North-Carolina, has heard a woman, in mourning for the death of a near relation, pronounce, in
her lamentations, the name Jehovah very distinctly.
He has also heard them at the green corn dance in
North-Carolia, pronounce the different syllables
Y He Ho Wah, one after another.   He has seen the
whole congregation set in a circle,[93] with a priest
in the centre, speaking, and frequently casting his
eyes up to heaven, whilst the assembly sat in the
most solemn silence.   And when the ceremonies
were ended, he has seen them all rise, and proceed,
with the priest at their head, to a river, and all
plunge into it and bathe themselves; after which
they returned to their respective homes.   These
ceremonies are a part of those belonging to the
green corn dance; and he was assured, that the
whole was a religious thanksgiving to God, for the
incoming of the fruits of the earth.   And he says,
that what is before stated respecting the syllables
of different words pronounced in the solemn dances,
is strictly correct, even at this day.   This testimony is of indubitable veracity.

In ancient times, the Cherokees had no conception of any one's dying a natural death.   They
universally ascribed the death of those who perished by disease, to the intervention or agency of evil
spirits, and witches, and conjurers, who had connexion with the Shina, or evil spirits.[94]   They
ascribe to their witches and conjurers, the power to
put on any shape they please, either of bird or beast,
but they are supposed generally to prefer the form

93 1 Josephus, 261, 298 ; 1 Samuel, ch. 26, v. 7.
94 Gen. ch. 41, v. 1, 24, ch. 44, v. 6 ; Exodus, ch. 7, v. 11,
ch. 8, v. 19, ch. 9, v. 11 ; Leviticus, ch. 20, v. 27 ; Num. ch.
22, v. 5, 9, 14, 25, 31, 35, ch. 23, v. 4, 30, ch. 24, v. 2, 3, 25, ch.
31, v. 8, 16 ; Deut. ch. 18, v. 9, 10, 11, 15 ; Numb. ch. 22, v.
27, ch. 23, v. 23 ; 1 Samuel, ch. 15, v. 23 ; 1 Kings, ch. 15, v.
40 ; 1 Kings, ch. 10, v. 19 ; Jeremiah, ch. 14, v. 14 ; Ezekiel,
ch. 12, v. 24, ch. 13, v. 6, 7, ch. 21, v. 21, 22, 23 ; Hosea, ch.
4, v. 12 ; 1 Dubois, 372 ; 2 Dubois, 81, 91, 125, 126.

of a cat or of an owl. They ascribe to them the power of passing from one place to another in as short a time as they please. To another set of priests, who are supposed to derive their power from the Good Spirit, they assign the knowledge of the divine will, the procurement of rain by supplication,[95] the giving of victory in a ball play, and the power to avert misfortune by conciliating the favour of God. Their witches and conjurers are supposed to receive their faculties from evil spirits, and are punished to this day with death.[96] Suspicion affixes to them the imputation of this crime. A person dying by disease, and charging his death to have been procured by means of witchcraft, or spirits, by any other person, consigns that person to inevitable death. They profess to believe that their conjurations have no effect upon white men. In ancient times they had a town called *Toquo*, which was a place of *refuge* for those who had committed capital offences, in which, if they took shelter, they could not be molested.[97]

In their hierarchal history, are some circumstances extremely attractive of attention. Sacrifices were as universally prevalent in America as in the old world, where they had spread over all countries. It must have sprung there from an origin of positive institution. There is nothing in nature that points it out or enjoins it; and no doubt it last came from the sacrifice made by Noah, on his disembarkation from the ark, on the subsidence of the grand cataclysma, or deluge.[98] When we find it in America, are we to imagine it commenced spontaneously, without an original, and extended itself universally

95 1 Samuel, ch. 12, v. 17, 18; 1 Kings, ch. 8, v. 36, ch. 18, v. 1; 2 Chron. ch. 6, v. 27.
96 Exodus, ch. 22, v. 18; Deut. ch. 18, v. 10.
97 Numb. ch. 35, v. 6, 11, 12, 13, 14, 15, 16, 17, 25, 26, 27, 28; Deut. ch. 19, v. 11, 12; Joshua, ch. 20.
98 Genesis, ch. 8, v. 20.

over the whole continent? Its conformity here to the same model which is in the old world, proves it to have come from thence, and the people of America with it.

Spiritualism, in the time of Moses, abstracted completely from the worship of the sun, or other created being, was at open war with the long established opinions of the world. It was restored by the pentateuch, founded upon it, and confined to the Israelites. Even among them it was preserved with the greatest difficulty. The golden calves built by the people at Sinai, the building of high places by Solomon, for Baal and Ashteroth, and the general idolatry to which the ten tribes afterwards addicted themselves, are full proofs of this remark. Spiritual theism made no proselytes in the adjacent countries; but always acted upon the defensive. It travelled only with the Israelites; and wherever we see it, whether in the old or in the new world, we may take it as a sure evidence, that those who possess it, have drawn their creeds mediately at least from the Mosaic writings. The aborigines of Tennessee spread from the south and southwest, towards the north and northeast: but the present race of Indians came from the north and northeast. The former had been long settled: the latter came recently into the country. These had no high places, or mounds, idols, human sacrifices, three-faced images, no fortifications or intrenchments, wells walled up from the bottom, bricks for building, nor any metallic tools or domestic utensils, no princes with despotic power, nor any political institutions which bear the least resemblance to those of the aborigines of Tennessee. In their manners, laws and customs, the new comers were in a few instances Hindoric; in a few others, Scythic; in all the rest, Hebraic. These and the ancient aborigines must have come from different sections of the old world: the aborigines from the south of Asia; the present race from the central parts of Asia, and by some passage near to the northeastern coast of America, over some isthmus which joins the two continents together, which by ice far protruded from its shores, prevents the access of navigation. The same isthmus which formerly afforded a passage to the mammoth of the north, whose body is found in the Frozen ocean and on the shores of Siberia, and whose bones are found in Tennessee. The same also which afforded a passage to the raindeer, the buffalo, the elk, the panther, the wolf, the fox, the racoon, the martin, the squirrel, and other animals of Siberia, which are precisely of the same species with the like animals in the northern and northwestern parts of America; and the same from whence flew the geese and ducks, in their southwardly migrations, over the ice which stopped Capt. Cook in his further progress in 1778, but in his view so as to inform him that, though he could go no farther, the country of their nativity was still more to the north, and could not be discovered but by pedestrian explorers. The arrival of the last emigrants had not been long enough to people the countries from California to the bay of Hudson, thence to the Northern ocean, and south southeastwardly through the present southeastern parts of the United States, as far as to James river, and afterwards to send to North and South Carolina as thick a population as was to the north of these countries, on the Susquehanna and the lakes. The tribes which were found in North-Carolina, had been lately from the mother stock. The Tuscaroras spake without any variation of dialect, the same language with the mother stock to the north; acknowledged their connexion with it; in times of distress, called upon them for assistance, and when sorely pressed by their enemies, took shelter under their wing, and made one of the six nations. They chiefly came into North-Carolina and Tennessee, from the north

and northeast, plainly designating the course of
their original, and migration. When, in the lapse
of ages, progressive population and the increased
number of animals had come through the Iberian
gates, as far as to the gateway into this continent,
the Scythians or Tartars, and perhaps the greatly
multiplied Israelites, anciently removed to the north
by the Assyrians, chose for their future residence,
the newly discovered regions of North-America.
They, with the northern animals of the old world,
whose augmented numbers called for new habitations, all entered with one accord into this passage,
and planted themselves in the land which Providence, in his goodness, had reserved for them.
Charlevoix, in his history of Canada, has stated
what father Grillan often informed him of, namely,
that after having laboured some time in the missions
of Canada, he returned to France. and went to
China.   As he was travelling through Tartary, he
met a Huron woman whom he had formerly known
in Canada.   She told him, that having been taken
in war, she had been conducted from nation to nation, until she arrived at the place where she then
was.   There was another missionary, said Charlevoix, passing by the way of Nantz, on his return
from China, who related the like story, of a woman
he had seen, from Florida in America. She informed him, that she had been taken and given to
those of a distant country, and by them again to
another nation, till she had been thus successively
passed from country to country, had travelled regions excessively cold, and at length found herself
in Tartary, and had there married a Tartar, who
had passed with the conquerors into China, and
had there settled.

Section 6.—*Of their Political Government, Laws, Civil Customs, Civil Traditions and Scientific Acquirements, Lingual Affinities and Games.*

Their darling passion is liberty.[h] To it they sacrifice every thing, and in the most unbounded liberty they indulge themselves through life. They are rarely chided even in infancy, and never chastised with blows. Reason, they say, will guide their children, when they are come to the use of it, and before that time they cannot commit faults. To chastise them, would be to debase the mind, and blunt the sense of honour, by the habit of a slavish motive to action. In manhood, command, subordination, dependence, were equally unknown : and by those who wish to possess their confidence, persuasion is avoided, lest their influence should seem a sort of violence offered to the will. They have no punishments but death. They have no fines, for they have no way of exacting them from freemen. When death is inflicted, it is rather on an individual or public enemy, than an act of judicial power on a subject or citizen. They have a supreme head, whom they call king; but his power is rather recommendatory, than coercive. He is revered as a father, more than feared as a monarch. The qualification for their head men is age, with experience, ability in the affairs of the nation, and fidelity in the discharge of the duties which devolve upon them. Yet there are in almost every tribe, some families respected as hereditary chiefs, unless they forfeit their title by misconduct. So of the tribes themselves, there are some which, on account of their numbers, and bravery, have a preëminence over the others. It is not exacted by pride, nor maintained by tyranny; and is never disputed where it is due. The great council is composed of their hereditary chiefs, with such whose capacity,

[h] A characteristical trait of the Hebrews. 1 Jos. 95, 180.

courage and virtue have elevated them to the same degree of consideration. The king is hereditary amongst the other southern nations, but not amongst the Cherokees, for with them he is elective. A part of the council is hereditary. The king has neither guards, power, or revenue. The council is no otherwise respected, than as their merit entitles them to it; and both may forfeit their rank and dignity by meanness and cowardice. None of the dignitaries, whether hereditary, or raised to office by merit, must have any power contrary to the will of the nation. In every village there is a chief, or head, whose authority extends to his own tribe or family. Amongst the Cherokees, not only the king, but the council is elective to supply deficiencies; though it is common to elevate the sons of any of the dignitaries to the rank of their fathers. The councils are attended by the whole nation, men, women and children. The progress of deliberation is frequently impeded, in order to consult the assembled nation. A few dissenting voices will often destroy the most salutary measures. The councils are public. The meeting is in a house privileged in every town for the purpose, in which to receive embassadors, deliver answers to them, to sing traditionary war songs, and to commemorate the dead. All things which concern the state are here performed, the same having been already digested in the great council. Here the orators display the talents which distinguish them for eloquence, and a knowledge of public affairs, in both of which some of them are admirable. None others are permitted to speak in the public councils. Out of them are selected the embassadors of the nation, and those who are appointed to treat of war and peace, or to form alliances with other nations. Precision of sentiment, metaphoric boldness of expression, vehemence of gesture, and propriety of manner, are exhibited. These are remembered with the greatest

accuracy for a long time. All the speeches delivered at treaties with foreign nations, are first repeated
by a head chief in a council at home, and sent in
the memory of another chief, or minister appointed
for the purpose, to be delivered at the negotiation.
These speeches are always repeated verbatim as
delivered. They use small shells or beads of different colours, which have different meanings, according to their colours or arrangement. These
are fixed on belts, which the orator wears around
the middle, and which are badges of his profession
of oratory, and credentials of his office of minister
or negotiator. A chief newly elected, and solemnly
invested into his office, is loved and respected by
his people, who safely confide in his measures. If
he is intelligent and skilful enough to gain the af-
fections of his captains and people, the former support his authority, and the latter execute his measures. A captain is the chief's right hand. He
must undertake every thing committed to him by
the chief, even at the hazard of his life. In this
consists his glory. If he is killed by the enemy,
the whole nation unites in avenging his death. A
chief is above all things to secure the confidence of
his counsellors. Without their assistance he is a
mere cipher. He therefore submits the subject of
deliberation to them without giving his own opinion.
When they have given theirs, he either approves of
it, or states his objections against it, with his reasons; but unless he covinces them that he is right,
and they are wrong, his opposition is never successful. But the confidence placed in their judgment, by giving them a choice of opinion, keeps
alive their zeal and activity, and procures him respect. A chief rules over his people only by calm
reason and friendly exhortation. In this he often
fails with the best intentions, and is compelled to
have recourse to artifice. He must be courteous,
friendly, hospitable, affable and kind to all, and

his house must be open to every Indian. Even strangers, who come upon business, put up at the chief's house, and are accommodated with the best the house affords. The embassadors of other nations must be lodged with the chief. It is the duty of the chief to keep the people from dispersing; but this he cannot do unless he is respected. In that case the Indians appear to be a flock without a shepherd.

All affairs of importance are laid before the grand council; and without its consent, no proposal can be put into execution. The council is convened on usual occasions by a runner; and when met, they sit *down upon the ground*, around a fire, and smoke a pipe. Cool deliberation always precedes a speech in the council. The principal chief opens the debate by a speech, setting forth the subjects upon which he desires the advice and opinion of the council, in a dignified manner, but shortly expressed, in plain and explicit terms. The speeches are in figurative language, picturing to the life the subjects under consideration. Is war to be declared? The orator represents the veins of his country's enemies as opened; the victims of war are at the stake; the fagots are collected, and the fire kindled; the tomahawk and scalping-knife are invoked, and called into action, till the picture of fancy seems to be realized. And in the same nervous strain is peace dressed off in beautiful apparel. The country is blessed with plenty; the tree of friendship is in blossom; the paths are cleared of thorns and briers; the knife and tomahawk are buried deep in the bowels of the earth, and the stains of blood are washed from the view of the beholder. Their speeches are solemn, animated, and fluent. The behaviour of the chiefs, and of the audience, consists with the dignity of the assembly, and the importance of the subject. No one interrupts the speaker. All sit silent and attentive, as in an act of devotion. Sometimes the subject is secret, and its source kept so, from the subordinate chiefs. The principal chief pretends that he has been inspired, that a *spirit* has come to him and delivered a bit of wampum, whispered in his ear, and again returned to his invisible abodes. The fiction is not discountenanced, because the good of the nation requires secrecy; and the chief is responsible only, for the truth and importance of the subject, which a supernatural communication often gives to the most trivial affair. Amongst the Cherokees are eight clans, or tribes—Wo-te-a, the paint; Ne-lus-te, the hollow leaf; Nank-a-lo-hee, a clan with the hair hanging loose; Neho-lo-hawee, the blind Savanna; Cheesqua, the bird; Howee, the deer; Nesonee, the clan with the rings of the ears cut off.[92]

On the death of a chief, the wampum is carefully preserved by the council, till a successor is elected. The sons of the chief cannot inherit the father's dignity, as they are not the royal blood, or next of kin to the father. The son of the chief's eldest sister, is generally the heir apparent. For it is a maxim with the Indians, that the children are related only to the mother. In general, some person who lived in intimacy with the deceased chief, and who hath the confidence of the nation, and is acquainted with public affairs, is chosen his successor.

Secondly—*Of their Laws.*

By the law and custom of the Cherokees, they are forbidden to intermarry, not only with their blood relations,[93] but even with the members of the same clan. The breach of this custom was formerly punished with death. But as they become more connected with the whites, by trade and intermixture, this severity is observed to wear off. But they

92 Numb. ch. 2, v. 2, 3, ch. 10, v. 5, 6, 14.
93 Leviticus, ch. 18, v. 6.

still whip for this offence. They count kin on the mother's side only; and are ranked in the clan of their mothers. In ancient times they allowed a man to have as many wives as he could clothe and feed; and they were all obliged, whilst he fulfilled these obligations, to be true and constant to him. But a few years ago, the nation resolved, in council, that in future a man should be allowed to have but one wife. If the wife was guilty of any infidelity, the husband was at liberty to take every article of property from her, and to turn her out to the world. This, and whipping at the pleasure of the husband, was the only punishment for adultery, though in their traditions there are traces of having stoned to death for this offence.[94] For they have a tradition, that the stone hillocks, which are at all the gaps in the mountains, and in other parts of the country, were originally erected by the casting of stones upon women who had been guilty of adultery, and that their bodies were under them. The same practice anciently prevailed in the Crimea, amongst the Tartars, whose law it was, to make a hole in the ground of depth enough to cover the adulteress up to her chin; then to stone her to death, and to cover her with stones, thrown by hand upon the body. This severity they too have relaxed in modern times, deeming the punishment disproportioned to the offence. In all other cases of parting, except for adultery, the wife is entitled to take away all her property. And in all cases of parting, the woman has a right to take with her all the children of the marriage. The husband has in all cases the right to correct the wife, by stripes, at his pleasure. In ancient times, the mother had a right to punish her own children, for any offence, with death: but if the father happened to kill his child by accident, he was punished with death, by the clan of the mother.[i] They in all cases punished accidental

94 Lev. ch, 20, v. 10; Deut. ch. 22, v. 22, 27.   i 1 Jos. 336.

homicide, as well as murder, with death. But the infliction of this punishment, is left to the clan of the party who was slain, and satisfaction is sometimes made by presents.[95] If the guilty person could not be reached, his nearest relations sometimes became the victims in his stead. The shaking of hands is a token of friendship, and the concurrence of two minds upon one and the same object.[96] The Cherokees had the law, or custom, of assigning to a certain woman the office of declaring what punishment should be inflicted on great offenders; whether, for instance, burning or other death, or whether they should be pardoned. This woman they called the pretty woman. Mrs. Ward exercised this office, when Mrs. Bean, about the year 1776, was taken from the white settlements on the upper parts of Holston. Being bound, and about to be burned on one of the mounds, the pretty woman interfered, and pronounced her pardon.

Civil Customs.

The war songs amongst the Cherokees are sung by the men, in their dances; but have no meaning at all, and are accommodated to a tune. The scalp dances belong to the women, who applaud the warriors for their bravery in destroying their enemy. In singing, they say how brave he was to destroy his enemies, and left them mourning.[50] The practice of scalping perhaps was planted in Scythia by the Hebrews, as well as the unlawfulness to eat swine,[60] after their removal thither by the Assyrians. So also, it is believed, was the doctrine of the soul's immortality, before it was known to the Greeks;[61]

95 Tacitus de Moribus Germanorum, sec. 21; Jos. Ant. b. 7, ch. 8, sec. 4; 2 Samuel, ch. 14, v. 7.

96 Tacitus de Moribus Germanorum, 12; Proverbs, ch. 17, v. 18, ch. 22, v. 26.

50 1 Sam. ch. 18, v. 6, 7, 60, ch. 18, v. 25, 27, ch, 29, v. 4; Jos. b. 1, ch. 10, sec. 2.

60 1 Sam. ch. 18, v. 27, ch. 29, v. 4

61 Herod. Melpomene, sec. 94.

and hence also they learned the unity of the God-head, or pure theism, when no other nation upon earth possessed it but the Hebrews; and it is strongly suspected, that the name Scythia originated from Cuthai, the river and district in Media, to which the captive Hebrews were removed by the Assyrians. For it is said by Herodotus[62] to have been originally peopled from Media; and if by emigrants from Cuthai, which the Greeks would call Cythai, it is very probable that they were called Cythians, and their country Cythia.[63]

When one chief intends to pay a visit to another, he sends him a piece of tobacco, with this message: "Partake of this tobacco, and look towards my dwelling, and thou shalt see me coming towards thee." Formerly their visits were conducted with great ceremony on both sides. The exchange of wampum is a test of friendship, as is the giving and receiving of presents, and smoking the calmet or pipe of friendship.

The Cherokee women are elegantly formed, have sprightly eyes, accompanied with modesty and chastity, which render them very far from uninteresting objects. They love their husbands; are attached to domestic duties and devotion to their children. With them the marriage contract is purchase.[97] The suiter either devotes his services for a time, to the parents of the maid whom he courts,[98] hunts for them, assists in making canoes, or offers them presents. The woman has not the power of refusing The price which he pays generally consists of wearing apparel, with which the bride is dressed out. On the appearance of the

62 Herod. Terp. 9.

63 Jos. Ant. b. 9, ch. 14, sec. 3, b. 10, ch. 9, sec. 7; Herodotus, 307.

97 Gen. ch. 24, v. 59, ch. 29, ch. 35, v. 11, 12; 1 Sam. ch. 18; Hosea, ch. 3, v. 2.

98 Genesis, ch. 29, v. 18, 29.

bridegroom, she is stripped of it, by her relations, who claim it, and in that state she is presented to him as his wife. He receives her with cold indifference, whilst she, with modesty and humility, retires to the hut which he has prepared for her reception. The culture of the farm, the preparing and dressing of food, and the bearing of burthens in their travels, are all imposed upon her. The husband stalks about, with his gun and pipe, regardless of the fatigue and pain which she endures. After she has served him as a slave, contributed to his pleasures as a mistress, borne him children, and taken care of his hut, he often takes another wife, and parts with her, as unfeelingly as if she had never existed. Such is the barbarous treatment which women experience, that they not unfrequently destroy their female offspring, that they may escape the hardships which have fallen on the mother. They use for the cure of disorders, what is called the Indian *sweat*, by pouring water on heated stones in a confined place, from whence the fumes arising, soon produces a copious perspiration. The same practice precisely has prevailed in Scythia, from the earliest times.[61] In the year 1781, when the small pox prevailed over all North-Carolina, the Catawbas applied this remedy for the cure of the disease, and jumping immediately afterwards into the river, destroyed a great part of the nation.

Civil Traditions.

They have a fabulous tradition respecting the mounds, which proves that they are beyond the events of their history. The mounds, they say, were caused by the quaking of the earth, and great noise with it. A ceremony used for the adoption

61 2 Herodotus, 375.
60 These foreskins were not prepuces, but the hair and skin which covered the forehead as explained. 1 Samuel, ch. 18, v. 25, 27, ch. 29, v. 4; Herod. Melpomene, section 63; Jos. book 6, chapter 11, section 2.

of their people into the family of Tuli-cula, who was an invisible person, and had taken a wife of one of their town's people. And at the time when his first son was born, this quaking of the earth and noise had commenced; but had ceased at the alarm whoop, which had been raised by two imprudent young men of the town. In consequence of which, the mounds had been raised by the quaking noise. Whereupon the father took the child and mother, and removed to near Brass-town, and had made the tracks in the rocks which are to be seen there.

Their Scientific Acquirements may be embraced by a brief enumeration.

The seven pointers, says Mr. Hicks, they call the bears. The morning star they call the torch-bearer. These stars served by night to guide them in their war expeditions. They have no division of time into seven days; nor any names for the days of the week. But they have 12 names for the 12 months of the year, and are ignorant of the number of days of which a month consisted. They have no names which the rivers bore, before they settled upon them. They have no peculiar veneration, says Mr. Hicks, for the number three; but their physicians have for the number 4 and 7, who say that after man was placed upon the earth, four and seven nights were instituted for the cure of diseases in the human body, and the seventh night as the limit for female impurity.

Their Lingual Affinities and Hebraisms.

The language of the Cherokees and of the southern tribes of the United States, are sometimes assimilated to those of their neighbours; whilst others are so widely diverged, as to have few or no traces of having ever been identified with a common original. Between the Chickasaw and Choctaw languages, and that of the Mexicans, there is in certain

J J

instances a strong analogy; whilst in those of the Cherokees and Creeks there is none. The languages of the Chickasaws and Choctaws differ from each other only in a few idioms, and pronunciation. The former has more guttural, the latter more nasal sounds. Both are easily recognized, even by a stranger, as speaking the same language. The same analogy exists between the Cherokees and Creeks, though in a less degree. Amongst the Mexicans, inca signified father; and the word has the same signification amongst the Chickasaws. The name of the Creeks for man, is *ishto*, and so it is in Hebrew. If they were never acquainted with the Romans, how comes it, that they have a name for them in their language? The same remark might be made with respect to the word Kenaai, for Canaan. Jehovah they call Y-he-ho-wah. The roof of the house they call toubanora; in the Hebrew it is debonaour. The nose they call nichiri; in Hebrew, neheri. The great first cause, Yo-he-wah; in Hebrew, Jehovah. Praise the first cause, in their language, halleluwah; in Hebrew, hallelujah. Father they call abba; the same in Hebrew. Now they call na; in Hebrew, na. To pray they call phale; in Hebrew, phalae. In their language, abel is manslaughter; the same in Hebrew. Wife, awah; in Hebrew, eve, or eweh. Winter, kora; in Hebrew, cora. God, Ale; in Hebrew, Ale, or Alohim. A high mountain, ararat; the same by the Indians of Penobscot

The following is a vocabulary of Cherokee names.

MEMBERS OF THE HUMAN BODY.

Cherokee.	English.
Geely,	Hair.
Eh-shoe,	Head.
Auh-can-to-lee,	Eye.
Cauh-yuneeh,	Chin.
Auho-lee,	Mouth.
Auh-ko-qua-leth,	Cheek.

Cherokee.	English.
Ro-ya-so-lee,	Nose.
Auh-ge-tau-canie,	Forehead.
Au-yale-ek,	Body.
Canna-che-ek,	Breast
Oas-quo-le-eh,	Belly.
Canno-kee-nie,	Arm.
Oo-wo-ya-nie,	Hand.
Taykaw-ya-sut-eh,	Fingers.
Can-cut-to-eh,	Thigh.
Canne-kanie,	Knee.
Gemnesh-kee-nie,	Leg.
Oo-law-se-la-nie,	Foot.
Tay-can-nan-tulle-eh,	Toes.
Au-ya-cha-nie,	Neck.
Au-kelle-ca-nie,	Back of the neck.
Au-squa-ca-nie,	Side.
Au-a-kas-ca-nie,	Hip.
Chu-clau-mo-kee,	Loins.
Can-qua-le-eh,	Buttock.
Oo-ge-sai-nie,	Fundament.
Wau-to-lee,	Penis.
Chu-le-ne-eh,	Testicles.
Oo-la-stulle-eh,	Ladies.

NAMES OF ANIMALS.

Keelee,	Dog.
Wauh-yauh,	Wolf.
Yonah,	Bear.
Chestee,	Rabbit.
Kayla,	Racoon.
Auh-wee,	Deer.
Wassauh,	Cat.
Yannasaw,	Buffalo.
Wau-cauh,	Cattle.
Su-quah,	Hog.
Yogah,	Beaver.
Chu-yauh,	Otter.
Chu-lar,	Fox.
Enolee,	Black fox.

Cherokee.	English.
Sunkee,	Mink.
Sale-to-kis-qua,	Muskrat.
Sullolee,	Squirrel.
Chesla-chee,	Mouse.
Oh-way-lee,	Rat.
Oh-culnee,	Badger.
Su-qua-oo-chas-tie,	Opossum.
Au-way-qua,	Elk.
So-quille,	Horse.
Au-wee-oo-ta-nank,	Sheep.
Auh-ne-soo-kee, } Auh-wee,	Goat.

NUMERALS.

Soquo,	One.
Tuller,	Two.
Choeh,	Three.
Nankee,	Four.
His-kee,	Five.
So-tullee,	Six.
Calle-quo-kee,	Seven.
Chu-na-lar,	Eight.
Sad-na-lar,	Nine.
Aua-sco-kee,	Ten.
Sut-too,	Eleven.
Tulle-too,	Twelve.
Cho-cut-too,	Thirteen.
Ne-cut-too,	Fourteen.
His-kee-cut-too,	Fifteen.
Tullar-too,	Sixteen.
Culle-qua-too,	Seventeen.
Nalar-too,	Eighteen.
So-and-lar-too,	Nineteen.
Tulle-sco-kee,	Twenty.
So-eh-cha-na,	Twenty-one.
Tulle-cho-na,	Twenty-two.
Cho-eh-cho-na,	Twenty-three.
Nankee-cho-na,	Twenty-four.
His-kee-cho-na,	Twenty-five.

Cherokee.	English.
So-tulle-cho-na,	Twenty-six.
Culle-quo-cho-na,	Twenty-seven.
Nalar-cho-na,	Twenty-eight.
So-a-nalar-cha-na,	Twenty-nine.
Cho-auh-sco-kee,	Thirty.
So-ah-cauh-lee,	Thirty-one.
Tulle-cauh-lee,	Thirty-two.
Cho-eh-cauhlee,	Thirty-three.

So continue cauhlee at the end of every number till you come to one hundred, which is,

Auh-sco-he-chu-que,	One hundred.

Of their Games.

The Cherokees have many games for their amusement, which are common to other tribes of the south. Amongst them is the game called the *ball play*. It is generally played at the time of the fall season. The moon presides over it as a tutelary spirit. In the time of Te-shy-ah-Natchee, two chiefs made a ball-play, at which all the red people attended, men, women and children. The contest between the parties was very severe for a long time, when one of them got the advantage by the superior skill of a young man. His adversary on the other side, seeing no chance of success in fair play, attempted to cheat, when, in throwing the ball, it stuck in the sky, and turned into the appearance which the moon hath, to remind the Indians, that cheating and dishonesty are crimes. When the moon becomes small and pale, it is because the ball has been handled by unfair play. They therefore for a long time never played at this game but on the full moon. Many of their customs are now disregarded, and the tradition of them is totally lost. The ball is now played, for the most part, without any regard to custom.

The mode of playing it is this: Two chiefs meet, and make up the game, each taking his choice of young men, against the others. An open plain is selected, at which the chiefs meet, and lay off the ground, about 400 yards in circumference, through which the ball passes. Equidistant from the extremes of the alley, the grappling sticks to catch the ball are placed. Each chief then retires to his party, consisting of equal numbers, from 11 to 30, on each side, who march up to the centre, whooping and yelling as if going to war. The first thing is to make up all the stakes, which are deposited in one pile. Each chief then addresses his party. He animates them with the glory of beating their adversaries, and the advantage of winning the stakes, which are all to be equally divided amongst the warriors. They are admonished to play fair, that the Great Spirit may not be offended with them. The chiefs then take their station, as judges of the game. The parties arrange themselves in the centre, and the ball is thrown up, each grappling it with his sticks, having a bow at the end to catch the ball. Another seizes it with his grappling stick, and runs away with it, to the post of his party, till at length some one, more active and swift, gets the ball too far ahead to be overtaken, till he arrives at the goal, which counts for his party one in the game. Thus the game is continued, sometimes one party carrying out the ball, sometimes the other, till the game is finished, which sometimes takes two or three hours; during which they display as much zeal and animation as if they were contending for prizes of the highest value, yelling, and giving each other the most dreadful falls, in order to stop their progress. The dress worn by the players, is a belt or wampum around the waist, with a flap of blue cloth. When the game is ended, the stakes are equally divided by the chiefs of the winning party. The one who carries out the most balls is dubbed a hero, and is huzzaed as if he had conquered an enemy. For to excel in this game, is a great mark of prowess in the chase or field of battle.

CHAPTER XI.

Of the Chickasaws.

AT the time of the Spanish invasion of Mexico, about the year of our Lord 1520, the Chickasaws, whom the Spaniards called *Chiccemecas*, are represented to have lived at the north and west of México, with other tribes of hunters, and had not recognized the Mexican monarch as their superiors.[100] They hold it as a certain fact, that their forefathers, in very remote ages, came from a far distant country, by the way of the west, where all the people were of one colour, And that in process of time, they moved eastwardly to their present settlements. The old Chickasaw Indians related to our traders, that now about 110 years ago, some of the old Chickasaws, or as the Spaniards call them, Chiccemecas, came from Mexico in quest of their brethren, as far north as the Aquapah nation, more than 130 miles above the Natchez, on the southeast side of the Mississippi river; but through French policy, they were either killed or sent back, so as to prevent their opening an intercourse with their brethren.

The Chickasaws and Choctaws have this tradition: That their forefathers came from the west, many years ago, in the time of No-hoo-la-pah, Tuskah-Hamah, or the beloved red chief. A great nation, say they, made war upon our tribes, who resided upon the great rivers, which run from the western mountains into the great waters of the south. With this nation we had long been connected in amity and friendship. We had associated with them in war, and in the chase, and often smoked together the pipe of peace. Their chiefs claimed kindred with the *sun*, and were more absolute than ours. We were permitted to eat with them, hunt

---

100 3 Rob, America, 312.

with them, go to war with them, but not to intermarry with them. The mingo, or head man, was
the brother of the *sun.* [01] No-hoo-to-ta-pah had a
son, who had distinguished himself as a great warrior in several battles against the nations of the west.
He had eclipsed all the children of the sun with
whom he fought, in annoying the enemy. After a
long and bloody war, carried on jointly with our
ally against the enemy, we returned victorious.
No-hoo-to-ta-pah had been the first in command,
but the victory had been achieved by his son, who,
in imitation of our allies, had been styled the
Morning Star. On our return through the country
of our allies, the brother of the sun entertained our
warriors, for several days; during which, our hero,
the *Morning Star,* was permitted to partake of the
feast of the sun, which was celebrated in honour of
the conquerors. Mora, the daughter of the king,
officiated as priestess. The Morning Star was the
first who was presented to receive consecration.
The ceremony ended in the captivation of the hero
and of the priestess. The moment was auspicious.
He could withstand the honours which were to
be administered to him, but must fall a victim to
the hand which had administered them. Mora
felt what she had communicated, and sympathized
with the heart which she subdued. The hero resolved to conquer for Mora; she wished no longer
to be a vestal, and to live only for the hero. But
she was the descendant of the sun, and her lover
the son of a subordinate chief. A connexion between them was impossible. She was sensible of
her divine origin. She knew that she could not
be obtained by the consent of her father. She determined to elope with her lover to his own tribe.
She professed herself willing to be the wife of the

101 The sovereigns of the Hindoos were of the race of
the sun and moon, those also of the Chinese, Ceylonese, Peruvians, Mexicans and Natchez. Cuvier, 115.

Morning Star. He was to take her from the temple of the sun. The old king, and No-hoo-to-ta-pah, were taking leave of each other in the long smoke; but *Mora* and the *Morning Star* were already on the wing. The brother of Mora had been jealous of the *Morning Star.* His courage and skill had entitled him to the first honours among the warriors. The brother of Mora could not bear the comparison. He concealed himself in an ambush to destroy the other as he returned home. And whilst Mora and the Morning Star conceived themselves safe, the wretch let fly an arrow, and the hero fell at the feet of Mora. She escaped whilst her brother scalped her lover. She wandered off, and was never more heard of. No-hoo-to-ta-pah immediately demanded the murderer. The demand was refused: and both sides resorted to war; by the brother of the sun for the loss of his daughter, and by No-hoo-to-ta-pah for the death of his son. And a bloody war ensued. They place their origin a long distance to the west of the Mississippi; and they have a tradition amongst them, that there were some of their conjurers, who dreaming of white people towards the sun-rising, in a fine country, they started, and were travelling for some years. Their leader, or magician, had a pole, along which he set up every night; and whichever way the pole leaned in the morning,[102] they kept their course all day. The pole constantly leaned towards the east, till they came to the east of Old-town. It then leaned towards the west, and they came back to Old-town and camped till the pole stood straight; and there they made the first settlement.

In the time of De Soto, in the year 1540, on the 17th of December of that year, he arrived at Chiccaça from Tuscaluça and Mavilla; and on the 8th of March, 1541, he was attacked by the Chiccaças. Marching to *Alimama,* on the 25th the Indians

102 Ezekiel, ch. 21, v. 21 ; Hosea, ch. 4, v. 12.

were seen walking upon the top of a strong fort, ready to meet him. In the battle at the fort they came in front by sevens and eights, each rank discharging its arrows and giving place to another, manifested a considerable acquaintance with tactics and evolutions. These circumstances serve to show, that they had been there a considerable time, and had built their towns and forts. A part of the Chickasaws, long after they had established themselves on the southeastern side of the Mississippi, advanced as far as the river Savannah, and settled upon it, on the side opposite Augusta. Chenubbee said, in his lifetime, that the Chickasaws were formerly settled opposite Augusta, on the Savannah river. Misunderstandings arising between them and the Creeks, a part of them removed towards the west, and settled where they now are. Another part of them, called the Lightwood-knots, went to war with the Creeks, and were reduced by them, and have lived with them ever since. Chenubbee was the principal chief of that tribe when he died, which was lately. The Chickasaws claimed the land opposite Augusta, in the year 1795, and presented a memorial on the subject to the government of the United States. The Chickasaws have not changed their religious character, by their intercourse with the whites. They have no religious ceremonies. They believe there is a great good spirit, or *first cause*, to whom they pay no kind of adoration. There is no form of worship amongst them. They are very credulous and superstitious. They believe in invisible genii, ghosts and apparitions. Their population in May, 1813, was about 2600, and they increased in the proportion of five births to one death. They have no coercive laws. If one man is indebted to another, he pays the debt as soon as he can. If, on the other hand, he does not pay it, nor make any exertion to pay it, he is never credited again. They have no accidents except in playing ball. If in that a man kills another, he is not hurt for it. But if he accidentally kills any other way than in playing ball, he must die for it. They have departed, in a great measure, from the custom they had, of killing an innocent person by way of retaliation, if he was one of the family of the guilty. Now they kill the guilty. Their government is hereditary: and it is also a democratic republic. They have a king and council, who do all the business, public and private. The title of king is hereditary, and he has the name without any authority, or any salary to support his kingly rank; and he has no distinction of rank shown him, more than a common man: the beggar and the king are equal. They have no laws, except retaliatory ones, and those of nature. The females are modest, and generally very virtuous. There is no instance of a young woman having a child before marriage. When they have the menses, they have a little house convenient to the dwelling house, in which they stay during their continuance. At the expiration of the time, they wash, and comb their hair, and put on clean clothes. They are much more easily delivered in childbirth[3] than white women, having very little pain. Frequently they have their children in the woods by themselves, hardly ever keeping their beds more than three or four hours after having a child. They are from a month to six weeks in their purification after childbirth.[4] Their marriage ceremonies are these: The man takes a bundle of some kind of clothing to the nearest relations of the woman, as a present for her and her relations. If the girl and her friends keep the presents, and wear the clothes, the contract is made; and the man may go, and claim and bed with her as his wife. But if the bundle or presents be returned, it is no match. Polygamy is sometimes practised amongst them.

3 Exodus, ch. 1, v. 19.   4 Leviticus, ch. 12, v. 2.

Some men have three or four wives; but the practice is now going into desuetude. A man or woman is at liberty, if either find fault with the other, to divorce themselves. Each party takes a share of the property they have, and the woman takes the children. In all cases, the children belong exclusively to the woman's family. The king's sister's son is heir apparent to the title, his mother being of the royal blood. The king's children have no claim to the soverignty, their mother not being of the blood royal. When they die, they are washed and dressed in the best apparel, wrapped up in a blanket, and then a grave is dug in a house, and the deceased put into it, with some of his most valuable effects, which he most prized in his lifetime. The relations mourn for twelve months. Females let their hair go loose[105] during the time of mourning, never tie, and scarcely ever comb. The Chickasaw and Creek languages have no similarity. They have not the same national origin. They cannot understand each other, except some few who have learned the language of the other. There is a great similarity between the languages of the Choctaws and Chickasaws. It is almost certain they were originally one and the same nation. There is so little difference between the two languages, that a Choctaw and Chickasaw can

105 The Hebrews, at the death of their friends or relations, wept, tore their clothes, smote their breasts, fasted and lay upon the ground, and went barefoot. The time of mourning was commonly seven days, but sometimes continued thirty. The whole time of mourning, the near relations of the deceased continued sitting in the houses, and ate upon the ground. The food they took was thought unclean, and even themselves were judged impure. Their faces were covered, and for all the time they could not apply themselves to any labour. They did not dress themselves, nor make their beds, nor uncovered their heads, nor shaved themselves, nor cut their nails, nor saluted any body. 1 Samuel, ch. 12, v. 16, 17, 20, ch. 13, v. 18, 19, ch. 14, v. 31, 36; 2 Samuel, ch. 18, v, 33, ch. 3, v. 31; Genesis, ch. 50, v. 11; Esther, ch. 4, v. 8.

converse together, and each in his own tongue, and be perfectly understood. The Choctaws have been much longer from the original nation, than the Chickasaws; and have an idea, that the first Choctaws came out of a hill in the Choctaw country, called Nanny-Wia. Some of the best imformed of them believe, that they and the Chickasaws came originally from one and the same nation.

The immense depopulation of the countries which the Indians inhabited, at the arrival of the Europeans, is to be ascribed to several causes. The first and principal one, is the want of political power in the tribes, to regulate the conduct of the members who compose them. Each tribe is answerable to other tribes and nations, for the conduct of all its members, who must either be surrendered, to atone for the injuries he does, or the whole tribe must be subjected to retaliation for his offences. And so little is it consonant to their practice, to call for the surrender of the guilty individual, though sometimes it is done, that their custom is to fall at once upon some part of the offender's tribe, without making any previous demand of him, and to take satisfaction at once for the wrong that has been done. Thus war is begun on both sides, without any decision of the national council, and without any consideration had by them of the policy or impolicy of the measure, having regard to existing circumstances. By such means they are frequently engaged in wars which are followed by very disastrous consequences. The same want of coercive power in the body politic. disables the tribe to concentre its force when war exists. Whoever chooses either to withhold or withdraw his military services, is at liberty to do so. One part of the nation retires from the contest, while the other is exposed to all the horrors and devastations of war. If peace be made, and one part of the nation dislike it, that part secedes from the rest and forms a new commu-

nity, which perseveres in hostilities till it is nearly
ruined. After some time, the discordant parts of
the new community separate for the like causes,
and again subdivide, forming other and less populous communities. For want of this controlling
power in one common political head, eternal dis-
cords, wars, divisions and subdivisions, waste away
each tribe, and reduce them, by incessant action, to
insignificance. The want of coercive power in one
common head, leaves every tribe free to quarrel
with its neighbour; causes of variance continually
arise; war follows, and all who are engaged in it
suffer impairment. The causes of difference multi-
ply in proportion to the number of tribes, affect all
of them in rotation, and constantly hold over them
the shadow of destruction. We are men like them,
governed by the same passions, and are similarly
affected by similar causes. We should learn from
their examples, the danger there is in having a head
too weak for the compression of all parts of the
body politic.

Another cause which has operated with incalcu-
lable effect in modern times, is the use of gunpowder
as subservient to the trade for peltry. The game
taken by snares, and by bows and arrows, was no
more than sufficed for the sustenance of the inhabitants; and under all the drawbacks which these
imposed on natural increase, the game multiplied,
and had become very abundant. Mansco, in 1769,
saw in one view at the French lick alone, thousands
of buffaloes, though at this time there is not one in
the whole state of Tennessee. That Indian population depends upon the game, is proved by the fact,
that they both disappear nearly at the same time;
and that their numbers decrease nearly in the same
ratio. When the European trader offered a reward
for skins and peltry, the great quantities which the
natives could supply, and the profitable returns
made for them, induced the Indians to abandon

their own manufactures for those of European fabrication; and in a little time they could no longer make those fabrics, which once they produced in large quantities. They killed the game for the skins, and left the carcases in the woods to spoil; and to do this with greater despatch and effect, guns with powder and ball wers put into their hands; and with these they involved the animal creation in almost universal destruction. To these were added the steel-trap, which was hardly less destructive amongst the amphibious race. The scarcity of game was soon perceptible, and the scarcity of food was the inevitable consequence. Those who were nearest to the place where it reigned, were obliged either to remove into the interior, or to perish for want of those necessaries which are essential to the preservation of human existence. Whatever country they left, European population at once occupied, and practised agriculture, which supported a population more than fifty times greater than the country could sustain before, and a much greater number of animals, of a new species, which had never been seen in it in ancient times. The face of the western world was entirely changed. In place of forests of large trees, and impenetrable thickets of canes and briers, beautiful plantations were opened to view, agriculture and its concomitant vocations took place of the spontaneous productions of the wilderness, and instead of the acorn and beach seed, has substituted the cereatia, wheat, rye, oats, barley, and the Indian corn. It has placed here the civilized man, instead of the wild one, and domestic animals, of all sorts, in place of the bear, the buffalo and the panther. Gunpowder is the prime agent in preparing the country for all these changes; and it may be said to have planted populous cities in the bosom of the wilderness. To it may attributed at once the destruction and the reproduction of the human species in the western world. It annihilated the Mexicans and the Peruvians, with the people of Hayti, and others within the limits of the Spanish conquests: but their numbers were replaced from the old world, and those who were extracted from them. In the northern and eastern parts of America, its effects have not been so instantaneous; but certainly not less efficacious. The navigator's needle opened the country to view; and brought to it the European, who with his firelock and gunpowder, astonished and expelled the dismayed inhabitants, and prepared the way for new settlers, who brought with them the art of printing, the nurse of every science and invention, and with it, that pure system of ethics, of which it has been foretold, that it shall penetrate into all the recesses of the globe. The invention of gunpowder, of the navigator's needle, and of printing, in the 13th and 14th centuries, of almost simultaneous birth, without the conjunction of whose powers these great changes could never have been effected, suggests the idea, that some invisible hand may have brought them to light for these ends, which they have actually accomplished; and that these simple agents may have been the preordained instruments for the stupendous alterations which they have produced. One thing, however, may be perceived, namely: That intellectual improvement, progressing for a century to come, with the same velocity and effusion that it has for a century past, will make the inhabitants, both of the old world and the new, compared with those of the patriarchal ages, seem to be the creatures of a new origin.

A third cause of Indian extinction is, the variolous diseases which they received from the Europeans, which, for want of knowing the treatment proper to be given, have been attended with the most frightful mortality, whenever they have prevailed amongst the Indians. A fourth cause is, the excessive use of ardent spirits; many have perished by this means, but not enough to have made a mainfest change in the general population of the continent. Nor indeed is there any good reason to believe, that as many of them perish from this cause, in proportion to their numbers, as the whites. For there is no instance, perhaps, to be adduced, of an Indian becoming a sot, and of sitting by his bottle till he is bloated to death: nor is there any red face amongst them, made by the scorching fumes of ardent liquors; nor of one covered all over with blotches from the same cause. Such, however, is the rapid decrease of the Indians, that in a few years we shall have no idea of the Indian figure, colour or countenance, unless from some paintings of the present day, which may happen to preserve the resemblance.

LL

NOTES.

A.

Mr. Childress, of Williamson county, saw in Philadelphia, a petrified woman in complete preservation. The stone was taken from a cave in Kentucky. The hair upon the head appeared coarse: the whole seemed to be covered with moss. The eyes were full; and the nails very plain, both on the hands and feet. The hair seemed, however, to be much finer than the black hair of an Indian.

A general officer of eminent merit and distinction in the American army, died in the early part of the year 1795, and was buried in the neighbourhood of lake Erie. Twelve or fifteen years afterwards his body was disinterred, for removal to his native state. It was found to be in part petrified, and would have been wholly so in a few years more.

When the foundations of Quebec were dug, a petrified savage was found. His quiver and arrows were undecayed and unpetrified.

Doctor Brown, late of Wilson country, saw in the museum at Philadelphia, a completely petrified bull. He was found about the year 1806, in the neighbourhood of the Ohio. All his parts are perfect, and all petrified. One of his hinder legs is bent as if in the act of making an effort to get out of the sink hole in which he was found, and into which he had been precipitated. He was of the English form and size, and probably had been received by the Indians from the English colonists. This phenomenon proves, that flesh may be converted into stone in a few years. If this bull belonged to the white settlers of Kentucky, where he was found, petrifaction must have taken place, and must have been completed, in less than thirty years. On the waters of the Ohio, every thing is subjected to the laws of petrifaction—men, quadrupeds, fish, shells, reptiles, insects, vegetables, wood, clay. -

A nest of yellowjackets with the young ones in it, all petrified, was taken from the Ohio river, and was seen by Mr. Hays, counsellor at law, in 1807.

In Europe, also, are many instances of petrified men, quadrupeds and trees. It may perhaps be a correct remark, that the greater part of them are north of the 45th degree of north latitude; but it is one suggested with great diffidence, for examination. Leaves of trees in rocks, and frogs and lizards in them, and fish adhering to rocks, with petrified tracks of animals, all seem to indicate a very sudden induration.

Mr. Molina saw pieces of hewn timber dug out of a little hill near Valparaiso, some of which were eight feet long, and have the visible marks of the European axe.

B.

On the bed of the Rio Brassos de Dios, which discharges itself into the gulf of Mexico, in the province of Texas, between the Colorado and Trinity rivers, was taken a small round ball, of a dark iron colour, of the size of two thirds of a billiard ball, or a little under the size of a grape shot. It is not quite as heavy as iron. The interior of some others which have been broken, contain materials of metallic brilliancy, tinged with sulphur, and very much resembling zinc. It was taken from a great number of similar balls lying on the bed of the river. Doubtless it received its form whilst in a state of fusion, and was rolled upwards by the steam of volcanic heat, till it came in contact with the water in the river, and instantly condensed, and cooled before its globular form was altered. The exterior surface was nearly smooth.

C.

In the county of Tuscaloosa, in the state of Alabama, a large rock was lately broken up, and in its interior was found a tooth with two rough prongs. The tooth was about two inches long, and one inch thick, and declines in width to the end, where it is about half as wide as at the commencement of the enamel above. On the lateral edges it is serrated. The enamel is of the colour of grey limestone, smooth and hard, and about the tenth of an inch thick. The materials within the coating are perfectly petrified

Just below the summit of the Allegheny mountains, near the road that leads from Pittsburgh to Philadelphia, are large beds of oyster shells adhering to the sides of the mountains.

Dezcabezado, a mountain of Chili, equal to Chimborazo of Quito, which was supposed to be the highest in the world, has upon it oyster shells, conchs, periwinkles, &c. in a calcined or petrified state. The mountains on both sides of the Andes, and parallel to them, at the distance of 25 or 30 miles, have strata which abound in marine productions, and often exhibit the impressions of animals and vegetables.

D.

On Quankey creek, near Halifax town in North-Carolina, 150 miles west of the seashore, at the depth of twenty-five feet below the surface, are beds of oyster shells, and a great collection of fish bones.

E.

In digging a well on the Sunfish, in Adams county, Ohio, a gentleman found an earthen pot below the surface a considerable depth.

Mr. Neville, in Pickaway county, in digging for water, met with blacksmith's cinders six or eight feet below the surface of the plane.

In removing the walls of Circleville, blacksmith's cinders were found.

In the state of Ohio, near Chillicothe, was found a stump, with the marks of the axe upon it, 90 feet below the surface.

On the Washita river, in the prairie Mar Rouge, Mr. Latting sunk a well, and at the depth of 19 feet, where the country is perfectly level, he found chumps of wood, with the ends put together, and coals on the chumps where the fire had acted.

In South-Carolina, Sumpterville district, Salem county, one mile below Cambden, in sinking a well, the diggers came to fire coals at the depth of 23 feet.

Mr. Burnett, of Cincinnati, in digging a well on his lot, within the wall of the old fort at Cincinnati, struck upon two stumps, a larger and a smaller one, at the depth of 93 feet below the surface. The largest was so injured by time, that it was doubtful to what family it belonged. The smaller one was in a state of better preservation, and is a sugar maple. Just before reaching the stumps, the workmen passed through a layer of black mud, which was very offensive. Lower down, pigments of a fine blue colour were thrown up in detached pieces. This was 20 or 30 feet below the level of the first bottom.

In the summer of 1819, not far from Franklinton on the Scioto, in digging a well, after the workman had descended sixty feet, he found a piece of brass, the remains of a boiler, and part of a tree, which had been partly burnt. In digging a well near

Williamsburg, on the east fork of the Little Miami, at the depth of thirty-six feet the workmen came to a fire place, charcoal, and fire brands, carefully laid together, and designed to be burnt or kindled.

In the countries near to Tennessee, are appearances of things covered deep in the bowels of the earth, which once grew upon the surface. They all point to a general cause, which at some time heretofore changed the face of nature in this part of the globe. The state of Illinois, on its eastern boundary, bordering on the river Ohio, is formed by a chain of small ridges, extending from ten to twelve miles west of the Ohio, gradually terminating in ground generally sloping, covered principally with beautiful oak timber, variegated with flat ground, maple swamps, and marshy branches. The creeks are principally confined in high banks nearly perpendicular, and without bluffs of rock on either side, the waters of which remain nearly still, flowing gently without any apparent current. At the distance of about thirty miles from the United States saline, the eye of the traveller is suddenly caught by the appearance of those extensive prairies for which Illinois and Missouri are so eminently and peculiarly identified. These prairies are different in extent, from one to twenty miles. The prairies are almost universally the highest lands to be found. They are skirted by oak and hickory timber, generally low and scrubby. Some of these prairies are very poor, having little or no vegetable mould, are flat, and much inclined to be wet during the spring and summer seasons. So soon as they receive the full force of the sun, the surface becomes hard, and large cracks are found in it. There are, however, but few of these poor prairies in Illinois, compared to the many that are rich and fertile, affording the means of making, by a little labour, the most extensive farms that can be made in any section of country upon the continent. The rich prairies have a vegetable mould on the surface, of irregular depths, from one to three feet, without visible change in appearance. The rich prairies seemed to be formed after the same order as those that are poor, which have been already described. The traveller seems to rise a little hill of considerable elevation above the woodland; but on arriving at the summit, he sees in prospect a widely extended plane. His view is only interrupted occasionally by a gently sloping ridge, or an irregular grove of timber. Some of the prairies are considerably rolling, others more gentle, exhibiting in their appearance an irregular or amphitheatrical form. It is universally and invariably found to be a fact, so far as experience goes, that the highest prairies are the best adapted to agricultural purposes. There are but few springs in Illinois affording pure water, they principally flowing from muddy ground and stagnant pools of water, in which Illinois, as well as Missouri, plentifully abounds. It is proved by all experience there, that the best water is found by *digging wells.* In the prairies, water is much more easily procured than in the timbered land. In the former, the farmer chooses an elegant site for his dwelling, and there sinks his well, it not being material where; for success almost invariably accompanies the attempt, when it often happens attempts to procure water in the timbered lands wholly fail. Hence it would seem that some material difference exists in the construction or in the composition of the prairie and timbered lands. In digging for water, generally, it is necessary to descend from twenty to thirty feet before it is procured. Some of the water, when found, is of excellent quality, but by far the greatest proportion is extremely indifferent and unhealthy. A great deal of the water of Illinois is very considerably impregnated with salts, which, when analyzed, are found to contain a considerable proportion of pure glauber salts. In digging for water, it is found necessary in many places to place in timber as the diggers descend, for the purpose of preventing the sand from falling in and covering the diggers. After passing through the stratum of vegetable mould, or top of the ground, there is frequently found a stratum of clay, which is of different colours in different places, being principally regulated by the fertility of the surface. In some places the clay is yellow, in others between a red and a yellow, verging towards a mulatto colour, and in places where the soil is sterile, the clay beneath is of a white colour. Wherever the clay is found, almost invariably beneath it is a stratum of sand, of yellowish tinge, composed of shining materials like flint. Beneath the sand is a stratum of tough clay, or rather mud, of a bluish cast, variegated with white or grey, and beneath this is found a clay of black mud, in which, after passing a few feet, water is found. The stratum covering the black mud is composed of very fine materials, remarkably tough in texture and appearance. And what is marvellously strange, in the black mud is found timber at the distance, in Illinois, of from twenty to thirty feet from the surface, some pieces of which are completely petrified, and others in a state verging to petrifaction. Hence it is inferred, that this black mud was at some period the surface of the common country, or the bottom of a lake or ocean. How this superabundance of ground is collected or formed above the stratum of mud in which the wood is found, is difficult to conjecture, except by reference to the general deluge, or some other of late date. The stratum of black mud is found in every part of the country where attempts have been made to procure water at nearly the same depth from the surface. Examples and proofs in abundance exist, of timber having been found in this mud, in different parts of the country, having sustained a complete decomposition. A well is in

St. Clair county, about ten miles eas'wardly of a small village called Lebanon, where a gentleman, digging for water, came on timber completely petrified, at the distance of twenty-nine or thirty feet from the surface. The timber was taken from the stratum of black mud above described. The increase above the black mud is too deep to admit of the supposition, that it was produced by the decay and rotting of timber and vegetables through a long succession of ages; nor would the rotting of timber have produced a stratum of tough clay and a stratum of almost pure sand, a stratum of clay varying in colour in different places, and finally a covering of vegetable mould of various thickness; and above all, by that process the timber would have been intermixed from the surface to where the timber is now found. The quality of the clay may be generally determined by the character of the surface, for where the land is poor the same quality is invariably infused into the clay beneath, and is discoverable by its being much finer in its texture, and whiter. It is known to the slightest observer, that timber, when rotten, tends to increase the vegetable mould, but never forms an entire stratum of sand, unmixed with alluvial, or more gross particles of dirt. At a place where Mr. Smith lives, in Loutre prairie, on the north side of the Mississippi, on the road leading from St. Charles to Franklin, about forty-five miles from the former, Mr. Smith was engaged in digging a well for water in the prairie, which is a high, fine tract of land, and at the distance of about seventy-five feet came upon the black mud. After having passed through the stratum of vegetable mould about three feet, he came to the clay, which was found about twenty-five or thirty feet. He passes next through sand, and a stratum of the same description of fine blue and white clay that is found in Illinois, and lastly the black mud. At the depth of seventy-nine feet from the surface, he drew up wood completely pet-rified, and in the mud were fire coals. Twenty-five miles northeast of St Charles, in digging a well, a grape vine was found completely petrified, thirty feet below the surface. The pores of the grape vine were clearly perceivable, though converted into stone.

In Halifax county, North-Carolina, eight miles southwest from the town of Halifax, a well was sunk on the plantation of Judge Haywood, in the year 1787. At the depth of fifty feet below the surface, in a bed or stratum of strong-scented black mud, the diggers came to the boughs of an oak, and it was some considerable distance before they could get through it. Sixteen miles southwest of that plantation, another well was dug at an earlier pe-riod, and at the depth of sixteen or eighteen feet, the workmen came to a poplar log lying horizon-tally. Sometimes fish and plants are found to-gether. If plants of another climate, they must have come with the fish from that climate. Sub-terranean intumescence might have raised the fish above water, but there would have been no plant with the fish. Water then must have been the cause of their removal and association, and that water bereft by tepidity of its vivifying principle. Why else did the fish die, but for want of cooling air in respiration? The coals so abundantly found in the earth support this idea.

Shell fish of the present races, found in limestone all over America and Europe, and marl composed of shells in the bays and rivers, and in the interior, show that the sea has once held dominion over these countries.

The remains of land and sea animals are often found together in the bowels of the earth. They did not grow where found; water must have brought them together, especially when accompanied by vegetable remains.

Fish and petrified plants have been found together: they must have been brought together by natation.

Amphibious and land animals have been found together, and must have met in the same way.

Marine shells and vegetable substances have been found together, and must have been united in the same way. Petrified wood and fossil bones were preserved in water, at first from putrefaction, and were overlaid by strata, by its violence and subsequent subsidence. The remains of large land and sea animals are found in very deep chalk beds, sometimes five hundred feet and more below the surface; and sometimes vegetable remains with them, demonstrative of the extreme turbidness of of the waters which involved them, of the vast depths and heights to which they plunged and ascended, and of the cavities which were filled with their deposites on their retrogradation. All the superincumbent crust at least has been raised by alluvial additions, taken perhaps from other countries now covered by the ocean, and from the beds and sides of the ocean itself. It is no doubt true, that the crust of the earth is incessantly increased, but the growth is too gradual and slow, to have superinduced that deep covering which we see above the black mud or former bed of the ocean. Coals burnt by the locaters of land thirty years ago, are now eighteen inches under ground. It was a matter of controversy in West Tennessee some time since, whether a certain tree had been marked as a corner in 1784. The marks of the axe were doubtful. The surveyor, when he laid off the tract in that year, had encamped, as he said, near to the corner the night before he made it, and on a certain elevation, and at a certain distance from it. There was no sign of fire at this spot. It was concluded to dig into the earth, and at the distance of eighteen inches they came to the coals and chumps, such as he described. Coals are frequently dug up at the distance of five feet under ground in Tennessee, and from thence to one hundred feet. At various distances are found the bones of animals, such as we have in modern times, and other articles which were once upon the surface. The earth increases: the oceanic waters decrease. But these phenomena cannot account for the deposites upon the bed of the ocean, now so deeply covered under the surface.

Fern and capillary plants have been found in Shale, in Rhode-Island. Impressions out of it, of the *palm tree* bark, at Wilkesbarre, and various species of palm in the sandy desert west of Grand Cairo, in thirty degrees of north latitude, evince plainly an accession from the south, for they are at least twenty or thirty, and in some instances forty or fifty degrees north of the climate of their nativity. So were the elephants in Europe, in the fiftieth degree of north latitude, and the crocodiles at Blenheim and Scanea. Elephant bones have been found in South-Carolina, Virginia and Maryland. Were they not floated from the south, as well as the tropical plants found at Zanesville? Fish have been found in large quantities, with their tails wreathed to one side, as if in pain for want of cool air. Why are not the like appearances in Chili or Patagonia? It is submitted, whether all these evidences do not establish a deluge from south to north, with many combustibles on fire, when it reached and involved them, an atmosphere extremely rarified, exceedingly high winds rushing into the vacuum, and the waters furiously agitated. The great comet, whose revolutionary period is 575 years, appeared, says Mr. Cavallo,[99] in the year 2349 before Christ, of course in the year of the world 1655. Turn into Mosaic years of thirty days to the month, the 575 solar years, and add them to the time of its appearance in 1766 or 1767 before Christ, at which

[99] V. 2, p. 241.

period it also appeared, making 583 years, 38 days, and it will reach to the year 1655 of the world. Supposing it to have appeared between the first and thirteenth of September, as it did in the year of our Lord 531,[100] and to have continued visible for several months, as did a comet in the time of Nero, 64 before Christ; another in 603, another in 1240, and a fourth in 1279; then the flood commencing in the second month of the next year, or 1656 of the world, answerable to November, this comet, was in view at the very time when the flood commenced. This exact concurrence at the precise period stated by the Mosaic history, not only evinces that the flood occurred at the point of time assigned for it, but also that the number of years from the creation was correct. Had he stated any other number, for instance 1655 or 1654, there would have been a chasm between that and the year 2349, in which the great comet appeared. But being 1656 of the world, or 2348 before Christ, there is no intervening chasm. Supposing the earth to have occupied a place in her orbit near where the track of the comet cut it in his passage towards or from the sun, thence may have been derived all the phenomena before described—the ignition of all the combustible materials in the southern regions of the globe more immediately exposed to its influence, extensive rarefaction of the atmosphere, and the loss of respiring vitality by its extreme tenuity and excalescense, a great rush of wind into the vacuum, and the pressure of the waters by the proximity of the comet from their place in the ocean. If a common conflagration will raise the winds, and if the heat of long continued fair weather in the hottest part of summer will set on fire the woods and thatched buildings of a country, as happened in Germany a few years ago, why not similar effects from similar, but infinitely more efficient causes?

With respect to marine shells on the tops of hills and mountains, there is a precise description of the cause in the first chapter of Genesis, if we would not be too fastidious to use so common a book. At first the earth was under the water, and afterwards rose up out of it. Darkness was upon the face of the deep, and the spirit of God moved upon the face of the waters.[101] And God said, let the waters under the heavens be gathered together in one place, and let the dry land appear; and it was so.[102] Then it arose from the water, the highest parts of the earth appearing first; for instance, the high mountains of Asia. Upon these were the deposites of sea animals, and upon the land were found land animals. The lands have gradually increased by the wise providence of God, as the animal creation wanted more room, whilst the seas have receded in the same ratio, those parts everywhere nearest to the ocean exhibiting the most numerous and the most recent signs of the former dominion of the ocean. When we see afterwards in layers the organic remains of land and sea animals embodied together, these are evidences of the deluge, for by no other means could they have been together.

The body of a tree has been found in Indiana ninety feet below the surface.

In digging the canal at Zanesville, in the state of Ohio, about the tenth of June, 1820, which was intended to connect the waters of the lakes with those of the Ohio, Mr. Atwater caused sixteen drawings to be made of tropical plants found there. Amongst them were, the leaf of the cocoa nut, the bearing palm leaf of twenty inches in length, the roots, trunk, limbs and leaves of the bamboo, the trunk, limbs, leaves, roots and even the blossoms of the cassia. The leaves and even the blossoms are fresh, uninjured and entire, showing very conclusively, as Mr. Atwater supposes, that they grew near the spot where they are now found.

101 Genesis, ch. 1, v. 2.   102 Genesis, ch. 1, v. 9.

The fossil bones of elephants are spread over the equatorial regions of America, where the elephant does not exist, and not at the foot of the palm trees in the burning planes of the Oronoko, but in the coldest and most elevated regions of the Cordilleras.

F.

In September, 1817, near Antrim, in Rockland county, a man in digging a drain through a miry swamp, discovered, about three feet from the surface of the earth, several pieces of teeth of enormous size. From the appearance, shape, and manner in which they are worn away, the animal must have lived to great age, and it is supposed belonged to the granivorous species. The largest piece appears to have belonged to the extreme back tooth of the under jaw, and is eight inches in length, four inches in breadth, and three in height from where it rested in the jaw bone to the head or top of the tooth. Though it evidently appears that one half has been worn away by mastication, yet it weighs three pounds, six ounces. The enamel is the principal part of the tooth that is preserved. The root is chiefly decayed, and upon being exposed to the air mouldered away. The teeth were full of marrow. There were found several large bones on Big Bone creek, in Kentucky, below the mouth of Big Miami. The horns were fifteen feet long, and weighed one hundred pounds, and the teeth and grinders from twelve to fifteen pounds.[103] 'Mr. Bell saw at the Blue licks in Kentucky, a rib of some huge animal, which reached from the ground to the roof of the house; also, a tooth as large as his head, and a big bone four feet long, and as large in circumference as his body. Many such bones are found near all the salines in that country.

103 Schnetz, 185.

G.

Medals representing the sun with rays of light,
have been found in the mounds. They are made
of very fine clay, and coloured in the composition
before they were hardened by heat, originally more
than three inches in diameter.

A stone of large size was found in Mexico, in
1790, containing a representation of the calendar.
The sculpture is in relievo, and well polished.
The concentric circles, with the numerous divisions
and subdivisions, are traced with mathematical exactness. In the centre of the stone, is sculptured
the hieroglyphic of the sun, surrounded by eight
triangular radii. The god of the country is figured
opening his large mouth armed with teeth, which
reminds us of a figure of a divinity in Indostan, the
image of Kala, or time. In the Hindoo sytem of
religion, are gods called Ashta-dik-pala-guru, who
presided over the eight principal divisions of the
world.[104]

In the city of Cusco in Peru, in South America,
was a temple standing in the time of the Spanish
invasion, in one of the apartments of which, towards
the east, was placed the image of the sun, consisting
of one gold plate which covered the whole breadth
of the chapel. This image was of a circular form,
representing the sun with his rays darting from him.
And in another part of the temple was the image of
the moon, of a round form, with a woman's face in
the middle of it.

When we come to the teocalli of Mexico, or high
mounds, which some call temples, one of them is
- called the house of the sun, the other the house of
the moon. They are built like those of Tennessee
and the neighbouring countries, wherever they are
square and precisely to the cardinal points. Like
them, they have a flat top. Images and altars were
upon them, and they have upon them the stone

104 2 Dubois, 214,

Knives with which the chests of human victims were opened. They leave us no doubt of the deities to whom they were dedicated, nor of the human sacrifices made upon them, nor of the perfect conformity to the models in India, Chaldea and Egypt, where also buildings of the like stupendous altitude have been erected to the cardinal points, with flattened tops, ascended like those of Mexico and Peru, by stairs on the outside. The time has been, when from the confines of Chili to the Alleghenies, and from the Stone mountains to the Savannah, the worship of the sun prevailed, and as we shall presently see, with all the peculiarities, emblems and rites which his worshippers in Asia observed and practised, and that it was maintained by a population which spread like the mounds, and with them from Mexico and Peru to the Alleghenies.

Other representations prove the worship of the moon also. Semicircles represent her. Copper plates perfectly round, thin, flat and smooth, without any thing to represent the rays of light, have been often found. Semicircular works, sometimes three or more joined together, always facing the east, are to be seen entirely unconnected with any other work. They are of earth, and only a few feet high.

Near the centre of the round fort at Circleville, which is described in the American Archaiologia, was a tumulus of earth about two feet in height, and several rods in diameter at the base. On its eastern side, and extending six rods from it, was a semicircular pavement, composed of pebbles, such as are now found in the bed of the Scioto river. The summit was nearly thirty feet in diameter, and there was a raised way to it, leading from the east, like a modern turnpike. The summit was level. The outline of the semicircular pavement, and the walk, is still discernible. In it, amongst other things, was the handle of a small sword, or large knife. Around the end where the blade had been inserted, was a ferule of silver. *No iron was found,* but the oxyde remained.

On the north side of the Ohio river, near the Scioto, and near three circular tumuli, is a high semicircular work, at this time not more than twenty feet of perpendicular height, and containing nearly an acre. This elevated circular work, with raised walks to ascend and descend to and from the elevated area, was not usual as a cemetery.

On the main branch of Paint creek, on the Ohio, where are very ancient and remarkable walls, gateways, wells, and stone elevations full of human bones and eliptical works, like those on the Mississippi and in Mexico,—is a work in the form of a half moon, set around the edges with stone, such as are now found one mile from the spot. Near the semicircular work is a very singular mound, five feet high, and thirty feet in diameter, composed chiefly of red ochre, an abundance of which is found in a hill at no great distance from the place. Hence the name of Paint creek.

Near the junction of Hargiss's creek with the Scioto, in the state of Ohio,—where are square and circular fortifications, walls and intrenchments of considerable extent, and gateways at proper intervals, with mounds in front of the gateways,—about the centre of the circular walls is the site of a once very remarkable mound of earth, with a semicircular pavement on its eastern side, nearly fronting the only gateway leading into the fort. This mound is now entirely removed, but the outline of the semicircular pavement may still be seen in many places.

H.

The Indians of North-Carolina, in the year 1730, had much veneration for the number three. The conjurers, in performing their exorcisms, after being blindfolded, went around the fire three times; then into the woods; and returning, went around again three times; then to the woods again a second time, where they remained half an hour, and performed the same exorcisms a third time. When a conjurer there was to discover stolen goods, he caused three fires to be made in regular form. He is hoodwinked with a deer skin, and stands in the centre of the three fires, and goes directly out of one of the three gaps, with a stick in his hand, with which he strikes the ground, and announces the thief. When one of them dies, they fast[105] three days successively around his grave. The mourners cut off more than one half of their hair, the women as well as the men; and there are women appointed and hired, who, during six months, lament the death of a king, crying with a loud voice three times a day, morning, noon and evening. Cutting off the hair in mourning was practised by the Persians, Jews, Thebans and Egyptians.[106] The custom of procuring hired mourners was kept up by the Hebrews particularly, as well as by other nations.[107] On Peace river, northwest of the lakes of Canada, near the mountains, a native of the country, about to embark on board of a boat with Mr. McKenzie, previous to his departure cut off a lock of his hair and divided it into three parts. He fixed one part to the hair and upper part of his wife's head, blowing upon it with all the violence in his power, and uttering certain cabalistical words. The other two he fixed with the same formality on the head of his two children.[108] Mr. Omstead, counsellor at law, of Franklin, in the county of Williamson in West Tennessee, saw a nation of Indians to the northwest,

105 2 Samuel, ch 12, v. 16; Joel, ch. 2, v. 16.
106 1 Herodotus, 204, 356; 2 Herodotus, 294; 5 Plutarch, 84; 3 Rollin, 86.
107 Job, ch 3, v. 8; Jeremiah. ch. 9, v. 17.
108 1 Samuel, ch. 20, v. 41; 1 Kings, ch. 9, v. 25; Daniel, ch. 6, v. 10, 13.

(perhaps the Pawnees,) who, like the Hindoos, celebrate the beginning of the year for *three* days, and sacrifice *three* white dogs. He was present at the festival and the sacrifice.

I.

In digging into a mound at Chillicothe, in the state of Ohio, the remains of a man were found. Over the place where his breast was supposed to have been, was a cross, and string of beads. The cross was completely converted into verdigrease. The trees which grew on the mound were of the same size as those of the surrounding woods.

When the Spaniards arrived in America, they found stones cut in the figure of the cross, which were reverenced by the Mexicans. The cross was a symbol of matter venerated amongst the Egyptians from the remotest antiquity. In India the temples are sometimes built in this form. It was amongst the Irish, who descended from the Hindoos, the symbol of knowledge.[109] The cross on the breast of the skeleton near Chillicothe, and that in the pottery in the small graves near Sparta, shows their Hindoo origin.

K.

The mounds are generally from five to ten and twelve feet high; and sometimes to the south, eighty or ninety; generally in the form of a cone. Those in the northern parts of the state of Ohio, are of inferior size, and fewer in number, than those along the river. They exist from the Rocky mountains in the west, to the Alleghenies on the east, and from the southern shore of lake Erie to the Mexican gulf. They are numerous and lofty in the south, and exhibit proofs of a common origin.[110]

On the Ohio, going downwards, the mounds appear on both sides erected uniformly on the highest

109 McCullough, 137. 110 Archailogia Americana, 167.

alluvians along the stream, at Marella, Portsmouth and Cincinnati. They are found at the junction of all the rivers along the Mississippi, in the most eligible positions for towns, and on the most extensive bodies of fertile land. Their number exceeds perhaps three thousand; the smallest not less than twenty feet in height, and one hundred in diameter at the base. They are found in that part of the country where the traces of numerous population might be looked for; from the mouth of the Ohio, on the east side of the river, to the Illinois river, and on the west side from the St. Francis to the Missouri. Nearly opposite St. Louis are traces of two large cities in the distance of five miles, on the Cahokia, which crosses the American bottom opposite St. Louis. There is a mound at New-Madrid three hundred and fifty feet in diameter at the base. There are large ones at St. Louis, one with two stages; another with three at the mouth of the Missouri. At the mouth of Cahokia are also mounds, in two groups. Twenty miles below are two groups likewise; but the mounds are of smaller size. There is one near Washington, in the state of Mississippi, one hundred and forty-six feet high; also at Baton-Rouge, and the bayou Manshac. The mound on Black river has two stages and a group around. On the plane between the Arkansas and the St. Francis, are several large mounds. The mounds are small on the northern lakes, and become more numerous as we go southwest, until we come to the Mississippi, where they are lofty and magnificent. These works, similar to the teocalli of Mexico, are not found north of the mound at Circleville, on the Scioto. They are very common and lofty in the Mississippi, thence to the gulf of Mexico, and around it, through Texas, into New Mexico and South America. They are in Alabama, and as far as the Savannah river. The size and number of these mounds, it is presumed, show the degree of population which existed at the time of their desertion, and from what heart or centre that population extended towards the extremities. And they show, what is now the principal object of inquiry, that the same religious creed and ceremonies extended over all the countries in which the mounds are seen, and possibly the same political institutions, perhaps the same empire.

In the county of St. Clair, in an extensive prairie called the Looking-glass prairie, about twenty-five miles from St. Louis, in Missouri, is a mound about thirty-five feet high above the common plane. It is perfectly circular, containing on the surface of its summit about three quarters of an acre. It rises from its base almost perpendicularly in some places, and the most gradual slope is difficult of ascent. The summit is almost level, being somewhat depressed in the centre, and covered with small sassafras bushes. The soil on the top is remarkably black and rich. Around this mound stand six others, being small, and similar to those we see in Tennessee, of the second order of those found in the country. A ditch near it is yet visible, of considerable length and breadth, from which the materials for the mound must have been taken. There are many small mounds in Illinois and Missouri.

It seems to be a well established fact, that the bodies of nearly all those buried in mounds were partially, if not entirely, consumed by fire before the mounds were built, says one writer.

This, says he, is made to appear by quantities of charcoal being found at the centre and base of the mounds, stones burnt and blackened, and marks of fire on the metallic substances buried with them.[r]

In a mound at Marella was found a human body, in 1819, with his face upwards, and his feet pointing to the northeast, and his head to the southwest. From the appearance of several pieces of charcoal

[r] Archailogia Americana, 118.

and bits of partially burnt fossil coal, and the black colour of the earth, it would seem that the funeral obsequies had been celebrated by fire; and whilst the ashes were yet hot and smoking, a circle of flat stones had been laid around and over the body. The circular covering is about eight feet in diameter, and the stones yet look black as if stained by fire and smoke. This circle of stones seems to have been the nucleus on which the mound was formed, as immediately over them is heaped the common earth of the adjacent plane, composed of clayey and coarse gravel. The mound was originally about ten feet high, and thirty feet in diameter at the base. From the length of some of his bones, the person is supposed to have been six feet in height. Those of the scull were uncommonly thick. Trees were upon the work, whose ages the annulars proved to have been four hundred or five hundred years; and on the ground were other trees, which appeared to have fallen from old age. Thick sculls are the effects of long exposure to a hot sun. But what is more material, the Hindoos burnt, the Hebrews buried, and the Scythians buried. Those who erected this mound over a burnt corpse, were not of the same nation with those who buried the great skeleton, eight feet in height, in White county. There are some mounds on Jonathan's creek of Muskingum, the bases of which are formed of well burnt brick, between four and five inches square; and in the bricks are charcoal cinders and pieces of calcined human bones. Above them the mound was composed of earth, showing that the dead had been burnt in the manner of several eastern nations, and the mound raised afterwards. The mounds over dead bodies, or their ashes, are generally conical to the top.

L.

On the two high mounds in the Mexican valley, dedicated to the sun and moon, and standing to the north of lake Cuscuco, were tops led to on the sides by a stair of large hewn stones; on which tops, the first travellers say, were statues covered with thin lamina of gold.

M.

The people who built the mounds used human sacrifices. The Wolf tribe of the Pawnee Indians yet follow the custom. Mr. Manuel Lea, during the summer of 1818, purchased a Spanish prisoner, a boy about ten years old, whom they intended to offer as a sacrifice to the *great star.* And they did put to death, by transfixing on a sharp pole, as an offering to the object of their adoration, the child of a Paddo woman, who, being a captive herself, and devoted to that sanguinary death, made her escape on horseback, leaving her new-born offspring behind.

N.

The worship of the lingham, or phallus, once prevailed over Egypt, Phenicia, Greece, Rome, and amongst the Moabites and Midianites, as well as in India. Being found in America. it affords an incontrovertible and prostrating evidence of the connexion which once existed between the old and the new world. Amongst the Egyptians, Greeks, and Hebrews, the representation of the phallus was of a large size, and was made sometimes of gold and silver, and sometimes of stone. Captain Cook saw traces of it in the Sandwich islands, where was left the custom of erecting mounds and the art of making feathered mantles, which emigration left there in the course of its progress to America. We can go upon the trace of the phallus from Tennessee to the Pacific islands, to India and to Egypt. In speaking of the Sandwich islands, the author of Cook's Voyages says, there are many idols, one of them the black figure of a man resting upon his toes and fingers, and that the islanders give place

Oo

in their houses to many ludicrous and obscene idols, like the priapus of the ancients.[112] Bacchus seems to have been the generative god of the Greeks, and Venus the generative goddess. The rites of both were celebrated with sorts of obscenity.[113] The like ceremonies were practised in the temple of Baol Peor.

There is a Mexican temple dedicated to the generative goddess, like the Ceres of the Greeks and Romans, the Isis of the Egytians, and the productive power of India.

A phallus, or priapus, was found in or near Chillicothe, not long since, and was presented to Mr. McCullough, who deposited it in the hall of the American Philosophical Society.

O.

Nine murix shells, the same as described by Sir William Jones, in the Asiatic Researches, have been found within twenty miles of Lexington, in Kentucky, in an ancient work.[114] Their component parts remained unchanged, and they were every way in an excellent state of preservation. These shells, so rare in India, are highly esteemed and consecrated to their god Meliadava, whose character is the same with the Neptune of Greece and Rome. This shell, amongst the Hindoos, is the musical instrument of the Tritons. The foot of the Siamese god Gaudme, or Budh, is represented by a sculpture in Ava, to be six feet in length, and the toes carved each to represent a shell of the murix. These shells have been found in many mounds which have been opened in every part of Ohio. And this proves that a considerable value was put upon them by their owners.[115]

112 1 Herodotus, 335, 336, 337, 338, 341; 1 Diodorus Siculus, 29; 2 Dubois, 200, 208, 282.
113 1 Rollin, 48.   114 Archailogia Americana, 241.
115 Archailogia Americana, 241.

One of the mounds near the lake, formerly the bed of the river, at the mouth of the Merimac, near St. Genevieve, is composed chiefly of shells. The inhabitants have taken away a great part of them for lime.

P.

In the county of Bourbon, in Kentucky, on the north side of Stone's fork, about five miles northeast of Paris, are seven piles of rocks placed in a direct line: they are from eight to ten feet in height, and from twenty-five to thirty feet in diameter; the base of a circular form, and terminating in a cone at the top. These piles are situated on a high and commanding eminence, formed by the bluff of the creek, and at the distance of from three hundred to four hundred yards from it. The piles are composed of broad flat stones, presenting evident marks of rock over which water had once run, and seemed to be of the same species of stone as that which is yet seen in the bottom of the creek. Some of the rock are large masses, and must have required the united exertions and patience of a number of persons to convey a single one to its place in the pile: and to have completed the whole of these monuments, at least one thousand men must have been employed twelve months. The piles are thrown up in loose array, indicating no specimens of art or of mechanic skill. All the rocks retain their native appearance, so far as any observation made enabled the beholder to discover.

Such were the monuments used in ancient times, by the people of Asia, to commemorate important events. Such monuments were used as well by the lettered Israelites when they passed the Jordan, and on other similar occasions, as by unlettered nations.[s] But what is far more striking, the number seven was with the people who set up these monuments

s Deut. ch. 27, v. 2, 4; Joshua, ch. 4, v. 3, 4, 5, 6, 7, 8, 9, 10, 1, 22.

a number of perfection, as it was with the people of India, Arabia, Egypt, and the Hebrews, and as it is with the Arabians and Hindoos to this day. There is no obvious cause in nature, or in natural history, for determining mankind to seven, as the number of perfection, more than to any other number. The seven days of the week is a cycle of positive institution, and so is the worship of the seven planets. This idea in America is a derivative one, emanating from a common source with others of the same family and connexions. That common sourse is India, where it has been from the earliest ages of the world. From thence it was carried by emigrant tribes to Gothland and Scandinavia, where the days were classed into sevens, and called by the names of their deities; the first of which being the sun, they called Sunday; the second being the moon, they called Moonday, or Monday; the next, Tuisto, the most ancient deity of the Germans and Scandinavians, gave name to Tuishday, or Tuesday. They had a god called Woden, hence Woden's-day, or Wednesday; another called Thor, hence Thor's-day, or Thursday. They had one called Frica, hence Frica's-day, or Friday; another called Seater, hence Seater's-day, or Saturday. Their neighbours, if not descendants, the Esquimaux, and the people seen by Capt. Wharring, about the 6th of August, 1820, in north latitude 73, to the south of Lancaster sound, paid adoration to the sun. If this be taken, as it certainly is, as an evidence that the Goths were of Hindoo extraction, it may perhaps be equally so, that those who built these piles were of Hindoo extraction also.

Q.

Near the junction of Hargess's creek with the Scioto, in the state of Ohio, where are very ancient works, the walls vary only a few degrees from north and south, east and west, but not more than the needle varies. Many surveyors from this circum-

325

stance, believe that the authors of these works were
acquainted with astronomy. The circle and square
exactly laid down, and no error could be detected
in their measurement.[17] On the American pyramids
there is a variation of 52 seconds. In 1794, the
pyramids of Egypt were examined, and there was
no variation from the north. Tycho Brahe, in 1576
and 1586, made observations in the island of Huen,
in the straits of the Baltic; and in 1671, another
skilful mathematician did the same. He found the
meridian then different in longitude by 18 minutes,
from the position Tycho Brahe had ascertained only
95 years before. Eighteen minutes for every 100
years, would have amounted to 7 degrees and 12
minutes, in 2400 years, the supposed time elapsed
since the erection of the Egyptian pyramids. It
follows then, from both these observations, that
there is a cyclar variation not perpetually progressive, and that the American mounds, when viewed,
had returned by the twentieth part of a century, to
that part of the cycle in which they were built;
though that at Bledsoe's lick is precisely at the
time in that point of the cycle in which it was built.
If this idea were pursued, and a cycle of time formed
which embraced the cold seasons and also the warm
ones, it might perhaps be found that there is a
regular alternation, and that the warm ones do not
incessantly advance without any retrogradation.
There are spaces of time in history, in which the
intensity of the weather is not complained of, and
others again in which, for a long course of time, its
severity is continually spoken of. There are periods in certain countries, when the vine and the
olive would grow, where in after times they refused
to grow, and vice versa. There were times when
part of certain northern seas were navigable for
centuries, and in after times the ice made them in-
navigable. In certain centuries the Baltic and

17 Archailogia Americana, 145.

Mediterranean have been covered with ice, which in former and latter ages were not so. In these cold centuries, whether alternate, or progressive, may have come hither those large animals whose bones we now find; and that too, not at a very great distance of time since their deposition, as they are yet upon the surface, uncovered, or only lightly covered, and undecayed by exposure to the sun, rain and air. In presence of the advancing warm seasons, they may have retired, like the raindeer and the auroch, from the wilds of Germany, which they inhabited in the times of Julius Cæsar. An advancement of the warm seasons incessantly, is irreconcilable with the tropical plants found below the surface at Zanesville, supposing them to have grown there; for on that supposition, the warm seasons must have retired. But assuming that, there is an alteration makes their growth there reconcilable with the operations of nature and the motions of the heavens; otherwise, these plants must have been removed in waters flowing from the south, which protected the blossoms from the rays of the sun. In the time of Tacitus, the Roman emperor, A. D. 276, the vine flourished in England; and from the year 1087 to 1154, and from 1377 to 1399, and thenceforward, would not grow there. In the time of Julius Cæsar, the vine would not grow there. Again, 300 years after it flourished there, and afterwards, in 1399, it would not, nor thenceforward. Snows were abundant at Rhegium, in the southern extremity of Italy, in the times of Spartacus and Crassus, 53 years before Christ. Snows were common in the Tarentine gulf in the time of Herodotus, 412 before Christ. The rebels taken and imprisoned at Capua in the time of Hannibal, about 220 before Christ, died there with cold. The olive and citron have grown there since since, with the utmost luxuriance. Supposing the warm seasons to be unceasingly progressive, it is not affected by any motion of the earth to the south, for the parallels would be changed; and if by some other cause, is not an alternation more agreeable to the course of nature, and in concert with the variations of the needle, and the inequality of seasons, which in some portions of time are more severe or more temperate than in others?

In Belmont county, in the state of Ohio, opposite the mouth of Little Grave creek in the state of Virginia, and nearly half a mile from the Ohio river, in the vicinity of several small mounds, was one about 15 or 16 feet high. Its top was flat, and its base about 40 feet in diameter. The timber in the vicinity was remarkably large. On it were the remains of three or four large trees, supposed to have been white oaks, from the relics of the bark which had fallen down and decayed. There were still growing upon it, several large poplars, some of them four or five feet in diameter within a foot of the ground, with several white oaks three or four feet in diameter, and other timber, such as beech, walnut, &c. An incision was made into the mound on the summit, descending perpendicularly. The first layer was a vegetable mould, about two feet through; the next was of dark clay, three feet through, resembling the clay of the river near that place, and below this was a layer of small stones of the size of walnuts, goose eggs, &c. rounded and smoothed by the water, having been brought, as was supposed, from the bed of the river a few miles distant, as there are none immediately contiguous. The layer of stones was three or four feet in thickness. Next was a stratum of earth resembling black marl, believed to be vegetable mould, about a foot deep; and next to this were several layers of human bones, laid transversely, in a great mass of decayed matter five or six feet thick. These bones, when exposed to the air, would moulder away, although they seemed solid when taken up.

The toe and finger nails were nearly, entire; the hair, long, fine, and of a dark brown colour, and almost rotten, but by letting the dirt dry and brushing it off, it would bear to be combed and straightened out. Under, the bones were flint stone, and spear or lance heads, four or five inches long, levelled from the middle to the edge, the edges converging to a point, in the form of the two longest sides of an isosceles triangle, the shortest side of the triangle being about two inches wide, at which commenced a flat prominence, or handle, to be inserted in the end of a pole. There were also found pieces of iron, from two to four feet long, straight and uncurved, the back of the blade flat, and one half or three quarters of an inch wide near the handle, regularly levelled on both sides to the edge, and tapering from the handle to the point, calculated both for thrusting and striking transversely. The iron was considerably oxidated, and when exposed to the air, dissolved and fell into small particles of rust, leaving only the handle, which was thick, and central parts adhering together. There were four or five of these swords, if we may so call them. The handle was round and cylindrical, and encircled with ferules or rings of silver. On the ferules were the representations of taropins or terobins, scored or carved in lines; and also birds with bushy tails, long necks, long legs, and feet like those of the turkey or flamingo. The bill was short and wide like that of a duck, only shorter, and tapering to a point from the sides. Upon them were also carved the following figures: First, a rectilinear isosceles triangle; secondly, a scalene triangle, some of these triangles approximating towards the equilateral, and others towards the right angled triangle; thirdly, a rectangular equilateral square, and a rectangular parallelogram, with each side equal to that laterally opposite it; fourthly, a perfect circle; and fifthly, an elipsis, perfectly and regularly proportioned.

The mould seemed to be of different shades and variegations; and near the bottom, and amongst the bones and mould, were found a great number of pieces of charcoal in a perfect state. This mound was opened in the spring of 1820.

With respect to the facing of the mounds to the cardinal points, the religion of the Hindoos enjoins, that the four sides of a pagoda should face the four cardinal points.[117]

R.

A stone tablet, fixed on a sculptured pillar, had on it some strokes taken for a Tartarean inscription. It was found in the savannas of Canada in 1746.

Letters of an unknown alphabet are inscribed upon a rock in the western parts of New-York.

There is a rock, called the Dighton rock, on Taunton river, near Dighton, in Massachusetts. It is a large rock in the margin of the sea, and upon it are inscriptions in strange characters, partly alphabetical and partly hieroglyphic. The letters are oriental, partaking of the characteristic forms of the Sanscrit and Talick, and written from right to left. It signifies whence the authors of the inscription came, their numbers and intercourse with the natives, and their intention to return whence they came. On landing, they paid their devotion to Budh, the genius of fecundity. Also, there is a symbol of Isis and Minerva. The head of a hawk indicates infinite wisdom; and there is represented the north wind, which conducted them to the spot. In another scene, there is a vessel, with its masts, flags, and long rudder, as in the oriental vessels at this day. There is the figure of a horse, which is the well known symbol of Carthage. There is a bust, upon the breast of which is a trident, emblematical of Neptune, or Vishnu, and also of the *oriental trinity*, of the good and evil, and of the

117 Robertson's India, 348.

PP

mediating powers—the same as Rama, Vishnu and
Siva, which, under one or another name, have been
found in the religions of all nations. The subject
generally seems intended to commemorate the arrival of a people there from the ocean and the east,
and who, having had intercourse with the natives,
had resolved to return, and written this on the rock,
to perpetuate the event; but whether from Phenicia,
Carthage, or elsewhere, is not ascertained. The
inscriptions are of great antiquity. That it is a
record of some fact, cannot be doubted, though the
hieroglyphics are many and crowded. There is
a method in it, which puts it beyond doubt, that it
was intended to perpetuate the remembrance of
facts. The oriental characters are to be found in
nearly all the alphabets.

Near Wheeling, in Virginia, on Grave creek, on
the lands of Mr. Tomlins, is one mound of a conical
form, 75 feet high. In the interior of this mound,
human bones were found, of uncommonly large size.
The mounds are a mile and a half from the Ohio.
Here also were found, mixed with bones, *two or
three plates of brass,* with characters inscribed upon
them resembling letters, but of what alphabet no
one could tell.

Inscriptions are engraven on a large stratum of
rocks on the southeast side of the river Ohio, about
two miles below the mouth of Indian or King's
creek, which empties into the Ohio fifty miles below
Pittsburgh. The greater part of the rocks lie nearly
in horizontal directions, and so close to the edge of
the river that at times the water entirely covers them.
A few yards, however, from the bank of the river,
there are several large masses of the same species
of rock, on which also are inscriptions. The inscriptions upon both are of the same kind, and apparently were made at the same time. In one of
the tamuli, near the place of inscription, was found,
amongst other things, a hard stone signet, of an

oval shape, two inches in length, with a figure in relievo resembling a note of admiration, surrounded by two raised rims. It is exactly the figure of the brand with which the Mexican horses were marked.

About the year 1806, in a field on Enoe river, in Orange county, North-Carolina, five or six miles above Hillsborough, part of a stone was ploughed up, which had been broken off from another part of it. It was perfectly transparent, of an octagonal shape, and the sides very smooth. It terminated in a cone. Between the commencement of the taper, which was towards the upper part of the stone, characters were cut resembling letters. One resembling the Roman L, but with a curved stroke [L] at the top, instead of a straight one across. The other characters were of different formation, but were not placed in a line either ascending or horizontal, but stood apart from each other. Afterwards the other, or lower part, was ploughed up, of the same form and thickness as the body above described was below the conical part of it. The whole seemed to be several feet in length, and was near an old Indian townhouse. Near the same place was found a circular piece of brass, of the size of the palm of the hand of a man of middle size. Characters were on it of the same form as those upon the stone.

An inscription, supposed by some to be Phenician, is said to have been found on a large block of granite in the middle of a cave in Guyana. And if the copy exhibited to the Baron de Humboldt were a faithful one, the inscription seems to have some resemblance to Phenician letters.

In the mounds near Natchez, on the earthenware there found are characters or letters.[18]

Malvenda, a Spanish writer, says, that the nations of St. Michael had tombstones with several ancient Hebrew characters upon them, as " Why is God gone away?" and " *He is dead, God knows.*"[19]

18 Shultz. 155.   19 Boudinot, 250.

There are said to be inscriptions, in unknown characters, on a rock in the middle of a river, which is apparent only in time of low water. The rock is in New river, and a few miles from Ashville. The fact is now put into a state of inquiry. The information was given to the writer by Robert Nall, Esquire, of the county of Hawkins, who lives on the main road 12 miles west of Rogersville. He says, that in the county of Ashe, in North-Carolina, on the north side of New river, four or five miles from the courthouse, just above the mouth of a creek which falls into the river on the east side, is a rock in the water, near the middle of the river, which in the time of low water is above the surface of the water. It is in the direction of southeast from the courthouse. On this rock are letters inscribed in a horizontal line, the letters being about an inch in length, and the line about eighteen inches in length. At the end of the line are Arabic numerals, or the figures which we now commonly use. On the rock is the impression of a man's hand and of a man's foot, of the track of a bear and of the track of a wolf, all very plain. The rock is hard blue river rock. To some who saw the figures, the idea was suggested, that the impressions were made at a time when the rock was in a plastic state. Many persons went to see the impressions, and all agreed that the characters were literal ones, and no one doubted of the fact; but none were acquainted with the letters, nor knew to what alphabet they belonged.

S.

In the county of Kenhaway, about four miles below the Burning spring, and near the mouth of Campbell's creek, in the state of Virginia, is a rock of great size, on which, in ancient times, the natives engraved many representations. There is the figure of almost every indigenous animal—the buffalo, the bear, the deer, the fox, the hare, and other quadrupeds of various kinds, fish of the various productions of the western waters, fowls of different descriptions, infants scalped, scalps alone, and men as large as life. The rock is in the river Kenhaway, near its northern shore, accessible only at low water, unless by the aid of water craft. When this was done the sculptors had not seen the horse, the cow, the hog, the sheep, or goat. It was done before their acquaintance with the Europeans, and tends strongly to support the supposition, that the ancient inhabitants had the use of metallic implements, which leads to an intercourse between them and those parts of the globe where metallurgy was understood and practised. The Indians known to us, have never possessed the sculptural art in as much perfection as was possessed by these ancient aborigines.

In the mouth of a cavern opposite or not very far from Hurricane, on the Ohio, on the northwest side, are engraved on the rock, 25 feet high, the figures of several animals, as of the bear and buffalo; and what is more remarkable, of the *lion and lioness*. These figures are done in a masterly style. You enter the cavern first through a small cavity nine feet wide and twelve feet high, then ascend a bench of a few feet and enter the aperture about the size of a door, into a most spacious cavern. The engraver must have seen the lion and lioness in Asia or Africa, or had seen at least the picture of them. If the latter, the painting itself must have come from the southern parts of Asia, or from Africa, or must have been there seen by him.

The facings of the stones in the pyramids near Cuernovaca, are adorned with hieroglyphic figures, among which are crocodiles spouting up water, and men sitting cross-legged, in the Asiatic manner.

On the pyramids of Papontla, the facings of the stones are adorned with hieroglyphics, in which serpents and crocodiles, carved in relievo, are discernible.

An owl carved in stone was found at Columbus, and sometimes are found stone axes; also are found, tools, with a very little silver and brass.

T.

In the ruins of the walls of the palace of Milla, in New Spain, curious paintings have been found, representing warlike trophies and sacrifices. When Cortes, in the year 1519, landed his troops at St. Juan de Ulloa, and was visited by some Mexican chiefs, with their trains, in a mission from Montezuma, during the interview some parties in the train of the Mexican chiefs had been diligently employed in delineating, upon white cotton cloths, figures of the ships, the horses, the artillery, the soldiers, and whatever else attracted their eyes as singular.[t] In the ruins of an ancient city within three miles of the Rio Gela, which is in the 27th degree of north latitude, near the gulf of California, the plane is covered with broken earthen pitchers and pots, prettily painted in red, white and blue. And from time immemorial, the people of Chili have used indigenous plants in dying, which communicate the liveliest and most durable colours to cloths, without any foreign production. Thirty years' use of a piece of blue cloth dyed there, made it lose nothing of the original lustre of its colours, which are red, yellow, green and black. They cannot be affected by exposure to the air or by the use of soap. There are plants and herbs in Chili which furnish all these colours. The paints in West Tennessee, on the rocks, must have come from thence; so also the silver ornaments and utensils found on the waters of the Ohio; and from Mexico and from the former came the black marble beads. The people have agreed with those of the south in their religion, sciences, manufactures, mechanic arts, fortifications, and in most of the articles which have passed in

[t] 2 Rob. Hist. Am. 265.

review before us. They were branches of the same stock: not so of the present race of Indians.

V.

In the possession of Mr. Mowbray, in the state of Louisiana, in the parish of St. Tammany, 20 miles from Madisonville, and in a northwardly direction from it, is a vessel of about the capacity of half a pint, and of the shape of an ordinary glass tumbler. The materials of which it is composed are of a dull transparency, of a grade between the most translucent and opaque china. The form of the hand which holds it on one side is visible on the other. One half of the vessel is stained with red, irregular blotches, like specks made by spattering from a brush, very ornamental to the cup. The vessel itself is of a milk white cast: the specks are of a bright red colour. No decorations are on the other side of the vessel. It was found in a mound within one or two miles of St. Louis, in the state of Missouri, which mound was covered with timber of an enormous size. There were in the mound two of these cups, together with about a peck of glazed beads, small, and of a white and brown colour. The mound was opened three or four years ago, about the year 1819 or 1820. The clay or sand was of a very fine texture, and the vessel highly polished.

An urn was found in a mound a few miles from Chillicothe. It very much resembled one found in a similar work in Scotland, which is thirteen inches high, and of a black appearance, as if it had been filled with oil. It was found in a tumulus, which contained arrow heads, ashes and calcined bones. The urns generally contain human bones which have been burnt in a hot fire. And from the appearance of the vessels, oil of some kind has been put into them with the bones. Some of these urns appear to have been made of a composition resembling that of which mortars for physicians are now manufactured by Europeans. There is one now in existence, and in possession of a gentleman residing on the Little Scioto, in Scioto county, Ohio. It contains about three quarts, and is brought to a perfect point at the bottom. About half way from the top to the bottom is a groove around its inside, and two ears. Through a hole a chain may be passed, on which to suspend it. It was found 12 feet below the surface, and is not injured by exposure to considerable heat.[19] The pottery found near the surface is rude, and such as the present Indians make; but at the bottom of mounds, or near the head of some distinguished personage, vessels are found in some instances equal to any now manufactured in any part of the world. Two covers of vessels were found in a mound in Ross county, in Ohio, very ingeniously wrought by the artist, and highly polished. They resemble almost exactly, and were quite equal to vessels of the same materials manufactured in Italy at the present time.

A number of pieces of glass, of singular workmanship, were lately found at Hamburgh, in the state of New-York. They were taken from an ancient barrow in the town of Hamburgh, where they were found deposited in an earthen pot. Contiguous to this spot, were also found a scull, and some other bones of the human frame, of *unusual size.* This mound, or supposed repository of the dead, is situated in an uncultivated part of the town, and several trees were growing upon it when the excavation was made, some of which were judged to be upwards of two feet in diameter. One of the pieces examined, (and they are all alike) is in the form of a large barrel-shaped bead, consisting of a tube, of transparent green glass, covered with an opaque course red enamel. Its length nine tenths of an inch, its greatest width six and a half tenths, and the bore of the tube two tenths of an inch.

19 Archailogia Americana, 228.

Near the circle of the bore of this tube, is an aperture, of the size of a large needle, perforating the tube from one end to the other. The enamel which covers the tube of transparent glass, appears to have been ornamented with paintings or figures resembling a spindle, or two inverted sections of a circle. But they are now hardly perceptible, as the head appears to have been considerably worn. But the circumstance most indicative of art, in the making of this bead, is a species of enamelling, which has been performed both on the external and internal surfaces of the tube previous to its being covered by the coarse red enamel. This second enamel is white; and as the external surface of the tube was not smooth, but in parallel veins, exhibits the appearance of a white vine between the green tube and red enamel. This enamelling seems to have been done, not by melting in any vitrious composition, as is practised at the present day, but by the effect of calcination for some time in a slow red heat. This will deprive glass, especially green glass, of its transparency, and render the surface white to a certain depth. The composition of the tube of glass seems to be simply a silicious sand, and an alkali, probably with a small addition of lime and vegetable ashes. It is hard, and will not receive scratches, like the lead glasses, whence it is concluded that there is no lead in the composition. Its colour seems also owing to the impurity of the materials employed, like the common window and bottle glass. And it is probably caused by a minute portion of iron in the state of an oxyde combined with the sand and alkali. The next enamel covering the tube, and the part in which these glasses were found, seem to have been constructed of similar materials, as they differ very little in colour, texture, or other external character. Possibly a very fusible brick clay, highly impregnated with oxyde of iron and pulverized fragments of green glass, are the principal ingredients of both. The earthen pot is manifestly constructed of different materials from those employed for brown pottery at the present period. It is a more imperishable substance, and of a vitrious appearance.

On Big river, in the state of Missouri, a similar discovery has been made. On opening an Indian grave on the river, several beads of glass of a similar nature were found. They were accompanied by many bones of the human frame, *of a most extraordinary size,* and which indicated a stature *eight feet* in height. This excavation was made near the bank of the river, where the soil is a rich alluvial, and covered by a heavy growth of fruit trees, such as are peculiar to the richest Ohio and Mississippi bottoms. A human body was found, in the year 1815, in one of the limestone caverns of Kentucky. It is a perfect exsiccation. All the fluids are dried up. The skin, bones, and other firm parts, are in a state of entire preservation. The outer envelope of the body was a deer skin, dressed in the usual way, and perhaps softened before its application by rubbing. The next covering was a deer skin, whose hair had been cut away by a sharp instrument resembling a hatter's knife. The remnant in the hair, and the gashes in the skin, nearly resemble the sheared felt of beaver. The next wrapping was of cloth made of *twine* doubled and twisted. But the thread does not appear to have been formed by the wheel, nor the web by the loom; the warp and filling seemed to have been crossed and netted by an operation like that of the fabrics of the northwest coast and the Sandwich islands. The innermost tegument is a mantle of cloth, like the preceding, but finished with large brown feathers, arrayed and fastened with great art, so as to be capable of guarding the living wearer from wet and cold. The plumage is distinct and entire, and the whole bears a near similitude to the feathered cloaks now worn by the nations of the northwestern waters of America. The body is in a squatting posture, with the right arm reclining forward, and its hand encircling the right leg. The left arm hangs down, with its hand inclined partly under the seat. The individual, who was a male, did not probably exceed the age of 14 at his death. There is a deep and extensive fracture of the scull near the occiput, which probably killed him. The skin has sustained little injury. It is of a dusky colour; but the natural hue cannot be decided with exactness, from its present appearance. The scalp, with small exceptions, is covered *with sorrel and foxy hair.* The teeth are white and sound. The hands and feet, in their shrivelled state, are slender and delicate. Some are inclined to the opinion, that this subject belonged to the Peruvian race.

In one of the mounds near Chillicothe, was discovered at the bottom, in a cavity, the remains of some chieftain. A string of ivory beads was around his neck, and on his breast a stone about three inches long, with a hole near each end, in order to fasten to the wearer's neck; rather thicker in the centre than at the extremities; flat on the side next the breast; the remainder of it round, and made of a species of black marble. Ever since the Mogul conquest of China, the emperor and the highest grades of his officers have worn such stones about their necks.

W.

Circleville is in Pickaway county, in the state of Ohio. It includes the whole of a circular fort and one half of a square one. The former had but one gateway on the inside of the fort, and a few yards from it was a small mound of earth, on which perhaps once stood a watch tower for the defence of the gate. In other mounds are human bones; in these none. The square fort is surrounded by only one wall; the circular one by two, having a deep ditch between them. The wall around the square fort is about twenty feet high; those of the latter are several feet higher. The forts are connected; and from appearances, the square fort was intended for the men and cattle, the circular fort for the women and children, and whatever was most valuable and sacred. On the outside of the inner wall of the circular fort, and half way up it, was a place around walled, where once stood a row of pickets. On the southwest of the circular fort, and adjoining it, is a mound nearly 100 feet higher than the surrounding plane, containing human bones of all sizes, from those of the largest man, to those of the smallest infant. The heads of these skeletons all lie towards the centre, and in a horizontal position. Near the centre of the circular fort was a small mound, near the bottom of which was a plate of isinglass above half an inch thick, eighteen or twenty inches wide, and from two and a half to three feet long; perfectly smooth on one side; and to appearance, had been used as a mirror. To it was attached *an iron plate*, an inch in thickness as was conjectured, because a substance resembling ore, exactly of its size, lay on it. In this mound was a large quantity of flint for arrows lying in heaps, together with a large knife. The handle of the knife was manufactured of the elk's horn, around which was a ferule of silver, uninjured, or nearly so. The blade had returned again to iron ore, but the shape and size was plainly discernible. Similar fortifications are found all over the regions west of the Alleghenies. The more fertile the soil, and the greater the natural advantages in their vicinity, the more numerous are the mounds and fortifications. In the front of each avenue leading to the square fort, were mounds where watch towers had been erected. There was a trench on the south side of the great mound. These erections are found on high ground, in commanding situations, and at the confluence of navigable waters. Very remarkable ones are found at the junctions of several streams of Licking creek, near Newark. On the high grounds in and about Columbus, near the junction of the Colchester branch of the Scioto river, the place where Hargis's creek enters the same river at Circleville. They are frequently found where one side is inaccessible, as the larger one on the Little Miami, where one side of the fort is a very high, perpendicular bank of rock. There are places of amusement near the fort at Circleville, and one very remarkable on the road from the place last mentioned to Chillicothe, 25 or 30 yards in length, and about 40 wide, with a ridge about two feet high all around, is perfectly smooth, and gently ascends towards the south. The walls of the fort at this place are as high, and the ditches as deep, as those of fort Oswego, on the south road of lake Ontario, which were in use in 1755. Indeed, the walls are as high, and the ditches as deep, as those of fort Stanwyx, at Rome, in New-York, in use 40 years ago.

The writers of antiquity, and particularly Josephus, whose history relates to the most ancient transactions of mankind, mentions fortifications made by walls[a] till about 136 years before Christ, when he mentions intrenchments also, and thenceforward very frequently.[b] This was about the time when such intrenchments came into general use in Asia, whence no doubt they came into use here.

X.

First we will speak of the coins of the aborigines found in the neighbouring countries, and then of metallic instruments and utensils also found there.

[a] 1 Josephus, 149, 166, 167, 202, 207, 292, 318, 319.

[b] Josephus Ant. b. 13, ch. 8, sec. 2, ch. 10, sec. 2, b. 14, ch. 4, sec. 1; Strabo, b. 16, p. 763—a ditch in the time of Pompey encompassed Jerusalem, 60 deep, 250 broad—b. 13, ch. 15, sec. 1.

First. On the farm of Mr. Edward Payne, near Lexington, were found two ancient coins; one was of gold, and sold for 13 dollars: the other was of brass. Each had a head reversed, and both were inscribed with characters not understood, but said to resemble Hebrew. The date of the gold coin was probably 1214, and the date of the brass piece 1009. A few miles below Mr. Payne, a gold piece was found, on the plantation of Mr. Chámbers, who says it was sold at Lexington for 13 dollars. It was inscribed in unknown characters; and, as Mr. Chambers thinks, was unlike any coin he had ever seen. He says, that a small piece of copper was found on his farm at the same time. The date 1214 could not relate to the hegira. If it related to the Christian era, it must have come from some of the modern kingdoms of Europe, which had adopted the use of the Arabic numerals. It is not known that the Persians ever used them. The most that can be made of the fact, is, a probability that these coins came to the country before the discovery of America by Columbus; for between 1214 and 1492, the time of his discovery, were 178 years, and before the Spaniards could have circulated it, many more years intervened prior to their intercourse with the nations on the continent. So that it must have circulated nearly 300 years, before it could have come hither from them, and by that time would have been worn out.

At Circleville a copper coin was taken from the central mound, from beneath the roots of a hickory growing on the mound, seven or eight inches in circumference. It has no resemblance in its devices to any British or other coins to which it hath been compared. A hickory six or eight inches in circumference, might have grown up long since the French settlements were on the Ohio and its waters.

On the plantation of Colonel William Sheppard, in the county of Orange, on the river Enoe, 6 miles above Hillsborough in North-Carolina, and near the remains of a town which had been deserted in very remote times, was picked up, about the year 1803 or 1804, a round piece of copper about the size of an American eagle. On both sides was a short line of letters, with parallel lines increasing in length till past the centre, whence they decreased in length to the bottom, accommodating themselves to the rounded shape of the copper. It was neatly executed. The letters were of some unknown alphabet. This copper was dropped again on the same plantation, where probably it now is. It was about the thickness of the coins called coppers. Similar pieces were sometimes given by the Spanish friars to their proselyted Indians.

. Gold and silver ornaments have been found in many of the tumuli in Ohio. Silver very well plated, has been found in several of the mounds: copper in many: pipe bowls of copper, hammered, and not welded together, but lapped over, have been found in them. A bracelet of copper was found in a stone mound at Chillicothe. It resembles the links of a common chain, the ends passed by each other, but were not welded together. Ornaments of silver and copper have not been found north of Newark. Below that place, vast numbers have been found. North of that place are no wells perforated in the rocks. Arrow heads of copper, some of them five or six inches in length, circular medals of copper, several inches in diameter, very thin, and much injured by time, have been found in the tumuli of Ohio. Iron has been found in some instances oxydized.

Out of a mound near the circle of the large fort at Circleville, was found the elk-horn handle of a small sword or long knife. Around the end where the blade had been inserted, was a ferule of silver; no iron was found, but an oxyde remained. Also, charcoal and wood ashes, in which those articles

lay, which were surrounded by several *bricks*, very
well burnt. A skeleton appeared to have been
burnt in a large and very hot fire, which had almost
consumed the bones of the deceased. The skeleton
was deposited a little to the south of the centre of
the tumulus. And 20 feet to the north of it, was
another. There was also a large mirror, three feet
in length, one and a half in breadth, and one inch
and a half thick. It was of isinglass. Also a plate
of iron, which had become an oxyde; but before
it was disturbed by the spade, resembled a plate of
iron. This skeleton had been burned like the former, and lay in charcoal and a considerable quantity of wood ashes.

An ornament of very pure gold was discovered,
a few years since, in Ross county, near Chillicothe,
lying in the palm of a skeleton's hand, in a small
mound.[a]

Not long since, a silver cup was taken from a
mound at Marietta, on the Ohio. It is in the possession of Mr. Hill, of St. Clair county, Illinois.
It is in the form of an inverted cone, measuring
three and a half inches across at top, two and a
half at bottom, and four inches in height. It is of
pure silver, and so skilfully wrought, that no traces
of the plating hammer are discernible. The bottom,
which is circular, has been separately forged, accu-
rately fitted to the sides, or barrel, and soldered on.
The line of attachment is plainly discernible. Its
interior surface has been gilt, or washed, with a
bright, yellow, untarnishable metal, which is undoubtedly gold; but that gilding is impaired in
some places. It was found in a mound at Marietta,
half a mile east of those remarkable fortifications
on the Muskingum. The mound is situated in a
woody plane, with a gentle declivity towards the
river, and a small stream washes its base. During
the autumnal rains, or the melting of the snow in

[a] Arch. Am. 176.

the spring, it runs with the velocity of a current. Thus it has gradually washed away the earth, and laid open the mound for a considerable space, and in this situation the cup was discovered. It was then in a bruised or shapeless mass, and foul from adhering clay; but being taken to a silversmith, was put into the shape it now presents, which was probably the shape it originally had. Its value by weight is about fifteen dollars. It bears no device or ornamental work of any kind, being a perfectly plain and heavy piece of workmanship. It it be not of European fabrication, the inference is inevitable, that some nation preceding the savages was formerly here, of far greater advancement in the arts of civilization than they ever possessed. But for fear of mistake, let us bear in mind that the French settled in Canada as early as the year 1608, and soon afterwards carried on trade extensively with all the Indians who lived on the waters of the Ohio.

Copper instruments and ornaments have also been found. In 1813 was found in a mound a piece of copper incrusted with erugo, half an inch thick It consists of thin plates of copper rolled up, encircling each other. It was about three inches in length, and one fourth of an inch in thickness. The plates were remarkably pure and fine. In the same mound a beautiful piece of marble was taken up in the year 1814. It was undoubtedly made and used for an ornament, being perforated with loop holes for fastening, which must have been bored by some hard instrument. The marble piece is about five or six inches in length, flat on one side, oval on the other, having an increasing width in the middle, the ends are apparently cut, and with some hard implement used for the purpose. The marble is of a dark dun colour, but the veins of the stones are very distinct. The magicians of India are provided with many articles against witchcraft, which they distribute amongst those who consult them. There are certain enchanted beads, *very thin plates of copper*, on which extraordinary figures are engraved, with inexplicable words and unknown characters. Amulets also, of various kinds, all which are worn by the Hindoos to serve as talismans, and to preserve them from every species of incantation. No other circumstance at present recollected, can account in the least degree for the plates of copper above mentioned.

In one of the tumuli on Grave creek, below Wheeling, near to the Ohio, were found, about 20 years since, sixty copper beads, made of a coarse wire, hammered out, and not drawn and cut off at unequal lengths. They were soldered together in an awkward manner, the centre of some of them uniting with the edges of others. They were incrusted with verdigrease, but the inside of them was pure copper.

Some copper pieces have been found in a mound near the Little Muskingum, four miles from Marietta, which appear to have been the front of a helmet, was orignally eight inches long and four broad, and has marks of having been attached to leather. It is much decayed and is now a thin plate, and appears to have been attached to the centre of it by a rivet, the hole for which appears both in the plate and ornament. At this place the remains of a skeleton were found. No part retained its form but a portion of the forehead or scull, which lay under the plate of copper. These bones are deeply tinged with green, and appear to have been preserved by the salts in the copper.

In an ancient mound of the streets of Marietta, in the margin of the plane near the fortifications, amongst other things, in 1819 were discovered three large circular bosses, or ornaments, for sword belts, or a buckler composed of copper, oval, and with a thick plate of silver. The front is slightly convex, with a depression like a cap in the centre. The measure, two inches and a quarter across the face of each. On the back side, opposite the depressed portion, is a copper rivet or nail, around which are two separate plates, by which they were fastened to the leather. Two small pieces of the leather were found lying between the holes of one of the bosses. They resemble the skin of an old mummy. The plates of copper are nearly reduced to rust. Around the rivet of one of them is a quantity of flax or hemp in a tolerable state of preservation. Near the side of the human body was a plate of silver, the upper part of a sword scabbard, six inches long, two wide, weighing one ounce. Three longitudinal ridges were on it, which perhaps corresponded with the edges or ridges of the sword. It had been fastened to the scabbard by three or four rivets, the holes of which yet remain in the silver. Two or three pieces of a copper tube were also found, filled with rust. These compose the lower end of the scabbard, near the point of the sword. There is no sign of the sword itself, except this appearance of rust. Near the feet was a piece of copper weighing three ounces. It seemed by the shape to have been used for a plumb or for ornament. Near one of the ends is a circular crease or groove for lying a thread. It is round, two inches and a half in length, one in diameter at the centre, and half an inch at each end. It is composed of small pieces of native copper pounded together; and in the cracks between the pieces, are several pieces of silver, one nearly of the size of a fourpenny piece or half a disme. This copper ornament was covered with a coat of green rust, and is considerably corroded. A piece of red ochre or paint, and a piece of iron ore, which has the appearance of having been partly vitrified or melted, were also found. The trees upon the mound, as evidenced by the annulars, were between 400 and 500 years of age, and on the ground beside them were other trees, in a state of decay, that appeared to have fallen from dotage.

From the ancient works where Circleville now stands, and from the mound there, were taken a few scattered human bones, a branch of a deer's horn, and a piece of earthenware containing muscle shells. At the distance of 500 feet from this pyramid, in the direction of north eight east, there is another, nine feet high, of a circular figure, nearly flat on the top. In it were found some human skeletons, *and a handful of copper beads*, which had been strung on a cravat of lint. There is another mound at the intersection of Third and Main streets; whatever it contained was deposited a small distance below a stratum of loam which is common to the town. The first artificial layer was gravel, considerably raised in the middle; the next, composed of large pebbles, was convex and of a uniform thickness; the last consisted of loam and soil. The strata were entire, and must have been formed after the deposites in the tumulus were completed. Amongst other articles were these: A bone ornamented with several carved lines; the sculpture representation of the *head or beak of a rapacious bird, perhaps an eagle;* a quantity of isinglass; *a small oval piece of sheet copper* with two perforations; a large oval piece of *some metal* with longitudinal grooves or ridges; a number of beads of bone or shell; the teeth of a carnivorous animal. probably those of a bear; *seven large marine shells,* belonging perhaps to the genus buccinum, cut in such a manner as to serve for domestic utensils, and nearly converted into a *state of chalk;* several copper articles, each consisting of two sets of circular concave and convex plates. The interior one of each sort connected with the other by a hollow axis, around which had been wound some *lint.* Other articles have been found there, consisting of pure copper, human bones of different sizes, sometimes enclosed *in rude stone coffins,* but oftener lying blended with the earth, surrounded by a portion of *ashes and charcoal.*[a] Iron and steel

a Arch. Am. 162.

utensils and ornaments have also been found. There was dug up from the central mound at Circleville, a fragment of some culinary vessel. It was evidently of cast iron, and showed the *marks of the mould.* It was covered on the lower side with the black smut contracted over the fire. It was found among ashes, and large pieces of charcoal.

In the large cemetery of Augusta were found four iron bracelets on the left arm of a female skeleton. They are formed with a loop at one extremity, and extend in an oval shape to a knob at the other end, which hitches into the loop. The elongated central part of the oval is the thickest, from which it gradually tapers to the clasp. These bracelets are much corroded, and the loops destroyed; but even their present state of preservation can only be accounted for by the fortunate circumstance, that the alluvial soil of the burying ground was free from mineral acids. There are in this state some ancient ivory bracelets from *Indostan,* which exactly resemble in shape those iron ones. It is a well known fact, that the dress and ornaments of the Hindoos have continued unchanged from the earliest periods of history. The aborigines had some very well manufactured swords and knives of iron, and possibly of steel.[a] A few years ago, near Blacksburg in Virginia, 80 miles from Marietta, was found about the half of a steel bow, which when entire would have measured five or six feet.

On the main branch of Paint creek in Ohio, near some very ancient works, and on the inside of a wall on the side of an elevated hill 300 feet high, which wall is of stone, around the brow of the hill there appears to have been a row of furnaces or smiths' shops, where the cinders now lie many feet in depth. The remains are four or five feet in depth even now in many places.

a Arch. Am.

Y.

' On the beach near the mouth of Muskingum, was discovered a curious ornament. It is made of white marble, in form a circle, about three inches in diameter. The outer edge is about one inch in thickness, with a narrow rim. The sides are deeply concave, and in the centre is a hole about half an inch in diameter, beautifully finished very smooth.

Z.

See letter *X*, upon which it is sufficient to remark, that the Mexicans buried with the dead the emblem which distinguished the god whom the deceased worshipped, and that they had a divinity called the god of the shining mirror. Mirrors of isinglass were common to the aborigines, and have been met with in many places. More or fewer of them have been found in Ohio. They were thick, otherwise they would not have reflected the light. Glass was not anywhere found in Ohio.

A.A.

Belonging to the works at Cincinnati was an excavation, or well, of the depth of twelve feet. The diameter from the top of the circular bank formed by throwing out the earth, is nearly fifty feet. It has the appearance of a half-filled well.

The principal wall at Marietta, amongst the works there, is sixty feet in diameter at the surface, and when the settlements were first made was at least twenty feet deep, but has been in part filled up from the washings of the sides by frequent rains. It was originally of the kind formed in the most early days, when the water was brought up by hand in pitchers and other vessels, by steps made on the side of the well.[a] The pond, or reservoir, near the

a 1 Jos. b. 7, ch. 12, sec. 4; Gen. ch. 16, v. 21, ch. 21, v. 26, ch. 24, v. 45, ch. 46, v. 45; Exodus, ch. 15, v. 27; Numb. ch. 21, v. 16, 17, 18; Judges, ch. 25, v. 19; 1 Chron. ch. 11, v. 17, 18; 2 Chron. ch. 26, v. 10; Samuel, ch. 17, v. 19; 1 Kings, ch. 1, v. 9, 38; Psalms, ch. 84.

northwest corner of the large fort was about 25 feet
in diameter, and the sides raised above the level of
the adjoining surface by an embankment of earth
three or four feet high. This was nearly full of
water, at the first settlement of the town, and remained so until lately. When the ground was
cleared near the well, a great many logs which lay
near, were rolled into it, to save the trouble of piling
and burning them. These with the annual deposite
of leaves and other trash for ages, had filled the
well nearly full, but still the waters rose to the
surface, and had the appearance of a stagnant pool.
In early times poles and rails have been pushed
down into the water, and deposites of rotten vegetables to the depth of 30 feet. An attempt was lately
made to drain it by cutting a ditch from the well
into the small covert way. The diggers went to
the depth of twelve feet, and let off the water to
that distance. The sides of the reservoir were
found not to be perpendicular, but projecting gradually towards the centre of the well in the form of
an inverted cone. *The bottom and sides are lined
with a stratum of very fine, ash coloured clay, about
eight or ten inches in thickness,* below which is the
common soil of the place, and above it, this vast
body of vegetation. On the outside of the parapet,
near the oblong square, is a considerable number of
fragments of ancient potter's ware, which are ornamented with lines, some of them quite curious and
ingenious, on the outside. They are composed of
clay and fine gravel, and have a partial glazing on
the inside. They seem to have been burnt, and
to have been capable of holding liquids. The
fragments, on breaking them, look quite black, with
brilliant particles appearing as they are held up to
the light. The ware near the river is composed of
shells and clay, and is not near so hard as this found
on the plane. Of twenty or thirty pieces picked up,
nearly all of them were found on the outside of the

parapet, as if they had been thrown over the wall purposely. This is an evidence that the parapet was crowned with a palisade. The chance of find. ing them on the inside of the parapet, was equally good, as the earth had been recently ploughed and planted with corn.

Several pieces of copper have been found in and near the ancient works at various times. One piece was in the form of a cup with low sides, the bottom very thick and strong. The avenues, or places of ascent, on the sides of the elevated squares, are ten feet wide, and at Waterford, not far from the banks of the Muskingum, was lately found a magazine of spear and arrow heads. They lay in a body occupying a space of eight inches in width and eighteen in length, and at one end about a foot from the surface of the earth, and eighteen inches at the other, as though they had been buried in a box, and one end had sunk deeper into the earth than the other. They appear never to have been used, and are of various lengths, from six to two inches; and have no shanks, but are in the shape of a triangle with two long sides. The walls and mounds were thrown up by dirt taken from the *surface*, and not from any other place. To make a *tank* was one of the most meritorious performances with the Hindoos, which contributed more readily than any thing else to remove the defilement of the soul,[a] and hence it is to be expected that they excelled in making them. In Persia and in India were vast numbers of *tanks*, or public reservoirs of water, under the care of public officers. They were made with great art. No less than 42.000 were in the single province of Chorazan.[b] They were of the like formation in Mesopotamia in ancient times, and also in Judea. The Scythians, or any other people north of the Persian empire, had no knowledge of them. The people

a 1 Dubois. 169, 184, 187; Gibbon, 302; Rob. Ind. 256.
b 1 Dubois, 184; Jos. Ant. b. 7, ch. 12, sec. 4.

who came hither and made them, learned the art from those countries or from Arabia. We do not find them anywhere but with the mounds in the shape of truncated pyramids, a sure proof that the man of large stature did not make them. The tanks are found where mounds for worship, circumvallatory enclosures, images, and the doctrines of transmigration are found; but not where these are undiscoverable.

Wells of the common form have been found under circumstances preclusive of the idea, that they were sunk by uncivilized men.

In Logan county, in Kentucky, on Muddy creek, which discharges itself into Green river on the south side, where old Philip Ashton formerly lived, in sinking a well for salt water, the workmen, after digging a few feet, came to a place where the rock was cut in the form of a well's mouth. By that they continued to dig out the dirt that had filled up the well, till at length they came to a dead *terebin* in a state of preservation; also gourds and corn cobs, and green persimons, in the mud just above the salt water.

On the Little Miami, four miles above Waynesville, in the neighbourhood of Mr. I. Vance, some moss and mud was removed to open a spring, and in doing this the workmen struck upon a regular wall. The ground here may have become alluvial in half a century; but the fact that there is such a wall, and its nature, it is said, indicates antiquity, and the existence of a people differing materially in knowledge from the present Indians. We ought still, however, to attend to the circumstance, that French settlements were in spots upon the Ohio from 1717 to 1758.

Mr. Sinks had a well sunk in the village of Williamsburg, on the east fork of the Little Miami. In passing down, the workmen went through different strata of clay, sand, gravel and stones, which had

Ss

the appearance of having been prepared and used. They continued to the depth of thirty-five or forty feet, to the extremity of a regular stone pavement, extending nearly across the diameter of the well, the stones of which bore evident impressions of having been subject to labour. Two or three feet below this pavement, they came to a poplar log, and soon after to a quantity of water, which rose so unexpectedly as to bury the workmen's tools.

Mr. McKibbon, at the head of the east fork of the Little Miami, thirty miles above Williamsburg, wishing to obtain water at a place which had been the resort of deer at a lick, selected a spot where he saw the best vein for water, and commenced digging. After passing two feet and a half he came to some logs of wood, and breaking through, fell into the water to his neck. Having regained his standing, he cautiously removed the timber, and found the cavity to be an old well, three or four feet in diameter. The walls of the well were smooth, and appeared to have been filled with beautiful fine sand and gravel to within four or five feet of the top, which had been covered with logs. Having removed the gravel and sand, he immersed a sycamore and filled up the excavation around it, leaving three feet. The water is impregnated with iron and fixed air. In the same neighbourhood has been discovered another ancient well, three feet in diameter, *walled up with stone.* Either from design or accident, it had been filled up with dirt near to its top. This well is yet to be opened and examined.

In Kentucky, a few years since, a man in ploughing, set his plough so as to make a furrow near a foot deep. He struck and ploughed up a smooth rock, which covered a well walled up with rock, and having within a fine stream of water.

General Walker, in digging for salt water, on Long creek of Salt river, fell upon an ancient well, carried down a solid limestone rock twelve or fifteen feet. Petrified buck horn, and earthen ware, were found at the bottom. Earthen pans or dishes which would have held three or four gallons, were found. Some were lying about the old well's mouth, and some with the dirt thrown out.

BB.

The Mexicans, when the Spaniards first arrived amongst them, had carpenters, masons, weavers, and founders. The pyramids of Cholula are constructed of alternate strata of brick and clay.[a] Bricks of peculiar fabrication have been found in a cave in Maury county, in this state, and on the Mississippi, as well as on the waters of the Ohio. The making of brick presupposes the use of the trowel, the plumb, the making of lime, and of the masonic art. The trowel presupposes metallurgy, fusion, forges, and smithery.

In the valley of Tenochtillon in Mexico, was a salt pit, in the time of Montezuma, about the year of our Lord 1519, where earthen vessels were used similar to those seen at the United States saline.

Mr. Bell saw at the United States saline, the fragments of large vessels, which had been composed of muscle shells and clay, the capacity of which must have been seventy or eighty gallons.

A copper mine was found some years ago on the Mississippi, below the falls of St. Anthony, where a large collection of mining tools were found several feet below the surface. Hence, probably, the ancient inhabitants on the waters of the Ohio were furnished with copper utensils and ornaments, as well as from the mines of Chili or Peru.

In Virginia, ten or fifteen years ago, General Mason had from the diggers of a grave there, a discovery which they made. It is stated to have been represented by them, that about four feet below the surface, on the side of elevated ground of

a 2 Humboldt, 120.

an acclivity of about ten degrees from the horizon, they struck a wall of stone from eight to nine feet thick. They followed it one hundred and sixty feet, and came to a corner; thence one hundred and forty feet at right angles, and came to another corner. They then pursued it no further, having found the ground that it enclosed. They dug into the interior, and three or four feet below the surface found great numbers of human bones in different apartments, both small and full grown, in regular rows, of the same stature as men of the present race. The wall was computed to be of the depth of at least nine feet, for so far they had gone. The cement was distinguishable, and was of a bluish cast. The stones were large, and also of a blue colour. The marks of the hammer upon the stone were also apparent.

In the year 1794, was discovered, in North-Carolina, a subterranean wall, about twelve miles above Salisbury, in Rowan county. It was parallel to a small branch, which ran into a creek about 300 yards below the wall. It is ten or twelve yards distant from the stream, and runs into a hill on the side of a branch, and upon the upper part of it. On this side of the rivulet and extending to it, was a cleared field. The rain water running from the hill to the branch, carried away in a gully, the soil above the wall, and exposed it to view. The inner side was then uncovered, as well as the outer, by digging. It is somewhat less than two feet thick. It is said, that as the hill rises, the wall rises, still keeping its upper part at the same distance below the surface as it was in the bottom. The wall is perfectly straight, except a small circular offset of about six feet, after which it is continued in its former direction. Some persons have dug ten or twelve feet by the side of the wall, without finding its bottom, or any alteration in its form. The stones of which it is composed, are all of a dark blue colour, containing iron, of the size and shape of small bricks, and exactly similar to others on the opposite hill, about the distance of 250 or 300 yards, where an abundance of the same sort of stones was to be seen in 1794. These stones, seven or eight inches long, are placed across the wall, and in the middle are stones of all sorts and shapes. There is between the stones a mortar, or cement, the outer side of which is of a ferruginous or dark colour; the inside, of the thickness of one sixth or eighth of an inch, was a pure white substance, of the precise colour of lime, made of burnt limestone, or oyster shells, and rendered adhesive by the addition of water; in which state being laid away, it had afterwards become dry and hard. When the outer stones do not exactly fit, there seems to be a small fragment of stone wedged in so as to fill the space. The mortar in some places is said to be an inch thick, where the stones do not exactly fit to one another. The wall seems to have been plastered on both sides with the same kind of mortar. He who has not seen it may think it a work of nature; but not him who has—one of whom is the writer. To look at it, and the hill above, and adjoining to it, will not fail to force the idea, of soil heaped in a diluted state, against, upon, and over the wall, without throwing it down. I would rather say, of settling against and reposing upon it, till it acquired a more solid consistence by exposure to the sun and wind. A lesser wall has since been discovered at the distance of five or six miles from this. It has been traced fifty or sixty feet. It is only seven inches thick, and all the stones reach quite across the wall. These walls are probably of the same age.

In 1783, in the county of Craven, in North-Carolina, at the plantation of General William Bryant, was a stream on which he had a mill. A point of land projected into the stream, against which the dam was made to abut. Into the bluff he cut twenty feet or more, for a site for the millhouse. At the bottom of this cavity, in red clay, the diggers found a hard glass bottle, of uncommon thickness, with a short neck, and the lower part flat, with ridges projecting on the sides, as if protruded by the pressure of the bottle to the ground when in a plastic state. Near the spot where the bottle was found; were a number of fire coals and some chumps. The bottle was fifteen or twenty feet at least below the surface of the bluff, and more than thirty feet from the margin of the stream.

Along the Ohio, where the river in many places swells over its banks, *hearths* and *fire-places* are seen, two, four and six feet below the surface It is supposed by some to be a long time since the dirt was deposited over them. Around them are immense quantities of muscle shells, bones of animals, &c. Upon the surface above these chimneys and fire-places, there grew, at the first settlement of the country by the whites, as large trees as any in the forest. The conclusion made by some, is, that a large space, probably 1000 years, has elapsed since these hearths were deserted. Muscle shells used in all the pottery of the ancient inhabitants, and found at all their dwellings, shows a much greater abundance of them produced in our waters in those days, than at the present; a much more agreeable taste in the muscle than at the present day, and of course a change in the waters themselves, to much more freshness now than then.

CC.

In Peru, the men have beards, and lighter complexions than the native inhabitants who reside on the elevated plane of Cusco. They came, as Baron Humboldt thinks, from eastern Asia, and from those nations which have been in contact with the inhabitants of Thibit and Tartary. Consider, that part of the ten tribes of Israel were carried into

Medea 735 before Christ, and the remnant in 677 before Christ; that part of them were settled on the north of the Euxine and on the east of the Caspian sea, and we shall not be at a loss to account for the traditions which prevailed in eastern Asia. When we find in the most northern and northeastern parts of America a great number of Biblical traditions coming down as late as to the time of the prophet Jonah, in the sixth century before Christ, mixed also with customs decidedly Scythic, we can be at no loss also in deciding upon the more recent emigrations of those nations, and of the countries from whence they have swarmed. And differing in all things from those in Mexico, and on the Mississippi, and on the waters of the Ohio, we shall find as little difficulty in pronouncing that they are not of the same races, and that they never had any intercourse with each other. That all came from Asia, indeed is true; and that their ancestors in Asia came from Medea, or its vicinity, is demonstrable; and furnishes a most signal proof of the correctness of the Mosaic history. See note *V*, last section but one.

DD.

See letter *V*, where the glass beads of New-York and Missouri are described, and instances given of skeletons of eight feet in length.

In Mason county, Virginia, in the year 1821, four skeletons were dug up, and three others found. The bones were remarkably large, and particularly the sculls, which can easily be slipped over the largest man's head. The upper jaw bone has two rows of teeth all around; the under but two, on the left side, and no sockets provided by nature in the bone for more. The sculls, with considerable quantities of broken ware, buck horns, and muscle shells, were all buried in lime two feet deep.

At fort Chartres was found a human scull of astonishing magnitude. A jaw bone was taken from the mound near Natchez, which the gentleman who saw it could with ease put over his face; also a leg bone which from the ground reached three inches above the knee.[a] Many other instances might be enumerated, to establish the position, that a race of men of much larger bulk than any in America at this day, formerly resided upon the Cumberland river and its waters, and upon the Tennessee and its waters, and below them, upon the Mississippi, as well as upon the rivers north of Cumberland and in some parts of Virginia.

But in some parts of the western country, there are evidences presented of the astonishing fact, that there has also been a race of men here, whose ordinary size did not in general exceed three feet. In 1818, Mr. Long, the proprietor of a farm on the south side of the Merimac river, fifteen miles from St. Louis, in the state of Missouri, discovered, on the site on which he had fixed his dwelling, a number of graves, the size of which appeared uncommonly small. He made a minute examination, which convinced him they were the remains of human beings much smaller than those of the present day. He seemed warranted in this conclusion, as well from the uniform appearance of the skeletons, the length of which in no case exceeded four feet, as from the teeth, which bore the evident marks of those belonging to adult persons. He communicated these facts to a gentleman of the place, who soon afterwards, with two other gentlemen, accompanied by Doctors Walker and Grayson, proceeded to the place of interment. They found in a wood adjacent to the house, a great number of graves, all situated in small tumuli or hillocks, raised about three feet above the surface. They examined several; the first of which, by actual measurement, was discovered to be only twenty-three inches in length. The grave was carefully covered up on both sides, as

[a] Schultz, 155; Brackenridge, 279.

well as at the head and feet, with flat stones. On
the bottom also a stone was fixed, on which the body
was lying, placed on the right side, with the head
to the east. Time had completely destroyed all
parts of the body, as well as decomposed the bones,
which, however, still preserved their relative situation. The teeth, which were expected to furnish
the best and perhaps only data to judge upon, were
found in a state almost perfect, being defended by
the enamel, which seems only to yield to chemical
decomposition. To the astonishment of all, they
proved to be the teeth of a being who, if it had not
attained the age of puberty, had unquestionably
arrived at that period of life when the milk teeth
yield to the permanent or second set. The *molares*
and *incisors* were of the ordinary size of second
teeth. The jaw bone seemed to have its full com-
plement, unless it was the dentis sapientiæ, better
understood by the term wisdom teeth, which make
their appearance from the age of 18 to 22 or 23.
The next grave examined, was an adjacent mound,
and measured 27 inches. It resembled, in every
respect, the first, except that the top of it was covered with flat stones placed horizontally. Several
others were opened, all of which presented a uniform
appearance; and none, although many were measured, proved to be in length more than four feet,
two or three inches. From these facts, it is said,
the mind is brought to the irresistible conclusion,
that these are the remains of beings, differing altogether from, and inferior in general size to our-
selves. There is a large growth of timber on these
mounds.

In certain ancient works near lake Erie, are
skeletons of people of small stature.

THE moon, or generative power, supposed to be the supplier of all the juices essential to animal existence and nourishment, was worshipped in ancient times all over the world, and was represented with a crescent, or horns, upon her head, to denote the horns of the moon. The greatest obscenities were practised at all her temples; at Babylon, at Aphek, at Alarbech, and other places. In Egypt, she was worshipped under the name of Isis. By the Greeks and Romans, she was called Ceres. In India, the productive power. By the Ephisians, Diana: and sometimes she was called Hecate, Trivia, Hebe, Luna. By the Carthagenians she was called Coelestes, Urania. By the Jews, the Queen of Heaven. By the Scythians, Artemposa; and by the Egyptians, sometimes, Atar. In Mexico was a temple dedicated to the generative goddess; a lively indication that the principles and objects of the Mexican worship were the same as in the ancient countries just mentioned.

Between Nootka sound and Cook's river, in the 57th degree of north latitude, in the hieroglyphic paintings on Cook's river, *a harp* is represented. They did not represent an imaginary figure, which accidentally turned out to be exactly similar to the harp of the Hindoos. They must have learned it from the people of Asia. The *vina*, or harp, of the Hindoos, was a musical instrument, greatly in fashion in India in ancient times, as it was also in Palestine in the times of David, Solomon, Isaiah and Ezekiel.*a*

a Dubois, 240: Job, ch. 21, v. 12, ch. 30, v. 31; Psalms, ch. 33, v. 2, ch. 43 v. 4 ch. 49, v. 4, ch 57, v. 8, ch. 71, v. 22, ch. 81, v 2; Daniel, ch. 3, v. 5; 1 Samuel, ch. 11, v. 5, ch. 16, v. 16; Isaiah, ch. 5, v. 12; Ezekiel, ch. 27, v. 18.

The vina of the Hindoos, and the harp of the scriptures, are the same.

The game of chess was invented in India, by the Brahmans, 601 years before Christ, with the design of admonishing kings, that they are strong only in the strength of their subjects. It was introduced into Persia in the time of Chosroes, the great enemy of the Roman power and of Justinian, between the years of our Lord 482 and 565. The Araucanians in the south of Chili, had this amongst other games, and called it *comicen.* It has been known to them from time immemorial, and they must have brought it from India or Persia.[a]

Mr. Clifford, late of Kentucky, had, in his lifetime, a pipe which was found in digging a trench on Sandusky river, in alluvial earth, six feet below the surface. The rim of the bowl is in high relief, and the front represents a handsome female face. The stone of which it is made is the real talc graphique, exactly resembling the stone of which the Chinese make their idols. No talc of this species is known to exist on this side the Alleghenies. This article of course must have been brought from a distance, probably from China, or its neighbourhood.

When Sir Hugh Paliser was governor of Newfoundland, the Moravian missionaries who were sent to the Esquimaux and Hudson's bay, were understood by the people there when speaking in the Moravian language. The Moravians were a Sclavonic race, which came from Silesia and Poland, and settled upon the Danube, and to the north of it, and probably also upon the Baltic and the north of it. The Esquimaux, Labradors, and the people of Hudson's bay, and those also of Nootka sound, Oonalashky and Prince William's sound, on the waters of the western coast of America, spake dialects of the same language. The Sclavonians are of the Tartar race, which came from the

a 7 Gibbon, 307; 2 Molinæ, 307.

ancient Scythians. They have emigrated to America on the eastern side, and have planted a language on the northeast and northwest of America, so evidently identified in its origin with that of the Moravians, spoken to this day in the northern parts of Europe, as to leave no doubt, that all those, both in America and Europe, who speak it, were people whose original parentage was one and the same, namely, tribes of Scythians, from the confines of China to the shores of Lapland, and from the Danube to Kamschatka. But not the same with the Hindoos, Persians, Chinese, Thibetans and Japanese, who came to the equatorial parts of America, and from thence extended their settlements towards the lakes of Canada and the river Savannah, till met by emigrants from the north, who passed through the country of the Esquimaux long since the original settlement of those people in their present abodes, and long since the climate had caused their degeneracy from the size of the ancient stock. They came perhaps through the same passage that the Esquimaux formerly did, taking with them some of the latter, either willingly or by compulsion, and made them compose a part of their retinue, and buried them in White county, on the lakes of Canada, and in the state of Missouri.

Men of the large stature of those whose skeletons are found in Tennessee and the adjoining countries, are not produced at this day in any of those countries, nor in any part of the United States. Nor are they to be found as far to the north as Hudson's bay or beyond it. Nor in the countries northwest of the lakes, which were passed through by Mr. McKenzie. Nor were any such seen by Clark and Lewis; nor are they produced in any part of America north of the southern frontiers of Chili. That they came hither from countries south of Chili, is barely possible. The distance is between 5000 and 6000 miles. Whence

then have they come, and at what period? All the
earliest writings of the world have spoken of men
of monstrous stature existing in the times they treat
of. ' The Mosaic writings, those who wrote the acts
of Joshua and David, Homer, Herodotus, Diodorus
Siculus, Plutarch, all mention them. All the Scythian tribes, including the Celts, Germans, Goths,
Gauls, Vandals, Franks, are treated of by subsequent historians, as well as those more ancient ones,
as men of gigantic stature.[a] And they continue to
be mentioned as men of great stature, till about the
sixth century of the Christian era, when that mark
of distinction seems to be dropped,[b] except as to the
Huns. The European tribes of gigantic men were
of tall stature, blue eyes, long flaxen hair, offensive
smell, and hairy. The Huns came into Europe in
the ninth century of the Christian era. They spake
a dialect of the Sclavonian language, as did the
Fins of Finland, who once occupied the north of
Asia and Europe. The Igors, who had the use
and knowledge of letters, were once settled on the
banks of the Irtish, where their inscriptions are yet
to be found.

A similar name and language are found in the
southern parts of Siberia. And the remains of the
Finnic tribes are scattered from the fens of the Oby
to the shores of Lapland. Extreme cold has di-
minished the size of the Laplanders from what it
anciently was, when they lived in more temperate
climates. The Esquimaux, it would seem, are descended from the ancient Huns. The large skeletons
we are speaking of, came from Scythia, the
ancient country of giants; not from the northern
nations of Europe, between the Danube and the
Baltic, the Rhine and the ocean; but from some

a Herod. Clio, 68; D. Siculus, 314; 4 Plutarch, 208; 1
Tacitus' Annals, sec. 64; Homer's Iliad.
b 1 Gibbon, 404; 7 Gibbon, 258; 1 Gibbon, 280, 290; 5
Gibbon, 200, 328; 6 Gibbon, 99.

part of Asiatic Tartary, where the climate is temperate, and congenial to the growth of human beings; from some climate between the 36th and 50th of north latitude; where the people have not the flaxen hair and blue eyes of the Gauls, Germans, Goths, Vandals and Franks. Not being able to bear the heat of a southern sun, they have stopped their conquests at the Mississippi and Natchez, and the countries adjacent to them, on the west. This was done before the influence of climate, and change of seasons all over the world, had reduced the human stature from its ancient gigantic bulk, to the ordinary stature of the men of this day.

The Huns were once settled in the countries on the north of the great wall of China; and before the Christian era, had extended their sway to the eastward as far as the ocean, westwardly as far as to the heads of the Irtish, and northwardly as far as to the ocean also. They were of dark complexion, having broad shoulders, flat noses, small black eyes, little or no beard, and were of tall stature. They were beaten in a general, decisive battle, by the Alans, about the year of our Lord 48, and were scattered in different directions to different parts of the world. One division settled on the east of the Caspian sea, where the ten tribes had been settled before their arrival, in the planes of Sogdiona, near to the Persians. They afterwards became civilized and luxurious. They extended their empire from the Caspian sea to the heart of India, about the year of our Lord 488. About the year of our Lord 558, they, as well as the Igors, on a branch of the Selinga, were subdued by the Turks. These nations were distinguished from all the other nations of Scythia, by the knowledge and use of letters in the Scythian character and language. Whether the Sogdoites learned these from the Israelites, will presently be examined. Another division of the Hans lived for some time on the Volga;

and in the year 405, they removed to the north, to escape from the Georgen, who had then conquered all the countries from the Corea to those on the west of the Irtish. The Huns were great archers; *adopted their captives taken in war;* each tribe had its mursa or chief, and they had no despotic ruler. They paid a tribute of one tenth for the support of government, *and they scalped their enemies.* Were not these the nations which came into America, bringing with them from the Irtish and from the planes of Sogdiona, their knowledge of letters and historical writings, both of which have been lost by time in the northern wilds of America, but at so late a period as to leave circumstantial traditions with their descendants of the facts related in their ancient writings? The climate inviting them, they came by degrees to the lakes, accompanied by some of the Esquimaux; and from thence to the countries on the Ohio and on the Cumberland, where the industry, arts and civilization of the inhabitants had heaped together the conveniences of life, which offered a rich spoil to their rapacity. The tuft of hair upon the heads of Indians of the present day,'must have been derived from those Huns who settled in India, and probably adopted the custom of the Hindoos, to leave a tuft of hair upon the head, which they have done from time immemorial to this day.[a] The effect of which is, that the head shaved all around the tuft, and constantly exposed to the sun and weather, and to the water in swimming, has produced the thick sculls which are found with the large skeletons in Tennessee; an effect known to be produced by similar causes in ancient times.[b]

The letters which are found in America inscribed on rocks, may be traced by reference to the history of the Hebrews. After the removal of the ten tribes into Medea and Mesopotamia, a part of them thence removed to a place on the Oxus, now called Haze-

a 2 Dubois, 95, 178.　　*b* Herod. Thalia, sec. 12.

ras; and Hazereth, no doubt, the Arsareth of Es-
dras. Thence they extended into Transoxiana, by
corruption called Sogdiana. They gave name to
Chorazon, after a city of that name on the east of
the Dead sea, the country from whence they had
been removed by the Assyrians; also Cashgar, for
Ashur; Samarcand, by corruption, for Samaria;
and Eighur, by corruption, for Igor. They settled
upon the mountains between India and Persia, and
upon the heads of the Indus, as far as to Kholen,
in the lesser Bucharia. The descendants of Dan,
Asher, Zebulon and Napthali, are there plainly
distinguishable at this day. The Affghans, on the
heads of the Indus, are descended of the Hebrews.
Their language is evidently a dialect of the scriptural Chaldaic. The people in all these countries
have been distinguished, by the earliest profane
historians, by their knowledge and use of letters.
These the Hebrews, the first settlers of the country,
planted there at least from the time of their arrival.
The neighbouring mountains of Imaus, before without a name, received one from them, after a city
near the lake of Genezerth. Those who belonged
to the tribe of Issachar, were called in their own
country by the popular name of Ischars, Isars,
Izors,[a] and by another corruption, Eughars, and
afterwards Igors. From the above-mentioned territory of this name, it is probable, those emigrated
who lived on the Irtish, and were distinguished by
their letters, from all the tribes of Scythia, and
were called Igors.[b] They were there settled long
before the subjection of their country by the Huns,
which was 201 years before the Christian era.
With a part of the Huns, they removed to the Volga
about the year of our Lord 48, to avoid the Alans;
and from thence, about the year of our Lord 405,
into the northern parts of Siberia, for fear of the

a Josephus' Antiquities, b. 8, ch. 13, sec. 6, sec. 8,
b 4 Gibbon, 360.

UE

Geougen.*a*   The remnant which the Huns left, afterwards became numerous by propagation, and spread to the mountains of Altai, in the centre of Scythia; and by successive changes, were called Igours, Ogors, Ocgurs, Tochars, Tartars. That part of them which removed to the northern parts of Siberia, after lingering for some time there, it is supposed, came into America, and made, in the latter country, inscriptions similar to those which they left on the Irtish, and in those parts of Siberia where they were once settled.   When they came to America, for want of settled habitations, and of the materials to write with, the culture of literature was inevitably lost. The great extent of the country and its various regions, as they were progressively discovered, incessantly invited them, as they now do us, to new migrations; and they had no time to preserve, by learning, the use of the letters which they had.   But those letters, and the greater frequency of their inscription in the northern parts of America, point out the direction and course of their migrations; which lead to the like inscriptions in Siberia and Tartary, where once lived, as may be fairly presumed, that people who came into America and made the inscriptions which we now see. We can trace them to the Igors, and to Sogdiona, and to Samaria.   The Cherokees and Creeks, as well as the Chickasaws, who are supposed to be the descendants of the Igors and the Huns, are of the common size of white men of the present day; having no beards; long, jet black hair, and black eyes, thick and blunt noses, short and blunt toes, the under part of the feet remarkably hollow, their fingers thin and long, white teeth; tapering, well formed legs and thighs, small ankles, their foreheads of the same form and size with those of the white people, their colour a reddish brown, or bright cop-

---

a 1 Herod. 3 0; 2 Herod. 326; 1 Gib. 352; 4 Gib. 660; 7 Gib. 204, 285, 293; 11 Gib. 406.

per, and they wear a tuft of hair upon the head. They brought with them both the Mosaic and prophetic writings, as well as those of the psalmist; for their traditions are taken for both, and Hal-le-lu-jah from the latter. If it be correct, as learned men have alleged, that tradition is adulterated after the lapse of two hundr. d years, and assumes the character of fable, then it is deducible from the fulness and particularity of their traditions when first made known to us, between 1606 and 1690, that they were within two hundred years from the period when the original was lost, from whence the traditions were taken.

When, about the year of our Lord 48, the Huns were broken up, and fled in different divisions to different quarters of the world, that part of them which came to Sogdiona, and there settled under the name of Nepthalites,[a] were no other, it is believed, than a part of those tribes of lettered men which the Huns had subdued on the Irtish two or three centuries before, and who again, upon this occasion, returned to their old country and friends, assuming the name by which those friends would the more readily recognize and receive them. The country was inhabited; yet they were received into it, without opposition, as a part of the people which belonged to the ancient tribe of Napthali, and who were called Nepthalites, by corruption, for Napthalites. By this name they were distinguished from the great body of the Huns, and gained admittance amongst the inhabitants of Sogdiona. The Chinese invaded and ruined them, after the middle of the third century of the Christian era; and at this period of adversity and distress, it has been suggested, that a part of these Nepthalites may have joined their brethren who had gone into Siberia[b] The Nepthalites who lived on the north of the Oxus, and on the borders of the Caspian sea,

<hr>

a 4 Gibbon, 368.   *b* 4 Gibbon, 370, 372.

so late as the period of the Chinese conquest, which was about the year of our Lord 367, must have heard of the Christian religion which had been established in Armenia ever since the year of our Lord 312, and has ever since continued there. These Nepthalites also must have learned some of its rites; yet in all the remains throughout the whole continent of America, there is not a single trait, or token, of the Christian religion. This circumstance strongly intimates, that the removal of those lettered men into America preceded the epoch of the Chinese conquests. There are not found in America any burials of bodies with their heads to the west; nor sign of the cross, for the infliction of punishment; no emblem of any baptismal initiation, except the immersion of prisoners, incorporated by adoption into the family of the captor, which was an emblem to signify that his old blood was washed away, and that he now had the blood of the adopting father.[a] The Huns practised adoption; so did the Hebrews and the Hindoos. There is not among our Indians any emblem of the resurrection; nor the tradition of any miraculous performance; nor, in short, any of those striking facts which are recorded in the New Testament, nor even of the destruction of the temple by the Romans, an event which dispersed the Jews into all parts of the world, and particularly into Mesopotamia and Medea, then under the power of the Parthians.[b] Numbers of these Jews had been converted to the Christian faith; and no doubt, maintained a correspondence with their brethren in Medea and on the Oxus. Nor is there to be found in America the vestige of any art or science, or improvement in either, which originated subsequently to the third century of the Christian era. The Roman coins are the latest. The Huns, when they fled from the Volga, in the year of our Lord 405,

a Exo. ch. 2, v. 10; Esther, ch. 2, v, 7, 15; 1 Dub. 340.
b Jos. War. b. 2, ch. 16, sec. 4.

being then identified with the Igors, or at least having the latter politically incorporated with them, were obliged to proceed to the Icy ocean, the countries to the west being all then settled; and there they did not remain long enough to lose their huge stature, by the intense cold of those climates; but before the occurrence of any diminution, they marched directly into some climate of America, which preserved their size as long as the rest of mankind retained theirs. The vast number of fortifications in all parts of Tennessee, Ohio and Kentucky, which are capable of being fortified, show that their wars with the aborigines were not immediately terminated, but were of long continuance. When these were finally ended, and these countries wholly abandoned to them, can only be inferred from the ages of the trees which have grown upon these fortifications since their desertion; and by these we are carried back to periods nearly 1000 years precedent to the commencement of this century; though the last aboriginal struggle for existence may have been several centuries later. Upon the whole, since every alphabet which ever has been in the world, beginning with the letters *alpha* and *beta*, contains within itself *demonstration* of a derivation with all others, from one common original; and since we can trace this art into Egypt prior to the time of the *exodus*, 1491 before Christ, and into India at a still earlier period,[a] there seems to be incontrovertible evidence, that the inscriptions in America were made by people from the old world; and very probably by Siberian descendants, from the Issachors and Napthalites. True, they have left in America but few tokens of a Sabbath day. But this may well be accounted for, by their loss of the use of letters; their want of written kalendars; their separation from the Levites, or regularly constituted priests of the nation, and their perpetual

a. Exodus, ch. 17; v. 14; 1 Dubois, 350, 379, 387, 388.

migrations for a long space of time, as they advanced slowly towards the southern and eastern regions of this continent. Nor is it left to reasoning, founded upon the existing circumstances of the world, to show us, that the Igours, when they removed from the Volga, in the year of our Lord 405, went to the Icy ocean and the north of Siberia; for we have express information of the fact from authentic history.[a] About the year 454, "the Igours of the north, issuing from the cold Siberian regions of the north, which produce the most valuable furs, spread themselves over the desert as far as the Borysthenes and Caspian gates, and finally extinguished the empire of the Huns." Another part of them, it is now hardly to be doubted, issuing from the same hive, came through the gates which opened into this continent, and over the peninsula which joins the two continents together; and through the country of the Esquimaux, a part of whom came with them, to lake Erie, the Calf-killer and the Missouri.

The coins found in Tennessee or Kentucky may be thus traced : From some place contiguous to the borders both of the Roman and Persian empires, where they contended for supremacy, and paid these coins to the soldiers who served in their armies, by whom they were circulated amongst the nations of Scythia, which deposited them, in their migrations, at the places where they are now found. Such wars were waged for a long time in the countries near to the heads of the Euphrates and the Tigris, and one of them after the division of the Roman empire into three parts, between 310 and 360 of the Christian era. The Persians were forced to conclude it by an invasion of the Massagetæ from the north and northeast. In these countries circulated both the Roman and the Persian coins, of the same dates with those which we now find in Tennessee and Kentucky; but none of a date subsequent to the middle of the third century of the Christian era.

a 6 Gibbon, 137.

The Mexicans did not descend from the people in the north of Europe, either the ancient Germans or Scandinavians, but from people who worshipped the sun. Like them, they had the zodiac for the mystical representation of their deities; and like the Egyptians, and the most ancient settlers of India, raised pyramids for his worship, decorated with representations of days, months, years, and the sun's path like the windings of a serpent, which they signified by the image of one. They had the arts of fortification and intrenchment, metallic tools and utensils; the science of astronomy and geometry in considerable perfection; and the mechanic arts; of all which the northern Indians were completely ignorant. They are glaring circumstances of difference, as well as their modes of warfare and political government. The Mexicans came to America at a much earlier period; but after the invention in Asia of the arts which they had practised here, and of the sciences which they had learned; after the invention of post roads and couriers, the game of chess, and intrenchment; after the ascertainment of the true length of the solar year; after the coins uttered in the time of Antoninus and Commodus; and after the time of the three simultaneous emperors of the Romans, if those coins were brought hither by the Mexicans. Or otherwise they must have become acquainted with these arts and sciences by an intercourse, kept up through the ocean, with those countries of the old world, which they had left. For the dates of which several arts and sciences, see the several heads in this volume, where they are mentioned.

ADDENDA.

Page 24.

INTRODUCTORY to a description of the salt works, it will be proper to take a view, in the first place, of the water courses near to which they are found.

The Cany Fork rises in the Cumberland mountain, near the Walton road, its head branches intersecting with the waters of Obed's river and the Calf-killer, in about an easterly direction from the town of Sparta, in the county of White, and flows in a southeastwardly direction for about fifteen or twenty miles, and thence gradually shapes its course to the south and southwest, until it receives into its bosom Cane creek, a small tributary stream, at the mouth of the Hickory valley, at which place it runs west, gradually inclining towards the north until it is discharged into the Cumberland river, near Carthage. This river from its source is rapid in its descent, passing over a rocky or pebbly bottom, affording numerous sites for mills and water machinery of every description. There are many places upon this stream where the water falls perpendicularly, or nearly so, 4 or 5 feet. The most considerable fall upon this stream, above the great falls, is near the mouth of the Hickory valley, and above the mouth of Cave creek. Here the bed of the river is composed of flat limestone rock, rising above the surface of the stream in rude disorder to the height of ten or fifteen feet. In viewing this point on the river, the observer is surprised and pleased with the grand and romantic scenery which surrounds him. On the western bank of the river rises in

Yv

prospect, a mountain about two hundred feet in height above the bed of the river, covered on its side and summit with beautiful small cedar, which in autumn contrasted with the yellow leaf of the oak and poplar, and the beautiful white foam meeting the eye for the distance of half a mile in a right line on the river, the impetuous rush of waters over the rocks at three or four points all in view, each falling from ten to fifteen feet, present a scene grand and sublime. The tributary streams of the Cany Fork, on the east side, are the Big Laurel and Bear creek, composed of large springs. These creeks, in their passage through the mountain, run with great rapidity, passing over pebbly bottoms and numerous round sand rocks, some of which are as large as a barrel, and others gradually diminishing in size to a pound weight or smaller, having thereon considerable falls of from five to twenty and thirty feet. Cane creek is also a tributary stream of the Cany Fork; it rises in the Cumberland mountain, within a few miles of Pikeville, in Bledsoe county, and runs a northeastwardly course, to its confluence with the Cany Fork, at the mouth of the Hickory valley. This stream, like all others of the mountain, in this section of the country, runs with great rapidity, falling in its passage down the mountain frequently twenty and thirty feet. This creek, shortly after it descends the mountain, passes over a large bed of stone coal, of considerable breadth and of excellent quality. The Cany Fork receives on its western bank, above the mouth of the Calf-killer river, White-oak creek, West's Fork, Polk-patch creek, Two-mile creek, Clifty and Lost creek. Nothing remarkable distinguishes these streams from the other tributary streams of the Cany Fork, all of them being rapid in their descent. Upon Lost creek are extensive falls, some of them thirty feet in perpendicular height. It affords water sufficient in quantity to propel water machinery about half of the year. This stream is about ten or twelve miles in length. It runs the whole extent with great rapidity. And nature, after exhibiting much variety in the romantic appearance of its falls, and the impetuosity of its current, has, as if weary of its passage, directed its course to the foot of a stupendous mountain, where the stream is ingulfed and lost in the silent grandeur of the surrounding objects. But few bottoms or low grounds are found on the Cany Fork, from its source to a considerable distance below the great falls. From its source to the great falls, meandering the stream, is a distance of fifty or sixty miles; and from thence to Carthage, about 100 miles, by the river. A phenomenon, strange in its nature, attends two or three points in the bed of the Cany Fork. In passing over large globular rocks, the water in the channel entirely disappears for the distance of a mile, rising in equal force below, with the channel above. At the mouth of Cave creek, in dry weather, in the fall season, the channel of the river dries up; and the waters above run up the mouth the mouth of Cave creek about 100 yards, and disembogues itself under the western bank, and again rises in the river at the distance of half a mile below. At a point on the Cany Fork, about six miles above the Hickory valley, is a bottom of level land, called the Big bottom. This on one side is limited by a mountain of considerable height, exhibiting immense cliffs, opposite to which, on the low grounds, are lying huge masses of rocks, ejected from the top of the pinnacle to the distance of 80 yards. The surface between the foot of the mountain and the point on which the rocks are, is too level for them to have rolled on, after having been precipitated from the mountain, showing conclusively that it has been the effect of some great convulsion of nature.

The Calf-killer river, on the northeast side of the Cany Fork, has its source in the Cumberland mountain, a little northeast of Sparta, and near the Walton road. It interlocks with the head streams of the Cany Fork, is rapid in its descent, shaping its course generally to the south and southwest, and is about thirty or forty miles in length. The point of confluence with the Cany Fork is on the north side, and about eight miles south of Sparta. Its principal tributary streams on the east side, are Bridge creek, Doe creek, Brush creek, Blue-spring creek, and Wildcat creek. On the west side, Plum creek, Cherry creek and Town creek. The latter forms a junction with the Calf-killer about half a mile below Sparta. About a mile below the town of Sparta, on the Calf-killer, is a fall of about fifteen feet, nearly perpendicular, where Captain Thomas B. Rice has in operation a grist and saw mills, and iron works. This is one of the most eligible sites in the western country for a national armory, or for any other description of water machinery in use in this country. In the neighbourhood of these falls are found inexhaustible mines of iron ore of good quality.

Upon the Calf-killer, above Sparta, are in operation six or seven salt works, at which considerable quantities of salt are made. It is about six miles above Sparta, upon the west side of the river, where the spot is nearest to the source of the river at which salt has been made. Also, about two miles above Sparta, is a salt establishment on the west side of the river. The other establishments on the river for the manufactory of salt, are between the former and latter points. Some of these are on the west, and some on the south side of the river. Two of the wells are situated from fifteen to twenty yards on the river; others are bored on the edge of the river. The salt water which is found by boring is from 50 to 180 feet under the surface of the earth, is of a darkish colour, and is generally pretty strongly impregnated with sulphur, it not being uncommon in descending to the salt water to pass

through streams and reservoirs of sulphur water.
It is, however, clearly ascertained, that the deeper
the salt water is found from the surface of the earth,
the less it is impregnated with sulphur. Several
of these wells, which from first appearances afforded
a plentiful supply of salt water, and held forth
flattering prospects of wealth to the owners by the
manufactory of salt, have partially failed to furnish
a supply of salt water, when on descending deeper
it has been found more abundant and strong, and
less impregnated with sulphur. Hence the conclusion eventually drawn is, that the deeper the descent
in quest of salt water, the better is its quality when
found, and the more plenteous the water. At the
establishment mentioned before as being six miles
from Sparta, large quantities of Epsom salts have
been manufactured, from the same water out of
which the common salt is made, equal in quality to
any in the world. The proprietor, who is a gentleman of sterling integrity, and whose veracity can
not for a moment be doubted, states that twenty or
thirty thousand pounds of salt per annum could
easily be made at his well.

The prerequisites necessary for the commencement of boring in the rock, are to sink a large pit,
by removing the earth from over the rock where the
boring is to be performed, making a vacuity about
eight feet square, which is secured by erecting a
pen of logs or frame extending from the rock to the
surface of the earth. A sweep or spring pole is
then prepared, the large end being fastened to the
ground, the small end extending over the well. To
the latter end a rope is fastened, one end of which
is fastened to a pole a little smaller in diameter
than the diameter of the hole intended to be bored
in the rock. On the lower end of this pole is fixed
an iron socket, with a cavity in the lower end, in
which cavity a screw is cut for the reception of the
auger. The auger is always made of steel, the end

applied to the rock having an edge in the centre, and the other end having a screw to attach it to the socket in which the screw is cut, attached to the pole. As the hole descends into the rock, the rope attached to the sweep or spring pole is lengthened, until a sufficient distance is bored in the rock to require another pole, when one is attached by screws, as the auger and pole first mentioned were. Thus those who perform the boring descend to the requisite depth. Three persons are generally employed in the act of boring, two remain at the sweep or spring pole, and put it in motion by moving it in a vertical position, which puts the pole and auger attached to the sweep as above, in motion, while one person in the pit below turns the pole to which the auger is attached, half round at each vertical motion of the spring pole above. In the mean time, water is applied to the hole pierced by the auger. Thus the boring is performed. The water is applied to the hole for the purpose of keeping the auger cool, and of reducing the dust made by boring to a consistence, that the same may be drawn out by a small pump, which is occasionally let down into the hole. If any of the poles break, which frequently occurs at the distance of a hundred feet and upwards in the rock, a socket is let down, and is driven around the part broken off, and is then screwed up and repaired. In descending to the salt water, it frequently happens that the streams of fresh and sulphur water are passed through. These are prevented from communicating with the salt water, by means of a tube made of copper, tin or wood, long enough to reach below those streams, the lower end of which being wrapped with some material that will close out the waters above; the salt water then rises in some wells to the top of the rock, in others it does not come nearer than fifty or sixty feet, whence it is drawn from them by the force of a pump It requires generally from one to two hundred gallons of water to make a bushel of salt, though as to the quantity, it is somewhat uncertain, much depending on the success in preventing the fresh water from mixing with the salt by the tube above mentioned. In descending through the rock, the strata or layers are generally next the surface composed of lime-stone rock from five to ten feet in thickness. At sixty feet in some, layers of sand rock mixed with limestone are passed. At about seventy-five or eighty feet, there is passed a stratum of materials, supposed to be lead, or some other mineral substance, it being of a soft consistence. frequently re. requiring a day to pass an inch. This stratum is generally found to be from one to three' or four inches in thickness. Owing, however, to the inattention of those engaged in boring for salt, no chemical experiment has has been made, to ascertain the quality of the mineral thus discovered. It is not unfrequent in boring for salt, to reach a cavity filled with gas, which produces an immense discharge of water, ejecting it to the height of seventy feet. Instances have happened after the explosion has subsided, that the pit sunk to the rock becomes filled with air so dense in its character and unhealthy in its nature, that it could not be inhaled without producing instant insensibility to every object around, depriving every person coming within its influence of motion, and threatening in its consequences the occurrence of instant death. The perforated hole by which the salt water is descended to, is of the width of three inches generally, but some are three and a half and four inches, and others only two and a half. Salt water rises at different points on the bed of the Calf-killer and of the Cany Fork, and is discovered by the resort of cattle to the spot to drink it. Several new discoveries have lately been made of water on the Cany Fork very strongly impregnated, and salt works are forming there which promise to afford \ery plentiful supplies.

Page 51.

About sixty miles west of the Cumberland mountain is a space three or four miles in width, and in some places more, extending from the Cumberland river nearly to the southern boundary of the state. Its direction is parallel to the Cumberland mountain and the river Mississippi. It is covered with a growth of cedars, and with rocks upon and just below the surface, some flat for a considerable distance, some lying obliquely with the upper part just above the surface in all directions, some with the extremities of the rock turned perpendicularly upwards, some with the corners of the sides and extremities only appearing. It is miry in all rainy seasons of the year. Salt licks and springs begin to appear about fifty miles below the foot of the Cumberland mountain, and within a space of forty miles from thence westwardly, and from the northern to the southern boundary, on both sides of the cedar flats. Animals lick away the clay near the springs, till for some considerable distance there is the appearance of banks, the clay between them and the springs having been taken away to the depth of a foot or more. The spring emits a thin water, of a whitish cast, which leaves on the side of the rock or gum in which it is contained, a mucilaginous coat or covering of a red colour. When the water of the spring falls upon the low ground, and is not carried off in the stream, it turns black and gives the same colour to the mud which imbibes it. In this space they are very numerous, and are usually called by the name of the first discoverer. Some believe that the water comes from the Cumberland mountain, and that the depth from the salt water to the surface decreases to the point where they break forth. Others are of opinion, that the water is collected on the elevated parts of the neighbourhood, and passing through layers of salt deposited there, soon afterwards issue from the earth. The taste is saline, and cows and other animals collect there to regale themselves with it, and to lick away the dirt from the banks which it impregnates. These springs are provided by creative wisdom to prevent the extinction of animals which cannot exist without the use of salt. Such animals resort to them from great distances; buffalo paths leading to them in some instances can be traced more than a hundred miles. Tennessee, both East and West, being far removed from the ocean, has an air not at all impregnated with saline particles: as a horse who travels all day in the rain, will not drink, because of the abundant absorption of water; so an animal who lives near the ocean, and constantly inhales an air abounding in saline impregnations, is so little desirous of more, that he will sometimes hardly lick salt when offered to him. But the case is far otherwise in Tennessee; and various consequences have followed which are too strikingly observable to escape the notice of a traveller as soon as he gets over the mountains and ridges between him and the ocean. Cows and horses, and all the granivorous animals, as well as some of the feline genus, are often in great distress for want of salt, running with great rapidity on hearing the fall of urine, to taste it, chewing up bridles and all sorts of leather which have been touched by sweat, and clothes and blankets in which there is the least perceptible tincture of salt. And in order to get the taste of salt, they bark the mulberry, and other trees from which can be extracted the smallest quantity of salt materials. And when salt is offered to them, they use it with the most voracious avidity. No such appearances are observable in countries near to the ocean, in which the air is sufficiently impregnated. Another consequence is, that in the freshened atmosphere of Tennessee, for want of a sufficient quantity of salt, to be inhaled into and incorporated with the system, those animals to which that article is most indispen-

W w

sable, decline in health, vigour and size. The deer and even the squirrels of Tennessee, as well as other animals, are smaller than the animals of the same species east of the mountains. The domestic animals raised here, unless plentifully supplied with salt, are of less bulk, activity and animation, than their kindred animals beyond the mountains, and after sometime will actually dwindle to death for want of its nourishment. The mammoth, it is probable, flourished here when the salt water of the ocean flowed to the oyster banks which we now see in the heart of the country; and when it retired, was compelled to resort to the salt springs, where not finding a plentiful supply, he often perished, and deposited his bones near them.

Of the Cascades of Tennessee.

A stream or rivulet in the county of White, in West Tennessee, known by the name of the Falling-water, is about forty yards wide, and empties into the Cany Fork of Cumberland, on the north side, forty or fifty miles above Carthage. The course of Falling creek is from northeast to southwest, having its source in the Cumberland mountain, and being in length, from the source to the mouth, twenty or thirty miles. The falls on this stream are seven or eight miles above its junction with the Cany Fork. In the course of one mile the descent is supposed to be three hundred feet. Several of these falls afford excellent seats for iron works, grist or saw mills, a national armory, or almost any machine which is brought into operation by water. The large fall is a perpendicular descent of water of the depth of two hundred feet, or as some think, of one hundred and fifty feet. The country on both sides of the stream, both above and below the fall, is nearly as level as the adjacent country generally: and what is very remarkable, the only difference in the aspect of the country as produced by the falls, appears to consist in the depth of the channel, which would seem to have been an excavation out of the solid rock. The perpendicular height of the clifts on each side of the stream, is about three hundred feet. The bottom of the channel below the falls, is almost inaccessible for many miles below the falls, and the descent to it is difficult and even dangerous. The width of the sheet of water which falls from the rock is about eighty feet, and produces a noise which can be heard for several miles. Three miles south of this, are the falls of Taylor's creek, which present similar appearances. These streams run parallel to each other, and fall about the same depth in the course of a mile. The principal fall on Taylor's creek is somewhat higher than that of Fallingwater. About eighty yards above the principal fall, the stream is about sixty feet wide, and falls over a rock ten feet. About forty yards further, the water falls twenty-five or thirty feet, and in forty yards more it pitches over a rock one hundred and fifty, some say two hundred, and others two hundred and fifty, feet. The descent to the foot of the rock is difficult and dangerous, but the grandeur of the spectacle richly compensates the hazard. Here the spectator finds himself almost shut out from the view of the heavens by the overhanging cliffs, three or four hundred feet high. The stream before him, falling from the last rock in sheets of foam, almost deafens him with the noise. A considerable wind is created by the fall, and the spray falls like mist for many yards around. Twenty yards below this, on the south side, is the most beautiful cascade of which the imagination can conceive. A creek, six or eight feet wide, falls from the summit of an over-hanging rock a distance of at least three hundred feet. A man standing on the brink of this rock, seen from below, appears no bigger than a child. Few have courage to venture so near the precipice as to look over it. The water in its descent is split into a thousand streams, and is often driven by the winds many yards around, making an artificial shower, which exhibits, when the sun shines, the colours of the rainbow. Between the sheet of water and the site of the rock from which it falls, both here and at the other high falls, is a considerable space of ground, on which a man may walk unmolested by the water: this ground is somewhat moist, but much impregnated with salt and nitre. In viewing this vast chasm, one hundred yards wide, three or four hundred deep, and many miles in length, the philosopher may inquire, how or by what means it was excavated in the solid rock; and the poet will exclaim, "*These are thy glorious works, Almighty Father!*"

The writer requested of Mr. Craighead and Mr. Nelson, two gentlemen of the bar, residents of Sparta, to ride to the falls for the purpose of viewing, and making a report upon them. With a readiness which ever marks the conduct of enlightened minds, they politely complied; and after an absence of a day and a half, having been at the falls with Mr. Eastland, a young gentleman of Sparta, and with Major Taylor, a member of the state legislature, distinguished for his discretion and good sense, they returned and made the preceding reports; the former by Mr. Nelson; the latter, respecting Taylor's creek, by Mr. Craighead. To these, by inquiry from Mr. Craighead, the writer has added the circumstances following: From the water upwards, on the face of the perpendicular rock, on the sides or banks of the creek, towards the water, are various strata of materials: first, limestone for thirty feet up; next, a stratum of slate or stone coal six or eight feet through; and upon this, rocks composed of flint and lime stone intermixed, and upon that the common mould.

It is conjectured by some, that these strata have been petrified, or converted into coal, since the ori-

ginal formation of the water course, by the same
cotemporary process which made the like conver-
sions in all parts of West Tennessee. Supposing
that at one time the surface of the earth corresponded
with a small elevation above them, to the surface of
the waters above and below the falls, the low lands
below must have been as discernible as any other
low lands of the country; but that the sediments
of inundation subsiding upon them, have elevated
their surface to an equality with that of the lands
above, and have produced the inequality of depth
from the surface below to the waters, compared with
the surface above to the waters; and that in forming
the superstrata below, those layers have been deposited, first of shells which have become limestone, and next of vegetable substances which have
become coal. And it is supposed to be a confirmation of this hypothesis, that indentations similar to those made by currents of water on the sides
of clay banks, are found on the sides of these limestone banks, at even distances on either side from
the level of the water. This theory supposes that
a strong current of water preserved the width of the
creek, and the same ancient bed and bottom which
it formerly possessed, and of course the same elevations and depressions of bottom which formerly be-
belonged to it. As a proof that no eruption ever
opened a passage for the waters of these creeks, it
is observed, that no fragments of rocks or other tokens of diruption are to be seen on their sides or
bottoms; and hence it is thought to be a reasonable
conclusion, that the materials for saxeous composition were borne down the current as fast as they
came to impede it, and before they could grow by
adhesion into an indissoluble mass.

Section 2, of chapter VI. *in page* 119.

In the state of Kentucky, near the state line, in the county of Barren formerly, but now Monroe, and between the towns of Williamsburg in Tennessee, and of Glasgow in Kentucky, and near the road leading from the one to the other, and about thirty miles from Williamsburg, are ancient mounds, the trees upon which are of equal size with those in the adjoining forest. They are placed three in a row on one side, and three in a parallel row on the other, making four rows in all, and the whole including a square area within; the height of their summits from eight to ten feet.

COMMENTARIES.

A Commentary on the Geological Phenomena in the western parts of West Tennessee.

In going from Jackson, in the western district of Tennessee, through the states of Mississippi and Alabama, and thence to Florence, near the Tennessee line, the alluvial land of the western district cannot fail to attract the attention of the traveller. There are marshes on the banks of every stream; dangerous quicksands; sluggish waters; and a sound made by the hoof of the horse when it strikes the ground. The falling of a tree at some distance will produce a tremulous motion of the earth to the distance of several hundred yards; and here are frequent shocks of earthquakes. In the banks of rivers, and under high bluffs, sticks or logs of wood are found sometimes petrified. And in digging wells through the sand, leaves and sticks of wood are often found; and also fire coals and pieces of pottery. Along the ridges dividing the head waters of Sandy river from the waters of Hatchie river, immense beds of marine shells on the top of the ground are presented to view. No fossil or mineral substance is found in what may be supposed to have been its primitive state. They all seem to have been acted upon by heat and moisture. The Chickasaw old towns furnish a great variety of marine substances. Calcareous limestone is everywhere found in that section of country, a few feet under ground; and the small streams are soon sunk or absorbed. Springs are scarce. Upon the ridges which separate the waters of Tennessee from those that fall into the bay of Mobile, a rough crystal-

1

lized sandstone, in combination with iron and flint stone, is often found. In going down the ridges, the steps or flats run horizontally around the hollows, not perpendicularly down the side of one eminence and up the adjacent; and on the flat lands below, there are evident traces of water having lain upon them. In going off the highlands adjacent to the prairies granted by congress to the French colonists in Alabama, the soil is chiefly composed of a black sediment, united with carbonate of lime, and a great variety of sea shells. The clam shell is here in abundance; and half oyster shells, petrified, may be found, from the size of a person's thumb nail to the weight of four or five pounds; although the place where they are is more than 150 miles from the nearest part of the sea. Some part of these prairies have their first growth of timber, if inferences may be drawn from appearances. The growth upon them is slow and durable; and no hillocs made of the roots of trees blown up can be seen, nor any holes out of which their roots could have come, or could have been burned. At the lower part of this settlement, are the White bluffs on the Tuscaloosa, nearly opposite to Demopolis. The bluff is a hundred feet high; its face presents layers of shells, fish bones, and various vegetable substances intermixed with a calcareous limestone. A well dug in Demopolis afforded nearly the same materials; but nowhere have any human bones in any such state of petrifaction been discovered. The prairie lands generally in that part of the country. Some perhaps are without timber, solely because what is called rotten limestone is near to the top of the ground. All the moisture contained in such lands, acquires certain properties from the limestone, which ascending in vapour, imbues the atmosphere with qualities very pernicious to human life. To raise this exhalation, a certain degree of heat and moisture is necessary.

In very wet places it does not rise abundantly, nor in very dry ones. In very wet summers, the high lands are most sickly; and in very dry seasons, the low, swampy lands are most unhealthy. On the impurities of this atmosphere, the long moss is cherished, and doubtless contributes much to free the air from those noxious qualities. This moss affords a gloomy covering for the timber, not only in the low lands, but also on the hills. This moss is indicative of certain qualities in the soil and air, wherever it is found. It extends in places, across the Mexican empire, the Arkansas, Mississippi, Florida, Georgia and South-Carolina, and is found in some few places in the lower parts of North-Carolina.

In almost every part of the country, various marine substances are found, even on the highest hills. Iron ores mixed with pebbles, and coarsely shot up, somewhat in crystallized shapes, and sometimes cemented in large masses, are fequently met with. No lava or any signs of volcanic eruption are seen. Some marine shells are also mixed, seemingly in a state of vitrification, instead of calcination. Sometimes passing over a rich soil, one comes unexpectedly to its edge, and in a few steps more will be upon a red clay bank, or gravel, or round pebbles, of various colours and sizes, completely smooth on the outside; and even in the midst of a rich flat, a whole sand-hill or bank of chalk will show itself. The productions are equally heterogeneous. In a narrow bottom of the Hatchie river, three miles above its confluence with the Tombeckbe, the spruce pine, the long-leaf, the hill pine, the cedar, the cypress, the bay tree, the holly, buckeye, ash, sugar tree, walnut, red oak, a species of the live oak, elm, sycamore, and sundry other trees, all grow. The same confusion generally obtains, except on the sandy hills, where the long-leaf pine is often the sole tenant of the forest. On the face of the sterile country, is a certain remarkable unevenness of the top of the earth, resembling a field prepared with hillocs for planting sweet potatoes. For ten or fifteen miles together the road passes through timbered flat land covered with these hillocs, and they are extremely tiresome to horses which travel over them. These mounds are about four inches high, and across the circular base from three to six feet. The top and sides are generally very sterile; and around the base, in wet weather, the water lies and kills the grass. The appearance of this land, which by the inhabitants is called "bumpy" land, is very much like the waves of a lake, when after a hard wind they have nearly subsided into a smooth surface. But on hills and rough places, it has an appearance very similar to small waves just rising before a light wind, or like those mounds, across soft parts of the road where tobacco hogsheads are rolled along. At least one third of that part of Alabama is covered by this bumpy land, which renders it forever unfit for cultivation. Some geologists believe that these hills were formed when the soil was in a state of solution, and covered with water; others, that they were made by earthquakes, as thousands were in the Chickasaw settlements in the time of the late earthquakes. Some think, that the prairies have been uncovered in modern times, and that alluvial soil between the Tennessee ridge and the Mississippi, was formed by successive deposites in various times since the great deluge; and as the waters of the river decreased from reaching the ridge to which they now are, and that the salt water or sea has also left these ridges and Alabama in times much more modern than the deluge. They think also, that the high bluffs and other deep coverings of marine or terrestrial animals or vegetables, were caused by the great deluge, which removed vast quantities of diluted soil from the south to the north, making a terrestrial continent in the latter, of materials swept from beyond the capes of Africa and of America by a furious and irresistible torrent, which penetrated almost to the centre of the globe, enlarging the ocean to the south of these continents from the 35th to the 90th degree of latitude, when at the same time in the northern hemisphere, the corresponding latitudes are composed of main and mountainous lands, washed up from the southward and deposited in rude confusion where we now see them, by the great deluge. Their opinion is also, that the southern capes of Africa and America received their present shape from vast bodies of water which rushed against, and were divided by them, in their progress to the north. They are of opinion that the southern parts of the southern hemisphere were acted upon by fire, by the too near approach of the great comet, whose revolutionary course did actually bring it in view at the time of the deluge. And that the fire took hold of all combustible materials, and consumed the same for some time, till the waters of the ocean were so heated as to expand and rise beyond their ancient barriers. That whirlwinds rushed into the rarified vacuum, and drove the waters before them with irresistible fury, and compelled them to fly to the northern regions; whither they carried on their bosom the diluted soil of the continent, which they had torn from its base in the south; and the lifeless inhabitants of the deep, whose wreathed tails denote the suffocating death they died, for want of cooling respiration, and whose remains in the deepest fissures of the earth, demonstrate that they endeavored to withdraw from the incalescence that oppressed them. And whither they carried likewise in their bosom, the fire coals which the flames had made; the tropical plants more to the north, which the flames had not reached; and the terrestrial animals, which the waters involved more to the north and laid them at depths in the northern regions of the earth.

The river Mississippi as near to its mouth as the 35th degree of north latitude, like all other great rivers, continually elevates its bed by the deposites which are made from above, and of course at this day is vastly above its ancient bottom. As the bottoms were elevated, so proportionably were the low lands on the side of the river. The evidence is, that both the bed of the river and these low lands cover trees which are at great depths below them. A constant decrease of waters, and increase of sediments by annual inundations, has formed by alluvian the whole country between the ridge and the river where it now is. The marshes are the remains of waters not yet completely drained off, but which in time will become dry land. It is not at all wonderful, that such articles as are here found in the bowels of the earth, namely, coals, pottery, &c. nor is it surprising, that great quantities of stone coal are on the sides and under the bed of the Mississippi; they are the product of vast quantities of timber lodged in past ages, where they now are in the form of coal, having been converted from wood to coal. Hence the frequency of earthquakes. The coals take fire, and by consumption make cavities, which emit a hollow sound when the surface is stricken by the fall of a tree, or by a horse's hoof in travelling or running. These subterranean fires are not always in action, but oftentimes are extinguished, and after long intervals are put again into action, by the appointed cause which Providence hath provided for its own wise purposes. Were not the impurities which are in the bowels of the earth, from materials which constantly accumulate, to be periodically purged away, the noxious effluvia arising from them would eventually so much increase in malignity, as to render the atmosphere too virulent for the sustentation of animal life. The choked up subterranean passages for water, would make ponds or lakes, impregnated with the same noxious qualities, which also would greatly add to the same deleterious causes in the atmosphere. Hence a necessity for the intervention of subterranean fires, at certain periods, to consume the materials which supply those noxious effluvia that come from them, and to open the subterranean passages for water which in the course of ages have become dammed up. The office of communicating this fire, is performed by the instrumentality of comets. They go near to the sun, and particularly the great comet of 1680, and return from him with electrical fluid or the elements of fire, and approaching the earth, and perhaps other worlds, in its course of 575 years, fills it with an ethereal matter, that raises into flame all things in the bowels of the earth that are capable of ignition : earthquakes are the consequence; more virulence for a time in the atmosphere; more water from the interior of the globe; and a more healthy atmosphere in succession. The evidences in support of these ideas are indispensable, because they are novel. And they are these : First, that electrical fluid is drawn from the sun, communicated to the comet and then to the earth; secondly, that earthquakes follow uniformly; thirdly, that pestilence follows; fourthly, that old springs burst out; fifthly, that there is more water than before; sixthly, that the atmosphere is more healthy than before.

First, that the electrical fluid is drawn from the sun, and communicated by means of the comet to the earth.

Immediately after the near approach of the great comet to the sun, so much of the fluid is drawn off as to cause a paleness, and sometimes darkness, which is not recovered from till after a lapse of 60 or 70 years, corresponding with the greater or less brilliancy of the comet. Julius Cæsar was killed in the senate-house 44 years before Christ. The great comet appeared at this time; the sun was frequently darkened,[7] and lost its light, and so continued for times upwards of fifty years, and how much longer is now not known. Virgil, in the place cited, says, "Who dares to say that the sun is false? He often warns of planned tumults, and of snares and meditated wars. He pitied Rome when Cæsar fell, and covered his shining head with the darkened colour of iron rust." Pliny, in the place cited, says, "The defects of the sun, such as that which happened when Cæsar was slain, and in the war of Anthony, became preternatural and longer by a continued paleness of almost the whole year." Plutarch upon Cæsar, says, "Around the sun too, the habitation of splendour, and in all that year his globe grew pale, and rising without brightness, he emitted a weak and thin warmth. Thus the air became clouded and heavy; when the fruits, sour and unripened, languished because of the coolness in the heavens, and were tasteless. . When Pliny speaks of the darkness at the death of Cæsar, and of that in the war of Anthony, comparing them with that of which he is then speaking, in which he says the defects are longer and more prodigious, &c. he probably speaks of the preternatural darkness mentioned by Adams, in his 2d volume, page 243, which took place in the year of Rome 757, and in the 5th year after the birth of Christ. At the same time were the earthquakes and inundations spoken of by this author, and Ferguson in his Roman Republic, vol. 5, pages 233, 249. And from the expression of Pliny we can learn, that these defects were of longer continuance and more like prodigies, than they had been in the time of Anthony's war, which was 34 years before the time he speaks of. These failures of light from the sun then had continued 52 years, and were occasional or period-

7 Ovid, Meta. b. 15, v. 782; Virg. Georg. b. 1, v. 467; Pliny, b. 2, ch. 80; Jos. Ant. b. 14, ch. 12, sec. 3; 2 Adams, p. 243; 5 Ferguson, 233, 249.

ical. And we are not told when they finally ceased. On the 12th of January, in the year 1679, a few months before the appearance of the same great comet in 1680, an unaccountable darkness took place at noonday, so that no person could see to read.

The like paleness of the sun occurred when the great comet appeared in the year 531 and in 1680, and probably in 618 before Christ, and indeed at every time of his appearance, had the circumstance been recorded. 10

Spots in the sun which precede or follow the appearance of a comet a short time, are not caused by the intervention of opaque bodies between us and the sun; for if that were the case, the paleness or darkness would be of short continuance, whereas that spoken of by the Roman authors was of very long continuance. In the time of Gallienus the Roman emperor, Anno Domini 260, there was a preternatural darkness. Soon after the appearance of the comet which was visible in 1811, a paleness of the sun followed also; a number of spots were seen in all parts of the sun's surface, which appeared and disappeared as he revolved around his axis. One near his centre disappeared in three days. Another in 24 hours. The first notice taken of these spots in the year 1818, was about the middle of April. They then covered a part of the sun's surface, about 200,000,000 of square miles, which is about 10,000 of square miles more than the superficies of this globe.

Secondly, the fluid drawn off from the sun is communicated to the earth by the agency of the comet.—The evidence of this is, the earthquakes which uniformly, and the inundations which sometimes follow, the appearance of the great comet, and of others. It appeared in 2349 before Christ, and immediately upon its heels followed the great del-

10 Plutarch, 86.

uge. It appeared in 1767 before Christ, and about
the same time the deluge of Ogyges. It appeared
again before Christ 1193. And again in 618. Historical evidences for those ages are defective. But
in the reign of Hezekiah, a great earthquake happened in Judea.[11] After its appearance, 44 before
Christ, a tremendous earthquake took place in Judea 37 years before Christ.[12] One in the Adriatic
in the time of Anthony's war; one in Judea 31
years before Christ; and others which happened
before the fall of Jerusalem, in Crete, Miletus,
Chios, Samos, Smyrna, Rome, Campania, Judea,
Laodecea, Hierapolis, Calliope in Lesser Asia.
These last mentioned cities were overturned. In
371 of the Christian era, a smaller comet appeared,
and was followed by a general earthquake in 377,
394 and 400. The great comet which appeared in
531 of the Christian era, was followed by an earthquake almost universal, in the year 541, and in the
year 544, which swallowed up Pompoliopolis, in
Mysia; and the earthquakes of that time were of
very long continuance. The great comet in the
year of our Lord 1106, was followed by an earthquake in 1110 in Shropshire, and in Sweden in
1112, at Antioch in 1114, in Lombardy for 40 days
in 1117. In 1456 a smaller comet appeared, and was
followed by an earthquake in Naples, where 40,000
perished in the same year. The comet of 1618
was followed by an earthquake at Bendah in the
East Indies in 1621, at Manilla in 1637, in Calabria in 1638, and in Germany in 1640. The great
comet in 1680 was followed by the Jamaica earthquake in 1687 and 1692. At Lima in 1687, at
Smyrna in 1688, felt in England in 1689; and
earthquakes in Sicily in 1692 and 1693. In 1744
a comet appeared, and in 1755 happened the earthquake in Portugal, in which at Lisbon alone 60,000

11 Amos. ch. 1, v. 1; Zach. ch. 14, v. 5.
12 Jos. War, b. 1, ch. 19.

perished, and numbers at other places, particularly in Morocco. A comet appeared in 1759, and in that year was an earthquake at Tripoli and in Syria, which extended 10,000 miles. Damos lost 6000 inhabitants, and the remains of Balbech were destroyed. In the same year, was an earthquake in Peru, another in Syria in 1760, and at Fez and Morocco in 1763. In 1764 a comet was observed at Rome by Cassina, and there was an earthquake at Constantinople in 1766; others also at Ragusa, Dalmatia, Albania and Naples, and in Martinico in 1767 and 1768, at Camera and at Buda in 1768, and in the Archipelago in 1770. In 1770 or 1771, a small comet appeared in North-Carolina, and the earth was soon afterwards shaken, by a considerable tremor, which lasted only a few seconds: In 1811, earthquakes followed the appearance of the comet in the latter part of that year. Some time afterwards another small comet appeared in the northwest, and small shocks of an earthquake almost immediately followed. In 1783, the appearance of a comet preceded the earthquakes of Calabria. Numerous other instances might be adduced.

Thirdly, that pestilence follows.—Sulphureous and noisome effluvia issue from the earth in the time of earthquakes, which in 1811 sickened the stomach, and excited a disposition to vomit, attended with a weakness and trembling of the knees; for which refer to what is said of our late earthquakes in another part of this work. A most dreadful pestilence followed the appearance of the great comet which appeared in 531, commencing in 542, spreading over the whole world, and continuing 50 years; it destroyed in the Roman empire above 100,000,000 of men,[13] and probably in America much the greater portion of its inhabitants. A like epidemic followed the comet and earthquakes of 1811. And it began and raged in 1815 and 1816.

13 4 Gibbon, 275.

Fourthly, that old springs are opened and new ones made in consequence of comets and earthquakes, is proved by the facts stated in the description of the earthquakes in 1811 and afterwards. Fifthly, that there is more water is proved by a reference to the same facts and statements. And sixthly, that the atmosphere is more healthy after the pestilence and its causes are removed, is proved by reference to the salubrity of the atmosphere in our own country since the year 1816. It is for these causes possibly, that the comet returns periodically, approaches near to the sun, and wheeling circularly around his circumference, flies off charged with heat and electric fluid, for the supply of the exhausted worlds which he is destined to visit. If paleness of the sun, and darkness, earthquakes, inundations and pestilence, follow in the train of comets, is it a forced idea, that the general deluge also was caused by that which appeared so near the time of its occurrence? The deluge began in the second month of the year 2348 before Christ; the comet appeared in the latter part of the year 2349, and probably in the latter part of the last months in that year, and for some months afterwards, and probably was visible at the very time when the deluge began. If ordinary approximation can thus affect the sun and this globe, would a much nearer one be incapable of destroying the globe; and short of that, of heating the waters of the ocean to overflowing; of removing the pressure and weight of the atmosphere; of rendering the air unfit for respiration in the more exposed parts of the globe; of reducing all vegetable substances to coal and cinders; and of floating in the agitated waters the tropical vegetables and animals which the flames did not reach, and of placing them as evidences for the conviction of modern times, in all the regions of the north?

A Commentary on the Colour of the American Indians.

In tracing the various arts and sciences which were transplanted from the old world into the new before the discovery of this continent by the Europeans, the whole theory is overturned in an instant, by a remark which many writers have made, and many others have repeated; which is, that uniformity of colour through all America, is a proof that they are all descended from one common origin peculiar to America, and not from any part of the old world. That therefore, the people of America have not proceeded from thence, and could not have received any part of the knowledge they possessed from that source.

It is proposed, therefore, to consider whether, supposing such uniformity to exist, it be a proof that all the American Indians descended from ancestors whose origin was in America; and of course that they are a distinct race of human beings from those found in the old world.

And secondly, it is proposed to be considered, whether the fact of uniformity of colour exists; for if not, the arguments founded upon it wholly fall to the ground.

First. It may be remarked in the outset, that it is as good reasoning to say, the ascertained fact of a descent from one set of common ancestors, proves that the difference of colour springs from climate, as to say that the difference of colour proves a descent from different ancestors. The same argument will prove as many different sets of common ancestors, as there are sets of men of different colours, when in all other respects there is no difference at all. In the brute creation, a difference of colour between the polar and the southern bear, for instance, induces no suspicion that these came from distinct sets of ancestors; yet in man the case is otherwise. There are, it is believed, as many va-

rieties of human complexions, as there are shades
between white and black. And the same argument
that makes one common ancestors for the Americans,
will make another and another for every shade in all
the climates of the old world. And for almost all the
islands of the old world. Reason alone would repel
the inference; but as conclusions from reasoning are
always questionable, it is safer to rely upon facts than
inferences; because the latter are irrefragable, and
show to demonstration that inferences which would
be correct, if the alleged causes or premises were
so, being not such as they are supposed to be, could
not arise from such causes. If it be shown, for
instance, that nations now white, came from ancestors who were black in remote times, or vice versa,
then the inference that a white posterity must have
proceeded, and does always proceed, from a white
ancestry, cannot be a true inference, and the change
of complexion must be referred to some other cause.
Consequently, a uniformity of complexion in any
country, will not prove that they have not come
from ancestors of another complexion. We may
learn causes from effects; but we must not assign
to effects, causes which do not produce them. We
may say that climate is the cause, but not the sameness of ancestorial colour; for the fact shows, that
it may not be so and has been otherwise.

Is it a fact then, that whole nations, by a change
of country, have proceeded from black ones; and
that black ones, by a similar change, have proceeded from white ones? for if so, a sameness of colour
all over America can only prove at most, the recency of their settlements in America, or that such
colour is peculiar to the country.

In the time of Herodotus, 413 before Christ, the
Indians, Ethiopeans and Egyptians were black.
Chaldea was colonized from Egypt, and mediately
also Persia, Greece and Phenicia. The colours of
these nations are now changed.

In the time of Sesostris, 1491 before Christ, an
Egyptian colony was left on the east of the Black
sea, which thence received its name.[20] The customs and peculiar manners of the Egyptians are
yet there, but no trace of their original colour.
They are now the fairest and best formed people
in the world. The Egyptians at this time are of
an olive complexion; but in the neighbourhood of
Nubia in Lybia are black. The rite of circumcision
is practised by the Mahometans of the Euxine, and
the curled hair and swarthy complexion of Africa,
has given place in Georgia, Mongrelia and Circassia, to a beautiful white, set off by the most well
formed limbs. and countenances of the most agreeable expression. In the time of Aloni, it had gradually altered, and at length the swarthy colour
wholly disappeared. A difference of colour did not
begin to prevail after the deluge, till many centuries,
when men had settled in different quarters and climates of the world. The Ethiopean woman married
by Moses, is not said to have been of a different complexion from him, and he did not differ in this circumstance from the Egyptians; for the daughters of
Ruel described him to their father as an Egyptian,
and not as a Hebrew, as they would have done had
the Hebrews been distinguished in this respect, at
that time, from the Egytians. Abraham's fear, because of the comeliness of his wife, did not arise
from any complexional distinction; and she had
come, as well as himself, from Mesopotamia. At
that time, it is probable, there was not any fixed
difference in this respect.

The Carthagenians went from Tyre 856 years,
before Christ, 605 years after the exodus of the
Israelites from Egypt, and 98 before the foundation of Rome. Their colour became darkened by
settling in Africa. Not more than a century and a
half before the Christian era, they were conquered

20 7 Gibbon, 321; Herod. b. 2, ch. 104, 105.

by the Romans, who settled in their country in vast numbers. This was for a long time considered the most splendid of their conquests. The colour of these colonists is now entirely lost.

The Israelites, after they left Egypt and settled in Judea, ceased after some centuries, to be of the same complexion with the Egyptians. David was of a ruddy countenance; and Tenia, the daughter of Absolam, was fair. The Jews of the present day have probably come down to us without inter-mixture, generally speaking, with the people of other countries, to this day. Their laws and religion strictly prohibited the formation of such connexions. The prohibition, it is well known, is a matter with them of the strictest observance. They are now in all parts of the world. If a sameness of ancestorial colour is uniformly transmitted to their posterity, then it is to be expected that in the different parts of the earth they are all of the same complexion. But the fact is far otherwise; and the inference drawn from such premises is not true, because it is not true that the sameness of ancestorial colour is uniformly transmitted to their descendants. Those Jews who live in southern European climates have changed their complexions into darker shades, whilst those of the temperate regions have become more white, and others in India have become more black.

On the Malabar coast, are great numbers of black Jews. They went thither earlier than the white ones: they colonized the coast of India long before the Christian era. [15] They are probably a part of the ten tribes, who were made captive in the 8th century before Christ, and were permitted to settle in India; when in a few centuries afterwards it became subject to the Persians who conquered the Assyrians, that made the ten tribes captive. Those tribes in India call themselves Isaelites, not Jews.

[15] Buchanan's Star in the East, 119.

Their ancestors were not subject to the kings of Judea, but of Israel. If the Israelites in the time of Moses were black, their descendants in the north of Europe are now white. If they were then white, their descendants in India are now black. The form of their countenances yet has a resemblance of the Jews of Europe. If we were now to say, that these Jews and Israelites did not all descend from Jacob, because of the great variety of complexion, which we see them possess in different parts of the globe, we should commit a great error; and therefore the inference is not true, that the posterity in all climates will have the same colour that their ancestors had in a far variant climate.

The Huns who were settled in ancient times on the eastern side of the Caspian sea, if indeed they are not the ten tribes mistaken for Huns, are supposed by writers,[18] after removing from the borders of China, to have experienced a change of features, which is attributed to the mildness of the climate, and were thence called the white Huns.[19]

The Vandals were of the same complexion with the Goths, and were a part of the same people who went from the Palus Mœotis at the time of the fall of Mithridates, and the conquest of his country by Pompey, about the year before Christ 63.[20] They went from the borders of the Asiatic Sarmatia. And the Sarmatians, it is remarked with surprise, had in the year of our Lord 324 the manners of the Asiatics, and the complexions of Europe. It is also said by writers, that the Alani, who lived between the Euxine and Caspian seas, were originally of a swarthy complexion, but by mixture of Sarmatic and German blood, had become whitened, and their hair had become tinged with yellow. The Goths had long hair.[22] It is easy to perceive from these

18 4 Gibbon, 368.   19, 4 Gib. 368, 369.   20 5 Gib. 192, 22 1 Gibbon, 392; 4 Gibbon, 368, 373; 5 Gibbon, 197.

3

instances, that the ancient Scythians were of an olive colour, and changed it by living some centuries in the countries to which they removed.

The Vandals and the Alani, in the year of Christ 429, crossed into Africa over the straits of Gibraltar, where it is remarked, the fair complexions of the blue-eyed Germans formed a singular contrast with the swarthy or olive hue which is derived from the neighbourhood of the torrid zone.[23] But their descendants are now of the same colour with the ancient and present inhabitants of the country. Difference of colour, therefore, is not primeval and inheritable, and unchangeable.

When the Persian army invaded Greece, in the year 490 before Christ, it was defeated at Marathon. Then, which was 1157 years after the time of Moses, difference of colours, though not mentioned in the early parts of the Bible, began to be noticed by Herodotus. It had commenced in the intermediate periods. The Persian army was composed of soldiers from all the provinces of Asia Minor, from all those on the shores of the Mediterranean, and those which composed the ancient empire of Babylon. The Egyptians, by their remoteness from Medea, and by their connexion and intercourse with the people of Ethiopia, still further removed towards the south, had received a deeper hue, which distinguished them from all the nations that served in the Persian army. And accordingly it is mentioned as a singular circumstance by Herodotus, that they were black men with curled hair. After this period, when distant countries to the north and south had become settled for centuries, a difference of colour became more and more common, and finally a matter of no singularity at all.

Again: The Hungarian language so nearly resembles the idiom of the ancient Fennic, as to demonstrate a derivation from it. The Fennic tribes

23 6 Gibbon, 16.

anciently resided on the confines of China. The
Tartar records say, they removed to the Irtish, and
were there called Ugri, or Igours. A similar name
and language is found in the southern parts of Siberia; and the remains of the Fennic tribes are
seen from the heads of the Oby, to the shores of
Lapland. The Hungarians and the Laplanders
are proved by this evidence, to be connected by
consanguinity, and to have descended from the
same parentage. The Russians also use the same
dialect. The Ugrian mountains, and the provinces
of Finland, attest the great extent of the Fennic
settlements. Yet how great is the difference at this
day, between the Hungarians or Russians, and the
Laplanders? The former are of a lofty stature,
fair complexion, and robust frames; whilst the
latter do not greatly exceed in stature four feet; and
are marked not only with a swarthy hue, but with
disproportioned limbs and features.[24]

A great number of islands lie scattered in the
Southern and Pacific oceans; from Madagascar,
on the east side of Africa, to the Marquesas and
Eastern islands, on the western coast of America,
and through an extent of 1300 leagues, north and
south. The inhabitants of these islands speak in
languages which are plainly and nearly allied to
each other, and all of them evidently dialects of
the Malays, who from the earliest times have lived on the continent of Asia.[30] These islands are
for the greater part at vast distances from the continent, and from each other. Their insular and
sequestered situations have excluded for a long series of ages, until discovered by European navigation, the intercourse of all the rest of the world, and
have prevented their borrowing the idioms of other
nations, and the names of things which are the pro-

24 10 Gibbon, 206, 224.
30 2 Cook's Voyages, 250; Introduction to the 1st vol. of
Cook's Voyages, 78.

ducts of other countries. Their languages, therefore, are nearly in their primitive purity, without
any except small dialectic variarions, the simple
effect of time, uncombined with other causes. By
this plain evidence, those islanders are proved to
have been descended from one common country and
parentage, the *Malays*. Their languages have
survived the wreck of time; but there is amongst
them as much variety of complexion, as there is of
situation. The inhabitants of Von Diemen's land,
in the year 1777, when Captain Cook visited them,
were black. Of New Zealand, black, yellow and
olive. Those at Wateoo were of a deeper cast;
of the Friendly islands, deeper than the copper
brown; at Fegee, darker than those of the Friendly islands. At Atooa the inhabitants were of a nut
brown colour. Should it be said, that these islanders proceeded from a common parentage, created
originally in their respective islands, and peculiar
to them respectively, the position would be in direct
contradiction to the evidence which shows them to
have been descended from a common mother country, that of the Malays. And consequently the
inference is not true, that the colonists and posterity
of all nations, are of the same colour with those of
the mother nation. On the contrary, it is true, that
removed to distant countries and climates, with a
long continuance there, is invariably followed by
a difference of colour from that of the mother stock.

And indeed, there seems to be as much diversity
of colour, as there is of countries and climates which
have been long settled. The colour of the Gedro-
sian Hindoos, in the time of Alexander the Great,
was swarthy: the Hindoos of the present age are
tawny, lighter or darker, according to the provinces
they inhabit. The agriculturalists of the south
who work in the sunshine, are nearly as dark as
the Caffres. The Brahmans, and those who work
in the shade, are lighter. The tint of the Brahman

approaches to the colour of copper, or to a bright infusion of coffee. Their women are still lighter than the males. Those who live on the hills or in forests, are much lighter than any of those already mentioned. In the Kongu country they are as light as the Spaniards or Portuguese.[31]

Secondly. The uniformity of colour which is said to pervade the whole continent of America, is next to be investigated.

And here we shall find, that there is not any such uniformity, except in the northern and eastern parts of the continent, for which a particular cause is assignable. But on the contrary, it will be seen, that there is a diversity of colour on this continent, as well as in the old world, and perhaps in a degree not much inferior to what is there observable.

The inhabitants at Nootka sound, in the northwestern parts of America, are nearly white, though of a pale cast. Those of Cape Denbigh, on the northwestern coast of America, a little whiter than copper. Those of Oonalshky are swarthy. At Prince William's sound, on the northwestern coast of America, the women and children are white, and the men brown. The Dogrib Indians, and the Stone-mountain Indians, are fairer than those of the south. The tribes of Indians on the upper branches of Peace river, on the south side of the Rocky mountains, and upon a river to the west of those mountains, which falls into the Pacific about 52° 20′ 48″ of north latitude, are not all of them of the same colour with those on the Atlantic ocean, or on the lakes of the St. Lawrence. In latitude 55° 5′ 36″, on the east side of the Rocky mountains, they are of low stature, not exceeding five feet, six or seven inches; their eyes a dark brown, the hair a dingy black. In 53° 3′ 17″, on the river on the west side of the Rocky mountains, they have grey eyes and flat noses. Others lower

31 1 Dubois, 276.

down, have eyes of a dark colour, tinged with red.
The same coloured eye still lower down, 52° 28′ 11″.
Others near the Pacific, have small grey eyes, with
a tinge of red, and the hair of a dark brown; and
those near the Pacific, are between the olive and
the copper colour, and have grey eyes.[33] The Indians of Chili, Peru, Cugo, Paraguay, and at the
straits of Magellan, all differ in colour from each
other. The Baroans, a people of Chili, who live
in the 39th degree of south latitude, are white, and
as well formed as the northern Europeans, with a
mixture of red. In one part of Chili, a reddish
brown prevails, of a clear hue, and the red changes
to white. The Chilians who inhabit the eastern
valleys of the Andes, are much redder than those
who dwell in the west. The southern nations of
America are in point of colour as distinguishable
from each other, as are the southern and northern
nations of Europe.[34]

What then is the cause of this variety of colour?
It is produced perhaps by the conjunct operation
of climate, face of the country, situation, food, and
manner of living. Each country, it is probable,
has a colour peculiar to itself, which the settlers of
that country will assume, after time enough has
elapsed to subject them to the full influence of the
causes which produce it. The deepest shades are
made by a vertical sun. Wherever that beams
upon the earth, unprotected by rivers, oceans, and
winds blowing their coolness. The country becomes
progressively arid and sandy. The parts of Africa
and Arabia which are the farthest from these refreshing causes, are examples of this remark.
From the like cause in a smaller degree, are the
countries affected which are further removed from
the solstice, but are similarly situated with respect
to rivers, oceans and winds. The same causes, for
instance, do not operate on the continent of America

33 2 McKenzie, 185, 205, 217, 267.   34 2 Mobna, 283.

with the full force which they have in the old world. Because in America, in the torrid zone, are large rivers in abundance, swelled to an enormous size by tributary rivers, of great size also, from all parts. They bear on their bosoms the cool waters which come from the snows of the Andes; which gives a refreshing coolness, to the air, in all the countries through which they pass. There is also the vicinity of tall mountains, covered with eternal snows; they cool and temper the air, and pour upon the earth continual streams of moisture. But in Africa, the countries under or near the equator, which have not these advantages, are parched, barren and sandy; and so perhaps are the large islands more to the east, which have not the same tempering causes. If the earth itself, and its surface, in the absence of such causes, can be changed by the intense heat of the sun; much sooner and more thoroughly can the bodies of men. The same effect as is produced by the curling-tongs applied to the hair, may doubtless be also produced by a heat nearly as great incessantly acting upon the human body for many centuries together.

Wherever in the torrid zone, there are winds from the ocean or rivers, and snows upon the mountains, and the earth is not parched into sand,—the air is cool, and the thermometer does not rise to the same height as it does in countries under or near the equator, not possessed of similar advantages. In the former, the people are not black, but tawny, or of an olive complexion. Where the country has some, but not all, of these advantages, and the mercury does not rise in the thermometer to the highest point, the people are black, and their hair not curled; as in small islands, where the internal as well as external parts are fanned by the sea-breezes. Where the islands are large and not thoroughly cooled by the winds, nor by internal rivers or lakes, or high mountains, the people are

black and their hair curled, especially if the country be converted into sand by the heat of the sun.
The colour is gradually bleached as the distance
widens from the torrid to the temperate zones, as
far as to the polar regions, where the cold operates
to darken the colour and to stint the growth. In
Mexico, New Spain, Peru, in the Amazon country,
Brazil and Guiana, are mountains covered with
snow, large rivers in the country, and immense
oceans in their vicinity. There is a cooling temperature. The thermometer is far below the highest attainable point in hot countries. The colour
of the inhabitants is that of copper, long black hair
and black eyes. In the space in Africa, from Senegal, Gambia, and to the islands on the east and
under or near the line, the colour is black, with
curled hair. Here is the hottest part of the earth :
the thermometer is at its highest point. The mouth
widened by the pain which is felt in the scorched
feet: the lip thickened by the unremitted influence
of the heat upon it: the calf of the leg drawn upwards, from the scorched soals of the feet: the
soals of the feet thickened, and the hollow of the
foot destroyed, by continual pressure upon burning
sands, and the scull thickened from daily exposure
to the glowing sunbeams of the climate,—all de-
clare the effects which are produced upon the human system. At Madagascar, the country is less
parched, and the colour is black. In New-Guinea,
which never had any known intercourse with Africa, and is two thousand leagues from it, the inhabitants are black, and the hair curled. From Gambia to the Moors northwardly, the people are not
black, but tawny: in Morocco, they are dark, but
lighter: in Spain, still more to the north, they are
dark, but lighter. In France, still lighter. In
England and Scotland they are beautifully white.
The same appearance in Denmark and Norway.
In all these instances, the colour whitens in pro-

portion to the distance of country from the torrid zone. From a point south of Circassia and Geor-, gia, and thence northwardly, the colours continual- ly whiten, till a portion of the human race is found, , not supposed to be equalled by any inhabitants of the globe, for symmetry of form and fairness of complexion. From the point of their residence, towards the west, through the whole extent of that. latitude, are the people of the same fair complexion, no matter whence they originally emigrated. In the torrid zone, the eye is universally black: in northern climates, it is black, grey, and blue. In the torrid zone, the hair is universally black: in northern climates, white, brown, yellow or black.

Mr. Shaw, a curious traveller it is true, has dis- covered in the heart of the Moorish tribes, inhabi- tants of a white complexion, and long flaxen hair; greatly resembling the race of the ancient Vandals, who settled in Africa. But high mountains, and cool air, preserve the colour of the inhabitants un- altered; and to these circumstances are to be attri- buted the present complexion and hair of these people. The people of mount Atlas were in the time of Procopius, distinguished by white bodies and yellow hair. Those found in Peru, upon the Andes, by the Europeans, exhibited the like ap- pearances. The Abyssinians preserve now, as they did two thousand years ago, the features and olive complexion of the Arabs. The Nubians, an African race, are pure negroes, as black as those of Senegal or Congo, with flat noses, thick lips, and woolly hair.[34] Hence it may be attempted to infer, that complexion is not the effect of climate. But in Abyssinia are high mountains, elevated lands, great rivers, the Red sea on one side, and the Southern ocean not far off. The same effects are produced here, as upon the settlers on the Andes, and upon those who live on the African mountains

34 8 Gibbon, 368, in a note.

near the Atlantic and the straits of Gibraltar.
The parched lands of Nubia, to the south, are
but poorly cultivated, to improve the complexion
of the inhabitants, nor would any change for the
better be ever effected there. The like causes operate there, as do in Congo or in Senegal. The
surface of Abyssinia is rugged and mountainous,
abounding in forests and morasses. Here are the
Nile and other large rivers, and the lake Dambea.
Here are the mountains of the Moon, the highest in
Africa. No wonder then, that the Arabian colour
does not become more dark. The temperature is
just such as to preserve it in the state it formerly
was.[34] The Baroans of Chili live in the mountains,
as far to the south as the people of Mongrelia in
Asia are to the north; where the country is cool
and refreshing; where snows frequently occur.

Famine also, and hunger, are amongst the operating causes contributing to a change of colour.[35]
The effects produced by it were eminently conspi-
cuous in the seige of Jerusalem by Titus, as related
by Josephus. Long continued hunger often occur-
ring in savage and uncultivated countries, together
with excessive heat or cold, may finally perhaps
bring on a fixed change of colour. Very poor persons, who live scantily, are apt to have something
of this cast. Civilization and food likewise contribute their aid. The savage lives in the open
field or woods, exposed by day and night to the
weather, oppressed by thirst and hunger, whilst
the civilized man sleeps in houses, feeds plentifully
and regularly, and is screened from both heat and
cold. The savage frequently experiences scantiness
of food, especially of the vegetable kind. The
culture of the earth, and its vegetable productions;

34 3 Gibbon, 119; 4 Gibbon, 310, 370, 373; 5 Gibbon,
163; 7 Gibbon, 340.
35 Job, ch. 30, v. 30; Lamentations, ch. 4, v. 8, 10; Psalm
119, v. 83.

the accommodation of supplies; neat, comfortable and plentiful living; houses, good lodgings, and generous liquors,—have, it is presumed, great influence upon the human form and complexion.

The subject is not yet exhausted; but it has become tiresome to the writer, and perhaps more so to the reader.

The regular conclusion from the foregoing premises seem to be, that the variety of colour is not the effect of descent from ancestors of the same colour, and that such variety prevails in America nearly in the same degree as in the old world. And that the general sameness of colour in the northern and eastern parts of America is attributable to the fact, that the present race of Indians have not been long enough in the country to have undergone a change of colour, by time and climate. And that the idea of as many sets of original ancestors as there are various colours of human beings, is as repugnant to experience and reason, as it is to the plain statements of the sacred writings.

A Commentary upon the Mammoth Bones.

WITH respect to the mammoth, it is proposed for inquiry, first, when was he here? secondly, where is he now? thirdly, for what cause did he retire, and what is the proof of that cause?

First.—His bones are near the surface of the earth, as well as great depths below it; and where near the surface, they are in a state of preservation. A great number of centuries would have decomposed them. A great number of centuries would have covered them far deeper in the earth. The French coin uttered in 1596, and found in the state of Massachusetts, on the 30th of July, 1631, a foot under ground, will show as well as numerous other evidences, that there is a continual enlargement of the outer crust of the earth, by the decay of vegetables, and the constant falling of an almost invisible dust, or by some other cause. There is, indeed, no instance of any very ancient deposite found upon the surface or near it. A foot in depth on the surface being less dense and compact than the foot in depth depth next below it, and than the foot next below that, may be estimated at not more than one third of its solidity. This French coin being then covered, in less than 41 years, to the depth of four inches, would in the course of a century, be covered ten inches. Of course, the Roman coin, or any other deposite, five feet under ground, on a hill or other place not liable to be overflown by water, must have lain there six centuries, or as many centuries as there are ten inches in solid depth. It is not pretended, that this is an accurate estimate; but only that it is founded upon accurate principles; and these lead to the general result, that the mammoth has been here within a few centuries. His bones are found undisturbed; which establishes the fact, that the country where found has not been inhabited by a dense population since he lived here;

and of course, that it was since the destruction of the aborigines who formerly peopled the country, and long since the Roman coin was deposited, that was found five feet under ground, at Fayetteville, on Elk river.

Secondly.—Where is the mammoth now? The body of a huge animal, supposed to be the mammoth, was seen in the ocean on the coast of Norway eighteen years ago, which must have come from this continent, no animals of the like kind being in Norway or the more northern parts of Europe. A complete carcase of the mammoth was discovered on the borders of the Frozen ocean, in 1799, near the mouth of a river in Siberia. It was seen and examined by Mr. Adams. It had a long main on its neck. The skin was extremely thick and heavy, and as much of it remained as required the exertions of ten men to carry away. More than thirty pounds of the hair and bristle was gathered. The hair consisted of three distinct kinds; one of these is a stiff black bristle, a foot or more in length; another is the inner bristle, or coarse flexible hair, of a reddish brown colour; and the third is a coarse, reddish brown wool, which grows among the roots of the hair. These are proofs demonstrable, that the animal was destined by nature for a frozen region; why else the long or flexible hair, and why the wool at its roots? His bones are not found to the south of 35°, nor to the east or west. He therefore never inhabited those countries, but the northern sections of the globe only, and the countries betwen the lakes and the 35th degree of north latitude, as were at the time he was here, probably, in a very different state from what they were in the year 1779, 1780, when we first came to settle West Tennessee. For what cause did he retire? The raindeer, the elk and the auroch have retired, since the days of Julius Cæsar, from the forest of Hyrconia, on the east of the Baltic; and the mammoth, at some time, from the wilds of Russia, where he once lived.[1] The raindeer exchanged his residence for the rocks of Spitsberg,[2] within ten degree of the north pole; and to the high arctic latitudes went also the mammoth, from both Siberia and America, in both which countries he was at the same time, and must have passed by land from one to the other. The mammoth also lived, in ancient days, in Poland, Germany, France, Holland and Hungary, and in Asiatic Russia,[3] in the same northern latitudes within which he lived in America, not going on either continent more to the south than the 35th degree of north latitude. By the writers of Europe, the departure of these animals, is supposed to have been caused by too great an augmentation of warmth in the climate; which is attributed to the clearing of the countries east of the Baltic, and towards the Volga, for the purposes of cultivation, and by excision of the forests, exposing the soil to the rays of the sun.[4] But it is to be remembered, that the bones of the raindeer, and of the mammoth, are also found in Tennessee and Kentucky, where the forests were not cleared for cultivation, during the lapse of centuries, before the settlements about the years 1775 and 1779. They have not returned to the uncleared wilds of these American climates, any more than to those of Europe. In searching for the cause of his departure, we can say, that it was not for want of vegetables to support him, if he lived upon vegetables; for ever since 1606, when the Europeans first came to settle in Canada, and some traversed the wilds of Kentucky and Tennessee, these countries abounded as much in vegetation as they could possibly have done at any former period, and so probably it had for centuries before. We can say also, it was not because he was destroyed

1 1 Cuvier, 253.   2 1 Gibbon, 347.
3 1 Cuvier, 253.   4 1 Gibbon, 347.

by any unrecorded deluge of modern times; for in Europe his departure has been since the commencement of historical records, and no such deluge has occurred there since the time when he was known to inhabit that continent; and moreover, if those climates were suited to his nature, he would, when his numbers were repaired by propagation, have resorted again to his native soil.   Nor has he been destroyed by pestilence; for without it he left Europe, and in America he would have returned again to the countries congenial to his wants and his convenience.   His departure, then, has probably been caused by a change of these climates from cold to warmth.   Here we are met with historical facts, which show that there has not been an unceasing increase of warm seasons.   These show, it is said, that excessively cold seasons prevailed from 400 before Christ to some time in the second century after it, and from thence that the warm seasons prevailed, till some time in the fourth century; thence the cold ones till some time in the tenth century; thence the warm ones till some time after 1399, and thence till some time after 1620, and thence the warm ones till 1810, and thence the cold ones which have progressively increased from that period, and even still progressively increasing; and for that reason, it is urged that the mammoth bones in Tennessee are of much more recent disposition, as shown by their nearness to the surface, than his bones in Russia or Germany.   In Tennessee, it is supposed, that he lived in the last cycle of cold seasons, from some point after 1399, and thence to 1620, the country not being cleared for cultivation, and so no obstacle to his return, when in Europe that obstacle prevented his return, and perhaps destroyed the food upon which he subsisted.

To try the correctness of this theory, we must inquire of these facts to support it.   First then, with respect to the time elapsed between 400 years

before Christ, to some point, say a century, before
276 of the Christian era. In the north of Scythia,
in the time of Herodotus,[5] it snowed incessantly;
and snows were common in the Tarentine gulf, in
the southern extremity of Italy.[6] Snows were
constantly falling around the Caspian sea.[7] The
rebels taken and imprisoned at Capua, in the
southern part of Italy, in the time of Hannibal,[8]
died of cold [9] The snows fell at Rheguim, in
the southern extremity of Italy, in the time of
Cressus.[10] The snows and ice, in the time of Julius
Cæsar, were excessive. In the time of Virgil,[11]
the rivers thrust forth beds of ice, the gloomy winter
broke the rocks with cold, and buried and bound
up the currents with ice,[12] the wine was frequently
frozen in great lumps, and the Barbarians often
passed the Rhine and the Danube with their wagons
on the ice. There were deep snows in Gallilee in
the time of Augustus.[13]

From some point in the 2d century of the Christian era, and from thence to the year 400, there are
some facts recorded. The vine was cultivated
successfully in England in 276 of the Christian era,
and for some time before and after that period, say
to the middle of the fourth century. From thence
to some period towards the commencement of the
tenth century, there are but few facts to guide us,
because of the decline of literature in those centuries. Very probably the cold predominated in
those centuries, and up to some period about the
commencement of the year 900. From 900 to 1399,
there are facts in support of the warm seasons.

5 412 before Christ.   6 Herod. Melp. 7.
7 1 Plut. 104 ; about 40 and thence to 53 before Christ.
8 2 Plut. 104 ; 200 before Christ.   9 1 Adams, 297.
10 From 40 to 53 before Christ ; 4 Plut. 205 ; 5 Plut. 320.
11 Died 18 before Christ.
12 1 Georg. 310 ; 3 Georg. 31 ; 4 Geog. 436; 1 Georg.
236 ; 3 Georg. 296.
13 1 Gibbon, 347 ; 3 Georg. 355 ; Ovid's Epistles, b. 4,
v. 9, 10.

The sea was open between Norway and Iceland, and from the latter to Greenland. The Norwegian navigators discovered and planted a colony on Iceland in the year 874; and in 982, the sea being still unfrozen, they discovered and established settlements on Greenland. The vine flourished in in England in 1087, and to 1154. We now come to a period subsequent to 1154, and thence to 1620.

In 1234, the Mediterranean sea, was frozen over, and the merchants passed with their merchandise in carts. In 1294, the sea between Denmark and Norway was frozen; and from Exslo, in Norway, they travelled on the ice to Jutland. In 1296, the sea between Norway and the promontory of Legurnit was frozen over, and from Sweden to Gothland. In 1306, the Baltic was covered with ice fourteen weeks, between the Danish and Swedish islands. In 1323, the Baltic was passable for foot passengers and horsemen for six weeks. In 1349, the sea was frozen over from Stralsand to Denmark. In 1402, the Baltic was quite frozen over, from Pimera near to Denmark. In 1408, the White sea, between Githland and Gelend, was frozen, and from Restoch to Gezour. In 1423, 1426, and 1459, the ice bore riding from Lubec to Prussia, and the Baltic was covered with ice from Meclenberg to Denmark. In this century the sea became covered with ice, and so for a long time continued, between Iceland and Greenland, and the colonists at the latter place all perished with cold. Trees formerly grew upon Iceland in abundance, no doubt nourished by a genial warmth of climate, which continued long enough to vegetate and to bring them to maturity. But when the cold seasons came, they perished. From 1584, and indeed all the time the first English colonies were settling in America, Doctor Williamson says, that the northwest winds prevailed along the coast as three to one, in comparison to what they did at the time he wrote the history of North-Carolina: The Indian records in North-Carolina, which Dr. Brickell saw there in 1730, and which were sticks of various lengths, with many notches cut into them of different appearance, and which he says the Indians well understood, related the fact, in which also all the nations agreed, that in 1608 the sound at Edenton was frozen over, and that the wild geese and ducks came upon the land to get acorns, and were killed in great numbers by the Indians.

In 1620, the sea between Constantinople and Ishodar was passable on the ice.

From some point after the year 1620, and prior to the year 1730, the warm centuries began to advance, and continued to do so till about the year 1810. Doctor Brickell was in North-Carolina in 1730, and for several years afterwards, till he returned to Ireland and published his history, about the year 1737. He says, that during the time he lived in North-Carolina, the winters were so mild, that the ice was hardly ever thick enough to bear a man, and that many of their stocks of cattle were subsisted by the herbage and vegetables in the woods which the cold weather was not intense enough to destroy. Mr. Jefferson likewise, who published his Notes on Virginia in 1782, advanced the opinion, that the snows were less frequent and deep than they formerly were; and that they did not then often lie, below the mountains, more than one, two or three days, and very rarely a week; although they were remembered to have been more frequent, deep and of long continuance.[8] The elderly informed him, that the earth used to be covered with snow in Virginia for three months in the year. The rivers, which in those ancient times, seldom failed to freeze over in the course of the winter, scarcely ever did so in 1781 or 1782, or in the years near to that period. This advancement of the warm sea-

8 Notes on Virginia, 148.

sons, and the constant conflict maintained in the
spring season for the mastery between the southern
and northwestern winds, had produced fluctuations
in the weather, which oftentimes proved very fatal
to fruit. Nor at the time he wrote, did the dissolution of the snows which lay on the ground through
the winter, produce, as formerly, those overflowings
of the rivers in the spring, which were so frequent
in ancient times.

From some point towards 1800 to this time, the
common opinion is, that the winters have increased
both in length and severity. The cotton plant, which
prior to that period grew here luxuriantly, will now
in some years hardly grow at all. Prior to 1800,
for many years back, the trees were often in bloom
between the middle and end of February, and were
seldom later than the 10th of March; and now the
blossoms are not unfolded till after the 20th of
March, and sometimes not till between the beginning and middle of April. In the year 1821, on the
evening of the 16th of April, snow fell for several
hours, and covered the ground. The clouds cleared
off, and the morning of the 18th was as cold as at
any time since the beginning of November. White
frosts appeared as late as the morning of the 20th.
The weather was so cold, that some of the most
experienced farmers in the neighbourhood of Nashville forbore to plant their corn, though the ground
was prepared for its reception, till the week after
the 22d of April. On the morning of the 4th of
May, 1821, in the neighbourhood of Nashville,
there was a considerable white frost; and in the
mountains, white frosts were seen in every month of
the year. It is advanced by some men of science,
in some of the western states, that the equatorial
climates did once include the place where, in digging
the Zanesville canal, plants of the tropical climates
were found. And they entertain the opinion, that
the cold seasons have progressed, and extended

themselves more to the south, for thirty years past. If this be meant as an evidence, in support of the position, that the cold seasons are in perpetual progression,—it is at war with the opinion of the European writers, before alluded to, that the *warm* seasons are perpetually progressive. It is at war, also with the fact, that the warm seasons predominated some time before and after the year of our Lord 276, 900, and thence to 1087; and from some point after 1620, and thence to 1810. And the position, that the warm seasons perpetually progress, is at war with the fact, that the cold centuries had the ascending from 400, to the 2d century of the Christian era, and then again from the 4th century to the 9th, and from 1234 to 1620. And if the facts be correctly stated, the inevitable conclusion must be, that there is an alternation of cold and warm seasons and centuries. And that the mammoth was here for the last time in the cold centuries which intervened from 1234 to 1620. His bones are not known to the writer, to have been found on the prairie lands, but frequently at saline springs, and hardly anywhere else; to which he resorted, no doubt, like the elk, the buffalo, and the deer, for the pleasure of drinking the salt water, and of tasting the saline particles at the lick. Whether the animals of the feline genus did so for the same purpose, the zoological naturalist will determine.

It has been suggested, that these variations are caused by a change alternately of the earth's polarity from north to west, and from north to east.

Such change of position would cause a deviation from the ancient meridians; and there is evidence both for and against this deviation. The pyramids were all built in India, Egypt and America precisely to the cardinal points. The variation of 52 seconds on the American pyramids, shows, that there is probably some variation. At Circleville, on the Scioto, in the state of Ohio, the walls of the fortifications vary a few degrees from the cardinal points, but not more than the needle varies. These works are some of them circular, and some square; and both the circle and the square were so exactly laid down, that no error could possibly be found in their measurement. The builders therefore intended to lay them to the cardinal points, and were too skilful to miss their aim: the variation is caused, not by their mistake, but in a change of polarity. In 1576 and in 1586, Tycho Broke made observations on the island of Huen, in the straits of the Baltic; and in 1671, another skilful mathematician did the same. He found the meridian then different in longitude, by 18 minutes from the position which Tycho Broke had ascertained only about 95 years before. A progressive variation of 18 minutes for every 100 years, would have amounted to 7 degrees, 12 minutes, by this time, from the time when history first speaks of the pyramids of Egypt.

The evidence against a change of position, is, that the pyramids of Egypt were examined in 1794, and stood exactly to the cardinal points. And unless 1794 was in that part of the cycle where the returning variation has gained the point at which the pyramids were built, this evidence is conclusive of the fact, that there is no change of polarity. But if there be a deviation, and intermediate points between the termini on the east and west of north, then if the point be for instance 6 degrees west of north when the erection was made, and there be at present no deviation, then it may be that the variation has attained 6 degrees, either in returning or advancing, at this time, as it had at the time of the erection; but if at this time, there be a variation of 5 degrees, then so much time has elapsed as is requisite to make up a variation of 5 degrees, from the 6th degree, the point in the cycle at which the erection was made. And could it be ascertained, what was the exact space of time that is taken up in passing from one terminus of the cycle to the other, then also it could be told precisely, by the deviation from the meridian, when the pyramid was built, by calculation of the time necessary for that width of that deviation. If the width of polar deviation be perpetually progressive, and if that deviation be nearly 18 minutes in a century, then in the space of 2400 years, during which time history has spoken of the Egyptian pyramids, there would in 1794 have been a deviation of 7 degrees and 18 minutes. There is then either no deviation, or it is not perpetually progressive.

It is suggested again, that the same cause which produces the cold and warm centuries in succession, also produces the variation in the direction of the magnetic needle. And in support of this opinion, the fact is adduced, that a returning diminution of the variation has commenced at the same time that the cold seasons have begun to advance. Mr. Far ley, an old surveyor in the county of Caswell, in North-Carolina, says, that he was formerly obliged to allow of five, six, or seven degrees more, to keep upon an old line, particularly upon those which were run in the time of Lord Granville, which was in 1756, and from thence to 1760 or 1761, when his office was open. And he says, that now the allowance is one or two degrees less, to enable him to keep upon the old line. The same remark is made by Col. Haraldson, another old surveyor in the county of Caswell

In 1728, a line in 36 degrees and 31 minutes, run west from Currituck, struck Blackwater 176 poles above the mouth of Nottoway. At Currituck, the variation of the compass was three degrees west. At the mouth of Nottoway, it was two degrees, thirty minutes. And some persons argue upon these premises, thus: If the variation increased from 1756 to 1819, which is 63 years, as far as seven degrees, and then two more backwards, it travelled at the rate of nine-degrees in 63 years, or one degree for every seven years, in this latitude. And for the time elapsed between 1756 and 1728, the year when the line was run from Currituck, there being four times seven years, the variation must have increased four degrees. And being in that year three degrees, must have commenced three times seven years from that period which leads to the year 1707. In 1819, the retrograde variation being two degrees, leads back to twice seven, as the commencing point of retrogradation, and fixes upon the year 1805, as the epoch of its commencement; and that is the year, they say, when the cold seasons also began to come forward. The warm temperature begins to increase, they say, precisely at the period when there is no variation of the needle, and increases gradually for a century; then begins to decrease, till the needle returns to the same point; after which, the cold predominates, and is excessive, till it again returns to the same point in its western route. And that, though the warm seasons begin to come forward at the point where there is no variation, they do not become decidedly predominant, till the variation has progressed for fifty years, or seven degrees and a fraction, corresponding with the year 1755. And that they continue so decidedly predominant, till the variation again returns to the point where the said seven degrees and a fraction were reached, corresponding with the year 1855, for some years prior to its arrival at this point. That thence forward the severity of the cold increases, till the needle reaches the point, when there is no variation, but in the intermediate space, sometimes holding a divided empire with the southern winds and warm temperature. And after the line is passed, where there is no variation, holds the exclusive dominion, which is exercised with all the rigour that can be conceived of, till there be again a return of milder laws; which is not till after the lapse of two hundred years; corresponding with the time which shall elapse between the years 1905 and 2005. The time which shall be elapsed between 1855 and 1905 being a space when the cold seasons will proceed with more and more severity every year, towards the sole sovereignty which they will acquire in 1905. Proceeding upon calculations founded on the same principles, they say that the needle must have pointed in 1807 as it did in 1803, in 1814 as it did in 1796, in 1820 as in 1789; and must point in 1827 as in 1782, in 1834 as in 1775, in 1843 as in 1768, in 1850 as in 1761, in 1857 as in 1754, in 1863 as in 1747, in 1870 as in 1740, in 1877 as in 1733, in 1884 as in 1726, in 1891 as in 1719, in 1898 as in 1712, and in 1905 as in 1705. And that its variation in 1712 was 1 degree; in 1719, 2 degrees; in 1726, 3 degrees; in 1733, 4 degrees; in 1740, 5 degrees; in 1747, 6 degrees; in 1754, 7 degrees; in 1761, 8 degrees; in 1768, 9 degrees; in 1775, 10 degrees; in 1782, 11 degrees; in 1789, 12 degrees; in 1796, 13 degrees; and in 1803, 14 degrees. Whether there be any correctness in these theoretical principles, happily it belongs not to the writer of history to determine. But if the variation at the mouth of Nottoway could now be ascertained, and if the old records of Edenton and Halifax supreme courts could be searched, and the surveys selected, which were made at the end of every seven years, from 1756 to 1823,—in cases of disputed boundary, the progress of the variation could be ascertained with the most exact certainty; and it would be known, unequivocably, whether in these theories, there be any thing of reality.

Another argument employed against a deviation perpetually progressive, is this: That such progressive deviation would ultimately make the ancient meridian of the place the equator of the same place, and would be productive of a continual change in the latitudes of places. And this change, it is said, is disproved by the latitudes of ancient cities and promontories, fixed by observations made 200 years ago; and now are in the same degrees of latitude they then were. If the fact be so, the argument is conclusive. There is no intention of disputing the fact. But it is worthy of notice, that the ending of any state line hitherto run, to any point or meridian, after the lapse of thirty or forty, or fifty years, have never been found to be in the latitude it was supposed to be in when the line was run to it, whenever it hath become necessary to make a further extension. Wyncook creek, in North-Carolina, near Currituck inlet, was deemed by astronomical observations made prior to June, 1665, to be in 36° 30' of north latitude. The line from the point was extended by Mosely and Swann; and where they ended, Jefferson and Fry began. In 1779, Walker began not where they ended, but to the south of it, and extended to the Tennessee river; and was supposed, by North-Carolina, to be more to the south than he ought to be. He was not supposed, by any one, to be more to the north than he ought to be. In 1808, Strother discovered that his line was nine miles north of 36° 30'; and Alexander lately made it to be 13, and even 14 miles more to the north than it ought to be. The boundary of North-Carolina also, after the lapse of many years, was found to be too far north; and the commissioners were obliged to begin at a point some miles to the south of the line where the former line ended. If the present latitudes of the first, second and third of those lines could now be ascertained, with the remarkable points at which they came to rivers or crossed the same, a body of light might be shed upon the subject, which might be of the greatest importance to science. But at present the conclusion most proper for the premises we have had under review, seems to be, that the mammoth lived here in very ancient times, and also in the time which elapsed between the year 1234 and 1620; that he was then removed to the north by a change of climate, and that such change is more probably alternate than forever progressive; and that, at some future period, this climate may be again fitted, in point of temperature, for his reception, if the then state of the population will admit of it; and that the cause of this alternation is yet amongst the undetected secrets of nature.

A Commentary on the Roman Coins found near Fayetteville.

First, was this a genuine Roman coin? Secondly, was it brought hither since the discovery of America by Columbus? Thirdly, was it driven to this continent in a storm from the east? Fourthly, was it brought by the ancestors of the present race of Indians from Siberia? Fifthly, by whom was it brought?

First—Was this a genuine Roman coin? Antoninus Pius, when he was adopted by Hadrean, agreed with the latter to adopt, as his successor, young *Aurelius*, of the age of 17 years; Pius himself being of the age of 56. He is represented on this coin as an aged man: Aurelius as about the age of 20. After the title of Augustus was bestowed on Octavianus, all his successors assumed it; as their adopted sons did that of Cæsar. It is added to the name of Antoninus on this coin; as well as the letters of the several offices which he united in himself, and which his successors also assumed and exercised—Chief Priest, Emperor of the Romans, and Consul the third time. The emperor, on the first day of every year, formally took upon himself the consulship; and at the end of every five years, the imperial dignity, and would then add another time to the date of that office. At the end of five years, for instance, he would say. a fifth time consul, and second time emperor. The adopted successor was called Cæsar, and to him was assigned other offices, which follow his name upon this coin. The other coin, with the image of Commodus, as already stated, exactly agreed with the history of his time. Considering these circumstances, with the roughness of the letters, suitable to the ancient coinage in the days of Antoninus, and not suitable to those about the time of Columbus; and considering also the little alloy in the silver, not agreeing with the coinage of modern days. There seems to be but little reason for doubting, but that these coins were of the date they purport to bear, in the years of our Lord 137 and 181.

Secondly—Was it brought hither since the discovery of America by Columbus? The forest of large trees which lately stood on the surface of the earth, under which this coin was found, was of an age greater than that which has followed the discovery of America by Columbus. Some of those trees could not be less than four hundred years of age, whereas not more than three hundred and thirty-eight have elapsed since the discovery of America by Columbus. A tree which stood on the top of the wall called the stone fort, and which was cut down in 1819, exhibited annulars which were 30 years from the time when Columbus came to America. This tree was not more than 20 or 25 miles from Fayetteville, and was of smaller growth than the trees which stood there. Another evidence of its antiquity is, that the prominent images upon this coin are not in the least impaired, or in any way defaced, or made dim or dull by rubbing with other money; neither are the letters on the edges. Had it been in circulation in Europe till after the time of Columbus, a space of more than 1450 years, its letters and images would have been worn away. It is believed, that no instance can be adduced, of a coin that circulated 1400 years without being impaired either in weight or appearance. The English nation reformed its coin in the time of William 3d. And in 1784, English shillings were spoken of as worn and defaced.[10] There is a continual waste of coins by wear and tear, which renders necessary a continual importation into countries which have no mines of their own, to repair this loss and waste. By rubbing and wearing, the coin contains less than the standard weight, and the price of

10 Smith's Wealth of Nations, 61, 67, 68.

goods is adjusted to the quantity of gold or silver which the coin actually contains, not to that which it ought to contain. The coins in the time of Antoninus were kept after his death, as talismans or relics, and were not in a state of circulation. But certainly there was no such reverence for the character or image of Commodus; nor could the coin which issued in his time, have been kept out of any pious regard for his memory. And besides such relics were out of fashion after the introduction of the Catholic religion. These evidences all concur in proof of the fact, that the coin in question must have been deposited where we now see it, before it had suffered any loss or waste by circulation, and within one or two centuries from the date it bears. The depth of the covering above it, proves the same thing. It is impossible to assent to the proposition, that it was brought to this country after the time of Columbus. It might have come by De Soto, or the French who were settled on the Hiwassee; by the Shawanese, from the Atlantic; or by the Cherokees, from Virginia; in short, by a thousand other channels, if it were not deposited before the time of De Soto and of the French settlements; but if they were, then it is wholly beside the purpose, to speak of either the French or Spanish.

Thirdly—Was it driven to America by a storm from the east? It must be taken for granted, that after the time of Antoninus there could not have been a Roman colony sent from Europe to settle in America; for the history of those times would have related a fact of such vast importance, with all its circumstances. And, besides, in those days there was not any navigation across the Atlantic ocean. The mariner's compass was not then in use; and fleets or trading vessels kept in sight of the coast, as they sailed from one part of the continent to another. If brought hither over the Atlantic ocean at all, it must have been in some vessel, driven by a storm from one continent to the other. Northwest winds are sometimes of six or eight weeks continuance; but a wind from the east has never been known, since the first settlement of the country, to have been of that continuance. Roman vessels also were not of structure and strength sufficient to have survived in a storm of such violence and duration on the Atlantic ocean.[11] Their vessels were small and ill built, and there was not storage enough in a small Roman vessel to hold provisions sufficient for the sustenance of the crew for five or six weeks. Every consideration combats the idea, that this coin came hither over the Atlantic ocean.

Fourthly—Was it brought by the ancestors of the present race of Indians from Siberia? This coin was near to very ancient intrenchments near Norris's creek, which contained within their enclosures, mounds such as are seen enclosed in ditches in other parts of the country. The ancestors of those Indians neither built mounds as places of worship, nor sunk intrenchments. They never wore dresses ornamented with silver buttons, such as are found abundantly a few miles from Fayetteville. It cannot be credited, that they were the importers of it into America from Siberia.

Fifthly—Who then brought it into America? It must have come by navigation, from the south and east of Asia, to the western coasts of America. In the time of Antoninus, and afterwards, the Romans traded with the Chinese by caravans, receiving their goods and carrying them to the Oxus, thence to the Caspian sea, thence down the nearest rivers to the Euxine, thence into the Mediterranean and to Rome. The Romans gave nothing but money in exchange. From China, it might have come to Molacca or Japan, thence to America, and through the gulf of Mexico, up the Mississippi and Ten-

11 1 Gibbon, 29, 30.

nessee, to Elk river. In the time of Antoninus, also, the Romans carried on war against the Persians in Armenia. The money there coined, was no doubt paid to the armies which were there employed, and from thence was carried into the neighbouring countries of India, and to those east of the Caspian and north of Indostan, thence by some nation to Mexico, or over land into the rivers which communicated with the immense population on the Mississippi and its numerous tributaries. It was once in the Roman empire; is now here, and could not have come by Atlantic navigation; nor did it come from Siberia, and of course it must have come by navigation over the Pacific and its islands. The Japanese navigation, and the crew of a cast-away vessel belonging to them, has been already noticed, as well as the importation of the emerald, which was alone the product of America. To these evidences of an ancient navigation through the Pacific, may be added, that the same manufactures of feathered mantles were produced both in Mexico and in the islands of the Pacific. Ivory was found in the islands of the Pacific when first visited by European navigation, which must have been carried thither by preceding navigators. That the oriental emerald was brought in ancient times from the Golden Chersonesus, and there sold to the western traders, who carried it to Arabia and Judea; and that to the Golden Chersonesus it must have come by navigation from America. The conductors of this navigation were the Malays. The evidence of this is, that all the islands in the Pacific speak languages which are clearly and nearly allied to each other, and all of them evidently derived from the mother language of the Malays. This great nation of ancient times carried on trade to Madagascar and to all the islands of the Pacific ocean, and could as easily sail to America as to the islands of the Pacific; and might have planted colonies in America, as they did in the Sandwich or Friendly islands, for instance. Thus it may have happened, that the inhabitants of America for a long time may have used the arts and have observed the religion of the Hindoos, till the crumbling to pieces of the Malayan empire. This sentiment agrees with all the phenomena we have noticed, and perhaps with all others that shall be presented to our view. The people upon Elk river then knew the value of money : it travelled from the ocean to Elk, upwards of three hundred miles from the ocean; because with the people who lived there, it was an article in demand, and came to be exchanged for their productions. They were in a state of civilization. The short answer, then, to the last question, is this : It came through the Pacific, by ancient navigation, from Japan, China, Molacça, or India.

Two pieces of copper coin, one of which is undoubtedly Roman, and probably the other likewise, were lately found, in the year 1823, at Fayetteville, amongst other curiosities left there by Mr. Colter, when he removed to Alabama. The smaller piece is of the diameter of the fourpenny pieces now current, but more than twice as thick, covered with a deep and dark erugo, which renders the letters and devices difficult to be seen. On the one side of the small piece, is a pair of scales in the centre, suspended from the ends of a beam, and between the two scales the letters PNR. and in the legend, LAVDIVS. IIII. The C which precedes the L is not visible. On the other side are the letters SC. about the centre, coarsely made; and on the legend, MI. COS.

On one side of the larger piece, the diameter of which is little less than an inch, is the head of a man or woman, with the face to the right, with three projecting prominences rising from the back and top of the head one fourth of an inch, in small blunt prongs, and from a cap which covers the head to the temples, where a riband descends from the forehead to the hinder part of the head, and there ends in a small knot. Before the face in the legend, are the letters **CARTFN**. On the other side is a human figure, naked, with his body and face turned to the left, one leg straight to the ground, the right leg raised so as by the leg and thigh to make an angle of seventy degrees. In his right hand, which with the arm is extended from the body about twenty degrees lower than a right angle, is something held, which is not at this time distinguishable; and in the left hand, which is also extended from the body, and to the elbow declines towards the ground, the part between that and the hand being raised, and from a part between the elbow and hand, where it touches a barbed instrument resting upon it, and the hand entwining it. This instrument is in the shape of a spear, the barbed part touching the ground and standing upon it, the upper part ending in two prongs placed at the end of a beam, rising perpendicularly from the two ends thereof, with a small knot in the centre, midway between the two prongs; the instrument itself is in a perpendicular position, on the left side of the figure

ERRATA.

In Page	For	Read
1	southwest	southeast
11	fifty to sixty	fifty or sixty
16	Phenomena	Phenomenon
29	melting	motion
32	agitations about	agitations above
	a dread calm	a dead calm
57	a spring of	a prong of
60	megil nox	megalonix
65	*The cold seasons,&c.* should have been placed at the end of the commentary on the mammoth bones.	
68	inea	inca
69	Seva	Siva
70	Trimurte	Trimurti
71	gurude	garudo
	Huelzittu pocli	Huelzetli pocli
	in the statues	on the statues
76	latter	former
77	fine pieces	five pieces
79	obsedion	obsidian
80	in which	on which
	Gbeze	Ghize
86	Jagpeli	Jaypeti
88	Alt	Atl
90	could other vessels	could not other vessels
93	obloquy	obliquity
97	various cetors	various colours
103	prosperity extended	prosperity it extended
105	like all other	like that of all other
109	lettered over	tilted over
111	lingomites	lingamites
113	Dozun	Dozier
120	Leleucidu	Seleucidæ
125	cedar piles	cedar poles
126	a foot long	an inch and a half long
	mastaden	mastodon
155	12 inches	an inch and a half
156	will be had	will be laid
161	in instance	in the instance
165	controvertible	incontrovertible
167	Bœtia	Bœotia
	the first Grecian history	the first in Grecian history
168	Antonius	Antoninus
	furnish datum	furnish a datum
169	in the two most	on the two most
171	as large any	as large as any
172	is in the rive	is on the river
174	pontifar	pontifex
198	Tonais	Tanais
208	Thibit	Thibet
211	their natural institutions	their national institutions

LIV

In Page	For	Read
213	Charazan	Chorazan
	Samarsand	Samaicand
216	and aided to	and added to
216, 217, 218, 219,	Lenopes	Lenapes
219	condition	tradition
	Indians a bark	Indians a book
223	stood in the mound	stood on the mound
226	an then says	another says
	Mohenens	Meherrins
236	Pekoos	Pekods
	Konoa	Kanaai
	Tenare	Tenase
237	Chola	Chota
	into new	on to new
	between	between then and
238	is transferred into	is transformed into
239	in 1756	in 1754
-	bloodless	boundless
240	he feel	he fell
	alleged conduct	alleged misconduct
	unoffensive	unoffending
	rattle snakes	rattle snake
250	performed	profaned
273	privileged	provided
280	produces	produce
295	cereatia	cerealia
307	happens attempts	happens that attempts
311	been togeth r	been brought together
314	in the bed of the Scioto	on the bed of the Scioto
3 5	usual as	used as
319	Marella	Marietta
322	with sorts	with all sorts
	murix	murex
326	in the Tarentine	on the Tarentine
328	regularly levelled	bevelled
	taropins or tarobins	tarapins or terebins
333	these ancient	those ancient
	Cuernovaca	Cuernavaca
	Papontla	Papantla
324	Milla	Mila
	in a mission	on a mission
347	for lying a thread	for tying a thread
355	Tenochtillon	Tenochtitlan
358	Thibit	Thibet
361	dentis sapientiæ	dentes sapientiæ
363	Alarbech	Atarbech
364	comicen	comican
367	Hans	Huns
368	Georgen	Geougen
369	Chorazon	Chorazan
	Kholn	Khoten
	Eughors	Eighars
371	for both	from both

Made in the USA
Monee, IL
20 May 2024

58698438R00252